The Scarecrow Author Bibliographies

1. John Steinbeck (Tetsumaro Hayashi). 1973.
2. Joseph Conrad (Theodore G. Ehrsam). 1969.
3. Arthur Miller (Tetsumaro Hayashi). 2d ed. 1976.
4. Katherine Anne Porter (Waldrip & Bauer). 1969.
5. Philip Freneau (Philip M. Marsh). 1970.
6. Robert Greene (Tetsumaro Hayashi). 1971.
7. Benjamin Disraeli (R.W. Stewart). 1972.
8. John Berryman (Richard W. Kelly). 1972.
9. William Dean Howells (Vito J. Brenni). 1973.
10. Jean Anouilh (Kathleen W. Kelly). 1973.
11. E.M. Forster (Alfred Borrello). 1973.
12. The Marquis de Sade (E. Pierre Chanover). 1973.
13. Alain Robbe-Grillet (Dale W. Frazier). 1973.
14. Northrop Frye (Robert D. Denham). 1974.
15. Federico García Lorca (Laurenti & Siracusa). 1974.
16. Ben Jonson (Brock & Welsh). 1974.
17. Four French Dramatists: Eugène Brieux, François de Curel, Emile Fabre, Paul Hervieu (Edmund F. Santa Vicca). 1974.
18. Ralph Waldo Ellison (Jacqueline Covo). 1974.
19. Philip Roth (Bernard F. Rodgers, Jr.). 1974.
20. Norman Mailer (Laura Adams). 1974.
21. Sir John Betjeman (Margaret Stapleton). 1974.
22. Elie Wiesel (Molly Abramowitz). 1974.
23. Paul Laurence Dunbar (Eugene W. Metcalf, Jr.). 1975.
24. Henry James (Beatrice Ricks). 1975.
25. Robert Frost (Lentricchia & Lentricchia). 1976.
26. Sherwood Anderson (Douglas G. Rogers). 1976.
27. Iris Murdoch and Muriel Spark (Tominaga & Schneidermeyer). 1976.
28. John Ruskin (Kirk H. Beetz). 1976.
29. Georges Simenon (Trudee Young). 1976.
30. George Gordon, Lord Byron (Oscar José Santucho). 1976.
31. John Barth (Richard Vine). 1977.
32. John Hawkes (Carol A. Hryciw). 1977.
33. William Everson (Bartlett & Campo). 1977.
34. May Sarton (Lenora Blouin). 1978.
35. Wilkie Collins (Kirk H. Beetz). 1978.
36. Sylvia Plath (Lane & Stevens). 1978.
37. E.B. White (A.J. Anderson). 1978.
38. Henry Miller (Lawrence J. Shifreen). 1979.
39. Ralph Waldo Emerson (Jeanetta Boswell). 1979.
40. James Dickey (Jim Elledge). 1979.
41. Henry Fielding (H. George Hahn). 1979.
42. Paul Goodman (Tom Nicely). 1979.

JAMES DICKEY:

A Bibliography, 1947—1974

by

Jim Elledge

Scarecrow Author Bibliographies, No. 40

The Scarecrow Press, Inc.
Metuchen, N.J., & London
1979

Library of Congress Cataloging in Publication Data

Elledge, Jim, 1950-
    James Dickey : a bibliography, 1947-1974.

    (The Scarecrow author bibliographies ; no. 39)
    Includes indexes.
    1.   Dickey, James--Bibliography.
Z8230. 2. E44   [PS3554. I32]   016. 811'5'4   79-10405
ISBN 0-8108-1218-5

For

Brad Hooper,

mentor and more.

TABLE OF CONTENTS

PREFACE

James Dickey: A Bibliography, 1947-1974 records the career
of one of the United States' most visible and widely acclaimed artists.
While principally a poet, James Dickey is also an accomplished nov-
elist, critic, film script writer, poetry editor of journals and an-
thologies, and on at least one occasion, an actor. Compiled by one
of his most ardent admirers, this record of all of Dickey's and his
critics' works--original publications and subsequent reprints and ex-
cerpts--will serve students, teachers, librarians, and lovers of lit-
erature as a facile guide to the first twenty-seven years of James
Dickey's career.

Although several other bibliographies dealing with Dickey and
his critics are available, each must be used with discretion since
they are limited in scope and contain errors and confusing entries,
conditions this bibliography was compiled to amend. Two will be
briefly reviewed to illuminate the advantages of James Dickey: A
Bibliography, 1947-1974.

Franklin Ashley's James Dickey: A Checklist (Gale, 1972)
lists all editions of Dickey's books, his pamphlets, and his works'
appearances in books and periodicals from 1951 to 1972. The check-
list is divided into classified sections, such as "Books, " "First
Book Appearances, " etc. Within each section, citations are ar-
ranged chronologically by each work's date of publication. In the
268 entries, Ashley recorded only Dickey's publications, including
photographs of the title pages of his books and pamphlets and repro-
ductions of several manuscript pages from Deliverance, Dickey's
first published novel. Ashley indicated where some reprints of
Dickey's works are located and when a few title changes occurred.

While Ashley painstakingly described Dickey's books and pam-
phlets, he made many errors in the other entries which will hinder
the user of his bibliography. In several instances, Ashley classified
works incorrectly. Dickey's review of Conrad Aiken's Sheepfold Hill
entitled "A Gold-Mine of Consciousness" is included in the section
for Dickey's poetry (#25), while Dickey's poem "The Common Grave"
is listed in the section for his stories (#1). Ashley included a cita-
tion for a poem, "Awaiting the Stone" (#34), which does not exist.
A periodical, Publishers Weekly, is incorrectly listed in the section
for articles and essays as Publishing World (#4).

Since this book is a checklist of only Dickey's published writ-
ing, the entire seventh section, for interviews, should not have been
included. Ashley compounds the confusion because in each citation,
the interviewer's name, when available, is given as the author.
Several of the entries, for example entries #2, #4, and #9, are to
articles in which Dickey is quoted but not interviewed. Another en-
try, for the film script of "Lord, Let Me Die, but Not Die Out, "
should not have been included. Appearing in the last section, "Un-
classified Separate Publications" (#4), it erroneously indicates that
Dickey wrote the script when, in actuality, Dickey is the subject of
the film.

Since Ashley's James Dickey: A Checklist is arranged chrono-
logically within each section and not alphabetically by the works' ti-
tles, one must know from the beginning in what year each work was
published. If the date is unknown, one must scan the entire section.
While this does not create too great a problem with many of the sec-
tions, which tend to be short, the section devoted to Dickey's poems
has 186 citations and presents a problem to the serious user. A
simple index of titles would have solved this problem.

Eileen Glancy's James Dickey: The Poet as Critic; An An-
notated Bibliography with an Introductory Essay (Whitston, 1971)
covers roughly the same period as Ashley's checklist, 1951 to 1970,
and was published the year before. However, Glancy's bibliography
records works by and about James Dickey. While comprised of
396 entries, 229 of them are to works by Dickey and 167 to works

about him and his publications.

Both Ashley's and Glancy's lists are arranged into subject areas first, then chronologically by dates of publication; both note where a few of Dickey's works, especially his poetry, have been reprinted; but Glancy's list is introduced by a 33-page essay in which Glancy discusses Dickey's poetry and its relationship to his theories of poetry.

While Glancy's list is the first major bibliography on Dickey to include citations to his critics' works, it is filled with many errors. Among the more blatant mistakes is Glancy's confusion with the identity of two of Dickey's earlier poems. According to Glancy in entry #A41, "A Beginning Poet, Aged Sixty-Five" and "To Landrum Guy, Beginning to Write at Sixty," are the same poem which, presumably, had undergone a title change. Not only are they actually different poems but "To Landrum Guy, Beginning to Write at Sixty" and "To a Beginning Poet, Aged Sixty" (a title which Glancy did not record) are the same poem which had undergone the title change she mistakenly attributed elsewhere.

Like Ashley, Glancy did not always identify Dickey's publications by their correct titles. His poem "On the Hill Below the Lighthouse" is recorded in Glancy's bibliography as "On a Hill Below the Lighthouse" (#A54). Entry #A182 is called "So Long," the poem's first line. Originally published without a title, it became "For the First Manned Moon Orbit."

Occasionally, incomplete bibliographic citations appear in Glancy's list. In the entry for Paul Carroll's The Poem in Its Skin (#B1), the book's publication date was omitted. Since Glancy did not indicate most title changes, many of her entries give false information. "At Mercy Manor" (#A196), a poem, is not included in Dickey's The Eye-Beaters, Blood, Victory, Madness, Buckhead and Mercy as her notation indicates. However his poem "Mercy," which was originally entitled "At Mercy Manor," is available in that volume. Similar cases abound.

Glancy's list purports to be annotated, but the remarks included in the second division, "Works About James Dickey," are usually only brief phrases quoted from the essay or review and which,

ix

consequently, do not give a total picture of the article cited. Although citations in the section "Book Reviews," the third section of "Works About James Dickey," is arranged chronologically beneath each book by Dickey, any information within an essay about a book other than the one under which the essay is listed is lost. As with Ashley's list, an index would have solved this problem and made use of the bibliography much easier.

James Dickey: A Bibliography, 1947-1974, a list of works by and about James Dickey, was compiled to correct errors and confusing entries appearing in Glancy's and Ashley's bibliographies and to ensure the greatest possible level of accessibility into the Dickey literature. Its most immediately identifiable advantages over the two earlier lists are its scope, the wide variety of notations it employs, the annotations and lists included with its citations, and its indexes.

Its 1262 entries record items in English language periodicals and books, as do Glancy's and Ashley's lists, but it also includes non-print materials; dissertations, theses, and term papers; non-English language publications; and "miscellanea"--for example, extensive collections of Dickey's manuscripts, letters, and recordings, parodies of his poems and poems about or dedicated to him, etc. Although James Dickey: A Bibliography, 1947-1974 covers approximately the same period of time as Glancy's and Ashley's works, it digresses to 1947 when, as a student, Dickey's first published poem, "Christmas Shopping, 1947," appeared, and continues to December 31, 1974. It provides its users about four times as many entries as Glancy's bibliography and about six times as many as Ashley's.

Both of its divisions, "Works by James Dickey" and "Works About James Dickey," include notations indicating where the materials cited have been anthologized, excerpted, and abstracted, and in which of Dickey's books the materials he wrote appear. While both Glancy and Ashley indicate some anthologies, they have done so haphazardly.

Entries in "Works About James Dickey" give a much fuller account of the critics' views than the similar division in Glancy's bibliography does. Annotations summarize the major points each critic made rather than merely quoting snippets from their comments, as Glancy so often did. Lists enumerating (1) all the works by Dickey and (2) all the persons, works, etc., mentioned in the text are also included in an effort to provide the user with a more detailed account of the text beyond that for which annotations are designed.

Finally, James Dickey: A Bibliography, 1947-1974 includes indexes to the entire volume which facilitate use of the bibliography.

I would like to take this opportunity to thank the committee of the Dean's Challenge Fund of Mundelein College, Chicago, for the stipend which partially funded this project. I also owe my gratitude to Peter J. Fay, Reference Librarian, Library of Congress; Holly Hall, Acting Chief, Rare Books and Special Collections, Washington University Libraries; Dorothy M. Harris, Director of Communications, The Southern Educational Communications Association; Willard A. Lockwood, Director, Wesleyan University Press; and the many anonymous librarians across the country who responded so well to my many requests for materials.

My parents, Richard and Mary Elledge; my sister, Judy Elledge; and my friends Nanci Ligon, Regina Delp, Kristine Kirkham, Bruce and Carol Meyer, and Ken Shivers will always have a warm place in my heart for their help and many kindnesses over the years.

Finally, Sylvia Y. Kaplan, an excellent teacher and a friend, who taught me the fundamentals and the love of research, and who guided me through a critical period of my life, has my eternal gratitude, as does Sister Rose Barry, B. V. M., my friend, who typed, and typed, and typed without complaint and always with a smile.

Jim Elledge
July 1978
Chicago

USER'S GUIDE

James Dickey: A Bibliography, 1947-1974 has two broad di-
visions--works by James Dickey and critical works by others--plus
a two-part index.   Each major section is subdivided.

In "Works by James Dickey," explanatory notes often accom-
pany bibliographic citations.   Following citations for works such as
poems and short stories, lists (indicated by "In") disclose in which
of Dickey's books the works may be found.   Other lists (introduced
by the abbreviation "Rept.") indicate in which anthologies his works
have been reprinted.

Citations to volumes by Dickey and to anthologies include con-
tents lists.   Entries for works which were published for the first
time in Dickey's books, not in periodicals, contain only the works'
titles and, below the titles, lists revealing their location in his
books or in anthologies, again introduced by "In" or "Rept." re-
spectively.

Entries in the second division, "Works About James Dickey,"
include bibliographic citations usually followed by 1) a list of Dickey's
works discussed or quoted in the criticism, 2) an annotation stating
the important points the critic discusses, and 3) a list of "items,"
i. e., persons, works, etc., mentioned in the text.   The list of
items is indicated by the abbreviation "Ref."   Page numbers in
either list disclose exactly where in the text Dickey's works or the
items were discussed.

Brackets enclosing all or a portion of the title of Dickey's
works signify 1) that the work was quoted or referred to in some
oblique manner but was not identified, or 2) that the title which the
critic uses is either incorrect, incomplete, or not specific enough
for the purposes of this bibliography.   When applicable, a note ex-

plaining where the criticism was originally published or subsequently reprinted or excerpted is included.

All references to Deliverance are to Dickey's novel. A notation in brackets always accompanies references to the film version, also entitled Deliverance. When both novel and film are discussed in the same text, notes in brackets explain which is which. Similarly, in a few other instances, individual works by Dickey have the same title, and all such works are arranged chronologically when listed together throughout this bibliography.

In some instances, only a portion of an article is about Dickey, with the rest devoted to one or more other writers. The bibliographic citations to such articles contain the page numbers of the entire article followed by brackets enclosing the page numbers on which material about Dickey is available.

In the two divisions, almost all citations have been verified by physical examination of the material cited. An asterisk (*) preceding an entry's number signifies a citation to a work which was unavailable. Whenever possible, an explanatory note about the material is included and followed by the source of the citation enclosed in brackets. When illustrations of any sort accompany cited materials, they are noted with the page numbers on which they appear and the person or persons responsible for them are identified.

Entries are given to more than a work's original publication. Anything reprinted or excerpted is given a second entry, for the reprint or excerpt source. When a title has changed, two entries, one for the original title and one for the second title, are also included. "See" references are always included to alert the user to alternate entries.

The "Index to Works by James Dickey" lists all of Dickey's published and "in-progress" works and indicates where references to, or discussions about, them may be located. Underlined numbers represent any "main entry," i.e., the work's original publication data. The "General Index" covers all entries' annotations and the items collected in the "Ref." lists.

LIST OF ABBREVIATIONS

abs.	abstract, abstracted in
Aut.	Autumn
col.	color
ed.	edition, editor
eds.	editors
exc.	excerpt, excerpted in
in.	inch, inches
ips.	inches per second
L. W. O.	library work order
min.	minutes
mono.	monaural
n.	footnote
n. d.	no date of publication, no date of production
n. p.	no place of publication, no publisher, no pagination
n. s.	new series
no.	number
orig.	originally published in
p.	page
pp.	pages
Ref.	reference, references
Rept.	reprint, reprinted in
rev.	revised
rpm.	revolutions per minute
sd.	sound
sec.	section
Spr.	Spring
stereo.	stereophonic
Sum.	Summer
vol.	volume
Win.	Winter

I: WORKS BY JAMES DICKEY

BOOKS AND PAMPHLETS

1 Babel to Byzantium: Poets and Poetry Now. New York: Far-
  rar, Straus, and Giroux, 1968.
  "Preface, " pp. ix-x.
  "I: Poets and Poetry Now, " pp. 1-230.
        "In the Presence of Anthologies, " pp. 3-13.
        "Randall Jarrell, " pp. 13-25.
        "David Ignatow, " pp. 25-28.
        "Kenneth Burke, " pp. 28-31.
        "Gene Derwood, " pp. 31-35.
        "Howard Nemerov, " pp. 35-41.
        "W. S. Graham, " pp. 41-45.
        "Samuel French Morris, " pp. 45-48.
        "Reed Whittemore, " pp. 49-52.
        "Allen Ginsberg, " pp. 52-55.
        "Donald F. Drummond, " pp. 56-58.
        "John Ashbery, " pp. 58-60.
        "Rolphe Humphries, " pp. 60-63.
        "Herbert Read, " pp. 63-65.
        "Katherine Hoskins, " pp. 65-69.
        "Philip Booth, " pp. 69-70.
        "Kenneth Patchen, " pp. 71-72.
        "May Sarton, " p. 73.
        "William Jay Smith, " pp. 74-75.
        "Robert Penn Warren, " pp. 75-77.
        "Richard Eberhart, " pp. 78-79.
        "Edwin Muir, " pp. 80-82.
        "Ted Hughes, " pp. 82-83.
        "Lawrence Durrell, " pp. 84-85.
        "Conrad Aiken, " pp. 85-93.
        "Margaret Tongue, " pp. 94-95.
        "Ellen Kay, " pp. 95-97.
        "James Merrill, " pp. 97-100.
        "E. E. Cummings, " pp. 100-106.
        "Emma Swan, " pp. 106-107.
        "Harold Witt, " pp. 108-109.
        "Winfield Townley Scott, " pp. 109-113.
        "Elder Olson, " pp. 113-116.
        "Nikos Kazantzakis, " pp. 116-119.
        "Thom Gunn, " pp. 120-123.
        "Brother Antoninus, " pp. 124-126.
        "Hayden Carruth, " pp. 127-129.
        "James Kirkup, " pp. 131-132.

3

"Anne Sexton, " pp. 133-134.
"Galway Kinnell, " pp. 134-135.
"Charles Olson, " pp. 136-139.
"William Stafford, " pp. 139-140.
"Lewis Turco, " p. 141.
"W. S. Merwin, " pp. 142-143.
"Theodore Weiss, " pp. 144-145.
"Josephine Miles, " pp. 146-147.
"Theodore Roethke, " pp. 147-152.
"Louis MacNeice, " pp. 152-154.
"Charles Tomlinson's Versions of Fyodor Tyutchev, " pp. 154-155.
"Marianne Moore, " pp. 156-164.
"John Logan, " pp. 164-167.
"John Frederick Nims, " pp. 168-170.
"Richard Wilbur, " pp. 170-172.
"Robert Duncan, " pp. 173-177.
"Horance Gregory, " pp. 177-179.
"I. A. Richards, " pp. 179-182.
"Yvor Winters, " pp. 182-186.
"Robert Graves, " pp. 186-187.
"Robinson Jeffers, " pp. 187-189.
"Ralph Hodgson, " pp. 189-190.
"Vernon Watkins, " pp. 190-191.
"William Carlos Williams, " pp. 191-192.
"J. V. Cunningham, " pp. 193-194.
"Louis Simpson, " pp. 195-197.
"William Meredith, " pp. 197-198.
"John Berryman, " pp. 198-199.
"Robert Frost, " pp. 200-209.
"Edwin Arlington Robinson, " pp. 209-230.
"II: Five Poems, " pp. 231-246.
"Christopher Smart: 'A Song to David, ' " pp. 233-235.
"Matthew Arnold: 'Dover Beach, ' " pp. 235-238.
"Gerard Manley Hopkins: 'The Wreck of the Deutschland, ' " pp. 238-241.
"Francis Thompson: 'The Hound of Heaven, ' " pp. 241-244.
"William Carlos Williams: 'The Yachts, ' " pp. 244-246.
"III: The Poet Turns on Himself," pp. 247-292.
"Barnstorming for Poetry, " pp. 249-256.
"Notes on the Decline of Outrage, " pp. 257-278.
"The Poet Turns on Himself, " pp. 278-292.
Much of Babel to Byzantium was previously published in The Suspect in Poetry (see no. 18).   It is indexed in Authors: Critical and Biographical References (see no. 1215).

2   Buckdancer's Choice.   Middletown, Conn.: Wesleyan University Press, 1965.
"Part 1, " pp. 11-20.
"The Firebombing, " pp. 11-20
"Part 2, " pp. 21-42.
"Buckdancer's Choice, " pp. 21-22.

It was subsequently filmed (see no. 529).

"Armor," pp. 45-46.
"In the Lupanar at Pompeii," pp. 47-48.
"Drowning with Others," pp. 49-50.
"A View of Fujiyama After the War," pp. 51-52.
"The Island," pp. 53-54.
"Section III," pp. 55-76.
   "Dover: Believing in Kings," pp. 57-63.
   "To His Children in Darkness," pp. 64-65.
   "A Screened Porch in the Country," pp. 66-67.
   "The Dream Flood," pp. 68-69.
   "The Scratch," pp. 70-71.
   "Hunting Civil War Relics at Nimblewill Creek," pp. 72-73.
   "The Twin Falls," p. 74.
   "The Hospital Window," pp. 75-76.
"Section IV," pp. 77-96.
   "The Magus," p. 79.
   "Antipolis," pp. 80-81.
   "The Change," p. 82.
   "Autumn," p. 83.
   "Snow on a Southern State," pp. 84-86.
   "To Landrum Guy, Beginning to Write at Sixty," pp. 87-88.
   "Facing Africa," pp. 89-90.
   "Inside the River," pp. 91-92.
   "The Salt Marsh," pp. 93-94.
   "In the Mountain Tent," pp. 95-96.

5 Exchanges: Being in the Form of a Dialogue with Joseph Trum-
bull Stickney. Bloomfield Hills, Mich.: A Bruccoli-Clark
Book, 1971.
A limited edition of 200 copies. It was originally published as
"Exchanges" (see no. 91).

6 The Eye-Beaters, Blood, Victory, Madness, Buckhead and
Mercy. Garden City, N.Y.: Doubleday and Co., 1970.
"Diabetes," pp. 7-9.
   "I.   'Sugar,'" pp. 7-8.
   "II. 'Under Buzzards,'" pp. 8-9.
"Messages," pp. 10-13.
   "I.   'Butterflies,'" pp. 10-12.
   "II. 'Giving a Son to the Sea,'" pp. 12-13.
"Mercy," pp. 14-16.
"Two Poems of Going Home," pp. 17-23.
   "I.   'Living There,'" pp. 17-19.
   "II. 'Looking for the Buckhead Boys,'" pp. 20-23.
"The Place," p. 24.
"Apollo," pp. 25-30.
   "I.   'For the First Manned Moon Orbit,'" pp. 26-29.
   "II. 'The Moon Ground,'" pp. 29-30.
"The Cancer Match," pp. 31-32.
"Venom," p. 33.
"Blood," pp. 34-35.
"In the Pocket," p. 36.
"Knock," p. 37.

"Victory," pp. 38-41.
"The Lord in the Air," pp. 42-43.
"Pine," pp. 44-46.
"Madness," pp. 47-49.
"The Eye-Beaters," pp. 50-55.
"Turning Away," pp. 56-63.

7 Helmets.   Middletown, Conn.: Wesleyan University Press, 1964.
   "Part One," pp. 9-30.
      "The Dusk of Horses," pp. 9-10.
      "Fence Wire," pp. 11-12.
      "At Darien Bridge," pp. 13-14.
      "Chenille," pp. 15-17.
      "On the Coosawattee," pp. 18-23.
         "I.   'By Canoe Through the Fir Forest,'" pp. 18-19.
         "II. 'Below Ellijay,'" pp. 19-21.
         "III. 'The Inundation,'" pp. 21-23.
      "Winter Trout," pp. 24-26.
      "Springer Mountain," pp. 27-30.
   "Part Two," pp. 31-54.
      "Cherrylog Road," pp. 31-35.
      "The Scarred Girl," pp. 36-37.
      "Kudzu," pp. 38-41.
      "The Beholders," pp. 42-43.
      "The Poisoned Man," pp. 44-45.
      "In the Marble Quarry," pp. 46-47.
      "A Folk Singer of the Thirties," pp. 48-54.
   "Part Three," pp. 55-80.
      "The Being," pp. 55-58.
      "Breath," pp. 59-61.
      "The Ice Skin," pp. 62-64.
      "Bums, on Waking," pp. 65-67.
      "Goodbye to Serpents," pp. 68-70.
      "In the Child's Night," pp. 71-72.
      "Approaching Prayer," pp. 73-80.
   "Part Four," pp. 81-93.
      "The Driver," pp. 81-83.
      "Horses and Prisoners," pp. 84-86.
      "Drinking from a Helmet," pp. 87-93.

8 Into the Stone and Other Poems.   In Poets of Today, vol. 7,
      edited by John Hall Wheelock, pp. 33-92.   New York:
      Charles Scribner's Sons, 1960.
   "Family," pp. 35-52.
      "Sleeping Out at Easter," pp. 37-38.
      "The Signs," pp. 39-41.
      "The Call," p. 42.
      "The Underground Stream," pp. 43-44.
      "The String," pp. 45-46.
      "The Game," pp. 47-48.
      "The Vegetable King," pp. 49-51.
   "War," pp. 53-64.
      "The Enclosure," pp. 55-56.

"The Jewel," pp. 57-58.
"The Performance," pp. 59-60.
"The Wedding," pp. 61-62.
"Mindoro, 1944," pp. 63-64.
"Death and Others," pp. 65-78.
    "Uncle," pp. 67-68.
    "Poem," pp. 69-70.
    "The Sprinter's Sleep," p. 71.
    "The Other," pp. 72-74.
    "Trees and Cattle," pp. 75-76.
    "Walking on Water," pp. 77-78.
"Love," pp. 72-79.
    "Awaiting the Swimmer," pp. 81-82.
    "Orpheus Before Hades," pp. 83-84.
    "On the Hill Below the Lighthouse," pp. 85-86.
    "Near Darien," pp. 87-88.
    "Into the Stone," pp. 89-90.
    "The Landfall," pp. 91-92.

9 Jericho: The South Beheld.   Birmingham, Ala.: Oxmoor
        House, 1974.
        "Introduction," pp. 15-17.
        "The Land and the Water," pp. 19-29.
        "Among the People," pp. 63-75.
        "The Traditions Web," pp. 109-121.
        "Epilogue," p. 157.
    Hubert Shuptrine's art work is included.

10 Metaphor as Pure Adventure: A Lecture Delivered at the
        Library of Congress, December 4, 1967.   Washington,
        D.C.: Library of Congress, 1968.
    It was aired by delayed broadcast on WGMS AM-FM.
    In: Sorties.

11 Poems.   Melbourne, Victoria, Australia: Sun Books Pty., 1968.
        "The Performance," pp. 9-10.
        "Walking on Water," pp. 11-12.
        "Into the Stone," pp. 13-14.
        "The Salt Marsh," pp. 15-16.
        "In the Mountain Tent," pp. 17-18.
        "Cherrylog Road," pp. 19-22.
        "The Scarred Girl," pp. 23-24.
        "The Poisoned Man," pp. 25-26.
        "The Ice Skin," pp. 27-28.
        "Approaching Prayer," pp. 29-34.
        "Slave Quarters," pp. 35-39.
        "The Sheep Child," pp. 40-41.
        "Snakebite," pp. 42-43.
        "A Letter," pp. 44-45.
        "Deer Among Cattle," p. 46.
        "The Leap," pp. 47-48.
        "Falling," pp. 49-55.
    Its "Foreword" is by Robert Clark (see no. 1000).

12 Poems 1957-1967.   Middletown, Conn. : Wesleyan University
          Press, 1967.
    "May Day Sermon to the Women of Gilmer County, Georgia, by
          a Woman Preacher Leaving the Baptist Church," pp. 3-13.
    A "miniature preview edition" of 500 copies published for promo-
    tional purposes.   Only the "Contents" page and the "Acknowledg-
    ments" page also appear here.   No other poems which appear in the
    actual collection, Poems 1957-1967 (see no. 13), were included.

13 Poems 1957-1967.   Middletown, Conn. : Wesleyan University
          Press, 1967.
    "Sermon," pp. 1-14.
          "May Day Sermon to the Women of Gilmer County,
              Georgia, by a Woman Preacher Leaving the Baptist
              Church," pp. 3-13.

    "Into the Stone," pp. 15-48.
          "Sleeping Out at Easter," pp. 17-18.
          "The Underground Stream," pp. 19-20.
          "The String," pp. 21-22.
          "The Vegetable King," pp. 23-25.
          "The Enclosure," pp. 26-27.
          "The Jewel," pp. 28-29.
          "The Performance," pp. 30-31.
          "The Wedding," pp. 32-33.
          "The Other," pp. 34-36.
          "Trees and Cattle," pp. 37-38.
          "Walking on Water," pp. 39-40.
          "Awaiting the Swimmer," pp. 41-42.
          "On the Hill Below the Lighthouse," pp. 43-44.
          "Near Darien," pp. 45-46.
          "Into the Stone," pp. 47-48.

    "Drowning with Others," pp. 49-110.
    "I," pp. 51-77.
          "The Lifeguard," pp. 51-52.
          "Listening to Foxhounds," pp. 53-54.
          "A Dog Sleeping on My Feet," pp. 55-56.
          "The Movement of Fish," pp. 57-58.
          "The Heaven of Animals," pp. 59-60.
          "A Birth," p. 61.
          "Fog Envelops the Animals," pp. 62-63.
          "The Summons," pp. 64-65.
          "In the Tree House at Night," pp. 66-67.
          "For the Nightly Ascent of the Hunter Orion over a Forest
              Clearing," pp. 68-69.
          "The Owl King," pp. 70-77.
              "I.   'The Call,'" p. 70.
              "II.   'The Owl King,'" pp. 71-72.
              "III.   'The Blind Child's Story,'" pp. 73-77.
    "II," pp. 78-86.
          "Between Two Prisoners," pp. 78-80.
          "Armor," pp. 81-82.

"Reincarnation (I)," pp. 196-197.
"Them, Crying," pp. 198-200.
"The Celebration," pp. 201-202.
"The Escape," pp. 203-204.
"The Shark's Parlor," pp. 205-208.
"III," pp. 209-233.
  "Pursuit from Under," pp. 209-211.
  "Fox Blood," pp. 212-213.
  "Fathers and Sons," pp. 214-217.
    "I.   'The Second Sleep,'" pp. 214-215.
    "II. 'The Aura,'" pp. 215-217.
  "Sled Burial, Dream Ceremony," pp. 218-219.
  "Gamecock," pp. 220-221.
  "The Night Pool," p. 222.
  "The War Wound," p. 223.
  "Mangham," pp. 224-225.
  "Angina," pp. 226-227.
  "Dust," pp. 228-229.
  "The Fiend," pp. 230-233.

"Falling," pp. 241-299.
"I," pp. 243-251.
  "Reincarnation (II)," pp. 243-251.
"II," pp. 252-287.
  "The Sheep Child," pp. 252-253.
  "Sun," pp. 254-255.
  "Power and Light," pp. 256-257.
  "The Flash," p. 258.
  "Adultery," pp. 259-260.
  "Hedge Life," pp. 261-262.
  "Snakebite," pp. 263-264.
  "Bread," pp. 265-266.
  "Sustainment," pp. 267-268.
  "A Letter," pp. 269-270.
  "The Head-Aim," p. 271.
  "Dark Ones," pp. 272-273.
  "Encounter in the Cage Country," pp. 274-275.
  "For the Last Wolverine," pp. 276-278.
  "The Bee," pp. 279-280.
  "Mary Sheffield," pp. 281-282.
  "Deer Among Cattle," p. 283.
  "The Leap," pp. 284-285.
  "Coming Back to America," pp. 286-287.
"III," pp. 288-299.
  "The Birthday Dream," pp. 288-289.
  "False Youth: Two Seasons," pp. 290-292.
    "I," pp. 290-291.
    "II," pp. 291-292.
  "Falling," pp. 293-299.

14 A Private Brinksmanship: An Address by James Dickey, Poet-
      in-Residence, San Fernando Valley State College, at the
      First Pitzer College Commencement, June 6, 1965.

Claremont, Calif.: Pitzer College 1965.
Also included in the imprint data is: "Vol. 3, no. 2. Nov.
1965." Its pages are unnumbered and its "Preface" is by John
Atherton, President of Pitzer College (see no. 987).

15 Self-Interviews, recorded and edited by Barbara and James
        Reiss. Garden City, N.Y.: Doubleday and Co., 1970.
    "Part One: 'The Poet in Mid-Career,'" pp. 21-80.
        "Creative Possibilities," pp. 23-37.
        "In Medias Res," pp. 39-50.
        "Teaching, Writing, Reincarnations, and Rivers,"
            pp. 51-79.
    "Part Two: 'The Poem as Something that Matters,'" pp. 81-185.
        "Into the Stone," pp. 83-100.
        "Drowning with Others," pp. 101-121.
        "Helmets," pp. 123-136.
        "Buckdancer's Choice," pp. 137-162.
        "'Falling,'" pp. 163-185.
    Its "Introduction" is by Barbara and James Reiss (see no. 1060).

16 Sorties. Garden City, N.Y.: Doubleday and Co., 1971.
    "Part I: 'Journals,'" pp. 1-152.
    "Part II: 'New Essays,'" pp. 153-227.
        "The Self as Agent," pp. 155-164.
        "A Statement of Longing," pp. 165-170.
            "The Son, the Cave, and the Burning Bush,"
                pp. 166-170.
        "Two Talks in Washington," pp. 171-208.
            "1: 'Metaphor as Pure Adventure,'" pp. 172-188.
            "2: 'Spinning the Crystal Ball,'" pp. 189-208.
        "Two Voices," pp. 209-224.
            "1: 'Edwin Arlington Robinson,'" pp. 210-213.
            "2: 'The Greatest American Poet: Theodore Roethke.'"
                pp. 214-224.
        "One Voice," pp. 225-227.

17 Spinning the Crystal Ball: Some Guesses at the Future of
        American Poetry; A Lecture Delivered at the Library of
        Congress, April 24, 1967. Washington, D.C.: Library
        of Congress, 1967.
    In: Sorties.

18 The Suspect in Poetry. Madison, Minn.: The Sixties Press,
        1964.
    I: "The Suspect in Poetry," pp. 7-38.
        "The Suspect in Poetry," pp. 9-11.
        "The Winters Approach," pp. 12-15.
            "I: Donald Drummond," pp. 12-14.
            "II: Ellen Kay," pp. 14-15.
        "Allen Ginsberg," pp. 16-19.
        "Thom Gunn," pp. 20-23.
        "Ned O'Gorman," pp. 24-25.
        "Robert Mezey," pp. 26-27.

"Charles Olson," pp. 28-31.
"Harold Witt," p. 32.
"Anne Sexton," pp. 33-35.
"Philip Booth," pp. 36-37.
II: "In the Presence of Anthologies," pp. 39-52.
"New Poets of England and America I (1957)," pp. 40-45.
"The Grove Press New American Poets (1960),"
     pp. 46-51.
III: "The Second Birth," pp. 53-100.
"The Second Birth," pp. 55-57.
"Theodore Roethke," p. 58.
"Kenneth Patchen," pp. 59-60.
"Howard Nemerov," pp. 61-67.
"Hayden Carruth," pp. 68-72.
"Randall Jarrell," pp. 73-84.
"E. E. Cummings," pp. 85-91.
"Elder Olson," pp. 92-94.
"Richard Eberhart," pp. 95-96.
"Brother Antoninus," pp. 97-99.
IV: "Toward a Solitary Joy," pp. 101-120.
"Gary Snyder," pp. 102-103.
"Galway Kinnell," pp. 104-105.
"John Logan," pp. 106-109.
"W. S. Merwin," pp. 110-111.
"William Stafford," pp. 112-113.
"David Ignatow," pp. 114-117.
"Toward a Solitary Joy," pp. 118-120.
Much of The Suspect in Poetry subsequently appeared in Babel
to Byzantium (see no. 1).

19 Two Poems of the Air.   Portland, Ore.: Centicore Press,
       1964.
"The Firebombing," pp. 1-38.
"Reincarnation," pp. 41-84. (The Roman numeral "II"
     was subsequently added to its title.)
A limited edition of 300 copies in carolingian script by Monica
Moselly Pincus.

20 Yevtushenko, Yevgeny. Stolen Apples. Translated by James
       Dickey, et al. Garden City, N.Y.: Doubleday and Co.,
       1971.
"Pitching and Rolling," pp. 17-19.
"Assignation," pp. 30-32.
"'In aircraft, the newest, inexorable models,'" pp. 37-38.
"Doing the Twist on Nails," pp. 39-40.
"'I dreamed I already loved you,'" pp. 48-49.
"'Poetry gives off smoke,'" pp. 67-69.
"In the Wax Museum at Hamburg," pp. 70-73.
"Idol," pp. 90-91.
"Old Bookkeeper," pp. 92-93.
"Kamikaze," pp. 103-105.
"At the Military Registration and Enlistment Center,"
     pp. 108-110.

"The Heat in Rome," pp. 119-123.
Anthony Kahn is given credit for helping Dickey with each of these translations.

POETRY

21 "Adam in Winter. " Choice, no. 2 (1962), pp. 14-15.

22 "Adultery. " Nation 202 (28 Feb. 1966), p. 252.
    In: Poems 1957-1967.
    Rept.: Hollander, John (no. 464); Poulin, A., Jr. (no.
    493); Weiss, M. Jerry (no. 524).

23 "After the Night Hunt. " Poetry 99 (Jan. 1962), pp. 239-240.

24 "The Angel. "
    It was published as the second part of "Angel of the Maze"
    (see no. 26).

25 "The Angel. " In Translations by American Poets, edited by
    Jean Garrigue, pp. 81, 83, 85, 87, 89. Athens, Ohio:
    Ohio University Press, 1970.
    The original poem, Louis Emié's "L'Ange, " appears in
    French on pages 80, 82, 84, 86, and 88.

26 "Angel of the Maze. " Poetry 86 (June 1955), pp. 147-153.
    Its two parts are entitled "The Maze" (see no. 166) and
    "The Angel" (see no. 24).

27 "Angina. " New Yorker 40 (15 Aug. 1964), p. 30.
    In: Buckdancer's Choice; Poems 1957-1967.

28 "The Anniversary. " Poetry 82 (June 1953), pp. 138-139.
    The author's name appears as "James L. Dickey. "

29 "Antipolis. " Poetry 97 (Dec. 1960), pp. 153-154.
    In: Drowning with Others.

30 "Apollo. "
    The title under which "For the First Manned Moon Orbit"
    (see no. 111) and "The Moon Ground" (see no. 170) were col-
    lected.
    In: The Eye-Beaters, Blood, Victory, Madness, Buck-
    head and Mercy.
    Rept.: Vas Dias, Robert (no. 520).

31 "Approaching Prayer. "
    In: Helmets; Poems 1957-1967; Poems.

15

32 "Armor." Hudson Review 14 (Win. 1961-1962), pp. 557-558.
        In: Drowning with Others; Poems 1957-1967.
        Rept.: Stevenson, Lionel (no. 509); Strand, Mark
    (no. 515).

33 "Assignation." In Stolen Apples, by Yevgeny Yevtushenko,
        pp. 30-32. Garden City, N.Y.: Doubleday and Co., 1971.
        Anthony Kahn is given credit for helping Dickey with this
    translation.

34 "At Darien Bridge." New Yorker 38 (1 Dec. 1962), p. 60.
        Although published with this title, it appeared on this page
    with four other poems under their collective title, "Poems of
    North and South Georgia" (see no. 194).
        In: Helmets; Poems 1957-1967.
        Rept.: Eastman, Arthur M. (no. 455).

35 "At Mercy Manor." Atlantic 224 (Dec. 1969), pp. 75-76.
        Its title was changed to "Mercy" (see no. 167).

36 "At the Home for Unwed Mothers." Quarterly Review of Liter-
    ature 12 (Fall-Win. 1962), pp. 55-56.

37 "At the Military Registration and Enlistment Center." In
        Stolen Apples, by Yevgeny Yevtushenko, pp. 108-110. Gar-
    den City, N.Y.: Doubleday and Co., 1971.
        Anthony Kahn is given credit for helping Dickey with this
    translation.

38 "The Aura." New Yorker 41 (5 June 1965), p. 38.
        It was collected as the second part of "Fathers and Sons"
    (see no. 100).
        Rept.: Cotter, Janet M. (no. 452).

39 "Autumn." New Yorker 36 (29 Oct. 1960), p. 42.
        In: Drowning with Others.

40 "Awaiting the Swimmer." Kenyon Review 21 (Aut. 1959),
        pp. 609-610.
        In: Into the Stone and Other Poems; Poems 1957-1967.
        Exc.: "Into the Stone" (see no. 334).

41 "The Bee." Harper's Magazine 232 (June 1966), pp. 80-81.
        In: Poems 1957-1967.
        Rept.: Rylander, John (no. 501).

42 "A Beginning Poet, Aged Sixty-Five." Quarterly Review of
    Literature 9 (Win. 1958), pp. 272-273.

43 "The Beholders." New Yorker 38 (1 Dec. 1962), p. 61.
        Although published with this title, it appeared on this page
    with four other poems under their collective title, "Poems of
    North and South Georgia" (see no. 194).

In: Helmets; Poems 1957-1967.
Rept.: Allen, Gay Wilson (no. 444).

44 "The Being." Poetry 102 (Aug. 1963), pp. 281-284.
    In: Helmets; Poems 1957-1967.
    Rept.: Rosenthal, M. L. (no. 500).

45 "Below Ellijay." Poetry 101 (Oct. -Nov. 1962), pp. 27-28.
    It was collected as the second part of "On the Coosawat-
    tee" (see no. 177).
    Rept.: "Poetry": The Golden Anniversary Issue (no. 491).

46 "Below the Lighthouse." Poetry 94 (July 1959), pp. 223-225.
    Its title was changed to "On the Hill Below the Light-
    house" (see no. 178).

47 "Between Two Prisoners." Yale Review 50 (Sept. 1960),
    pp. 86-88.
       In: Drowning with Others; Poems 1957-1967.
       Rept.: Allen, Gay Wilson (no. 444); Eastman, Arthur
    (no. 455); Lapides, Frederick R. (no. 470); Millet, Fred B.
    (no. 481); Stevenson, Lionel (no. 507).

48 "A Birth." New Yorker 36 (13 Aug. 1960), p. 30.
    In: Drowning with Others; Poems 1957-1967.
    Rept.: McCullough, Francis Monson (no. 476); "Prize
    Winner" (no. 494).

49 "The Birthday Dream." Nation 201 (27 Sept. 1965), p. 170.
    In: Poems 1957-1967.

50 "The Blind Child's Story."
    Originally published as the second part of "The Owl King"
    (see no. 183), it subsequently became its third part (see
    no. 184).

51 "Blood." Poetry 114 (June 1969), pp. 149-150.
       In: The Eye-Beaters, Blood, Victory, Madness, Buckhead
    and Mercy.

51a "Blowgun and Rattlesnake." Texas Quarterly 6 (Aut. 1963),
    pp. 158-160.

52 "Bread."
    In: Poems 1957-1967.
    Rept.: Eastman, Arthur (no. 455).

53 "Breath." New Yorker 39 (9 Nov. 1963), p. 48.
    In: Helmets.

54 "Buckdancer's Choice." New Yorker 41 (19 June 1965), p. 36.
    In: Buckdancer's Choice; Poems 1957-1967.
    Rept.: Calhoun, Richard James (no. 449); Eastman,

Arthur M. (no. 455); Ellman, Richard (no. 456); Engle, Paul
(no. 457); Greenfield, Stanley B. (no. 460); Hughes, Langston
(no. 465); "The New Yorker" Book of Poems (no. 485).
Exc.: "A James Dickey Sampler" (no. 467).

55 "Bums, on Waking." New Yorker 39 (7 Sept. 1963), p. 34.
In: Helmets; Poems 1957-1967.
Rept.: Lieberman, Laurence (no. 472); "The New Yorker"
Book of Poems (no. 485); Stevenson, Lionel (no. 510).

56 "Butterflies."
It was published as the first part of "Messages" (see
no. 168).

57 "By Canoe Through the Fir Forest." New Yorker 38 (16 June
1962), p. 32.
It was collected as the first part of "On the Coosawattee"
(see no. 177).
Rept.: "The New Yorker" Book of Poems (no. 485);
Stevenson, Lionel (no. 509).

58 "The Call." Hudson Review 12 (Win. 1959-1960), p. 560.
In: Into the Stone and Other Poems.
Rept.: Hall, Donald (no. 462).
It was subsequently collected as the first part of "The
Owl King" (see no. 184).

59 "Camden Town." Virginia Quarterly Review 46 (Spr. 1970),
pp. 242-243.

60 "The Cancer Match." Poetry 114 (June 1969), pp. 158-159.
In: The Eye-Beaters, Blood, Victory, Madness, Buckhead
and Mercy.

61 "The Celebration." Harper's Magazine 230 (June 1965), p. 50.
In: Buckdancer's Choice; Poems 1957-1967.
Rept.: Carruth, Hayden (no. 450); Stevenson, Lionel
(no. 512).

62 "The Change." Kenyon Review 23 (Win. 1961), p. 71.
In: Drowning with Others.

63 "Chenille."
In: Helmets; Poems 1957-1967.
Rept.: Ellman, Richard (no. 456).

64 "Cherrylog Road." New Yorker 39 (12 Oct. 1963), p. 51.
In: Helmets; Poems 1957-1967; Poems.
Rept.: Brinnin, John Malcolm (no. 447); Crotty, Robert
(no. 453); Hieatt, A. Kent (no. 463); Lieberman, Laurence
(no. 472); Martz, William J./Beginnings (no. 477); Martz,
William J./The Distinctive (no. 478); "The New Yorker"
Book of Poems (no. 485); Simpson, Louis (no. 505); Strand,

Mark (no. 515); Thompson, Ruth (no. 517); Walsh, Chad
(no. 522); Williams, Miller (no. 527).

65   "The Child in Armor." Poetry 82 (June 1953), p. 137.
     The author's name appears as "James L. Dickey."

66   "Children Reading." In "Children's Book Section," New York
     Times Book Review (1 Nov. 1964), p. 1.

67   "A Child's Room." Quarterly Review of Literature 10 (Win.
     1960), pp. 247-248.

68   "Christmas Shopping, 1947." Gadfly 3 (Win. 1947), p. 59.
     The author's name appears as "Jim Dickey."

69   "Coming Back to America." New Yorker 41 (18 Sept. 1965),
     p. 57.
          In: Poems 1957-1967.
          Rept.: "The New Yorker" Book of Poems (no. 485).

70   "The Common Grave." New Yorker 40 (24 Oct. 1964), p. 54.
          In: Buckdancer's Choice; Poems 1957-1967.
          Rept.: Strand, Mark (no. 515).

71   "The Confrontation of the Hero (April, 1945)." Sewanee Review 63
     (July-Sept. 1955), pp. 461-464.
          The author's name appears as "James L. Dickey."

72   "The Courtship." Mutiny, no. 12 (1963), pp. 97-98.

73   "The Crows." In New World Writing, edited by Stewart
     Richardson and Corlies M. Smith, vo. 21, pp. 50-51.   New
     York: J. B. Lippincott and Co. , 1962.

74   "The Cypresses." Quarterly Review of Literature 9 (Win.
     1958), pp. 268-270.

75   "Dark Ones." Saturday Evening Post 240 (8 Apr. 1967), p. 72.
          In: Poems 1957-1967; "Education Via Poetry" (see
     no. 292).

76   "Deer Among Cattle." Shenandoah 16 (Sum. 1965), p. 78.
          In: Poems, 1957-1967; Poems.
          Rept.: Meiners, R. K. (no. 817).

77   "Diabetes." Poetry 114 (June 1969), pp. 151-155.
          The title under which "Sugar" (see no. 232) and "Under
     Buzzards" (see no. 247) were published.
          In: The Eye-Beaters, Blood, Victory, Madness, Buckhead
     and Mercy.

78   "A Dog Sleeping on My Feet." Poetry 99 (Jan. 1962),
     pp. 238-239.

In: Drowning with Others; Poems 1957-1967.
Rept.: Corrington, John William (no. 451); Drachler,
Jacob (no. 454); Millet, Fred B. (no. 481); Wallace, Robert
(no. 521).

79 "Doing the Twist on Nails." In Stolen Apples, by Yevgeny
Yevtuchenko, pp. 39-40. Garden City, N.Y.: Doubleday and
Co., 1971.
Anthony Kahn is given credit for helping Dickey with this
translation.

80 "Dover: Believing in Kings." Poetry 92 (Aug. 1958),
pp. 283-290.
In: Drowning with Others; Poems 1957-1967.

81 "The Dream Flood."
In: Drowning with Others.

82 "Drinking from a Helmet." Sewanee Review 71 (July-Sept.
1963), pp. 451-457.
In: Helmets; Poems 1957-1967.
Rept.: Lieberman, Laurence (no. 472).

83 "The Driver." New Yorker 39 (7 Dec. 1963), p. 54.
In: Helmets; Poems 1957-1967.
Rept.: Carruth, Hayden (no. 450); Stevenson, Lionel
(no. 510).

84 "Drowning with Others." Partisan Review 27 (Fall 1960),
pp. 636-637.
In: Drowning with Others; Poems 1957-1967.
Rept.: Leary, Paris (no. 471); Millet, Fred B.
(no. 481).

85 "Drums Where I Live." New Yorker 45 (29 Nov. 1969), p. 56.

86 "The Dusk of Horses." New Yorker 38 (1 Dec. 1962),
pp. 60-61.
Although published with this title, it appeared on this
page with four other poems under their collective title,
"Poems of North and South Georgia" (see no. 194).
In: Helmets; Poems 1957-1967.
Rept.: Allen, Gay Wilson (no. 444); Lieberman, Laurence
(no. 472); "The New Yorker" Book of Poems (no. 485);
Stevenson, Lionel (no. 509); Sullivan, Nancy (no. 928); Walsh,
Chad (no. 523).

87 "Dust."
In: Buckdancer's Choice; Poems 1957-1967.
Rept.: Crotty, Robert (no. 453); Schorer, Mark (no. 504).

88 "The Enclosure." Poetry 94 (July 1959), pp. 218-220.
In: Into the Stone and Other Poems; Poems 1957-1967.

89   "Encounter in the Cage Country." New Yorker 42 (11 June
      1966), p. 34.
          In: Poems 1957-1967.
          Rept.: Lieberman, Laurence (no. 472); Poulin, A., Jr.
      (no. 493).

90   "The Escape." New Yorker 40 (18 July 1964), p. 30.
          In: Buckdancer's Choice; Poems 1957-1967.

91   "Exchanges." Atlantic 226 (Sept. 1970), pp. 63-67.
          It was subsequently published in limited edition (see
      no. 5) and on the verso of a poster (see no. 554). The
      comment "being in the form of a dialogue with Joseph
      Trumbull Stickney (1874-1904)," which appears below the
      title, subsequently became, in somewhat altered form, the
      subtitle of the limited edition.

92   "The Eye-Beaters." Harper's Magazine 237 (Nov. 1968),
      pp. 134-136.
          In: The Eye-Beaters, Blood, Victory, Madness, Buckhead
      and Mercy.

93   "Faces Seen Once." Hudson Review 17 (Aut. 1964), pp. 414-
      416.
          In: Buckdancer's Choice; Poems 1957-1967.
          Exc.: "A James Dickey Sampler" (no. 467).

94   "Facing Africa." Encounter 16 (Apr. 1961), p. 41.
          In: Drowning with Others; Poems 1957-1967.
          Rept.: Spender, Stephen (no. 506).

95   "Falling." New Yorker 42 (11 Feb. 1967), pp. 38-40.
          In: Poems 1957-1967; Poems; "'Falling.'" (see no. 301).
          Rept.: Hollander, John (no. 464); Hutchins, Robert M.
      (no. 467); Lieberman, Laurence (no. 472); "The New Yorker"
      Book of Poems (no. 485); Rodman, Selden (no. 499).

96   "False Youth: Autumn: Clothes of the Age." Atlantic 228
      (Nov. 1971), p. 67.
          Rept.: Stalker, James C. (no. 1076).

97   "False Youth: Summer." Harper's Magazine 231 (Sept. 1965),
      p. 115.
          It was collected as the first part of "False Youth: Two
      Seasons" (see no. 98).
          Rept.: Stevenson, Lionel (no. 512).

98   "False Youth: Two Seasons."
          The title under which "False Youth: Summer" (see no.
      97) and "False Youth: Winter" (see no. 99) were collected.
          In: Poems 1957-1967.
          Rept.: Weiss, M. Jerry (no. 525).

99   "False Youth: Winter." New Yorker 42 (26 Feb. 1966),
      p. 44.
         It was collected as the second part of "False Youth:
      Two Seasons" (see no. 98).
         Rept.: Lieberman, Laurence (no. 472).

100 "Fathers and Sons."
         The title under which "The Second Sleep" (see no. 215)
      and "The Aura" (see no. 38) were collected.
         In: Buckdancer's Choice; Poems 1957-1967.

101 "The Father's Body." Poetry 89 (Dec. 1956), pp. 145-149.

102 "Fence Wire." New Yorker 38 (24 Feb. 1962), p. 36.
         In: Helmets; Poems 1957-1967.
         Rept.: Carruth, Hayden (no. 450); "The New Yorker"
      Book of Poems (no. 485); "Prize Winner" (no. 494).

103 "The Fiend." Partisan Review 32 (Spr. 1965), pp. 206-209.
         In: Buckdancer's Choice; Poems 1957-1967; "Buck-
      dancer's Choice" (see no. 274).
         Rept.: Lieberman, Laurence (no. 472); Schorer, Mark
      (no. 503); Trilling, Lionel (no. 518); Williams, Miller
      (no. 527); Williams, Oscar (no. 528).

104 "The Firebombing." Poetry 104 (Mar. 1964), pp. 63-72.
         In: Buckdancer's Choice; Poems 1957-1967; Two Poems
      of the Air.
         Rept.: Calhoun, Richard James (no. 449); Lieberman,
      Laurence (no. 472); Poulin, A., Jr. (no. 493); Untermeyer,
      Louis (no. 519).
         Exc.: "A James Dickey Sampler" (no. 467); Lowenfels,
      Walter (no. 475); "The Poet Turns on Himself" (no. 378).

105 "The First Morning of Cancer." Poetry 90 (May 1957),
      pp. 97-102.

106 "The Flash."
         In: Poems 1957-1967.
         Rept.: Crotty, Robert (no. 453); James Dickey Reads
      His Poems (no. 1223); "James Dickey: Worksheets"
      (no. 146).
         Several manuscript revisions of the poem were pub-
      lished as "James Dickey: Worksheets."

107 "The Flight." Beloit Poetry Journal 6 (Sum. 1956), pp. 16-19.

108 "Fog Envelops the Animals." Virginia Quarterly Review 37
      (Spr. 1961), pp. 224-225.
         In: Drowning with Others; Poems 1957-1967.
         Rept.: Poems from "The Virginia Quarterly Review"
      (no. 489).

109 "A Folk Singer of the Thirties." Poetry 102 (Aug. 1963),
       pp. 286-291.
          In: Helmets; Poems 1957-1967.

110 "For the Death of Vince Lombardi." Esquire 76 (Sept. 1971),
       p. 142.
          Rept.: Weibusch, John (no. 526).

111 ["For the First Manned Moon Orbit."] Life 66 (10 Jan. 1969),
       pp. 22a, 22c-22d.
          It was originally published without a title but was sub-
          sequently given this title. It was collected as the first
          part of "Apollo" (see no. 30).

112 "For the Last Wolverine." Atlantic Monthly 217 (June 1966),
       pp. 70-71.
          In: Poems 1957-1967.
          Exc.: "'Falling.'" (see no. 301).

113 "For the Linden Moth." Quarterly Review of Literature 13
       (Win. -Spr. 1964), pp. 38-40.
          Rept.: Quarterly Review of Literature (no. 495).

114 "For the Nightly Ascent of the Hunter Orion Over a Forest
       Clearing." New Yorker 37 (2 Dec. 1961), p. 58.
          In: Drowning with Others; Poems 1957-1967.
          Rept.: Brinnin, John Malcolm (no. 447).

115 "Fox Blood." Quarterly Review of Literature 13 (Win. -Spr.
       1964), pp. 37-38.
          In: Buckdancer's Choice; Poems 1957-1967.
          Rept.: "Prize Winner" (no. 494); Quarterly Review of
          Literature (no. 495).

116 "The Game." Poetry 94 (July 1959), pp. 211-212.
          In: Into the Stone and Other Poems.

117 "Gamecock." Virginia Quarterly Review 41 (Spr. 1965),
       pp. 232-233.
          In: Buckdancer's Choice; Poems 1957-1967.
          Rept.: Calhoun, Richard James (no. 449); Corrington,
          John William (no. 451); Poems from "The Virginia Quart-
          erly Review" (no. 489).

118 "The Gamecocks." Poetry 99 (Jan. 1962), pp. 240-242.

119 "Genesis." Commentary 25 (May 1958), p. 427.

120 "Giving a Son to the Sea."
          It was published as the second part of "Messages" (see
          no. 168).

121 "Goodbye to Serpents." New Yorker 39 (21 Sept. 1963), p. 47.

In: Helmets; Poems 1957-1967.
Rept.: "The New Yorker" Book of Poems (no. 485).

122 "The Ground of Killing." Sewanee Review 62 (Oct. 1954),
pp. 623-624.

123 "Haunting the Maneuvers." Harper's Magazine 240 (Jan.
1970), p. 95.
Rept.: Stevenson, Lionel (no. 514).

124 "The Head-Aim." Virginia Quarterly Review 41 (Spr. 1965),
pp. 233-234.
In: Poems 1957-1967.
Rept.: James Dickey Reads His Poems (no. 1223);
Poems from "The Virginia Quarterly Review" (no. 489).

125 "The Heat in Rome." In Stolen Apples, by Yevgeny
Yevtushenko, pp. 119-123. Garden City, N.Y.: Doubleday
and Co., 1971.
Anthony Kahn is given credit for helping Dickey with
this translation.

126 "The Heaven of Animals." New Yorker 37 (18 Nov. 1961),
p. 48.
In: Drowning with Others; Poems 1957-1967; "Drowning
with Others" (see no. 290).
Rept.: Allen, Gay Wilson (no. 444); Carrol, Paul
(no. 998); Crotty, Robert (no. 453); Ellman, Richard
(no. 456); Genthe, Charles (no. 459); Heyen, William
(no. 1105); Lieberman, Laurence (no. 1034); Lief, Leonard
(no. 473); Poulin, A., Jr. (no. 493); Roberts, Michael
(no. 498); "A Sampling of His Poetry" (no. 502); Strand,
Mark (no. 515); Walsh, Chad (no. 523); Williams, Miller
(no. 527).
Exc.: "Drowning with Others" (see no. 290).

127 "Hedge Life." New Yorker 41 (4 Sept. 1965), p. 34.
In: Poems 1957-1967.

128 "Horses and Prisoners." Hudson Review 16 (Aut. 1963),
pp. 384-385.
In: Helmets; Poems 1957-1967.
Rept.: Stevenson, Lionel (no. 510).

129 "The Hospital Window." Poetry 99 (Jan. 1962), pp. 236-237.
In: Drowning with Others; Poems 1957-1967.
Rept.: Drachler, Jacob (no. 454); Kostelanetz, Richard
(no. 469); Leary, Paris (no. 471); Lieberman, Laurence
(no. 472); Martz, William J. (no. 477); Meserole, Harrison
T. (no. 479).

130 "Hunting Civil War Relics at Nimblewill Creek." Sewanee
Review 69 (Jan.-Mar. 1961), pp. 139-141.

In: Drowning with Others; Poems 1957-1967.
Rept.: Drachler, Jacob (no. 454); Hall, Donald
(no. 461); Meserole, Harrison T. (no. 479).

131 "'I dreamed I already loved you. '" In Stolen Apples, by
Yevgeny Yevtushenko, pp. 48-49. Garden City, N. Y. :
Doubleday and Co. , 1971.
Anthony Kahn is given credit for helping Dickey with
this translation.

132 "The Ice Skin. " New Yorker 39 (28 Dec. 1963), p. 37.
In: Helmets; Poems 1957-1967; Poems.
Rept.: Clark, Robert (no. 635); Lieberman, Laurence
(no. 472); "The New Yorker" Book of Poems (no. 485).

133 "Idol. " In Stolen Apples, by Yevgeny Yevtushenko, pp. 90-91.
Garden City, N. Y. : Doubleday and Co. , 1971.
Anthony Kahn is given credit for helping Dickey with
this translation.

134 "'In aircraft, the newest, inexorable models. '" In Stolen
Apples, by Yevgeny Yevtushenko, pp. 37-38. Garden City,
N. Y. : Doubleday and Co. , 1971.
Anthony Kahn is given credit for helping Dickey with
this translation.

135 "In the Child's Night. " Virginia Quarterly Review 39 (Aut.
1963), pp. 590-591.
In: Helmets.

136 "In the Lupanar at Pompeii. " Kenyon Review 23 (Fall 1961),
pp. 631-633.
In: Drowning with Others; Poems 1957-1967.
Rept.: Walsh, Chad (no. 523).

137 "In the Marble Quarry. " New Yorker 38 (1 Dec. 1962), p. 60.
Although published with this title, it appeared on this
page with four other poems under their collective title,
"Poems of North and South Georgia" (see no. 194).
In: Helmets; Poems 1957-1967.
Rept.: Eastman, Arthur (no. 455); Lieberman, Laurence
(no. 472); "A Sampling of His Poetry" (no. 502).
Exc. : "Helmets" (see no. 321).

138 "In the Mountain Tent. " New Yorker 37 (28 Oct. 1961), p. 54.
In: Drowning with Others; Poems 1957-1967; Poems.
Rept.: Ganz, Margaret (no. 458); Genthe, Charles
(no. 459); Greenfield, Stanley B. (no. 460); Martz, William
J. (no. 478); Poulin, A. , Jr. (no. 493).

139 "In the Pocket. "
In: The Eye-Beaters, Blood, Victory, Madness, Buck-
head and Mercy.

Rept.: Graham, John (no. 1103); Knudson, R. R.
(no. 468).

140 "In the Tree House at Night." New Yorker 37 (24 June 1961),
p. 30.
In: Drowning with Others; Poems 1957-1967.
Rept.: Adams, Hazard (no. 443); Eastman, Arthur
(no. 455); Lieberman, Laurence (no. 472); Roberts, Michael
(no. 498); Thompson, Ruth (no. 517); Walsh, Chad (no. 523).

141 "In the Wax Museum at Hamburg." In Stolen Apples, by
Yevgeny Yevtushenko, pp. 70-73. Garden City, N. Y.:
Doubleday and Co., 1971.
Anthony Kahn is given credit for helping Dickey with
this translation.

142 "Inside the River." Poetry 97 (Dec. 1960), pp. 156-157.
In: Drowning with Others; Poems 1957-1967.
Rept.: Knudson, R. R. (no. 468).

143 "Into the Stone." Poetry 94 (July 1959), pp. 225-226.
In: Into the Stone and Other Poems; Poems 1957-1967;
Poems.

144 "The Inundation."
It was originally entitled "On the Inundation of the
Coosawattee Valley" (see no. 179) and was later collected
as the third part of "On the Coosawattee" (see no. 177).

145 "The Island." Sewanee Review 68 (Jan.-Mar. 1960), pp. 89-90.
In: Drowning with Others.

146 "James Dickey: Worksheets." Malahat Review, no. 7 (July
1968), pp. 113-116.
It is four manuscript revisions of "The Flash" (see
no. 106).

147 "The Jewel." Saturday Review 42 (6 June 1959), p. 38.
In: Into the Stone and Other Poems; Poems 1957-1967.
Rept.: Lieberman, Laurence (no. 472).

148 "Joel Cahill, Dead." Beloit Poetry Journal 8 (Sum. 1958),
pp. 18-19.

149 "Kamikaze." Playboy 18 (Oct. 1971), p. 152.
Rept.: Yevtushenko, Yevgeny (see no. 20).
Anthony Kahn is given credit in Stolen Apples for helping
Dickey with this translation but not in Playboy.

150 "King Crab and Rattler." Gadfly 3 (Spr. 1948), pp. 104-105.

151 "Knock." New Yorker 44 (25 Jan. 1969), p. 92.
In: The Eye-Beaters, Blood, Victory, Madness, Buck-
head and Mercy.

152 "Kudzu." New Yorker 39 (18 May 1963), p. 44.
        In: Helmets; Poems 1957-1967.
        Rept.: Hollander, John (no. 464).

153 "The Landfall." Poetry 94 (July 1959), pp. 213-215.
        In: Into the Stone and Other Poems.

154 "The Leap."
        In: Poems 1957-1967; Poems.
        Rept.: Kostelanetz, Richard (no. 469).

155 "A Letter." Sewanee Review 70 (July-Sept. 1962), pp. 416-
     417.
        In: Poems 1957-1967; Poems.
        Rept.: Stevenson, Lionel (no. 509).

156 "The Lifeguard." New Yorker 37 (5 Aug. 1961), p. 24.
        In: Drowning with Others; "The Poet Turns on Himself"
     (see no. 378); Poems 1957-1967; "Drowning with Others"
     (see no. 290).
        Rept.: Eastman, Arthur (no. 455); Kostelanetz, Richard
     (no. 469); Leary, Paris (no. 471); Lieberman, Laurence
     (no. 472); Martz, William J. (no. 478); Meserole, Harrison
     T. (no. 479); "The New Yorker" Book of Poems (no. 485);
     Peck, Richard (no. 487); Perrine, Laurence (no. 488);
     "Prize Winner" (no. 494); Stevenson, Lionel (no. 508);
     Sweetkind, Morris (no. 516); Thompson, Ruth (no. 517).

157 "Listening to Foxhounds." New Yorker 36 (26 Nov. 1960),
        p. 48.
        In: Drowning with Others; Poems 1957-1967.
        Rept.: Corrington, John William (no. 451); "A Sampling
     of His Poetry" (no. 502); Simpson, Louis (no. 505); Steven-
     son, Lionel (no. 507).

158 "Living There." Harper's Magazine 238 (May 1969), pp. 52-
     53.
        It was collected as the first part of "Two Poems of
     Going Home" (see no. 245).

159 "Looking for the Buckhead Boys." Atlantic 224 (Oct. 1969),
        pp. 53-56.
        It was collected as the second part of "Two Poems of
     Going Home" (see no. 245).

160 "The Lord in the Air." New Yorker 44 (19 Oct. 1968), p. 56.
        In: The Eye-Beaters, Blood, Victory, Madness, Buck-
     head and Mercy.

161 "Madness." New Yorker 45 (26 Apr. 1969), p. 40.
        In: The Eye-Beaters, Blood, Victory, Madness, Buck-
     head and Mercy.
        Rept.: "The New Yorker" Book of Poems (no. 485).

162 "The Magus." New Yorker 36 (24 Dec. 1960), p. 30.
        In: Drowning with Others; Poems 1957-1967.

163 "Mangham." Kenyon Review 27 (Sum. 1965), pp. 476-477.
        In: Buckdancer's Choice; Poems 1957-1967.

164 "Mary Sheffield." Shenandoah 15 (Win. 1964), pp. 52-53.
        In: Poems 1957-1967.

165 "May Day Sermon to the Women of Gilmer County, Georgia,
        by a Woman Preacher Leaving the Baptist Church."
        Atlantic Monthly 219 (Apr. 1967), pp. 90-97.
           In: Poems 1957-1967 (see no. 12); Poems 1957-1967.
           Rept.: Burnett, Whit (no. 448); Calhoun, Richard James
        (no. 449).
           Exc.: Lieberman, Laurence (no. 472).

166 "The Maze."
        Originally published as the first part of "Angel of the
        Maze" (see no. 26).

167 "Mercy."
        It was originally entitled "At Mercy Manor" (see no. 35).
           In: The Eye-Beaters, Blood, Victory, Madness, Buck-
        head and Mercy.

168 "Messages." New Yorker 45 (2 Aug. 1969), p. 30.
        Its two parts are entitled "Butterflies" (see no. 56) and
        "Giving a Son to the Sea" (see no. 120).
           In: The Eye-Beaters, Blood, Victory, Madness, Buck-
        head and Mercy.

169 "Mindoro, 1944." Paris Review 7 (Aut. -Win. 1960),
        pp. [122-123].
        The pages on which this appears are unnumbered.
           In: Into the Stone and Other Poems.

170 "The Moon Ground." Life 67 (4 July 1969), p. 16c.
        It was collected as the second part of "Apollo" (see
        no. 30).

171 "The Movement of Fish." New Yorker 37 (7 Oct. 1961),
        p. 58.
           In: Drowning with Others; Poems 1957-1967.
           Rept.: Carruth, Hayden (no. 450); "The New Yorker"
        Book of Poems (no. 485).

172 "Near Darien." Quarterly Review of Literature 10 (Win.
        1960), pp. 249-251.
           In: Into the Stone and Other Poems; Poems 1957-1967.
           Rept.: Quarterly Review of Literature (no. 495).

173 "The Night Pool." Virginia Quarterly Review 41 (Spr. 1965),

pp. 231-232.
In: Buckdancer's Choice; Poems 1957-1967; "Education Via Poetry" (see no. 292); "Buckdancer's Choice" (see no. 274).
Rept.: Poems from "The Virginia Quarterly Review" (no. 489).

174   "Of Holy War." Poetry 79 (Oct. 1951), p. 24.
The author's name appears as "James L. Dickey."
Rept.: Poetry (no. 490).

175   "Old Bookkeeper." In Stolen Apples, by Yevgeny Yevtushenko, pp. 92-93. Garden City, N.Y.: Doubleday and Co., 1971.
Anthony Kahn is given credit for helping Dickey with this translation.

176   "On Discovering that My Hand Shakes." Quarterly Review of Literature 12 (Fall-Win. 1962), pp. 59-60.

177   "On the Coosawattee."
The title under which "By Canoe Through the Fir Forest" (see no. 57), "Below Ellijay" (see no. 45), and "The Inundation" (see no. 144) were collected.
In: Helmets; Poems 1957-1967.

178   "On the Hill Below the Lighthouse."
It was originally entitled "Below the Lighthouse" (see no. 46).
In: Into the Stone and Other Poems; Poems 1957-1967.
Rept.: Hall, Donald (no. 462); Hollander, John (no. 464); Lapides, Frederick R. (no. 470).

179   "On the Inundation of the Coosawattee Valley." Yale Review 52 (Dec. 1962), pp. 234-235.
Its title was subsequently changed to "The Inundation" (see no. 144).

180   "Orpheus Before Hades." New Yorker 35 (5 Dec. 1959), p. 52.
In: Into the Stone and Other Poems.
Rept.: Allen, John Alexander (no. 445); Berry, David C. (no. 581).

181   "The Other." Yale Review 48 (Mar. 1959), pp. 398-400.
In: Into the Stone and Other Poems; Poems 1957-1967.
Rept.: Hollander, John (no. 464).

182   "The Owl King."
Originally published as the first part of "The Owl King" (see no. 183), it subsequently became its second part (see no. 184).

183   "The Owl King." Hudson Review 14 (Win. 1961-1962),

pp. 550-556.
Its two parts are entitled "The Owl King" (see no. 182) and "The Blind Child's Story" (see no. 50). An earlier poem, "The Call" (see no. 58), was subsequently added (see no. 184).

184 "The Owl King."
The title under which "The Call" (see no. 58) and "The Owl King" (see no. 183) were collected.
In: Drowning with Others; Poems 1957-1967.
Rept.: Leary, Paris (no. 471).

185 "Paestum." Shenandoah 14 (Win. 1963), pp. 7-10.

186 "The Performance." Poetry 94 (July 1959), pp. 220-221.
In: Into the Stone and Other Poems; Poems 1957-1967; Poems; "Into the Stone" (see no. 334).
Rept.: Crotty, Robert (no. 453); Ellman, Richard (no. 456); Engle, Paul (no. 457); Hall, Donald (no. 461); Hall, Donald and Pack, Robert (no. 462); Heyen, William (no. 1105); Lieberman, Laurence (no. 472); Strand, Mark (no. 515).

187 "Pine." New Yorker 45 (28 June 1969), p. 89.
Its two parts are entitled "Sound" and "Smell." It was collected as the first and second parts of "Pine" (see no. 188) with the titles of each part omitted.

188 "Pine."
The title under which "Pine" (see no. 187) and "Pine: Taste, Touch, and Sight" (see no. 189) were collected.
In: The Eye-Beaters, Blood, Victory, Madness, Buckhead and Mercy.

189 "Pine: Taste, Touch, and Sight." Poetry 114 (June 1969), pp. 160-162.
It is divided into three untitled, but numbered, parts. It was collected as the third, fourth, and fifth parts of "Pine" (see no. 188).

190 "Pitching and Rolling." In Stolen Apples, by Yevgeny Yevtushenko, pp. 17-19. Garden City, N.Y.: Doubleday and Co., 1971.
Anthony Kahn is given credit for helping Dickey with this translation.

191 "The Place." New Yorker 45 (1 Mar. 1969), p. 40.
In: The Eye-Beaters, Blood, Victory, Madness, Buckhead and Mercy.

192 "Poem." Quarterly Review of Literature 9 (Win. 1958), pp. 270-271.
In: Into the Stone and Other Poems.
Rept.: Quarterly Review of Literature (no. 495).

193 "A Poem About Bird-Catching by One Who Has Never Caught a
     Bird. " In New World Writing, edited by Stewart Richardson
     and Corlies M. Smith, vol. 21, pp. 53-54. New York:
     J. B. Lippincott and Co. , 1962.

194 "Poems of North and South Georgia. " New Yorker 38 (1 Dec.
     1962), pp. 60-61.
         The title under which five of Dickey's poems--"In the
     Marble Quarry" (see no. 137), "The Dusk of Horses" (see
     no. 86), "At Darien Bridge" (see no. 34), "The Beholders"
     (see no. 43), and "The Poisoned Man" (see no. 196)--were
     originally published.

195 "'Poetry gives off smoke. '" In Stolen Apples, by Yevgeny
     Yevtushenko, pp. 67-69. Garden City, N. Y. : Doubleday
     and Co. , 1971.
         Anthony Kahn is given credit for helping Dickey with
     this translation.

196 "The Poisoned Man. " New Yorker 38 (1 Dec. 1962), p. 61.
         Although published with this title, it appeared on this
     page with four other poems under their collective title,
     "Poems of North and South Georgia" (see no. 194).
         In: Helmets; Poems 1957-1967; Poems.
         Rept. : Baylor, Robert (no. 446); Walsh, Chad (no. 523).

197 "Power and Light. " New Yorker 43 (11 Mar. 1967), pp. 60-61.
         In: Poems 1957-1967.
         Rept. : Lieberman, Laurence (no. 472).

198 "The Prodigal. " Poetry Northwest 1 (Spr. -Sum. 1960),
     pp. 10-13.

199 "Pursuit from Under. " Hudson Review 17 (Aut. 1964),
     pp. 412-414.
         In: Buckdancer's Choice; Poems 1957-1967.
         Rept. : Lieberman, Laurence (no. 472); Stevenson,
     Lionel (no. 511).

200 "The Rafters. " Quarterly Review of Literature 13 (Win. -Spr.
     1964), pp. 40-42.

201 "The Rain Guitar. " New Yorker 47 (8 Jan. 1972), p. 36.

202 "The Red Bow. " Sewanee Review 65 (Oct. -Dec. 1957),
     pp. 627-634.

203 "Reincarnation. " New Yorker 40 (7 Mar. 1964), p. 51.
         The title subsequently included "(I)" (see no. 204).
         In: Buckdancer's Choice.
         Rept. : Corrington, John William (no. 451).

204 "Reincarnation (I). "

Originally, the title did not include the Roman numeral (see no. 203).
In: Poems 1957-1967.
Rept.: Corrington, John William (no. 451); Williams, Miller (no. 527).

205 "Reincarnation (II)."
In: Two Poems of the Air; Poems 1957-1967.
Rept.: Martz, William J. (no. 478); Poulin, A., Jr. (no. 493).

206 "Remnant Water." New Yorker 49 (10 Mar. 1973), p. 36.

207 "Reunioning Dialogue." Atlantic 231 (Jan. 1973), pp. 46-49.

208 "The Rib."
In: Drowning with Others.

209 "Root-Light, or the Lawyer's Daughter." New Yorker 45 (8 Nov. 1969), p. 52.

210 "The Salt Marsh." New Yorker 37 (16 Sept. 1961), p. 46.
In: Drowning with Others; Poems 1957-1967; Poems.
Rept.: Calhoun, Richard James (no. 449); "A Sampling of His Poetry" (no. 502).

211 "The Scarred Girl." New Yorker 39 (1 June 1963), p. 36.
In: Helmets; Poems 1957-1967; Poems.
Rept.: Allen, John Alexander (no. 445); Thompson, Ruth (no. 517); Walsh, Chad (no. 523).

212 "The Scratch." Quarterly Review of Literature 10 (Win. 1960), pp. 251-253.
In: Drowning with Others.
Rept.: Allen, Gay Wilson (no. 444); Quarterly Review of Literature (no. 495).

213 "A Screened Porch in the Country."
In: Drowning with Others; Poems 1957-1967.

214 "Sea Island." Gadfly 3 (Spr. 1948), p. 104.

215 "The Second Sleep." Kenyon Review 26 (Spr. 1964), pp. 302-303.
It was collected as the first part of "Fathers and Sons" (see no. 100).

216 "Seeking the Chosen." Times Literary Supplement (25 Nov. 1965), p. 1069.
It was published here with several other poets' works under their collective title, "Poems of the Sixties--4."

217 "The Shark at the Window." Sewanee Review 59 (Apr.-June

1951), pp. 290-291.
The author's name appears as "James L. Dickey."

218 "The Shark's Parlor." New Yorker 40 (30 Jan. 1965),
pp. 32-33.
In: Buckdancer's Choice; Poems 1957-1967.
Rept.: Lieberman, Laurence (no. 472); Martz, William
J. (no. 478); Miles, Josephine (no. 480); "The New Yorker"
Book of Poems (no. 485).

219 "The Sheep-Child." Atlantic Monthly 218 (Aug. 1966), p. 86.
The hyphen in its title was subsequently omitted.
In: Poems 1957-1967; Poems.
Rept.: Calhoun, Richard James (no. 449); Ellman,
Richard (no. 456); Hutchins, Robert M. (no. 466); Lieber-
man, Laurence (no. 472); Poulin, A., Jr. (no. 493);
Stevenson, Lionel (no. 513); Williams, Miller (no. 527).
Exc.: "'Falling'" (see no. 301).

220 "The Signs." Poetry 94 (July 1959), pp. 215-218.
In: Into the Stone and Other Poems.

221 "Slave Quarters." New Yorker 41 (14 Aug. 1965), pp. 28-29.
Lines 8-14, 49-53, 60-65, 110, and 171-172 and parts
of lines 82, 83, 109, 111, and 170, all of which appear in
subsequent versions, do not appear in the original.
In: Buckdancer's Choice; Poems 1957-1967; Poems.
Rept.: "The New Yorker" Book of Poems (no. 485);
Poulin, A., Jr. (no. 493).

222 "Sled Burial: Dream Ceremony." Southern Review, n.s. 1
(Jan. 1965), pp. 125-126.
The colon in the title was subsequently exchanged for a
comma.
In: Buckdancer's Choice; Poems 1957-1967.
Rept.: Heyen, William (no. 1105).

223 "Sleeping Out at Easter." Virginia Quarterly Review 36 (Spr.
1960), pp. 218-219.
In: Into the Stone and Other Poems; "The Poet Turns
on Himself" (see no. 378); Poems 1957-1967; "Into the
Stone" (see no. 334).
Rept.: Engle, Paul (no. 457); Poems from "The
Virginia Quarterly Review" (no. 489).
Exc.: "Into the Stone" (see no. 334); "The Poet Turns
on Himself" (see no. 378).

224 "Snakebite." New Yorker 43 (25 Feb. 1967), p. 44.
In: Poems 1957-1967; Poems.

225 "Snow on a Southern State."
In: Drowning with Others.

226 "A Sound through the Floor." Quarterly Review of Literature
     12 (Fall-Win. 1962), pp. 57-59.

227 "Springer Mountain." Virginia Quarterly Review 38 (Sum.
     1962), pp. 436-441.
          In: Helmets; Poems 1957-1967; "Helmets" (see no. 321).
          Rept.: Lieberman, Laurence (no. 472); Poems from
     "The Virginia Quarterly Review" (no. 489); Poulin, A., Jr.
     (no. 493).

228 "The Sprinter's Mother." Shenandoah 6 (Spr. 1955), pp. 17-18.

229 "The Sprinter's Sleep." Yale Review 47 (Sept. 1957), p. 72.
          In: Into the Stone and Other Poems.

230 "The Step." Literary Review 5 (Sum. 1962), pp. 474-475.

231 "The String." Poetry 94 (July 1959), pp. 222-223.
          In: Into the Stone and Other Poems; Poems 1957-1967.
          Rept.: Lieberman, Laurence (no. 472).

232 "Sugar."
          It was published as the first part of "Diabetes" (see
     no. 77).

233 "The Summons." Virginia Quarterly Review 37 (Spr. 1961),
     pp. 222-223.
          In: Drowning with Others; Poems 1957-1967.
          Rept.: Garrigue, Jean (no. 707); Poems from "The
     Virginia Quarterly Review" (no. 489); Stevenson, Lionel
     (no. 508).

234 "Sun." New Yorker 42 (28 Jan. 1967), p. 32.
          In: Poems 1957-1967.
          Rept.: Lieberman, Laurence (no. 472); Poulin, A.,
     Jr. (no. 493).

235 "Sustainment." Yale Review 54 (June 1965), pp. 547-548.
          In: Poems 1957-1967.
          Rept.: Stevenson, Lionel (no. 512).

236 "The Swimmer." Partisan Review 24 (Spr. 1957), pp. 244-
     246.

237 "Them, Crying." New Yorker 40 (9 May 1964), p. 42.
          In: Buckdancer's Choice; Poems 1957-1967; "Education
     Via Poetry" (see no. 292).
          Rept.: Stevenson, Lionel (no. 511).
          Exc.: "Buckdancer's Choice" (see no. 274).

238 "To a Beginning Poet, Aged Sixty." Atlantic Monthly 205
     (May 1960), p. 69.
          Its title was subsequently changed to "To Landrum Guy,
     Beginning to Write at Sixty" (see no. 241).

239   "To Be Edward Thomas." Beloit Poetry Journal Chapbook,
      no. 5 (Sum. 1957), pp. 10-15.

240   "To His Children in Darkness."
      In: Drowning with Others.

241   "To Landrum Guy, Beginning to Write at Sixty."
      It was originally entitled "To a Beginning Poet, Aged
      Sixty" (see no. 238).
      In: Drowning with Others.
      Rept.: Wallace, Robert (no. 521).

242   "Trees and Cattle." New Yorker 36 (16 July 1960), p. 34.
      In: Into the Stone and Other Poems; Poems 1957-1967.
      Rept.: Hall, Donald (no. 462).

243   "Turning Away." Hudson Review 19 (Aug. 1966), pp. 361-368.
      In: The Eye-Beaters, Blood, Victory, Madness, Buck-
      head and Mercy.

244   "The Twin Falls." Chicago Choice 1 (Spr. 1961), p. 52.
      In: Drowning with Others.
      Rept.: Molloy, Paul (no. 482).

245   "Two Poems of Going Home."
      The title under which "Living There" (see no. 158) and
      "Looking for the Buckhead Boys" (see no. 159) were col-
      lected.
      In: The Eye-Beaters, Blood, Victory, Madness, Buck-
      head and Mercy.

246   "Uncle." Quarterly Review of Literature 10 (Win. 1960),
      pp. 253-254.
      In: Into the Stone and Other Poems.

247   "Under Buzzards."
      It was published as the second part of "Diabetes" (see
      no. 77).

248   "The Underground Stream." New Yorker 36 (21 May 1960),
      p. 42.
      In: Into the Stone and Other Poems; Poems 1957-1967.
      Rept.: Hollander, John (no. 464).

249   "The Vegetable King." Sewanee Review 67 (Apr.-June 1959),
      pp. 278-280.
      In: Into the Stone and Other Poems; Poems 1957-1967.

250   "Venom." Poetry 114 (June 1969), pp. 156-157.
      In: The Eye-Beaters, Blood, Victory, Madness, Buck-
      head and Mercy.

251   "Via Appia." Chicago Choice 1 (Spr. 1961), pp. 50-51.

252 "Victory." Atlantic Monthly 222 (Aug. 1968), pp. 48-50.
        In: The Eye-Beaters, Blood, Victory, Madness, Buck-
        head and Mercy.

253 "A View of Fujiyama After the War." Poetry 97 (Dec. 1960),
        pp. 154-156.
        In: Drowning with Others.

254 "The Vigils." Beloit Poetry Journal 6 (Fall 1955), pp. 21-23.

255 "Walking on Water." New Yorker 36 (18 June 1960), p. 44.
        In: Into the Stone and Other Poems; Poems 1957-1967;
        Poems.
        Rept.: Hall, Donald (no. 462); Stevenson, Lionel
        (no. 507).

256 "Walking the Fire Line." Mutiny, no. 12 (1963), pp. 96-97.

257 "Wall and Cloud." In New World Writing, edited by Stewart
        Richardson and Corlies M. Smith, vol. 21, p. 52. New
        York: J. B. Lippincott and Co., 1962.

258 "The War Wound." New Yorker 40 (12 Sept. 1964), p. 54.
        In: Buckdancer's Choice; Poems 1957-1967.
        Rept.: Schorer, Mark (no. 504); Williams, Oscar
        (no. 528).

259 "The Wedding." Quarterly Review of Literature 10 (Win.
        1960), pp. 248-249.
        In: Into the Stone and Other Poems; Poems 1957-1967.

260 "Whitten and the Kite." Gadfly 4 (Sum. 1949), p. 26.

261 "Why in London the Blind Are Saviors." Poetry 102 (Aug.
        1963), pp. 284-286.

262 "Winter Trout." Paris Review 8 (Win.-Spr. 1964),
        pp. [98-99].
        The pages on which this appears are unnumbered.
        In: Helmets; Poems 1957-1967.
        Rept.: Stevenson, Lionel (no. 511).

263 "The Work of Art." Hudson Review 10 (Fall 1957),
        pp. 400-402.

PROSE

264 "After."
  In: Deliverance.

265 "Allen Ginsberg."
  Reviews of Howl and Kaddish originally in "From Babel
  to Byzantium" (see no. 310), pp. 508-510, and "Confession
  Is Not Enough" (see no. 280) respectively.
  In: The Suspect in Poetry; Babel to Byzantium.
  Exc.: Riley, Carolyn (see no. 496).

266 "Among the People."
  In: Jericho; "Jericho: The South Beheld" (see no. 343).
  Exc.: "Small Visions from a Timeless Place" (see
  no. 405).

267 "Anne Sexton."
  Reviews of To Bedlam and Part Way Back and All My
  Pretty Ones originally in "Five First Books" (see no. 304),
  pp. 318-319, and "Dialogues with Themselves" (see
  no. 287), respectively.
  In: The Suspect in Poetry; Babel to Byzantium (the re-
  view of All My Pretty Ones was omitted).
  Exc.: Riley, Carolyn and Harte, Barbara (see no. 497;
  only the review of To Bedlam and Part Way Back was
  excerpted).

268 "Arnold: 'Dover Beach.'" In Master Poems of the English
  Language: Over One Hundred Poems Together with Intro-
  ductions by Leading Poets and Critics of the English Speak-
  ing World, edited by Oscar Williams, pp. 713-715. New
  York: Trident Press, 1966.
  Its title was subsequently changed to "Matthew Arnold:
  'Dover Beach'" (see no. 361) and was collected with four
  other essays under the title "Five Poems" (see no. 305).

269 "Barnstorming for Poetry." New York Times Book Review (3
  Jan. 1965), pp. 1, 22-23.
  It was collected with two other essays under the title
  "The Poet Turns on Himself" (see no. 379).
  In: Babel to Byzantium.

270 "Before."

Originally published, with other portions of Deliverance, as "Two Days in September" (see no. 426), pp. 78-81.
In: Deliverance.

271 [No entry.]

272 "Blowjob on a Rattlesnake." Esquire 82 (Oct. 1974), pp. 174-178, 368.

273 "Brother Antoninus."
A review of The Crooked Lines of God originally in "The Suspect in Poetry or Everyman as Detective" (see no. 413), pp. 669-671.
In: The Suspect in Poetry; Babel to Byzantium.
Exc.: Riley, Carolyn (see no. 496).

274 "Buckdancer's Choice."
Two poems, "The Night Pool" (see no. 173), and "The Fiend" (see no. 103), appear here, and one, "Them Crying" (see no. 237), is excerpted.
In: Self-Interviews.

275 "Camping." New York Times Book Review (10 June 1973), pp. 6, 22.

276 "Charles Olson."
A review of The Maximus Poems originally in "The Death and Keys of the Censor" (see no. 285), pp. 322-324.
In: The Suspect in Poetry; Babel to Byzantium.
Exc.: Riley, Carolyn (see no. 496).

277 "Charles Tomlinson's Versions of Fyodor Tyuchev."
A review of Versions from Fyodor Tyuchev originally in "Toward a Solitary Joy" (see no. 423), p. 613.
In: Babel to Byzantium.

278 "Christopher Smart: 'A Song to David.'"
It was originally entitled "Smart: 'A Song to David'" (see no. 406).
In: Babel to Byzantium.

279 "Comments to Accompany Poems 1957-1967." Barat Review 3 (Jan. 1968), pp. 9-15.

280 "Confession Is Not Enough." New York Times Book Review (9 July 1961), p. 4.
The review of Allen Ginsberg's Kaddish (see no. 265) appears in The Suspect in Poetry and Babel to Byzantium.
Exc.: "A Mutiny Alert" (see no. 836).
Also reviewed are: Charles Olson's The Maximus Poems and The Distances and Harvey Shapiro's Mountain, Fire, and Thornbush.

281 "Conrad Aiken."
     Reviews of Sheepfold Hill and The Morning Song of Lord
     Zero originally entitled "A Gold-Mine of Consciousness"
     (see no. 315) and "That Language of the Brain" (see
     no. 416), respectively.
     In: Babel to Byzantium.
     Exc.: Riley, Carolyn (see no. 496; only the review of
     The Morning Song of Lord Zero is excerpted).

282 "Correspondences and Essences." Virginia Quarterly Review
     37 (Aut. 1961), pp. 635-640.
     Reviews of the following appear in The Suspect in Poetry
     and Babel to Byzantium: Hayden Carruth's Journey to a
     Known Place (see no. 320), William Stafford's West of Your
     City (see no. 437), and Theodore Roethke's I Am! Says
     the Lamb and Words for the Wind (see no. 417).
     Also reviewed are: William Goodreau's The Many Is-
     lands, Arthur Freeman's Apollonian Poems, Thomas
     Kinsella's Poems and Translations, Maxine W. Kumin's
     Halfway, and George Garrett's Abraham's Knife.

283 "Creative Possibilities."
     In: Self-Interviews.

284 "David Ignatow."
     Reviews of The Gentle Weight Lifter and Say Pardon
     originally in "Some of All of It" (see no. 407), pp. 325-
     326, and "The Death and Keys of the Censor" (see no. 285),
     pp. 325-326, respectively.
     In: The Suspect in Poetry; Babel to Byzantium.

285 "The Death and Keys of the Censor." Sewanee Review 69
     (Apr.-June 1961), pp. 318-332.
     Reviews of the following appear in The Suspect in Poetry
     and Babel to Byzantium: The New American Poetry 1945-
     1960 (see no. 318), Charles Olson's The Maximus Poems
     (see no. 276), Howard Nemerov's New and Selected Poems
     (see no. 327), and David Ignatow's Say Pardon (see
     no. 284).
     Reviews of the following appear in Babel to Byzantium:
     Lewis Turco's First Poems (see no. 355), W. S. Merwin's
     The Drunk in the Furnace (see no. 431), Theodore Weiss'
     Outlanders (see no. 420), and Josephine Miles' Poems 1930-
     1960 (see no. 348).
     Also reviewed are: Robert Bagg's Madonna of the Cello
     and Charles H. Philbrick's Wonderstrand Revisited.

286 "Delights of the Edge." Mademoiselle 79 (June 1974),
     pp. 118-119.
     Exc.: "The Honorable Jester" (see no. 324).

287 "Dialogues with Themselves." New York Times Book Review
     (28 Apr. 1963), p. 50.

The review of Anne Sexton's All My Pretty Ones appears in The Suspect in Poetry (see no. 267).
Also reviewed are: Richard Emil Braun's Children Passing and Charles Gullans' Arrivals and Departures.

288   "Donald Drummond. "
        Its title was subsequently changed to "Donald F. Drummond" (see no. 289).
        A review of The Battlement originally in "From Babel to Byzantium" (see no. 310), pp. 514-515.
        In: The Suspect in Poetry (the first part of "The Winters Approach" [see no. 440]).

289   "Donald F. Drummond. "
        It was originally entitled "Donald Drummond" (see no. 288).
        In: Babel to Byzantium.

290   "Drowning with Others. "
        Two poems, "The Lifeguard" (see no. 156), and "The Heaven of Animals" (see no. 126), appear here.   The latter poem is also excerpted.
        In: Self-Interviews.

291   "E. E. Cummings. "
        A review of 95 Poems originally in "The Human Power" (see no. 328), pp. 511-516.
        In: The Suspect in Poetry; Babel to Byzantium.
        Exc. : Riley, Carolyn (see no. 496).

292   "Education via Poetry. " In Teaching in America: Proceedings of the Fifth Annual Conference of the National Committee for Support of the Public Schools, April 2-4, 1967, pp. 34-43. Washington, D. C. : National Committee for Support of the Public Schools, 1967.
        Three poems--"Them, Crying" (see no. 237), "The Night Pool, " (see no. 173), and "Dark Ones" (see no. 75)--appear here.

293   "Edwin Arlington Robinson. "
        It was originally entitled "Edwin Arlington Robinson: The Many Truths" (see no. 295).
        In: Babel to Byzantium.

294   "Edwin Arlington Robinson. "
        It was originally entitled "The Poet of Secret Lives and Misspent Opportunities" (see no. 376).
        In: Sorties.

295   "Edwin Arlington Robinson: The Many Truths. " In Selected Poems of Edwin Arlington Robinson, edited by Morton Dauwen Zabel, pp. xi-xxviii.   New York: Macmillan Co. , 1965.

Its title was subsequently changed to "Edwin Arlington
Robinson" (see no. 293).
Rept.:   Murphy,   Francis (no.   483); Owen, Guy
(no. 486).

296 "Edwin Muir."
A review of Collected Poems originally in "In the
Presence of Anthologies" (see no. 331), pp. 310-312.
In: Babel to Byzantium.

297 "Elder Olson."
A review of Plays and Poems 1948-1958 originally in
"The Human Power" (see no. 328), pp. 509-511.
In: The Suspect in Poetry; Babel to Byzantium.

298 "Ellen Kay."
A review of A Local Habitation originally in "Five
Poets" (see no. 307), pp. 119-120.
In: The Suspect in Poetry (the second part of "The
Winters Approach" [see no. 440]); Babel to Byzantium.

299 "Emma Swan."
A review of Poems originally in "The Human Power"
(see no. 328), pp. 501-502.
In: Babel to Byzantium.

300 "Epilogue."
In: Jericho; "Jericho: The South Beheld" (see no. 343).

301 "'Falling.'"
It was originally entitled "The Poet Tries to Make a
Kind of Order" (see no. 377). (The sections on "Sun,"
"The Bee," and "The Leap" and the poem "Falling" do not
appear in the original version.)
One poem, "Falling" (see no. 95), appears here and
two others, "The Sheep Child" (see no. 219) and "For the
Last Wolverine" (see no. 112), are excerpted.
In: Self-Interviews.

302 "First and Last Things." Poetry 103 (Feb. 1964), pp. 316-
324.
Reviews of the following appear in Babel to Byzantium:
Robert Graves' New Poems (see no. 394), Robinson Jeffers'
The Beginning and the End and Other Poems (see no. 397),
Ralph Hodgson's Collected Poems (see no. 384), Vernon
Watkins' Affinities (see no. 429), and William Carlos
Williams' The Collected Later Poems (see no. 433).
Also reviewed are: Gene Frumkin's The Hawk and The
Lizard, Rolf Fjelde's The Imagined Word, R. G. Everson's
Blind Man's Holiday, Frederick Seidel's Final Solutions,
Jean Burden's Naked as the Glass, and Charles Baudelaire:
The Flowers of Evil.

303   "First Novelists," edited by Irene Land.   Library Journal 95
        (1 Feb. 1970), pp. 516-522 [517].
            Remarks by Dickey concerning Deliverance are added to
        comments by other novelists about their own first works.
        Exc.: Kinsman, Clare D. (see no. 1029).

304   "Five First Books."   Poetry 97 (Feb. 1961), pp. 316-320.
            Reviews of the following appear in The Suspect in Poetry
        and Babel to Byzantium: Anne Sexton's To Bedlam and
        Part Way Back (see no. 267) and Galway Kinnell's What a
        Kingdom It Was (see no. 311).
            The review of Gary Snyder's Myths and Texts (see
        no. 312) appears in The Suspect in Poetry.
            Also reviewed are: Bruce Cutler's The Year of the
        Green Wave and George Starbuck's Bone Thoughts.

305   "Five Poems."
            The title under which "Smart: 'A Song to David'" (see
        no. 406), "Arnold: 'Dover Beach'" (see no. 268), "Hop-
        kins: 'The Wreck of the Deutschland'" (see no. 325),
        "Thompson: 'The Hound of Heaven'" (see no. 422), and
        "Williams: 'The Yachts'" (see no. 438) were collected.
            In: Babel to Byzantium.

306   "Five Poets."   Poetry 89 (Nov. 1956), pp. 110-117.
            Reviews of the following appear in Babel to Byzantium:
        Samuel French Morse's The Scattered Causes (see no. 399)
        and Reed Whittemore's An American Takes a Walk (see
        no. 388).
            Also reviewed are: Ernest Sandeen's Antennas of
        Silence, Wilfred Watson's Friday's Child, and Charles
        Bell's Delta Return.

307   "Five Poets."   Poetry 94 (May 1959), pp. 117-123.
            Reviews of the following appear in The Suspect in
        Poetry and Babel to Byzantium: Ellen Kay's A Local Habi-
        tation (see no. 298) and Harold Witt's The Death of Venus
        (see no. 319).
            The review of Margaret Tongue's A Book of Kinds (see
        no. 359) appears in Babel to Byzantium.
            Also reviewed are: Alan Stephens' The Sum and William
        Pillin's Passage After Midnight.

308   [Foreword].
            It is untitled.
            In: Exchanges.

309   "Francis Thompson: 'The Hound of Heaven.'"
            It was originally entitled "Thompson: 'The Hound of
        Heaven'" (see no. 422).
            In: Babel to Byzantium.

310   "From Babel to Byzantium."   Sewanee Review 65 (July-Sept.

1957), pp. 508-530.
Reviews of the following appear in The Suspect in Poetry
and Babel to Byzantium: Donald F. Drummond's The Bat-
tlement (see nos. 288 and 289) and Allen Ginsberg's Howl
(see no. 265).
Reviews of the following appear in Babel to Byzantium:
John Ashbery's Some Trees (see no. 344), Rolphe Hum-
phries' Green Armor on Green Ground (see no. 398), Herbert
Reed's Moon's Farm (see no. 322), and Katherine Hoskins'
Villa Narcisse (see no. 350).
Also reviewed are: Poets of Today III, Richard Lyon's
Men and Tin Kettles, Neil Weiss' Changes of Garments,
and Lenore G. Marshall's The Center Is Everywhere.

311 "Galway Kinnell."
A review of What a Kingdom It Was originally in "Five
First Books" (see no. 304), pp. 319-320.
In: Babel to Byzantium.
Exc.: Riley, Carolyn (see no. 496).

312 "Gary Snyder."
A review of Myths and Texts originally in "Five First
Books" (see no. 304), pp. 316-317.
In: The Suspect in Poetry.

313 "Gene Derwood."
A review of The Poems of Gene Derwood originally in
"Some of All of It" (see no. 407), pp. 330-333.
In: Babel to Byzantium.

314 "Gerard Manley Hopkins: 'The Wreck of the Deutschland.'"
It was originally entitled "Hopkins: 'The Wreck of the
Deutschland'" (see no. 325).
In: Babel to Byzantium.

315 "A Gold-Mine of Consciousness." Poetry 94 (Apr. 1959),
pp. 41-44.
A review of Conrad Aiken's Sheepfold Hill (see no. 281)
which appears in Babel to Byzantium.

316 "The Greatest American Poet." Atlantic 222 (Nov. 1968),
pp. 53-58.
Its title was subsequently changed to "The Greatest
American Poet: Theodore Roethke" (see no. 317). It is
Dickey's memoir of Roethke and a review of Allen Seager's
The Glass House, a biography of Roethke.

317 "The Greatest American Poet: Theodore Roethke."
It was originally entitled "The Greatest American Poet"
(see no. 316).
In: Sorties.

318 "The Grove Press New American Poets (1960)."

A review of The New American Poetry: 1945-1960 originally in "The Death and Keys of the Censor" (see no. 285), pp. 318-322.
In: The Suspect in Poetry; Babel to Byzantium (the first part of "In the Presence of Anthologies" [see no. 332]).

319 "Harold Witt. "
A review of The Death of Venus originally in "Five Poets" (see no. 307), pp. 122-123.
In: The Suspect in Poetry; Babel to Byzantium.

320 "Hayden Carruth. "
Reviews of The Crow and the Heart and Journey to a Known Place originally in "The Suspect in Poetry or Every-man as Detective" (see no. 413), pp. 671-673, and "Correspondences and Essences" (see no. 282), pp. 637-639, respectively.
In: The Suspect in Poetry; Babel to Byzantium.

321 "Helmets. "
One poem, "Springer Mountain" (see no. 227), appears here, and another, "In the Marble Quarry" (see no. 137), is excerpted.
In: Self-Interviews.

322 "Herbert Reed. "
A review of Moon's Farm originally in "From Babel to Byzantium" (see no. 310), pp. 523-524.

323 "The High Cost of Fame: Reflections on the Bitch Goddess by Nine Authors Who Have Scored with Her. " Playboy 18 (Jan. 1971), pp. 123-127 [124].

324 "The Honorable Jester. " Christian Science Monitor (17 Dec. 1974), p. 11.
An excerpt from "Delights of the Edge" (see no. 286).

325 "Hopkins: 'The Wreck of the Deutschland.'" In Master Poems of the English Language: Over One Hundred Poems Together with Introductions by Leading Poets and Critics of the English Speaking World, edited by Oscar Williams, pp. 801-803. New York: Trident Press, 1966.
Its title was subsequently changed to "Gerard Manley Hopkins: 'The Wreck of the Deutschland'" (see no. 314) and to "Introduction" (see no. 335). It was collected with four other essays under the title "Five Poems" (see no. 305).

326 "Horace Gregory. "
A review of Medusa in Gramercy Park originally in "The Stillness at the Center of the Target" (see no. 411), pp. 493-494.

327 "Howard Nemerov."
     Reviews of The Salt Garden and New and Selected Poems
     originally in "Some of All of It" (see no. 407), pp. 333-
     336, and "The Death and Keys of the Censor" (see no. 285),
     pp. 331-332, respectively.
     In: The Suspect in Poetry; Babel to Byzantium.
     Exc.: Riley, Carolyn and Harte, Barbara (see no. 497;
     only the review of New and Selected Poems was excerpted).

328 "The Human Power." Sewanee Review 67 (Sum. 1959),
     pp. 497-519.
     Reviews of the following appear in The Suspect in Poetry
     and Babel to Byzantium: E. E. Cummings' 95 Poems (see
     no. 291) and Elder Olson's Plays and Poems 1948-1958
     (see no. 297).
     A review of Ned O'Gorman's The Night of the Hammer
     (see no. 364) appears in The Suspect in Poetry.
     Reviews of the following appear in Babel to Byzantium:
     James Merrill's The Country of a Thousand Years of Peace
     and Other Poems (see no. 342), Emma Swan's Poems (see
     no. 299), Winfield Townley Scott's The Dark Sister (see
     no. 439), and Nikos Kazantzakis' The Odyssey: A Modern
     Sequel (see no. 368).
     Also reviewed are: Tania van Zyl's Shadow and Wall,
     John Edward Hardy's Certain Poems, Louis O. Coxe's The
     Wilderness and Other Poems, and Robin Skelton's Third
     Day Lucky.

329 "I. A. Richards."
     A review of The Screens and Other Poems originally in
     "The Stillness at the Center of the Target" (see no. 411),
     pp. 494-496.
     In: Babel to Byzantium.

330 "In Medias Res."
     In: Self-Interviews.

331 "In the Presence of Anthologies." Sewanee Review 66 (Apr. -
     June 1958), pp. 294-314.
     Reviews of the following appear in The Suspect in Poetry
     and Babel to Byzantium: The New Poets of England and
     America (see no. 367), Philip Booth's Letter from a Dis-
     tant Land (see no. 375), Kenneth Patchen's When We Were
     Here Together (see no. 352), and Richard Eberhart's Great
     Praises (see no. 389).
     Reviews of the following appear in Babel to Byzantium:
     Ted Hughes' The Hawk in the Rain (see no. 415), May
     Sarton's In Time Like Air (see no. 362), William Jay
     Smith's Poems 1947-1957 (see no. 435), Robert Penn War-
     ren's Promises: Poems 1954-1956 (see no. 396), Edwin
     Muir's Collected Poems (see no. 296), and Lawrence Dur-
     rell's Selected Poems (see no. 354).
     Also reviewed are: Mavericks, Kingsley Amis' A Case

of Samples, Poets of Today IV, Peter Kane Dufault's For Some Stringed Instrument, Arthur Gregor's Declensions of a Refrain, Thomas Merton's The Strange Lands, Daniel Berrigan's Time Without Number, and Richmond Lattimore's Poems.

332 "In the Presence of Anthologies."
        The title under which "New Poets of England and America I (1957)" (see no. 367) and "The Grove Press New American Poets (1960)" (see no. 318) were collected.
        In: The Suspect in Poetry; Babel to Byzantium.

333 "In the Terrified Radiance." New York Times Book Review (24 Sept. 1972), p. 4.
        A review of Stanley Burnshaw's In the Terrified Radiance.

334 "Into the Stone."
        Two poems, "Sleeping Out at Easter" (see no. 223) and "The Performance" (see no. 186), appear here. The former and another poem, "Awaiting the Swimmer" (see no. 40), are also excerpted.
        In: Self-Interviews.

335 "Introduction." In The Wreck of the Deutschland, by Gerard Manley Hopkins. Boston: David Godine: 1971.
        It was originally entitled "Hopkins: 'The Wreck of the Deutschland'" (see no. 325). The pages on which this appears are unnumbered.

336 "Introduction." In James Dickey: A Checklist, compiled by Franklin Ashley, p. xi. Detroit: Gale Research Co., Book Tower, 1972.

337 "Introduction."
        In: Jericho.
        Exc.: "Jericho: The South Beheld" (see no. 343).

338 "J. V. Cunningham."
        A review of To What Strangers, What Welcome originally in "Orientations" (see no. 374), pp. 648, 650.
        In: Babel to Byzantium.

*339 "James Dickey, National Book Award in Poetry, 1966: Acceptance Speech." New York, 1966.
        A copy of the "mimeographed (or possibly multilithed)" speech Dickey gave during the NBA. It was printed on "three sheets of white 8 1/2" x 11" paper with material on the rectos only."
        In: Ashley, Franklin (see no. 1127).
        *[This citation is from Franklin Ashley's James Dickey: A Checklist, p. 97 (see no. 1127).]

340 "James Dickey Tells About Deliverance. "   Literary Guild Mag-
     azine (Apr. 1970), pp. 6-7.

341 "James Kirkup. "
         Review of The Prodigal Son originally in "The Suspect in
     Poetry or Everyman as Detective" (see no. 413), pp. 673-
     674.
         In: Babel to Byzantium.
         Exc. : Riley, Carolyn (see no. 496).

342 "James Merrill. "
         A review of The Country of a Thousand Years of Peace
     and Other Poems originally in "The Human Power" (see
     no. 328).
         In: Babel to Byzantium.
         Exc. : Riley, Carolyn and Harte, Barbara (see no. 497).

343 "Jericho: The South Beheld. "   Southern Living (Oct. 1974),
     pp. 1A-16A.
         A collection of portions of "Introduction" (see no. 337),
     "The Land and the Water" (see no. 353), "Among the
     People" (see no. 266), and "The Traditions Web" (see
     no. 425), with the entire "Epilogue" (see no. 300).

344 "John Ashbery. "
         A review of Some Trees originally in "From Babel to
     Byzantium" (see no. 310), pp. 515-517.
         In: Babel to Byzantium.
         Exc. : Riley, Carolyn and Harte, Barbara (see no. 497).

345 "John Berryman. "
         A review of 77 Dream Songs originally in "Orientations"
     (see no. 374), p. 648.
         In: Babel to Byzantium.
         Exc. : Riley, Carolyn (see no. 496).

346 "John Frederick Nims. "
         A review of Knowledge of the Evening originally in
     "Stillness at the Center of the Target" (see no. 411),
     pp. 485-487.
         In: Babel to Byzantium.

347 "John Logan. "
         It was originally entitled "A Note on the Poetry of John
     Logan" (see no. 369).
         A review of Ghosts of the Heart.
         In: The Suspect in Poetry; Babel to Byzantium.

348 "Josephine Miles. "
         A review of Poems 1930-1960 originally in "The Death
     and Keys of the Censor" (see no. 285), pp. 330-331.
         In: Babel to Byzantium.
         Exc. : Riley, Carolyn (see no. 496).

349 "Journals. "
　　　　　In: Sorties.

350 "Katherine Hoskins. "
　　　　　Reviews of Villa Narcisse and Excursions originally in
　　　　　"From Babel to Byzantium" (see no. 310), pp. 527-528,
　　　　　and "Of Mind and Soul" (see no. 371), pp. 10, 12, respec-
　　　　　tively.
　　　　　In: Babel to Byzantium.

351 "Kenneth Burke. "
　　　　　A review of Book of Moments originally in "Some of All
　　　　　of It" (see no. 407), pp. 328-330.
　　　　　In: Babel to Byzantium.
　　　　　Exc. : Riley, Carolyn and Harte, Barbara (see no. 497).

352 "Kenneth Patchen. "
　　　　　A review of When We Were Here Together originally in
　　　　　"In the Presence of Anthologies" (see no. 331), pp. 302-303.

353 "The Land and the Water. "
　　　　　In: Jericho.
　　　　　Exc. : "Jericho: The South Beheld" (see no. 343);
　　　　　"Small Visions from a Timeless Place" (see no. 405).

354 "Lawrence Durrell. "
　　　　　A review of Selected Poems originally in "In the Pres-
　　　　　ence of Anthologies" (see no. 331), pp. 312-313.
　　　　　In: Babel to Byzantium.

355 "Lewis Turco. "
　　　　　A review of First Poems originally in "The Death and
　　　　　Keys of the Censor" (see no. 285), p. 327.
　　　　　In: Babel to Byzantium.

356 "A Look into Your Future ... Life Style. " Today's Health 51
　　　　　(Apr. 1973), pp. 54, 65.

357 "Louis MacNiece. "
　　　　　A review of Solstices and Eighty-Five Poems originally
　　　　　in "Toward a Solitary Joy" (see no. 423), pp. 610-612.
　　　　　In: Babel to Byzantium.
　　　　　Exc. : Riley, Carolyn (see no. 496).

358 "Louis Simpson. "
　　　　　A review of Selected Poems originally in "Orientations"
　　　　　(see no. 374), pp. 650, 656.
　　　　　In: Babel to Byzantium.

359 "Margaret Tongue. "
　　　　　A review of A Book of Kinds originally in "Five Poets"
　　　　　(see no. 307), pp. 120-121.
　　　　　In: Babel to Byzantium.

360 "Marianne Moore. "
        Reviews of A Marianne Moore Reader and Tell Me, Tell
     Me originally in "The Stillness at the Center of the Target"
     (see no. 411), pp. 499-503, and "What the Angels Missed"
     (see no. 432), respectively.
        In: Babel to Byzantium.
        Exc.: Riley, Carolyn (see no. 496).

361 "Matthew Arnold: 'Dover Beach. '"
        It was originally entitled "Arnold: 'Dover Beach'" (see
     no. 268).
        In: Babel to Byzantium.

362 "May Sarton. "
        A review of In Time Like Air originally in "In the Pres-
     ence of Anthologies" (see no. 331), pp. 306-307.
        In: Babel to Byzantium.

363 "Metaphor as Pure Adventure. "
        A lecture originally published as a pamphlet (see no. 10).
        In: Sorties.

364 "Ned O'Gorman. "
        A review of The Night of the Hammer originally in "The
     Human Power" (see no. 328), pp. 502-503.
        In: The Suspect in Poetry.

365 "New Essays. "
        The title under which "The Self as Agent" (see no. 401)
     and "The Son, the Cave, and the Burning Bush" (see
     no. 408) were collected.
        In: Sorties.

366 "The New Literature. " In The University and the New Intel-
     lectual Environment, pp. 66-84. New York: St. Martin's
     Press, in association with York University, 1968.
        This is the seventh of the Frank Gerstein Lectures,
     York University Invitation Series. It was delivered in
     November 1967.

367 "New Poets of England and America I (1957). "
        A review of The New Poets of England and America
     originally in "In the Presence of Anthologies" (see no. 331),
     pp. 294-299.
        In: The Suspect in Poetry; Babel to Byzantium (the
     second part of "In the Presence of Anthologies" [see
     no. 332]).

368 "Nikos Kazantzakis. "
        A review of The Odyssey: A Modern Sequel originally
     in "The Human Power" (see no. 328), pp. 516-519.
        In: Babel to Byzantium.

369 "A Note on the Poetry of John Logan." Sewanee Review 70
     (Apr. -June 1962), pp. 257-260.
          Its title was subsequently changed to "John Logan" (see
     no. 347).
          A review of Ghosts of the Heart.

370 "Notes on the Decline of Outrage." In South: Modern Southern
     Literature in Its Cultural Setting, edited by Louis D. Rubin,
     Jr. and Robert D. Jacobs, pp. 76-94. Garden City, N.Y.:
     Doubleday and Co., 1961.
          It was collected with three other essays under the title
     "The Poet Turns on Himself" (see no. 379).
          In: Babel to Byzantium.

371 "Of Mind and Soul." New York Times Book Review (18 June
     1967), pp. 10-12.
          The review of Katherine Hoskins' Excursions appears in
     Babel to Byzantium (see no. 350).
          Also reviewed is John L'Heureux's Rubrics for a Revolu-
     tion.

372 "An Old Family Custom." New York Times Book Review (6
     June 1965), pp. 1, 16.

373 ["One Voice"]. In The Distinctive Voice: Twentieth-Century
     American Poetry, edited by William J. Martz, pp. 227-
     228. Glenview, Ill.: Scott, Foresman, and Co., 1966.
          Originally, it did not have a title, being an "introduction"
     to five of Dickey's poems: "Cherrylog Road" (see no. 64),
     "In the Mountain Tent" (see no. 138), "The Lifeguard" (see
     no. 156), "Reincarnation (II)" (see no. 205), and "The
     Shark's Parlor" (see no. 218).
          In: Sorties.

374 "Orientations." American Scholar 34 (Aut. 1965), pp. 646,
     648, 650, 656, 658.
          Reviews of the following appear in Babel to Byzantium:
     Louis Simpson's Selected Poems (see no. 358), William
     Meredith's The Wreck of the Thresher and Other Poems
     (see no. 436), John Berryman's 77 Dream Songs (see
     no. 345), Robert Duncan's Roots and Branches (see no. 391),
     and J. V. Cunningham's To What Strangers, What Welcome
     (see no. 338).
          Also reviewed are: Randall Jarrell's The Lost World,
     Donald Hall's A Roof of Tiger Lillies, and Melville Cane's
     To Build a Fire.

375 "Philip Booth."
          A review of Letter from a Distant Land originally in "In
     the Presence of Anthologies" (see no. 331),
     pp. 300-301.
          In: The Suspect in Poetry; Babel to Byzantium.

376   "The Poet of Secret Lives and Misspent Opportunities." New
        York Times Book Review (18 May 1969), pp. 1, 10.
            Its title was subsequently changed to "Edwin Arlington
        Robinson" (see no. 294).
            A review of Louis O. Coxe's Edwin Arlington Robinson:
        The Life of Poetry.

377   "The Poet Tries to Make a Kind of Order." Mademoiselle 71
        (Sept. 1970), pp. 142-143, 209-210, 212.
            Its title was subsequently changed to "'Falling'" (see
        no. 301).
            A paragraph about adultery on page 143 was subsequently
        omitted.

378   "The Poet Turns on Himself." In Poets on Poetry, edited by
        Howard Nemerov, pp. 225-238. New York: Basic Books,
        1966.
            Originally it was a lecture for the Voice of America
        Forum. It was collected with two other essays under the
        title "The Poet Turns on Himself" (see no. 379).
            Two poems, "Sleeping Out at Easter" (see no. 223) and
        "The Lifeguard" (see no. 156), appear here, and the former
        poem and "The Firebombing" (see no. 104) are excerpted.
            In: Babel to Byzantium.
            Rept.: Crotty, Robert (no. 453).
            Exc.: Engle, Paul (see no. 457); "Poets on Poetry"
        (see no. 492).

379   "The Poet Turns on Himself."
            The title under which "Barnstorming for Poetry" (see
        no. 269), "Notes on the Decline of Outrage" (see no. 370),
        and "The Poet Turns on Himself" (see no. 378) were col-
        lected.
            In: Babel to Byzantium, pp. 247-292.

380   "A Poet Witnesses a Bold Mission." Life 65 (1 Nov. 1968),
        p. 26.

381   "Poets and Poetry Now."
            A collection of book reviews.
            In: Babel to Byzantium.

382   "Preface."
            The pages on which this appears are unnumbered.
            In: Babel to Byzantium.

383   "Process of Writing a Novel." Writer 83 (June 1970),
        pp. 12-13.
            An excerpt from a speech delivered during a session of
        the National Book Award in 1970.

384   "Ralph Hodgson."
            A review of Collected Poems originally in "First and

Last Things" (see no. 302), p. 321.
In: Babel to Byzantium.

385 "Randall Jarrell. "
A review of Selected Poems originally in "Some of All
of It" (see no. 407), pp. 339-348.
In: The Suspect in Poetry; Babel to Byzantium.
Rept.: Lowell, Robert (no. 474).

386 "Reading. " Mademoiselle 76 (Jan. 1973), pp. 133-134.
An essay on the works of Bruce Cummings (W. N. P.
Barbellion).

387 "Reality's Shifting Stages: Reviews by Five Hands. " Kenyon
Review 27 (Spr. 1965), pp. 378-384 [382-384].
A review of Clair McAllister's Arms of Light appearing
with four other reviews by different people.

388 "Reed Whittemore. "
A review of An American Takes a Walk originally in
"Five Poets" (see no. 306), pp. 115-117.
In: Babel to Byzantium.

389 "Richard Eberhart. "
A review of Great Praises originally in "In the Presence
of Anthologies" (see no. 331), pp. 309-310.
In: The Suspect in Poetry; Babel to Byzantium.

390 "Richard Wilbur. "
A review of Advice to a Prophet originally in "The
Stillness at the Center of the Target" (see no. 411),
pp. 489-491.
In: Babel to Byzantium.

391 "Robert Duncan. "
Reviews of The Opening of the Field and Roots and
Branches originally in "The Stillness at the Center of the
Target" (see no. 411), pp. 491-493, and "Orientations"
(see no. 374), p. 658, respectively.
In: Babel to Byzantium.
Exc.: Riley, Carolyn (see no. 496; only the review of
The Opening of the Field is excerpted).

392 "Robert Frost. "
It was originally entitled "Robert Frost, Man and Myth"
(see no. 393).
In: Babel to Byzantium.
Exc.: Riley, Carolyn (see no. 496).

393 "Robert Frost, Man and Myth. " Atlantic Monthly 218 (Nov.
1966), pp. 53-56.
Its title was subsequently changed to "Robert Frost"
(see no. 392).

An essay on Frost and a review of Lawrence Thompson's
Robert Frost: The Early Years.

394 "Robert Graves."
A review of New Poems originally in "First and Last
Things" (see no. 302), pp. 318-319.
In: Babel to Byzantium.

395 "Robert Mezey."
A review of The Lovemaker originally in "Toward a
Solitary Joy" (see no. 423), pp. 609-610.
In: The Suspect in Poetry.

396 "Robert Penn Warren."
A review of Promises: Poems 1954-1956 originally in
"In the Presence of Anthologies" (see no. 331), pp. 307-
309.
In: Babel to Byzantium.
Exc.: Riley, Carolyn (see no. 496).

397 "Robinson Jeffers."
A review of The Beginning and the End and Other Poems
originally in "First and Last Things" (see no. 302),
pp. 320-321.
In: Babel to Byzantium.
Exc.: Riley, Carolyn and Harte, Barbara (see no. 497).

398 "Rolphe Humphries."
A review of Green Armor on Green Ground originally in
"From Babel to Byzantium" (see no. 310), pp. 520-523.
In: Babel to Byzantium.

399 "Samuel French Morse."
A review of The Scattered Causes originally in "Five
Poets" (see no. 306), pp. 110-112.
In: Babel to Byzantium.

400 "The Second Birth."
Remarks originally in "In the Presence of Anthologies"
(see no. 331), pp. 313-314.
In: The Suspect in Poetry.

401 "The Self as Agent." In The Great Ideas Today, 1968, edited
by Robert M. Hutchins and Mortimer J. Adler, pp. 91-97.
Chicago: Encyclopaedia Britannica, 1968.
It was collected with another essay under the title "New
Essays" (see no. 365).
In: Sorties.
Rept.: *The Year's Developments in the Arts and Sci-
ences: A Symposium on Contemporary Poetry.   Chicago:
Encyclopaedia Britannica, 1968.
*[This citation is from Franklin Ashley's James Dickey:
A Checklist, p. 44 (see no. 1127) and is described there

as "an offprint from The Great Ideas Today, 1968 in printed
wrappers. "]

402 "September 15th. "
       Portions were originally published with slight differences
in "Two Days in September" (see no. 426), pp. 83-103.
       In: Deliverance.

403 "September 14th. "
       Portions were originally published in "Two Days in
September" (see no. 426), pp. 81-83.
       In: Deliverance.

404 "September 16th. "
       Portions were originally published with slight differences
in "Two Days in September" (see no. 426), pp. 103-108.
       In: Deliverance.

405 "Small Visions from a Timeless Place. " Playboy 21 (Oct.
1974), pp. 152-154, 220-221.
       A collection of excerpts from "Among the People" (see
no. 266), "The Land and the Water" (see no. 353), and
"The Traditions Web" (see no. 425).

406 "Smart: 'A Song to David. '" In Master Poems of the English
Language: Over One Hundred Poems Together with Intro-
ductions by Leading Poets and Critics of the English Speak-
ing World, edited by Oscar Williams, pp. 339-340. New
York: Trident Press, 1966.
       Its title was subsequently changed to "Christopher Smart:
'A Song to David'" (see no. 278) and was collected with
four other essays under the title "Five Poems" (see
no. 305).

407 "Some of All of It. " Sewanee Review 64 (Apr. -June 1956),
pp. 324-348.
       Reviews of the following appear in The Suspect in Poetry
and Babel to Byzantium: Randall Jarrell's Selected Poems
(see no. 385), David Ignatow's The Gentle Weight Lifter
(see no. 284), and Howard Nemerov's The Salt Garden (see
no. 327).
       Reviews of the following appear in Babel to Byzantium:
W. S. Graham's The Nightfishing (see no. 430), Gene Der-
wood's The Poems of Gene Derwood (see no. 313), and
Kenneth Burke's Book of Moments (see no. 351).
       Also reviewed are: Thomas McGrath's Figures from a
Double World, Edwin Honig's The Moral Circus, Howard O.
Sackler's Want My Shepherd, and David Waggoner's Dry
Sun, Dry Wind.

408 "The Son, the Cave, and the Burning Bush. " In New Ameri-
can Poets, edited by Paul Carroll, pp. 7-10. Chicago:
Follet, Big Table, 1968.

It is an introduction to this anthology and was collected with another essay under the title "New Essays" (see no. 365).

In: Sorties (also given the title "A Statement of Long-ing" here [see no. 410]).

409   "Spinning the Crystal Ball: Some Guesses at the Future of American Poetry."

A lecture originally published as a pamphlet (see no. 17).

In: Sorties.

410   "A Statement of Longing."

A second title for "The Son, the Cave, and the Burning Bush" (see no. 408).

In: Sorties.

411   "The Stillness at the Center of the Target."   Sewanee Review 70 (July-Sept. 1962), pp. 484-503.

Reviews of the following appear in Babel to Byzantium: Richard Wilbur's Advice to a Prophet (see no. 390), Robert Duncan's The Opening of the Field (see no. 391), Horace Gregory's Medusa in Gramercy Park (see no. 326), I. A. Richards' The Screens and Other Poems (see no. 329), Yvor Winters' Collected Poems (see no. 442), Marianne Moore's A Marianne Moore Reader (see no. 360), and John Frederick Nims' Knowledge of the Evening (see no. 346).

Also reviewed are: Nissim Ezekiel's The Unfinished Man, Jon Stallworthy's The Astronomy of Love, and Peter Viereck's The Tree Witch.

412   "The Suspect in Poetry."

Remarks originally in "The Suspect in Poetry or Every-man as Detective" (see no. 413), pp. 660-661.

In: The Suspect in Poetry.

413   "The Suspect in Poetry or Everyman as Detective." Sewanee Review 68 (Oct. -Dec. 1960), pp. 660-674.

Reviews of the following appear in The Suspect in Poetry and Babel to Byzantium: Thom Gunn's The Sense of Move-ment (see no. 421), Brother Antoninus' The Crooked Lines of God (see no. 273), and Hayden Carruth's The Crow and the Heart (see no. 320).

The review of James Kirkup's The Prodigal Son (see no. 341) appears in Babel to Byzantium.

Also reviewed are: Carol Hall's Portrait of Your Niece and Other Poems, Melvin Walker LaFollette's The Clever Body, R. G. Everson's A Lattice for Momos, John Press' Guy Fawkes Night and Other Poems, and Hyam Plutzik's Apples from Shinar.

414   "Teaching, Writing, Reincarnations, and Rivers."

In: Self-Interviews.

415 "Ted Hughes."
        A review of The Hawk in the Rain originally in "'n the
        Presence of Anthologies" (see no. 331), pp. 301-302.
        In: Babel to Byzantium.

416 "That Language of the Brain." Poetry 103 (Dec. 1963),
        pp. 187-190.
        A review of Conrad Aiken's The Morning Song of Lord
        Zero (see no. 281).

417 "Theodore Roethke."
        A review of I Am! Says the Lamb and Words for the
        Wind originally in "Correspondences and Essences" (see
        no. 282), p. 640.
        In: The Suspect in Poetry; Babel to Byzantium (the
        first part of "Theodore Roethke" [see no. 419]).

418 "Theodore Roethke." Poetry 105 (Nov. 1964), pp. 119-122.
        A review of Sequences, Sometimes Metaphysical.
        In: Babel to Byzantium (the second part of "Theodore
        Roethke" [see no. 419]).

419 "Theodore Roethke."
        The title under which "Theodore Roethke" (see no. 417)
        and "Theodore Roethke" (see no. 418) were collected.
        In: Babel to Byzantium.
        Exc.: Riley, Carolyn (see no. 496).

420 "Theodore Weiss."
        A review of Outlanders originally in "The Death and
        Keys of the Censor" (see no. 285), pp. 329-330.
        In: Babel to Byzantium.

421 "Thom Gunn."
        A review of The Sense of Movement originally in "The
        Suspect in Poetry or Everyman as Detective" (see no. 413),
        pp. 662-664.
        In: The Suspect in Poetry; Babel to Byzantium.

422 "Thompson: 'The Hound of Heaven.'" In Master Poems of
        the English Language: Over One Hundred Poems Together
        with Introductions by Leading Poets and Critics of the Eng-
        lish Speaking World, pp. 817-819. New York: Trident
        Press, 1966.
        Its title was subsequently changed to "Francis Thompson:
        'The Hound of Heaven'" (see no. 309) and was collected
        with four other essays under the title "Five Poems" (see
        no. 305).

423 "Toward a Solitary Joy." Hudson Review 14 (Win. 1961-1962),
        pp. 607-613.
        The review of Robert Mezey's The Lovemaker (see
        no. 395) appears in The Suspect in Poetry.

Reviews of the following appear in Babel to Byzantium:
Louis MacNiece's Solstices and Eighty-Five Poems (see
no. 357) and Charles Tomlinson's Versions from Fyodor
Tyutchev (see no. 277).

Also reviewed are: Thomas Vance's Skeleton of Light,
John Masefield's The Blue Bells and Other Poems, John
Hall Wheelock's The Gardener, Poets of Today VIII, Mar-
vin Solomon's The Royal Tiger Face, Paul Blackburn's The
Nets, John Wain's Weep Before God, and John Ciardi's In
the Stoneworks.

424   "Toward a Solitary Joy."
Remarks originally in "Toward a Solitary Joy" (see
no. 423), p. 607; "From Babel to Byzantium" (see no. 310),
pp. 529-530; and "The Suspect in Poetry or Everyman as
Detective" (see no. 413), p. 674.
In: The Suspect in Poetry.

425   "The Traditions Web."
In: Jericho.
Exc.: "Jericho: The South Beheld" (see no. 343);
"Small Visions from a Timeless Place" (see no. 405).

426   "Two Days in September."   Atlantic 225 (Feb. 1970),
pp. 78-108.
It was subsequently published in Deliverance as "Before"
(see no. 270), "September 14th" (see no. 403), "September
15th" (see no. 402), and "September 16th" (see no. 404).

427   "Two Talks in Washington."
The title under which two lectures, "Metaphor as Pure
Adventure" (see no. 363), and "Spinning the Crystal Ball"
(see no. 409), were collected.
In: Sorties.

428   "Two Voices."
The title under which "Edwin Arlington Robinson" (see
no. 294) and "The Greatest American Poet: Theodore
Roethke" (see no. 317), two essays, were collected.
In: Sorties.

429   "Vernon Watkins."
A review of Affinities originally in "First and Last
Things" (see no. 302), p. 319.
In: Babel to Byzantium.

430   "W. S. Graham."
A review of The Nightfishing originally in "Some of All
of It" (see no. 407), pp. 336-339.
In: Babel to Byzantium.

431   "W. S. Merwin."
A review of The Drunk in the Furnace originally in

"The Death and Keys of the Censor" (see no. 285),
pp. 327-329.
  In: The Suspect in Poetry; Babel to Byzantium.
  Exc.: Riley, Carolyn (see no. 496).

432 "What the Angels Missed." New York Times Book Review (25
     Dec. 1966), pp. 1, 16.
       A review of Marianne Moore's Tell Me, Tell Me (see
     no. 360).

433 "William Carlos Williams."
       A review of The Collected Later Poems originally in
     "First and Last Things" (see no. 302), pp. 321-322.
       In: Babel to Byzantium.
       Exc.: Riley, Carolyn (see no. 496).

434 "William Carlos Williams: 'The Yachts.'"
       It was originally entitled "Williams: 'The Yachts'" (see
     no. 438).
       In: Babel to Byzantium.

435 "William Jay Smith."
       A review of Poems 1947-1957 originally in "In the
     Presence of Anthologies" (see no. 331), p. 307.
       In: Babel to Byzantium.

436 "William Meredith."
       A review of The Wreck of the Thresher and Other Poems
     originally in "Orientations" (see no. 374), p. 656.
       In: Babel to Byzantium.

437 "William Stafford."
       A review of West of Your City originally in "Corres-
     pondences and Essences" (see no. 282), p. 639.
       In: The Suspect in Poetry; Babel to Byzantium.

438 "Williams: 'The Yachts.'" In Master Poems of the English
     Language: Over One Hundred Poems Together with Intro-
     ductions by Leading Poets and Critics of the English Speak-
     ing World, edited by Oscar Williams, pp. 901-902. New
     York: Trident Press, 1966.
       Its title was subsequently changed to "William Carlos
     Williams: 'The Yachts'" (see no. 434) and collected with
     four other essays under the title "Five Poems" (see
     no. 305).

439 "Winfield Townley Scott."
       A review of The Dark Sister originally in "The Human
     Power" (see no. 328).
       In: Babel to Byzantium.

440 "The Winters Approach."
       The title under which "Donald Drummond" (see no. 288)

and "Ellen Kay" (see no. 298) were collected.
   In: The Suspect in Poetry.

441 "Your Next-Door Neighbor's Poems." Sewanee Review 72
     (Apr. -June 1964), pp. 307-321.
     The following are reviewed: Charles Edward Eaton's
Countermoves, Anthony Ostroff's Imperatives, Robinson
Jeffers' The Beginning and the End, Robert Hazel's Poems
1951-1961, Allen Grossman's A Harlot's Hire, Paul Roche's
The Rank Obstinancy of Things, Robert Pack's Guarded by
Women, Anne Ridler's Selected Poems, Richard Eberhart's
Collected Verse Plays, and Octavio Paz's Sun-Stone.

442 "Yvor Winters."
     A review of Collected Poems originally in "The Stillness
at the Center of the Target" (see no. 411), pp. 496-499.
     In: Babel to Byzantium.

ANTHOLOGIES

443 Adams, Hazard. <u>Poetry: An Introductory Anthology.</u> Boston:
 Little, Brown and Co., 1968.
  "In the Tree House at Night," pp. 342-343.
  Biographical note, p. 379.

444 Allen, Gay Wilson; Rideout, Walter B.; and Robinson, James
 K., eds. <u>American Poetry.</u> New York: Harper and Row,
 1965.
  "The Beholders," pp. 1019-1020; "Between Two Prison-
 ers," pp. 1014-1016; "The Dusk of Horses," pp. 1018-1019;
 "The Heaven of Animals," pp. 1013-1014; "The Scratch,"
 pp. 1016-1018.

445 Allen, John Alexander, ed. <u>Hero's Way: Contemporary Poems
 in the Mythic Tradition.</u> Englewood Cliffs, N.J.: Prentice-
 Hall, 1971.
  "Orpheus Before Hades," pp. 95-96; "The Scarred Girl,"
 pp. 409-410.

446 Baylor, Robert and Stokes, Brenda, eds. <u>Fine Frenzy: En-
 during Themes in Poetry.</u> New York: McGraw-Hill Book
 Co., 1972.
  "The Poisoned Man," pp. 240-241.

447 Brinnin, John Malcolm and Read, Bill, eds. <u>Twentieth Cen-
 tury Poetry: American and British, 1900-1970.</u> New York:
 McGraw-Hill Book Co., 1970.
  "Cherrylog Road," pp. 90-94; "For the Nightly Ascent
 of the Hunter Orion Over a Forest Clearing," pp. 88-90.

448 Burnett, Whit, ed. <u>This Is My Best in the Third Quarter of
 the Century.</u> Garden City, N.Y.: Doubleday and Co.,
 1970.
  "May Day Sermon to the Women of Gilmer County,
 Georgia, by a Woman Preacher Leaving the Baptist Church,"
 pp. 66-75.
  A biography and a bibliography appear on p. 987 and a
 letter from Dickey (see no. 532) is included.

449 Calhoun, Richard James and Guilds, John Caldwell, eds. <u>A
 Tricentennial Anthology of South Carolina Literature, 1670-
 1970.</u> Columbia, S.C.: University of South Carolina Press,

1971.
"Buckdancer's Choice," pp. 572-573; "The Firebombing,"
pp. 561-569; "Gamecock," pp. 574-575; "May Day Sermon
to the Women of Gilmer County, Georgia, by a Woman
Preacher Leaving the Baptist Church," pp. 547-558; "The
Salt Marsh," pp. 570-571; "The Sheep Child," pp. 559-560.
A biography is included on p. 546.

450   Carruth, Hayden, ed. The Voice That Is Great Within Us:
      American Poetry of the Twentieth Century. New York:
      Bantam Books, 1970.
          "The Celebration," pp. 495-496; "The Driver," pp. 494-
      495; "Fence Wire," pp. 492-493; "The Movement of Fish,"
      pp. 491-492.

451   Corrington, John William and Williams, Miller, eds. Southern
      Writing in the Sixties: Poetry. Baton Rouge: Louisiana
      State University Press, 1967.
          "A Dog Sleeping on My Feet," pp. 13-14; "Gamecock,"
      pp. 12-13; "Listening to Foxhounds," pp. 14-16; "Reincar-
      nation [(I)]," pp. 16-17.

452   Cotter, Janet M. , ed. Invitation to Poetry. Cambridge,
      Mass.: Winthrop Publishers, 1974.
          "The Aura," pp. 309-310.
          Commentary about "The Aura" in included on p. 311.

453   Crotty, Robert; McRoberts, Robert L.; and Clark, Geoffrey,
      eds. Workshop: A Spontaneous Approach to Literature.
      Menlo Park, Calif.: Cummings Publishing Co. , 1971.
          "Cherrylog Road," pp. 202-205; "Dust," pp. 208-209;
      "The Flash," p. 210; "The Heaven of Animals," pp. 200-
      201; "The Performance," pp. 206-207; "The Poet Turns on
      Himself," pp. 187-199.
          Questions for discussion are included on pp. 211-212.

454   Drachler, Jacob and Terris, Virginia R. , eds. The Many
      Worlds of Poetry. New York: Alfred A. Knopf, 1969.
          "A Dog Sleeping on My Feet," p. 229; "The Hospital
      Window," p. 59; "Hunting Civil War Relics at Nimblewill
      Creek," pp. 123-124.

455   Eastman, Arthur, et al. , eds. The Norton Anthology of Poetry.
      New York: W. W. Norton, 1970.
          "At Darien Bridge," p. 1153; "Between Two Prisoners,"
      pp. 1151-1152; "Bread," pp. 1154-1155; "Buckdancer's
      Choice," pp. 1155-1156; "In the Marble Quarry," pp. 1153-
      1154; "In the Tree House at Night," pp. 1150-1151; "The
      Lifeguard," pp. 1149-1150.

456   Ellman, Richard and O'Clair, Robert, eds. The Norton An-
      thology of Modern Poetry. New York: W. W. Norton and
      Co. , 1973.

"Buckdancer's Choice," p. 1034; "Chenille," pp. 1032-
1033; "The Heaven of Animals," pp. 1031-1032; "The Per-
formance," pp. 1030-1031; "The Sheep Child," pp. 1034-
1036.
Explanatory footnotes and a biography are included on
pp. 1028-1030.

457   Engle, Paul and Carrier, Warren. Reading Modern Poetry.
Rev. ed. Glenview, Ill.: Scott, Foresman and Co., 1968.
"Buckdancer's Choice," pp. 89-90; "The Performance,"
pp. 87-88; "The Poet Turns on Himself" [exc.], pp. 92-93;
"Sleeping Out at Easter," pp. 90-92.
Biographical and bibliographical note is included on
p. 442.

458   Ganz, Margaret and Ebel, Julia, eds. The Enduring Voice:
Concerns in Literature, Present and Past. New York:
Macmillan Co., 1972.
"In the Mountain Tent," p. 385.
Questions for discussion on "In the Mountain Tent" are
included on p. 386.

459   Genthe, Charles and Keithley, George, eds. Themes in Amer-
ican Literature. Lexington, Mass.: D. C. Heath and Co.,
1972.
"The Heaven of Animals," pp. 88-89; "In the Mountain
Tent," pp. 391-392.

460   Greenfield, Stanley B. and Weatherhead, A. Kingsley, eds.
The Poem: An Anthology. 2d ed. New York: Appleton-
Century-Crofts, 1972.
"Buckdancer's Choice," p. 488; "In the Mountain Tent,"
p. 487.
Explanatory footnotes for "Buckdancer's Choice" are
included.

461   Hall, Donald, ed. Contemporary American Poetry. Balti-
more: Penguin Books, 1962.
"Hunting Civil War Relics at Nimblewill Creek,"
pp. 78-80; "The Performance," pp. 77-78.
A biography is included on pp. 7-8.

462   _____ and Pack, Robert, eds. New Poets of England and
America: Second Selection. New York: The World Pub-
lishing Co., 1962.
"The Call," p. 208; "On the Hill Below the Lighthouse,"
pp. 210-211; "The Performance," pp. 211-212; "Trees and
Cattle," pp. 209-210; "Walking on Water," pp. 206-207.

463   Hieatt, A. Kent and Park, William, eds. The College An-
thology of British and American Poetry. 2d ed. Boston:
Allyn and Bacon, 1972.
"Cherrylog Road," pp. 651-654.
Explanatory footnotes are included.

464 Hollander, John, ed.   Poems of Our Moment.   New York:
     Pegasus, 1968.
          "Adultery," pp. 63-64; "Falling," pp. 64-71; "Kudzu,"
     pp. 60-62; "On the Hill Below the Lighthouse," pp. 55-56;
     "The Other," pp. 58-60; "The Underground Stream,"
     pp. 56-57.

465 Hughes, Langston and Bontemps, Arna, eds.   The Poetry of
     the Negro, 1746-1970.   Rev. and updated ed.   Garden City,
     N. Y. : Doubleday and Co. , 1970.
          "Buckdancer's Choice," pp. 579-580.

466 Hutchins, Robert M. and Adler, Mortimer J. , eds.   The
     Great Ideas Today, 1968.   Chicago: Encyclopaedia
     Britannica, 1968.
          "Falling," pp. 110-113; "The Sheep Child," pp. 108-109.

467 "A James Dickey Sampler. "   Milwaukee Journal (20 Mar.
     1966), sec. 5, p. 4.
          "Buckdancer's Choice" [exc.]; "Faces Seen Once" [exc.];
     "The Firebombing" [exc.].

468 Knudson, R. R. and Ebert, P. K. , eds.   Sports Poems.   New
     York: Dell Publishing Co. , 1971.
          "In the Pocket," p. 43; "Inside the River," pp. 93-94.

469 Kostelanetz, Richard, ed.   Possibilities of Poetry: An An-
     thology of American Contemporaries.   New York: Dell
     Publishing Co. , 1970.
          "The Hospital Window," pp. 311-312; "The Leap,"
     pp. 313-314; "The Lifeguard," pp. 308-310.

470 Lapides, Frederick R. and Shawcross, John T. , eds.   Poetry
     and Its Conventions: An Anthology Examining Poetic Forms
     and Their Themes.   New York: The Free Press, 1972.
          "Between Two Prisoners," pp. 354-355; "On the Hill
     Below the Lighthouse," pp. 19-20.

471 Leary, Paris and Kelly, Robert, eds.   A Controversy of
     Poets: An Anthology of Contemporary American Poetry.
     Garden City, N. Y. : Doubleday and Co. , 1965.
          "Drowning with Others," pp. 77-78; "The Hospital
     Window," pp. 78-80; "The Lifeguard," pp. 69-70; "The
     Owl King," pp. 70-77.

472 Lieberman, Laurence, ed.   The Achievement of James Dickey:
     A Comprehensive Selection of His Poems with a Critical
     Introduction.   Glenview, Ill. : Scott, Foresman and Co. ,
     1968.
          "Bums, on Waking," pp. 44-46; "Cherrylog Road,"
     pp. 37-40; "Drinking from a Helmet," pp. 46-51; "The
     Dusk of Horses," pp. 33-34; "Encounter in the Cage
     Country," pp. 75-76; "Falling," pp. 78-84; "False Youth:

Winter," pp. 76-77; "The Fiend," pp. 65-69; "The Fire-
bombing," pp. 52-59; "The Hospital Window," pp. 31-32;
"The Ice Skin," pp. 42-44; "In the Marble Quarry,"
pp. 41-42; "In the Tree House at Night," pp. 29-30; "The
Jewel," pp. 24-25; "The Lifeguard," pp. 27-29; "May Day
Sermon to the Women of Gilmer County, Georgia, by a
Woman Preacher Leaving the Baptist Church" [exc.],
p. 22; "The Performance," pp. 25-27; "Power and Light,"
pp. 73-75; "Pursuit from Under," pp. 63-65; "The Shark's
Parlor," pp. 60-63; "The Sheep Child," pp. 69-71; "Springer
Mountain," pp. 34-37; "The String," pp. 23-24; "Sun,"
pp. 71-73.
    A biography appears on page ix, and the introduction (see
no. 1034) covers pages 1-21.
    Illustrated with a photograph of Dickey on the cover by
Christopher Dickey and a sketch on the back cover by
Richard Koppe.

473   Lief, Leonard and Light, James F., eds.   The Modern Age:
      Literature.   2d ed.   New York: Holt, Rinehart, and Win-
      ston, 1972.
          "The Heaven of Animals," pp. 658-659.

474   Lowell, Robert; Taylor, Peter; and Warren, Robert Penn,
      eds.   Randall Jarrell, 1914-1965.   New York: Farrar,
      Straus, and Giroux, 1967.
          "Randall Jarrell," pp. 33-48.

475   Lowenfels, Walter, ed.   Where Is Vietnam?   American Poets
      Respond: An Anthology of Contemporary Poems.   Garden
      City, N.Y.:   Doubleday and Co., 1967.
          "The Firebombing" [exc.], pp. 28-29.

476   McCullough, Francis Monson, ed.   Earth, Air, Fire, and
      Water: A Collection of Over 125 Poems.   New York:
      Coward, McCann, and Geoghegan, 1971.
          "A Birth," p. 63.
          A biography appears on p. 174.

477   Martz, William J.   Beginnings in Poetry: A Motley Book of
      Poems.   Chicago: Scott, Foresman and Co., 1965.
          "Cherrylog Road," pp. 166-169; "The Hospital Window,"
      pp. 165-166.
          Explanatory footnotes are included.

478   Martz, William J.   The Distinctive Voice: Twentieth Century
      American Poetry.   Glenview, Ill.:   Scott, Foresman and
      Co., 1966.
          "Cherrylog Road," pp. 230-233; "In the Mountain Tent,"
      p. 230; "The Lifeguard," pp. 228-229; ["One Voice"],
      pp. 227-228; "Reincarnation [(II)]," pp. 236-243; "The
      Shark's Parlor," pp. 233-236.

479 Meserole, Harrison T.; Sutton, Walter; and Weber, Brom,
       eds. American Literature: Tradition and Innovation,
       vol. 2. Lexington, Mass.: D. C. Heath and Co., 1969.
          "The Hospital Window," pp. 3683-3684; "Hunting Civil
       War Relics at Nimblewill Creek," pp. 3684-3686; "The
       Lifeguard," pp. 3683-3684.

480 Miles, Josephine, ed. The Ways of the Poem. Rev. ed.
       Englewood Cliffs, N.J.: Prentice-Hall, 1972.
          "The Shark's Parlor," pp. 357-360.

481 Millet, Fred B.; Hoffman, Arthur W.; and Clark, David R.,
       eds. Reading Poetry. 2d ed. New York: Harper and
       Row, Publishers, 1968.
          "Between Two Prisoners," pp. 143-144; "A Dog Sleeping
       on My Feet," pp. 340-341; "Drowning with Others,"
       pp. 339-340.
          Questions for discussion and comments on "Between Two
       Prisoners" appear on pp. 145-146.

482 Molloy, Paul, ed. Beach Glass and Other Poems. New York:
       Four Winds Press, 1970.
          "The Twin Falls," p. 117.

483 Murphy, Francis, ed. Edwin Arlington Robinson: A Collec-
       tion of Critical Essays. Englewood Cliffs, N.J.: Prentice-
       Hall, 1970.
          "Edwin Arlington Robinson: The Many Truths,"
       pp. 77-94.

484 Nemerov, Howard, ed. Poets on Poetry. New York: Basic
       Books, Publishers, 1966.
          "The Poet Turns on Himself," pp. 225-238.
          A biography appears on page v.

485 "The New Yorker" Book of Poems; Selected by the Editors of
       "The New Yorker." New York: The Viking Press, 1969.
          "Buckdancer's Choice," pp. 86-87; "Bums, on Waking,"
       p. 88; "By Canoe Through the Fir Forest," pp. 92-93;
       "Cherrylog Road," pp. 114-116; "Coming Back to America,"
       pp. 135-136; "The Dusk of Horses," p. 182; "Falling,"
       pp. 216-220; "Fence Wire," p. 226; "Goodbye to Serpents,"
       pp. 278-279; "The Ice Skin," pp. 311-312; "The Lifeguard,"
       pp. 386-387; "Madness," pp. 407-410; "The Movement of
       Fish," p. 451; "The Shark's Parlor," pp. 635-637; "Slave
       Quarters," pp. 644-648.

486 Owen, Guy, ed. Modern American Poetry: Essays in Criti-
       cism. Deland, Fla.: Everett-Edwards, 1972.
          "Edwin Arlington Robinson: The Many Truths," pp. 1-19.

487 Peck, Richard, ed. Sounds and Silences: Poetry for Now.
       New York: Delacorte Press, 1970.
          "The Lifeguard," pp. 88-90.

488   Perrine, Laurence and Reid, James M. , eds.   One Hundred
      American Poems of the Twentieth Century.   New York:
      Harcourt, Brace and World, 1966.
          "The Lifeguard," pp. 277-279.
          Commentary by Laurence Perrine is included (see
      no. 1056).

489   Poems from "The Virginia Quarterly Review," 1925-1967.
      Charlottesville: The University Press of Virginia, 1969.
          "Fog Envelops the Animals," pp. 93-94; "Gamecock,"
      pp. 102-103; "The Head-Aim," p. 104; "The Night Pool,"
      pp. 100-101; "Sleeping Out at Easter," pp. 89-90; "Springer
      Mountain," pp. 95-99; "The Summons," pp. 91-92.

490   Poetry 121 (Oct. 1972), p. 7.
          "Of Holy War."

491   "Poetry":   The Golden Anniversary Issue.   Chicago: The
      University of Chicago Press, 1967.
          "Below Ellijay," pp. 27-28.

492   "Poets on Poetry."   Writer 82 (Mar. 1969), p. 30.
          "The Poet Turns on Himself" [exc.].

493   Poulin, A. , Jr. , ed.   Contemporary American Poetry.   Bos-
      ton: Houghton Mifflin Co. , 1971.
          "Adultery," pp. 73-74; "Encounter in the Cage Country,"
      pp. 69-70; "The Firebombing," pp. 82-89; "The Heaven of
      Animals," pp. 72-73; "In the Mountain Tent," pp. 65-66;
      "Reincarnation (II)," pp. 90-98; "The Sleep Child," pp. 70-
      72; "Slave Quarters," pp. 76-81; "Springer Mountain,"
      pp. 66-69; "Sun," pp. 75-76.
          A biography appears on pp. 368-369.
          Illustrated with a photograph of Dickey by Rollie
      McKenna, p. 64.

494   "Prize Winner."   New York Times Book Review (27 Mar.
      1966), p. 2.
          "A Birth"; "Fence Wire"; "Fox Blood"; "The Lifeguard."
          A notice of Dickey's winning the NBA is included.
          Illustrated with a photograph of Dickey by Sam Faulk.

495   Quarterly Review of Literature 19 (Spr. -Sum. 1974).
          "For the Linden Moth," pp. 265-266; "Fox Blood,"
      pp. 264-265; "Near Darien," pp. 212-213; "Poem,"
      pp. 202-203; "The Scratch," pp. 213-215.

496   Riley, Carolyn, ed.   Contemporary Literary Criticism: Ex-
      cerpts from Criticism of the Works of Today's Novelists,
      Poets, Playwrights, and Other Creative Writers, vol. 1.
      Detroit: Gale Research Co. , Book Tower, 1973.
          Excerpts of the following: "Allen Ginsberg," p. 118;
      "Brother Antoninus," p. 96; "Charles Olson," pp. 262-263;

"Conrad Aiken," p. 3; "E. E. Cummings," p. 68; "Galway
Kinnell," p. 167; "James Kirkup," p. 169; "John Berryman,"
p. 33; "Josephine Miles," p. 215; "Louis MacNiece," p.
186; "Marianne Moore," pp. 226-227; "Robert Duncan,"
p. 82; "Robert Frost," p. 111; "Robert Penn Warren,"
p. 352; "Theodore Roethke," p. 290; "W. S. Merwin,"
pp. 211-212; "William Carlos Williams," p. 370.

497   and Harte, Barbara, eds. Contemporary Literary
Criticism: Excerpts from Criticism of the Works of To-
day's Novelists, Poets, Playwrights, and Other Creative
Writers, vol. 2. Detroit: Gale Research Co., Book
Tower, 1974.
     Excerpts of the following: "Anne Sexton," p. 390;
"Howard Nemerov," pp. 305-306; "James Merrill,"
pp. 272-273; "John Ashbery," p. 16; "Kenneth Burke,"
p. 87; "Robinson Jeffers," p. 214.

498 Roberts, Michael, ed. The Faber Book of Modern Verse.
3d ed. rev. with a supplement of poems chosen by Donald
Hall. London: Faber and Faber, 1965.
     "The Heaven of Animals," pp. 372-373; "In the Tree
House at Night," pp. 373-375.

499 Rodman, Selden, ed. One Hundred American Poems: Master-
pieces of Lyric, Epic, and Ballad from Pre-Colonial Times
to the Present. 2d ed. New York: New American Library,
1972.
     "Falling," pp. 209-216.

500 Rosenthal, M. L., ed. The New Modern Poetry: British and
American Poetry since World War II. New York: The
Macmillan Co., 1967.
     "The Being," pp. 44-46.

501 Rylander, John and Rylander, Edith, eds. What's in a Poem?
Encino and Belmont, Calif.: Dickenson Publishing Co.,
1972.
     "The Bee," pp. 259-261.

502 "A Sampling of His Poetry." Life 61 (22 July 1966), p. 70.
     "The Heaven of Animals"; "In the Marble Quarry";
"Listening to Foxhounds"; "The Salt Marsh."

503 Schorer, Mark, ed. Galaxy: Literary Modes and Genres.
New York: Harcourt, Brace and World, 1967.
     "The Fiend," pp. 391-394.

504   , ed. The Literature of America: Twentieth Century.
New York: McGraw-Hill Book Co., 1970.
     "Dust," pp. 732-733; "The War Wound," pp. 731-732.

505 Simpson, Louis, ed. An Introduction to Poetry. 2d ed. New

York: St. Martin's Press, 1972.
"Cherrylog Road," pp. 353-355; "Listening to Foxhounds,"
pp. 352-353.

506 Spender, Stephen; Kristol, Irving; and Lasky, Melvin J., eds.
Encounters: An Anthology from the First Ten Years of
"Encounter" Magazine. New York: Basic Books, Pub-
lishers, 1953-1963.
"Facing Africa," pp. 551-552.

507 Stevenson, Lionel, et al., ed. Best Poems of 1960: Bore-
stone Mountain Poetry Awards, 1961; A Compilation of
Original Poetry Published in Magazines of the English-
Speaking World in 1960, vol. 13. Palo Alto, Calif.:
Pacific Books, Publishers, 1962.
"Between Two Prisoners," pp. 37-38; "Listening to
Foxhounds," pp. 39-40; "Walking on Water," pp. 41-42.

508 _____. Best Poems of 1961: Borestone Mountain Poetry
Awards, 1962; A Compilation of Original Poetry Published
in Magazines of the English-Speaking World in 1961, vol.
14. Palo Alto, Calif.: Pacific Books, Publishers, 1962.
"The Lifeguard," pp. 43-44; "The Summons," pp. 45-46.

509 _____. Best Poems of 1962: Borestone Mountain Poetry
Awards, 1963; A Compilation of Original Poetry Published
in Magazines of the English-Speaking World in 1962, vol.
15. Palo Alto, Calif.: Pacific Books, Publishers, 1963.
"Armor," pp. 43-44; "By Canoe Through the Fir
Forest," pp. 45-46; "The Dusk of Horses," pp. 47-48;
"A Letter," pp. 41-42.

510 _____. Best Poems of 1963: Borestone Mountain Poetry
Awards, 1964; A Compilation of Original Poetry Published
in Magazines of the English-Speaking World in 1963, vol.
16. Palo Alto, Calif.: Pacific Books, Publishers, 1964.
"Bums, on Waking," pp. 42-43; "The Driver," pp. 44-
45; "Horses and Prisoners," pp. 7-8.

511 _____. Best Poems of 1964: Borestone Mountain Poetry
Awards, 1965; A Compilation of Original Poetry Published
in Magazines of the English-Speaking World in 1964, vol.
17. Palo Alto, Calif.: Pacific Books, Publishers, 1965.
"Pursuit from Under," pp. 37-39; "Them, Crying,"
pp. 40-42; "Winter Trout," pp. 34-36.

512 _____. Best Poems of 1965: Borestone Mountain Poetry
Awards, 1966; A Compilation of Original Poetry Published
in Magazines of the English-Speaking World in 1965, vol.
18. Palo Alto, Calif.: Pacific Books, Publishers, 1966.
"Celebration," pp. 5-6; "False Youth: Summer,"
pp. 25-26; "Sustainment," pp. 27-28.

513 _____. Best Poems of 1966: Borestone Mountain Poetry
Awards, 1967; A Compilation of Original Poetry Published
in Magazines of the English-Speaking World in 1966, vol.
19. Palo Alto, Calif.: Pacific Books, Publishers, 1967.
"The Sheep Child," pp. 37-39.

514 _____. Best Poems of 1970: Borestone Mountain Poetry
Awards, 1971; A Compilation of Original Poetry Published
in Magazines of the English-Speaking World in 1970, vol.
23. Palo Alto, Calif.: Pacific Books, Publishers, 1971.
"Haunting the Maneuvers," pp. 30-31.

515 Strand, Mark, ed. The Contemporary American Poets:
American Poetry since 1940. New York: The World Pub-
lishing Co., 1969.
"Armor," pp. 66-67; "Cherrylog Road," pp. 67-70; "The
Common Grave," pp. 70-72; "The Heaven of Animals,"
pp. 64-65; "The Performance," pp. 63-64.

516 Sweetkind, Morris, ed. Getting into Poetry. Boston: Hol-
brook Press, 1972.
"The Lifeguard," pp. 328-330.

517 Thompson, Ruth and Thompson, Marvin, eds. The Total Ex-
perience of Poetry: An Introductory Anthology. New York:
Random House, 1970.
"Cherrylog Road," pp. 127-130; "In the Tree House at
Night," pp. 130-132; "The Lifeguard," pp. 132-134; "The
Scarred Girl," pp. 134-135.

518 Trilling, Lionel, ed. The Experience of Literature: A Reader
with Commentaries. Garden City, N.Y.: Doubleday and
Co., 1967.
"The Fiend," pp. 1310-1313.

519 Untermeyer, Louis, ed. 50 Modern American and British
Poets, 1920-1970. New York: David McKay Co., 1973.
"The Firebombing," pp. 140-149.
A biography containing some critical commentary appears
on pp. 313-314.

520 Vas Dias, Robert, ed. Inside Outer Space: New Poems of
the Space Age. Garden City, N.Y.: Doubleday and Co.,
1970.
"Apollo," pp. 63-66.

521 Wallace, Robert and Taaffe, James G., eds. Poems on
Poetry: The Mirror's Garland. New York: E. P. Dutton
and Co., 1965.
"A Dog Sleeping on My Feet," pp. 242-243; "To Landrum
Guy Beginning to Write at Sixty," pp. 239-240.

522 Walsh, Chad. Doors into Poetry. 2d ed. Englewood Cliffs,

N. J. : Prentice-Hall, 1970.
"Cherrylog Road," pp. 305-308.

523 _____, ed. Today's Poets: American and British Poetry Since the 1930's. New York: Charles Scribner's Sons, 1964.
"The Dusk of Horses," pp. 294-295; "The Heaven of Animals," pp. 289-290; "In the Lupanar at Pompeii," pp. 292-294; "In the Tree House at Night," pp. 290-292; "The Poisoned Man," pp. 297-298; "The Scarred Girl," pp. 295-297.
A biography appears on p. 414.

524 Weiss, M. Jerry, ed. Man to Himself. Menlo Park, Calif.: Cummings Publishing Co. , 1970.
"Adultery," pp. 95-96.
A biography appears on p. 316.
Illustrated with a photograph of Dickey by Wayne Miller, p. 97.

525 _____. Perspectives on Man: Kaleidoscope. Menlo Park, Calif. : Cummings Publishing Co. , 1970.
"False Youth: Two Seasons," pp. 103-105.
A biography appears on p. 389.

526 Wiebusch, John, ed. Lombardi. Chicago: Follett Publishing Co. , 1971.
"For the Death of Lombardi," pp. 206-210.

527 Williams, Miller, ed. Contemporary Poetry in America. New York: Random House, 1973.
"Cherrylog Road," pp. 73-74; "The Fiend," pp. 71-73; "The Heaven of Animals," pp. 74-75; "Reincarnation (I)," p. 70; "The Sheep Child," pp. 69-70.
A biography appears on p. 69.
Illustrated with a photograph of Dickey by Christopher Dickey, p. 69.

528 Williams, Oscar, ed. The Pocket Book of Modern Verse: English and American Poetry of the Last Hundred Years from Walt Whitman to the Contemporaries. Newly rev. by Hyman J. Sobiloff. New York: Washington Square Press, 1972.
"The Fiend," pp. 516-521; "The War Wound," pp. 112-113.

FILMS

529 Deliverance.　John Boorman, producer and director; James
　　　Dickey, writer.　Warner Brothers, 1972.　109 min. , sd. ,
　　　col.
　　　　　The film version of Deliverance was filmed at and near
　　　the Chattooga River in Georgia.　Dickey not only wrote its
　　　screenplay but also appeared in it as Sheriff Bullard.
　　　Other major roles were played by Jon Voight (as Ed Gentry),
　　　Burt Reynolds (as Lewis Medlock), Ned Beatty (as Bobby
　　　Trippe), Ronny Cox (as Drew Ballinger), Billy McKinney
　　　(as the Mountain Man), and Herbert "Cowboy" Coward (as
　　　the Toothless Man).　Vilmos Zsigmond was its photographer,
　　　and Eric Weissberg and Steve Mandel played its music,
　　　"Dueling Banjos" (see no. 1240).

*530 [An unidentified documentary about aircraft carriers].　Gruman
　　　Aircraft.
　　　　　*[This data is from John Logue's "James Dickey De-
　　　scribes His Life and Works as He 'Moves Toward Hercules, '"
　　　p. 46 (see no. 1109).]

*531 [An unidentified documentary based on John Fitzgerald Ken-
　　　nedy's A Nation of Immigrants].
　　　　　*[This data is from John Logue's "James Dickey De-
　　　scribes His Life and Works as He 'Moves Toward Hercules, '"
　　　p. 46 (see no. 1109).]

PUBLISHED CORRESPONDENCE

532 Burnett, Whit, ed.　This Is My Best Third Quarter of the
　　　Century.　Garden City, N. Y. :　Doubleday and Co. , 1970.
　　　To Whit Burnett, p. 65.

533 Mutiny 4 (Fall-Win. 1961-1962), p. 5.
　　　To Jane Esty (see no. 1166).

534 Poetry 89 (Mar. 1957), pp. 391-392.
　　　To Rolfe Humphries (see no. 1178).

535 <u>Sewanee Review</u> 69 (Apr. -June 1961), pp. 353-354.
          To Brother Antoninus (see no. 1168).

536 <u>Sewanee Review</u> 69 (July-Sept. 1961), pp. 512-513.
          To Brother Antoninus (see no. 1169).

537 <u>Sewanee Review</u> 73 (Jan. -Mar. 1965), pp. 177-178.
          To Charles Edward Eaton (see no. 1165).

RECORDS

*538 "Consultant in Poetry for 1966-68, for His Last Official Public Appearance in the Library, Reading His Poems with Comment in the Coolidge Auditorium on May 6, 1968, Under the Auspices of the Library of Congress." 1 tape. Library of Congress, 1968, 10 in. reel, 7 1/2 ips., stereo.

"Chenille"; "The Eye-Beaters"; "The Lord in the Air"; "May Day Sermon to the Women of Gilmer County, Georgia, by a Woman Preacher Leaving the Baptist Church"; "Victory."

Dickey was introduced by L. Quincy Mumford, Librarian of Congress. During the reading, Dickey omitted the word "Georgia" from his "May Day Sermon to the Women of Gilmer County, Georgia, by a Woman Preacher Leaving the Baptist Church."

*[This citation is from contents notes provided by Peter J. Fay, reference librarian, Library of Congress.]

*539 "James Dickey." Applause Productions, [n.d.]. 2 discs, 12 in., 33 1/3 rpm., mono., 4 sides.

"Fog Envelops the Animals"; "The Lifeguard"; "The Performance."

Although other works are included, they are unidentified.

*[This citation is from N.I.C.E.M.'s Index to Educational Records, 1975, p. 426.]

540 "James Dickey Reads His Poetry." Caedmon Records, 1971, disc TC1333, 12 in., 33 1/3 rpm., stereo.

"The Celebration"; Deliverance [exc.]; "Diabetes"; "Encounter in the Cage Country"; "Falling"; "For the Last Wolverine"; "Hunting Civil War Relics at Nimblewill Creek"; "In the Tree House at Night"; "Mercy"; "Messages"; "The Scarred Girl."

Slipcase notes are by Richard Howard (see no. 1222).

Illustrated with a photograph of Dickey on the cover by Christopher Dickey.

*540a Library of Congress, Washington, D.C.

During his tenure as poetry consultant, Dickey made several recordings of his works for which the bibliographic control is minimal or does not exist.

*[This citation is from information provided by Peter J. Fay, reference librarian, Library of Congress.]

73

*541 "The Poems of James Dickey (1957-1967)." Spoken Arts,
      1967, disc SA984, 12 in., 33 1/3 rpm.
          "A Birth"; "Cherrylog Road"; "The Firebombing"; "Fog
      Envelops the Animals"; "The Heaven of Animals"; "The
      Hospital Window"; "In the Mountain Tent"; "The Lifeguard";
      "On the Hill Below the Lighthouse"; "The Performance";
      "The Sheep Child"; "Sun"; "To His Children in Darkness."
          This reading was directed by Luce Klein, and slipcase
      notes are by Paul Kresh.
          *[This citation was compiled from data in The National
      Union Catalog ...: Music and Phonorecords, vol. 1,
      p. 620 and Robert W. Hill's "James Dickey: A Checklist,"
      p. 216 (see no. 1130).]

*542 "Reading His Poems in the Recording Laboratory of the Li-
      brary of Congress, Apr. 29, 1960." LWO 3092.
          "Awaiting the Swimmer"; "Between Two Prisoners";
      "Drowning with Others"; "The Enclosure"; "Fog Envelops
      the Animals"; "The Game"; "In the Tree House at Night";
      "The Landfall"; "The Magus"; "The Performance"; "Sleeping
      Out at Easter"; "The String"; "Trees and Cattle"; "Uncle";
      "The Underground Stream"; "The Vegetable King."
          *[This citation is from Mary Lillis Latimer's "James
      Dickey: A Bibliography," p. 15 (see no. 1131).]

*543 "Reading His Poems with Comment in the Coolidge Auditorium
      on Oct. 3, 1966, Under the Auspices of the Library of
      Congress; First Official Program as 1966-67 Consultant in
      Poetry." 1 tape. Library of Congress, 1966, 10 in. reel,
      7 1/2 ips.
          "Bums, on Waking"; "Encounter in the Cage Country";
      "Falling"; "The Hospital Window"; "Hunting Civil War
      Relics at Nimblewill Creek"; "In the Mountain Tent";
      "Kudzu"; "The Lifeguard"; "The Night Pool"; "Reincarna-
      tion [(I)]"; "The Scarred Girl"; "The Sheep Child"; "To His
      Children in Darkness"; "The Vegetable King"; "Winter
      Trout."
          Dickey was introduced by John G. Lorenz, Deputy Li-
      brarian of Congress.
          *[This citation is from contents notes provided by Peter
      J. Fay, reference librarian, Library of Congress.]

*544 "Reading His Poems with Comment on Nov. 8, 1965, in the
      Coolidge Auditorium of the Library of Congress Under the
      Auspices of the Gertrude Clarke Whittall Poetry and Litera-
      ture Fund." LWO 4697.
          "Adultery"; "At Darien Bridge"; "The Celebration";
      "Cherrylog Road"; "Faces Seen Once"; "Falling"; "Fathers
      and Sons: II, The Aura"; "The Firebombing"; "The Heaven
      of Animals"; "The Performance"; "The Shark's Parlor";
      "Slave Quarters"; "The String"; "Sun."
          Dickey was introduced by Roy P. Basler.
          *[This citation is from Mary Lillis Latimer's "James
      Dickey: A Bibliography," p. 15 (see no. 1131).]

*545   "Reading His Poetry with Comment at the University of Vir-
          ginia on April 17, 1968. "   3 tapes.   University of Virginia,
          1968, 7 1/2 in. reels, 7 1/2 ips.
              "Adultery"; "Chenille"; "Cherrylog Road"; "Encounter in
          the Cage Country"; "Hunting Civil War Relics [at Nimble-
          will Creek]"; "The Scarred Girl"; "The Sheep Child"; "Vic-
          tory. "
              Dickey was introduced by an unidentified person.   Al-
          though this reading was recorded by the University of Vir-
          ginia, it was given in the same year to the Library of
          Congress.
              *[This citation is from contents notes provided by Peter
          J. Fay, reference librarian, Library of Congress.]

*546   "Treasury of 100 Modern American Poets. "   vol. 15, Spoken
          Arts, [n. d.], disc. 12 in. , 33 1/3 rpm.
              The poems included are unidentified.
              *[This citation is from N. I. C. E. M. 's Index to Educa-
          tional Records, 1975, p. 709.]

SPECIAL COLLECTIONS

547   Rare Books Department, John M. Olin Library, Washington
      University, St. Louis, Missouri.
          Books, records, dissertations, theses, term papers,
      letters, clippings, programs, publishers' notices, galley
      proofs, letters, manuscripts, revisions, etc. are included.

MISCELLANEA

548   The American Literary Anthology/I: The First Annual Collec-
      tion of the Best from the Literary Magazines. New York:
      Farrar, Straus, and Giroux, 1968.
          Dickey was one of several poets who selected the poems
      appearing in this anthology.

549   Esquire 75 (Jan. 1971).
          Beginning with this issue, Dickey is poetry editor.

550   New Orleans Review 1 (Fall 1968).
          Beginning with this issue, Dickey is one of the members
      of the advisory editorial board.

551   New York Quarterly, no. 4 (Fall 1970).
          Beginning with this issue, Dickey is one of the members
      of the advisory board.

552   Shenandoah 15 (Aut. 1963).
          Dickey was one of the advisory editors for this issue.

553   Shenandoah 16 (Aut. 1964).
          Beginning with this issue, Dickey is one of the advisory
      editors.

*554 Wafer, Ralph and Burnside, Dianne. "Environmental Self-
      Consciousness." New Orleans, 1971.
          A poster on which "Exchanges: Being in the Form of a
      Dialogue with Joseph Trumbull Stickney" (see no. 91) ap-
      pears on the reverse side.
          *[This citation is from Franklin Ashley's James Dickey:
      A Checklist, p. 37 (see no. 1127).]

II: WORKS ABOUT JAMES DICKEY

PERIODICAL LITERATURE

555 Aarons, Leroy F. "Ex-Adman Dickey: Don't Just Wait for
Oblivion." Washington (D. C.) Post (10 Sept. 1966), p. 6.
Buckdancer's Choice.
A personality piece concerned with Dickey's appointment
as poetry consultant at the Library of Congress, his pub-
lishing career, and his views on the relationship between a
poem and its reader. Biographical data is included in this
essay-interview.
Ref. : Van Heflin.
Photograph of Dickey by Arthur Ellis.

556 "About James Dickey." Literary Guild Magazine (Apr. 1970),
p. 7.
Buckdancer's Choice; Deliverance; Poems 1957-1967.
Biographical data and career information are given.
Photograph of Dickey by Christopher Dickey.

557 Adams, Phoebe. Atlantic 221 (May 1968), p. 114.
Favorable review of Babel to Byzantium containing 24
words.

558 _____. Atlantic 225 (Mar. 1970), p. 146.
Favorable review of The Eye-Beaters, Blood, Victory,
Madness, Buckhead and Mercy containing 15 words.

*559 After Dark 5 (Sept. 1972), p. 61.
A review of the film version of Deliverance.
*[This citation is from Multi Media Reviews Index, 1972,
p. 59.]

560 Aigner, Hal. "Deliverance." Film Quarterly 26 (Win. 1972-
1973), pp. 39-41.
Deliverance [film], pp. 39, 41.
Characterization in and plot of the film version of
Deliverance are discussed at length. Theme of survival is
investigated in relation to the plot and to the epilogue.
Flaws are identified.
Ref. : Ned Beatty, p. 40; John Boorman, pp. 39, 41;
Herbert "Cowboy" Coward, p. 40; Ronny Cox, p. 40; The
Culpepper Cattle Co. [film], p. 39; Bill McKinney, p. 40;
Burt Reynolds, pp. 39, 40; The Treasure of the Sierra
Madre [film], p. 39; Vilmos Zsigmond, p. 41.
Illustrated with a still, p. 40.

561 Algren, Nelson. "Tricky Dickey. " Critic 28 (May-June 1970),
          pp. 77-79.
               Deliverance, pp. 77-79; ["Falling"], p. 78.
               A personal account of the effects Deliverance had on this
          reviewer.
               Photograph of Dickey by Christopher Dickey, p. 78.

562 Allen, Henry. "A Poetry Reading for 10, 000. " Washington
          (D. C.) Post (29 Jan. 1972), sec. C, pp. 1, 6.
               Dickey's participation in the poetry recital "Yevtushenko
          and Friends" is favorably mentioned although, as a whole,
          the concert was uneventful.
               Ref. : Sarah Bernhardt, p. 6; Barry Boys, p. 1; Sol
          Hurok, p. 6; Iris Kones, p. 6; Stanley Kunitz, pp. 1, 6;
          Viveca Lindfors, p. 1; Eugene McCarthy, pp. 1, 6;
          McCarthy's "Vietnam Message, " p. 6; Vladimir Mayakovsky,
          p. 1; The Rolling Stones, p. 1; Albert Todd, p. 1; Andrei
          Vozesensky, p. 6; Richard Wilbur, pp. 1, 6; William
          Wordsworth, p. 1; Yevgeny Yevtushenko, pp. 1, 6;
          Yevtushenko's "Babi Yar, " p. 6; Yevtushenko's "Bombs
          for Balalaikas, " p. 6; Yevtushenko's Stolen Apples, p. 1
          (see no. 20).

563 Allen, Morse. "Modern Poets. " Hartford (Conn.) Courant.
          Courant Magazine (20 May 1962), p. 14.
               "The Change"; Drowning with Others; "For the Nightly
          Ascent of the Hunter Orion Over a Forest Clearing. "
               Favorable review of Drowning with Others containing
          133 words.

564 American Literature 40 (Nov. 1968), p. 436.
               ["Allen Ginsberg"].
               Unfavorable review of Babel to Byzantium containing
          95 words.

565 Armour, Robert. "Deliverance: Four Variations of the Amer-
          ican Adam. " Literature/Film Quarterly 1 (July 1973),
          pp. 280-285.
               Deliverance [novel], pp. 280, 282, 285; Deliverance
          [film], pp. 280, 282, 285.
               The emergence of the archetypal American Adam is ex-
          plored in Deliverance and in its film version. Each of the
          suburbanites is shown to exhibit, wholly or partially, the
          archetype's characteristics.
               Ref. : Nick Adams, p. 280; Daniel Boone, pp. 280, 282;
          John Boorman, pp. 282, 284; Natty Bumppo, pp. 280, 282;
          Carl Jung, p. 282; R. W. B. Lewis' The American Adam:
          Innocence, Tragedy, and Tradition in the Nineteenth Cen-
          tury, pp. 280, 282, 285n; Ike McCaslin, p. 280.
               Illustrated with stills, pp. 281, 283.

566 Arnett, David Leslie. Abstract of "James Dickey: Poetry and
          Fiction. " In Dissertation Abstracts International; A: The

Humanities and Social Sciences 34 (Oct. 1973), p. 1889.
"Below Ellijay"; Deliverance; Drowning with Others;
Helmets; Into the Stone and Other Poems.
In the author's dissertation (see no. 1115), recurring
images and themes, the development of major themes through
several volumes, and the use of religious concepts in
Dickey's oeuvre are discussed. Its first chapter is a sur-
vey of Dickey's critics' works, and an interview, "James
Dickey and the Writing of Deliverance," is appended.
Ref.: David Leslie Arnett's "James Dickey and the
Writing of Deliverance" (see no. 1091); Jesus.

567 Arnold, Gary. "Deliverance: A Gripping Piece of Work."
Washington (D. C.) Post (5 Oct. 1972), sec. B, pp. 1, 19.
Deliverance [novel], pp, 1, 19; Deliverance [film],
pp. 1, 19.
Although the film version of Deliverance is successful on
a suspense-adventure tale level, it is faulted for its lack of
emotional and social revelations, its inability to establish
characters, and its poor acting. The merits of the novel
are compared with the film's shortcomings.
Ref.: Ned Beatty, p. 19; John Boorman, pp. 1, 19;
Boorman's Hell in the Pacific [film], p. 1; Boorman's Leo
the Last [film], p. 1; Boorman's Point Blank [film], pp. 1,
19; Ronny Cox, p. 19; The Hired Hand [film], p. 1; McCabe
and Mrs. Miller [film], p. 1; Bill McKinney, p. 1; Burt
Reynolds, p. 19; George Stevens, p. 1; Stevens' A Place in
the Sun [film], p. 1; Jon Voight, p. 1, 19; Vilmos Zsigmond,
p. 1.
Illustrated with stills, pp. 1, 19.

568 _____. "Sticking with the Money." Washington (D. C.) Post
(5 Oct. 1972), sec. B. , p. 19.
Deliverance [film].
Ned Beatty, who played the role of Bobby in the film
Deliverance, discusses his success in the film industry
after the film's release. The entry of Deliverance in the
Atlanta Film Festival is noted.

569 Aronson, James. Antioch Review 30 (Fall-Win. 1970-1971),
pp. 463-465 [463-464].
Deliverance, p. 464; "The Firebombing," p. 464; "The
Heaven of Animals," p. 464.
Review of Self-Interviews concerned with Dickey's obses-
sion with technique, his insecurity with his poetic vision,
and his philosophical comments.
Exc.: Contemporary Literary Criticism (see no. 1062).

570 "Arts and Letters Body Elects Barzun as Head." New York
Times (3 Feb. 1972), p. 24.
Dickey is listed with twelve other newly elected mem-
bers of the National Institute of Arts and Letters.

*571 Ashman, Richard A. New Orleans Poetry Journal.
          *[According to Dickey in Self-Interviews, pp. 46-47,
      Ashman was the first person to mention Dickey in a pub-
      lication. All efforts to discover this reference have been
      unsuccessful.]

*572 Audience, no. 50 (Aug. 1972), p. 20.
          A review of the film version of Deliverance.
          *[This citation is from Multi Media Reviews Index,
      1972, p. 59.]

573 "Author Feels Responsible for Deaths." Los Angeles Times
      (19 Sept. 1973), sec. 1-A, p. 15.
          Deliverance [novel]; [Deliverance] [film].
          Dickey responds to the drownings in the Chattooga River
      popularized by Deliverance and its film version.
          Orig.: "Just like Deliverance" (see no. 754). (Only
      remarks by Dickey were reprinted here.)

574 Avant, John Alfred. Library Journal 95 (1 Mar. 1970),
      pp. 902-903.
          "The Eye-Beaters," p. 903; "Madness," p. 903; "Mercy,"
      p. 903; ["The Moon Ground"], p. 902.
          Favorable review of The Eye-Beaters, Blood, Victory,
      Madness, Buckhead and Mercy containing 135 words.
          Rept.: "The Library Journal" Book Review: 1970 (see
      no. 988).

575 _____. Library Journal 95 (1 Mar. 1970), p. 912.
          Unfavorable review of Deliverance containing 158 words.
          Ref.: Edgar Rice Burroughs; Ernest Hemingway.
          Rept.: "The Library Journal" Book Review: 1970 (see
      no. 989).

576 Baker, Donald W. "The Poetry of James Dickey." Poetry
      111 (Mar. 1968), pp. 400-401.
          "Adultery," p. 401; "The Bee," p. 401; "The Being,"
      p. 401; "The Birthday Dream," p. 401; Buckdancer's
      Choice, p. 400; "Cherrylog Road," p. 401; "Coming Back
      to America," pp. 400-401; "Deer Among Cattle," p. 401;
      Drowning with Others, p. 400; "Falling," p. 401; "Falling,"
      [sec. of Poems 1957-1967], p. 400; "The Firebombing,"
      p. 401; Helmets, p. 400; Into the Stone and Other Poems,
      p. 400; "The Leap," pp. 400-401; "Listening to Foxhounds,"
      p. 401; "May Day Sermon to the Women of Gilmer County,
      Georgia, by a Woman Preacher Leaving the Baptist Church,"
      p. 401; "The Performance," p. 401; Poems 1957-1967,
      p. 400; "Reincarnation (II)," p. 401; "The Scarred Girl,"
      p. 401; "The Shark's Parlor," p. 401; "The Sheep Child,"
      p. 401; "Sun," p. 401.
          Notes on Dickey's nostalgic mythology, poetic techniques,
      and obsession with the metaphysical in Poems 1957-1967.
      Emphasis is on the effect of his career in advertising on

"Falling." List of major themes are included.
  Ref.: W. H. Auden, p. 400; Auden's Doom is Dark,
p. 400; The Wanderer, p. 400; The Seafarer, p. 400.

577 Baro, Gene. "The Sound of Three New Poetic Voices." New
  York Times Herald Tribune. Book Review (30 Oct. 1960),
  p. 10.
       Dickey's metaphysical motifs in Into the Stone and Other
  Poems are the causes of three effects in his poetry: an
  extremely personal quality, elaboration, and pretentiousness.

577a "Beat Poetry." New York Times Book Review (24 Sept. 1961),
  p. 48.
       ["Confession Is Not Enough"].
       The editor's remarks, prefacing two letters (see
  nos. 1188 and 1196), trace the literary feud prompted by
  Dickey's criticism of beat poetry.
       Ref.: the Beats; John J. Gill's [letter] (see no. 1172);
  Allen Ginsberg's Kaddish; Charles Olson's The Maximus
  Poems; Selden Rodman's [letter] (see no. 1189).

578 Bedient, Calvin. "Gold-Glowing Mote." Nation 210 (6 Apr.
  1970), pp. 407-408.
       Deliverance, pp. 407-408; "Two Days in September,"
  p. 408.
       Dickey's novel Deliverance is more limited than his
  poetry since it doesn't produce an awareness. It aims at,
  but misses, profundity. Its theme, narrative, and action,
  all of which are discussed at length, save it.
       Ref.: Kingsley Amis, p. 407; Emily Brontë, p. 407;
  William Golding, p. 407; Golding's Pincher Martin, p. 407;
  Robert Graves, p. 407; Thomas Hardy, pp. 407-408; Karl
  Jaspers, p. 408; D. H. Lawrence, p. 407; Novalis,
  p. 408; Obadiah's [epigraph used in Deliverance], p. 408;
  Muriel Spark, p. 407; Wallace Stevens, p. 408; Peter
  Taylor, p. 408; Henry David Thoreau, p. 408; John Updike,
  p. 407; Robert Penn Warren, p. 407.

579 Beidler, Peter G. "'The Pride of Thine Heart Hath Deceived
  Thee': Narrative Distortion in Dickey's Deliverance."
  South Carolina Review 5 (Dec. 1972), pp. 29-40.
       Deliverance, pp. 29-38.
       Evidence is provided to prove that Ed Gentry, the nar-
  rator of Deliverance, killed an innocent man at the summit
  of the cliff which he had scaled. He is viewed as one who
  distorts the truth for self-serving reasons. His relation-
  ship to the novel's epigraph from Obadiah is explored. Re-
  pudiations of various critics' attacks on Deliverance conclude.
       Ref.: John Alfred Avant's [Library Journal review],
  p. 36 (see no. 575); Calvin Bedient's "Gold-Glowing Mote,"
  p. 37 (see no. 578); Wayne C. Booth's The Rhetoric of
  Fiction, p. 39; Walter Clemons' "James Dickey, Novelist,"
  p. 39 (see no. 637); Benjamin DeMott's "The 'More Life'

School and James Dickey," p. 35 (see no. 664); Stephen
Farber's "Deliverance: How It Delivers," p. 39 (see
no. 685); Paul Edward Gray's "New Fiction in Review,"
pp. 38-39 (see no. 714); Carolyn Heilbrun's "The Masculine
Wilderness of the American Novel," p. 36n. (see no. 726);
Henry James, p. 35; Obadiah's [epigraph used in Deliver-
ance], p. 37; Richard Patrick's "Heroic Deliverance,"
p. 36 (see no. 855); Christopher Rick's "Man Hunt,"
p. 35-36 (see no. 876); Charles Thomas Samuels' "What
Hath Dickey Delivered?," p. 29 (see no. 890); Tarzan,
pp. 34, 36; Johnny Weismuller, p. 34.

580   Bennett, Joseph. "A Man with a Voice." New York Times
       Book Review (6 Feb. 1966), p. 10.
            "Angina"; Buckdancer's Choice; "The Common Grave";
       "The Fiend"; "The Firebombing"; "Gamecock"; "Mangham";
       "The Shark's Parlor"; "Slave Quarters."
            Unity, clarity, controlled emotion, intensity, and con-
       flicts within the poems' subjects characterize Buckdancer's
       Choice. The recurrent theme of death is noted.
            Exc.: A Library of Literary Criticism (see no. 1005).

581   Berry, David C. "Harmony with the Dead: James Dickey's
       Descent Into the Underworld." Southern Quarterly 12 (Apr.
       1974), pp. 233-244.
            "Armor," pp. 238-239, 244; Buckdancer's Choice,
       p. 243; "Drinking from a Helmet," pp. 242, 244; "The
       Driver," p. 243; Drowning with Others, pp. 238-239;
       "Falling" [sec. of Poems 1957-1967], p. 235; "The Fire-
       bombing," pp. 243-244; Helmets, pp. 241-242; "Horses and
       Prisoners," p. 241; "Hunting Civil War Relics at Nimble-
       will Creek," pp. 239-240; "In the Tree House at Night,"
       p. 238; ["Into the Stone"], pp. 236-237; Into the Stone and
       Other Poems, pp. 234, 236-237; "The Island," p. 240;
       "Orpheus Before Hades," pp. 234-235; "Poem," pp. 236,
       244; "The Sprinter's Mother," pp. 235-236; "The String,"
       pp. 236-237, 244; "The Underground Stream," pp. 237,
       239, 244; "A View of Fujiyama After the War," p. 240.
            The Orphic experience--the poet's descent into the realm
       of the dead, contact with a ghost, and celebration of the
       knowledge gained from the descent and contact--is examined
       in Dickey's family and war poems. "Orpheus Before Hades"
       is reprinted in full, pp. 234-235.
            Ref.: Bible, p. 244; Robert Bly's "The Work of James
       Dickey," pp. 235, 235n. (see no. 589); Eurydice, p. 242;
       Heraclitus, p. 244; Janus, p. 235; Laurence Leiberman's
       "The Worldly Mystic," pp. 235, 235n. (see no. 796);
       Orpheus, pp. 233-236, 240-241, 244; Rainer Maria Rilke,
       pp. 239-242; Rilke's Brife II: 1914-1926, pp. 233, 233n.;
       Rilke's Sonnets to Orpheus, pp. 233, 233n., 241; Walter A.
       Strauss' Descent and Return, pp. 233-234, 233n.

582   Berry, David Chapman, Jr. Abstract of "Orphic and Narcis-

sistic Themes in the Poetry and Criticism of James Dickey,
1951-1970. " In Dissertation Abstracts International; A:
The Humanities and Social Sciences 34 (Feb. 1974),
p. 5158.
Babel to Byzantium; Buckdancer's Choice.
In the author's dissertation (see no. 1116), Dickey's
celebration of life, his expansional technique, and the re-
lationship between the poem and its creator are studied.
Ref. : Apollo; Dionysus; Narcissus; Orpheus.

583   Berry, Wendell.   "James Dickey's New Book. "   Poetry 105
(Nov. 1964), pp. 130-131.
"Bums, on Waking, " p. 130; "Cherrylog Road, " p. 130;
"Drinking from a Helmet, " p. 130; "The Dusk of Horses, "
p. 130; "Fence Wire, " p. 130; "The Ice Skin, " p. 130;
"The Scarred Girl, " p. 130; "Springer Mountain, " p. 130.
Sympathy lies at the core of Helmets, and an over-
worked technique taints several poems.   Dickey's use of
rhythm is mentioned.
Exc. : A Library of Literary Criticism (see no. 1005).

584   Bishop, David R.   America 126 (18 Mar. 1972), p. 297.
["Edwin Arlington Robinson"]; ["The Greatest American
Poet: Theodore Roethke"]; "Metaphor as Pure Adventure";
"The Self as Agent"; Sorties.
While the journal section of Sorties is uneven and un-
revealing, its essays, described as precise, expressive,
and sensitive, reaffirm Dickey's lofty place in American
letters.

584a   Bledsoe, Jerry.   "What Will Save Us from Boredom?"
Esquire 80 (Dec. 1973), pp. 227-233.
[Deliverance] [novel], p. 233; Deliverance [film],
pp. 227-233.
The rise in drownings from "shooting the rapids" of the
Chattooga River, a sport popularized by the film Deliver-
ance and termed the "Deliverance Syndrome" by many, is
investigated.   A brief history of the area and Dickey's re-
action to the accidents are added to this report of events
leading to one young man's death.   Dickey's appearance at
the Atlanta premiere of Deliverance is noted.
Ref. : Jack Ambrose, pp. 229, 231-233; Howard Banchek,
p. 233; Walt Belcher, p. 232; June Black, pp. 230, 233;
Jimmy Carter, p. 230; Chattooga River, pp. 227, 229, 233;
Cherokee Indians, p. 229; Huck Finn, p. 229; Sonny Foster,
p. 232; The Godfather [film], p. 233; Lloyd Hunter,
pp. 231-233; Virgil Justus, p. 231; J. C. Moore, p. 231;
Earl "Preach" Parsons, p. 230; Harry Reeves, pp. 227,
229, 232; Hazel Reeves, pp. 227, 229, 232-233; Tommy
Reeves, pp. 227, 229, 231-233; Burt Reynolds, pp. 228,
230; Charles Roessler, p. 233; Bill Sills, pp. 229, 231-
233; Marc J. Silverman, p. 233; Michael Smith, p. 233;
Claude Terry, p. 230; Sam Wood, pp. 229, 231-233; Doug

Woodward, p. 230; Chester York, pp. 232-233.
Illustrated with a still, p. 228.

585 Blumenfeld, Yorick. New York Times Book Review (6 Feb.
     1972), pp. 30-31 [31].
          Dickey is listed as one of the translators of Stolen
     Apples.

586 Bly, Robert. "Buckdancer's Choice." Sixties, no. 9. (Spr.
     1967), pp. 70-79.
          [Note: The title given this essay in the table of con-
     tents is "The Collapse of James Dickey."]
          Buckdancer's Choice, p. 70; Drowning with Others,
     p. 79; "The Escape," p. 78; "The Fiend," pp. 75-76;
     "[The] Firebombing," pp. 72-77; "[In the] Mountain Tent,"
     p. 79; "The Shark's Parlor," p. 78; "Slave Quarters,"
     pp. 70-72, 76-77, 79; "Sled Burial, [Dream Ceremony],"
     p. 78.
          Dickey is severely criticized because he displays a
     hunger for power and lacks a sense of social responsibility
     and compassion in Buckdancer's Choice. His language and
     rhythm are also criticized.
          Ref.: Anton Chekhov, p. 70; Count Ciano, p. 74; John
     Dos Passos, p. 79; Fortinbras, p. 76; Robert Frost,
     p. 78; Hamlet, p. 76; Lyndon B. Johnson, p. 77; Rudyard
     Kipling, p. 79; The New Yorker, p. 79; Rainer Maria
     Rilke, p. 78; Marquis de Sade, p. 70; The Saturday Evening
     Post, p. 70; Leo Tolstoy, p. 70; Ivan Turgenev, p. 70;
     William Butler Yeats, p. 77.

587 _____. "The Collapse of James Dickey."
          This essay is often referred to as "The Collapse of
     James Dickey" although this title is only given to the essay
     in the table of contents. The title "Buckdancer's Choice"
     (see no. 586) appears at the beginning of the essay.

588 _____. "Prose vs. Poetry." Choice, no. 2 (1962),
     pp. 65-80 [66-68].
          ["Armor"], p. 66; ["The] Heaven of Animals," p. 67;
     ["The Hospital Window"], p. 66; ["Hunting Civil War Relics
     at Nimblewill Creek"], p. 66; "In the Mountain Tent,"
     p. 67; "The Owl King [: II, The Owl King]," pp. 67-68.
          Drowning with Others is a striking volume due to Dickey's
     strong imagination and abhorrence of clichés. Only his
     verboseness, which appears to be diminishing as his oeuvre
     progresses, is a handicap.

589 _____ [Crunk?]. "The Work of James Dickey." Sixties,
     no. 7 (Win. 1964), pp. 41-57.
          ["Armor"], p. 42; ["The Change"], p. 46; "Death" [sec.
     of Into the Stone and Other Poems], p. 41; "Dover:
     Believing in Kings," pp. 44, 51; ["The Dream Flood"],
     p. 46; Drowning with Others, pp. 43, 52, 54; "Fog Envelops

the Animals," pp. 52-53; ["For the Nightly Ascent of the Hunter Orion Over a Forest Clearing"], p. 49; ["The Game"], p. 56; "The Heaven of Animals," pp. 47-48, 56; ["Hunting Civil War Relics at] Nimblewill [Creek]," pp. 41-42; ["In] the Tree House [at Night]," pp. 42-43, 48-49, 51-52; "Inside the River," p. 49; Into the Stone and Other Poems, pp. 41-42, 52, 57; ["The Jewel"], pp. 56-57; "The Land Fall," p. 52; "Listening to Foxhounds," p. 41; "The Owl King," pp. 44, 56; ["The Owl King: III, The Blind Child's Story"], p. 45; ["The Owl King: II, The Owl King"], p. 44; ["Poem"], p. 42; "The Rib," pp. 46, 49-50; "The Salt Marsh," pp. 48-49, 51; "The Scratch," pp. 43-44; ["A Screened Porch in the Country"], pp. 47, 51; ["The Signs"], pp. 43, 56; "Sleeping Out at Easter," p. 51; "The Sprinter's Sleep," p. 42; ["The Summons"], p. 52; ["The Twin Falls"], pp. 53, 55; "The Vegetable King," p. 53.

Dickey's originality is praised. His poems' spirituality, the devices employed for elements of metamorphosis, their flights of fantasy, and their narcissism are discussed. Death and war and images of clowns and animals are seen as major traits. Dickey's Southern heritage is identified, and his rhetoric, especially his use of meter and adverbs, is criticized.

Ref.: Thomas Aquinas, p. 56; Geoffrey Chaucer, p. 55; Chaucer's Canterbury Tales, p. 55; John Ciardi, pp. 55, 57; Hart Crane's "Repose of Rivers," p. 53; Charles Darwin, pp. 46, 56; Grimm Brothers, p. 46; Randall Jarrell, pp. 56-57; Howard Nemerov, p. 55; John Frederick Nims, p. 55; George Joseph Seidel, p. 55; Anne Sexton, p. 55; Karl Shapiro, p. 55; Saint Teresa, p. 55; Reed Whittemore, p. 55; William Butler Yeats, p. 54.

590   Booklist 66 (1 May 1970), p. 1077.
        Favorable review of Deliverance containing 126 words.

591   Booklist 66 (15 June 1970), p. 1251.
        Buckdancer's Choice.
        Favorable review of The Eye-Beaters, Blood, Victory, Madness, Buckhead and Mercy containing 108 words.

592   Booklist 67 (15 Mar. 1971), p. 582.
        Favorable review of Self-Interviews containing 99 words.
        Ref.: Mademoiselle.

593   Booklist 67 (1 Apr. 1971), p. 656.
        Favorable review of Self-Interviews containing 43 words.

594   Booklist 67 (15 July 1971), p. 949.
        Deliverance.
        Favorable review of the L. P. record James Dickey Reads His Poetry containing 121 words.
        Ref.: Richard Howard's [remarks on the slipcase] (see no. 1222).

595   Booklist 68 (15 Jan. 1972), p. 411.
            Self-Interviews.
            Favorable review of Sorties containing 79 words.

596   Booklist and Subscription Books Bulletin 60 (1 May 1964),
            p. 813.
            Favorable review of Helmets containing 55 words.

597   Booklist and Subscription Books Bulletin 61 (1 Nov. 1964),
            p. 240.
            ["Allen Ginsberg"]; ["Anne Sexton"]; ["Brother Antoninus"];
            ["The Grove Press New American Poets (1960)"]; ["Howard
            Nemerov"]; ["New Poets of England and America I (1957)"];
            ["Theodore Roethke"]; ["Thom Gunn"].
            Favorable review of The Suspect in Poetry containing
            103 words.
            Ref. :   The Hudson Review; Poetry.

598   Booklist and Subscription Books Bulletin 62 (1 Dec. 1965),
            pp. 350-351.
            Favorable review of Buckdancer's Choice containing 81
            words.

599   Booklist and Subscription Books Bulletin 63 (1 June 1967),
            p. 1027.
            Favorable review of Poems 1957-1967 containing 68
            words.

600   Booklist and Subscription Books Bulletin 65 (1 Sept. 1968),
            p. 32.
            Favorable review of Babel to Byzantium containing 103
            words.

601   "Books of the 1960's: U. S. A. " Times Literary Supplement
            (25 Nov. 1965), p. 1084.
            Buckdancer's Choice; Drowning with Others; Helmets;
            Into the Stone and Other Poems.
            Volumes of Dickey's verse are included in a list of
            significant books.

602   Bornhauser, Fred.   "Poetry by the Poem. " Virginia Quarterly
            Review 40 (Win. 1965), pp. 146-152 [149-150].
            Helmets, p. 150.
            Criticism is aimed at the anapestic rhythm and the
            spatially isolated lines of Helmets.   Its subjects and
            themes are deemed successful.

603   Brockman, Zoe.   "Valuable Poetry Study. "   Gastonia (N. C.)
            Gazette (21 Apr. 1968), sec. P, p. 4.
            Babel to Byzantium; Buckdancer's Choice; Into the Stone
            and Other Poems; ["Marianne Moore"]; Poems 1957-1967;
            ["Randall Jarrell"]; ["Robert Frost"]; The Suspect in Poetry;
            ["Theodore Roethke"].

89   Periodical Literature

Dickey is cited for the unique intensity and intelligence
displayed in Babel to Byzantium.   Biographical data and
descriptions of several of his volumes are included.
  Ref. :   Richard Howard's [unidentified remarks]; Richard
Kostelanetz's [unidentified remarks].

604   Broyard, Anatole.   "Dickey's Likes and Dislikes. "   New York
      Times (17 Dec. 1971), p. 37.
         ["Journals"]; ["The Son, the Cave, and the Burning
      Bush"]; Sorties.
         Dickey is criticized for the searching, unoriginality, and
      unsophistication of Sorties.
         Ref. :   T. S. Eliot; Edward Hopper; Sylvia Plath; Trans-
      ition.

605   Buckley, Peter.   "Deliverance. "   Films and Filming 19 (Oct.
      1972), p. 46.
         Deliverance [film].
         Survival theme, homosexual motif, tension building
      devices, and scenes of terror in the film version of
      Deliverance are discussed.   Plot summary and credits are
      given.
         Ref. :   Ned Beatty; John Boorman; Peter Brook's Lord of
      the Flies [film]; Ronnie Cox; William Golding; Psycho [film];
      Burt Reynolds; Straw Dogs [film]; Jon Voight.

606   Bulletin from Virginia Kirkus' Service 28 (1 July 1960),
         p. 549.
         Favorable review of Into the Stone and Other Poems
      containing 41 words.
         Ref. :   John Hall Wheelock's "Introductory Essay: Some
      Thoughts on Poetry" (see no. 1089).

607   Bulletin from Virginia Kirkus' Service 31 (15 Dec. 1963),
         pp. 1177-1178.
         "The Performance, " p. 1177; ["On the Coosawattee: I,
      By Canoe Through the Fir Forest"], p. 1177.
         Mixed review of Helmets containing 224 words.
         Ref. :   Henry David Thoreau, p. 1178.

608   Burke, Herbert.   Library Journal 85 (1 Sept. 1960), p. 2947.
         Into the Stone and Other Poems; [unidentified passage].
         Favorable review of Into the Stone and Other Poems
      containing 71 words.
         Ref. :   William Carlos Williams.

609   Burns, Gerald.   "Poets and Anthologies. "   Southwest Review
      53 (Sum. 1968), pp. 332-336 [332-333].
         "Adultery, " p. 332; ["Allen Ginsberg"], p. 333;
      "Approaching Prayer, " p. 333; Babel to Byzantium, p. 333;
      Buckdancer's Choice, p. 332; ["Charles Olson"], p. 333;
      "The Driver, " p. 332; "Falling" [sec. of Poems 1957-1967],
      p. 332; ["Francis Thompson: 'The Hound of Heaven'"],

p. 333; Helmets, p. 332; ["Howard Nemerov"], p. 333;
["John Ashbery"], p. 333; ["Kenneth Patchen"], p. 333;
["Matthew Arnold: 'Dover Beach'"], p. 333; ["May Day
Sermon to the Women of Gilmer County, Georgia, by a
Woman Preacher Leaving the Baptist Church"], p. 333;
"Notes on the Decline of Outrage," p. 333; "The Owl King,"
p. 333; Poems 1957-1967, p. 332; ["Randall Jarrell"],
p. 332; ["Reed Whittemore"], p. 333; ["Richard Eberhart"],
p. 333; ["Robert Duncan"], p. 333; ["Robert Penn Warren"],
p. 333; ["William Carlos Williams: 'The Yachts'"], p. 333.
Dickey's words are too superficial as illustrated by
Poems 1957-1967, and his criticism in Babel to Byzantium
is best when it concerns poets not poetry. Successful
poems and prose are noted.
Ref.: W. H. Auden, p. 332; Auden's Collected Shorter
Poems, p. 332.

610 Burns, Richard K. Library Journal 89 (1 Mar. 1964),
p. 1095.
Helmets.
Favorable review of Helmets containing 223 words. An
explanation of the helmet image is included.

*611 Calendo, J. "Deliverance." Inter/View, no. 27 (Nov. 1972),
p. 41.
A review of the film version of Deliverance.
*[This citation is from International Index to Film Peri-
odicals, 1972, p. 147.]

612 Calhoun, Richard. "On Robert Bly's Protest Poetry."
Tennessee Poetry Journal 2 (Win. 1969), pp. 21-22 [21].
Included are comments defending Dickey against Bly's
attack on him.
Ref.: Robert Bly's "Buckdancer's Choice" (see no. 586).

613 _____. "'His Reason Argues with His Invention': James
Dickey's Self-Interviews and The Eye-Beaters." South
Carolina Review 3 (June 1971), pp. 9-16.
["Apollo: I, For the First Manned Moon Orbit"],
p. 16; Babel to Byzantium, p. 9; Buckdancer's Choice,
p. 13; "The Cancer Match," p. 15; Deliverance, p. 9;
"Diabetes: I, [Sugar]," p. 12; ["Diabetes: II,] Under
Buzzards," pp. 13, 15; Drowning with Others, pp. 11, 13;
["Drowning with Others"], pp. 10-11; "The Eye-Beaters,"
pp. 12, 15; The Eye-Beaters, Blood, Victory, Madness, Buck-
head and Mercy, pp. 9, 11-13, 15; "Falling," p. 14; "Falling"
[sec. of Poems 1957-1967], p. 13; "The Firebombing," p. 13;
["The Heaven of Animals"], p. 10; Helmets, p. 13; Into
the Stone and Other Poems, p. 13; ["J. V. Cunningham"],
pp. 9-10; "The Lifeguard," p. 11; ["The Lord in the Air"],
p. 12; ["Messages"], p. 12; ["Messages: II,] Giving a Son
to the Sea," p. 15; ["Pine: I"], p. 12; "The Poem as
Something that Matters," p. 10; Poems 1957-1967, pp. 10,

13; "The Poet in Mid-Career," p. 10; "Power and Light,"
p. 14; ["Randall Jarrell"], p. 9; Self-Interviews, pp. 9-11,
13, 15; "Two Poems of Going Home," p. 14; ["Two Poems
of Going Home: I,] Living There," p. 14; ["Two Poems of
Going Home: II,] Looking for the Buckhead Boys," pp. 13,
15-16; ["William Carlos Williams"], p. 10.

The strengths and weaknesses of Self-Interviews and the
themes of death, aging, and illness in The Eye-Beaters,
Blood, Victory, Madness, Buckhead and Mercy are investi-
gated.   A brief examination of the reincarnation motif of
five volumes of Dickey's poetry is included.   The quoted
portion of the title is from "The Eye-Beaters."

Ref.: James Agee, p. 11; T. S. Eliot, p. 11;
Heraclitus, p. 11; Randall Jarrell, p. 12; John Keats,
p. 11; Life, p. 16; Robert Lowell's Life Studies, p. 13;
Malcolm Lowry, p. 11; Marshall McLuhan, p. 9; Wolfgang
Mozart, p. 11; Barbara Reiss and James Reiss' "Introduc-
tion", p. 9 (see no. 1960); Stephen Spender's "The Making
of a Poem," p. 11; Allen Tate's "Ode to the Confederate
Dead," p. 11.

Rept.: James Dickey: The Expansive Imagination (see
no. 993).

614 _____ . "Whatever Happened to the Poet-Critic?" Southern
Literary Journal, n. s. 1 (Aut. 1968), pp. 75-88.

["Allen Ginsberg"], p. 76; Babel to Byzantium, pp. 75,
77, 79, 82-83, 86; "Barnstorming for Poetry," p. 85;
["E. E. Cummings"], pp. 78, 83-84; ["Edwin Arlington
Robinson"], pp. 78, 81, 84; ["Edwin Arlington Robinson:
The Many Truths"], p. 84; ["Harold Witt"], p. 81;
["Howard Nemerov"], pp. 78-79; ["I. A. Richards"], p. 87;
["In the Presence of Anthologies"], p. 79; ["J. V. Cunning-
ham"], p. 87; ["James Merrill"], p. 76; ["Marianne
Moore"], p. 78; "Notes on the Decline of Outrage," p. 85;
"The Poet Turns on Himself," pp. 81-85; "Preface," p. 76;
["Randall Jarrell"], p. 87; ["Richard Wilbur"], p. 76;
["Robert Frost"], pp. 78, 80-81; ["Robert Graves"], p. 86;
"Sleeping Out at Easter," p. 81; The Suspect in Poetry,
p. 75; ["Theodore Roethke"], pp. 78, 81-84; ["Thom Gunn"],
p. 76; [unidentified passage], p. 75; ["William Carlos
Williams"], p. 87; ["William Carlos Williams: 'The
Yachts'"], p. 82; ["William Meredith"], p. 81; ["Yvor
Winters"], p. 86.

Returning subjectivity and personality to poetry, the
target of Dickey's criticism in Babel to Byzantium is
academicism, the opposite of subjectivity and personality.
Several major poet-critics are discussed as are points of
concern for the critic, such as the voice of the poet and
the reader's belief in the poem.

Ref.: W. H. Auden, p. 79; Robert Bly, p. 80;
Dionysios, p. 75; T. S. Eliot, pp. 77-80, 83, 86; Eliot's
"The Love Song of J. Alfred Prufrock," p. 87; Eliot's On
Poetry and Poets, p. 77; Robert Frost, p. 78; Frost's

"The Secret Sits," p. 78; Northrop Frye, pp. 76, 87; Allen
Ginsberg, p. 79; T. E. Hulme, p. 85; Randall Jarrell,
pp. 75-79, 84-85, 87; Jarrell's Poetry and the Age, p. 78;
Murray Krieger, pp. 76, 87; D. H. Lawrence, p. 75;
Robert Lowell, pp. 78, 80; W. S. Merwin, pp. 80-81;
Charles Olson, p. 79; Walter Pater, p. 86; Edgar Allan
Poe, p. 75; John Crowe Ransom, pp. 75, 77; Theodore
Roethke, pp. 80-81; The Sewanee Review, pp. 75, 79; Anne
Sexton, p. 80; Karl Shapiro, pp. 76, 79, 86; Louis Simp-
son, p. 80; W. D. Snodgrass, p. 80; William Stafford,
p. 80; Wallace Stevens, p. 78; Allen Tate, pp. 75-77,
85-86; Robert Penn Warren, p. 77; René Wellek, pp. 76,
78, 78n. , 85; Walt Whitman, pp. 75, 78; William Carlos
Williams, p. 79; Yvor Winters, p. 84; Thomas Wolfe,
p. 82; James Wright, p. 80.
    Rept. James Dickey: The Expansive Imagination (see
no. 995).

615 Canby, Vincent. "James Dickey's Deliverance Arrives. " New
     York Times (31 July 1972), p. 21.
         Deliverance [novel]; Deliverance [film].
         The theme of survival and the influences of the charac-
     ters' experiences are central to Deliverance and its film
     version.   The film lacks in realism and has static dialog
     and rough narrative.   Credits for the film are included.
         Ref. : Ned Beatty; John Boorman; Ronny Cox; Ernest
     Hemingway; McCabe and Mrs. Miller [film]; Burt Reynolds;
     Jon Voight; Irving Wallace; Vilmos Zsigmond.
         Illustrated with a still.
         Rept. : "The New York Times" Film Reviews, 1971-1972
     (see no. 996).   (Its title was subsequently omitted.)

616 Carleton Miscellany 6 (Win. 1965), pp. 123-124.
         ["Allen Ginsberg"], p. 123; ["The Suspect in Poetry"],
     p. 123; The Suspect in Poetry, p. 123; ["Toward a Solitary
     Joy"], p. 123; ["The Winters Approach: I, Donald Drum-
     mond"], p. 123; ["The Winters Approach: II, Ellen Kay"],
     p. 123.
         An observation of Dickey's inconsistencies in The Suspect
     in Poetry.

617 Carnes, Bruce Marshall.   Abstract of "James Dickey: The
     Development of His Poetry. " In Dissertation Abstracts
     International; A: The Humanities and the Social Sciences
     32 (Feb. 1972), p. 4602.
         Buckdancer's Choice; Deliverance; Drowning with Others;
     The Eye-Beaters, Blood, Victory, Madness, Buckhead and
     Mercy; "Falling" [sec. of Poems 1957-1967]; Helmets; Into
     the Stone and Other Poems.
         In the author's dissertation (see no. 1117), death and an
     accompanying guilt are proven to be Dickey's major theme.
     It is traced through his works in its various guises.
         Ref. : Gerard Manley Hopkins.

618   Carrico, Paul. "Violence: Real and Mediate." Media and
      Methods 9 (Oct. 1972), pp. 65-69, 71, 86 [67-68].
      Deliverance [film], pp. 67-68.
      Violence displayed in the film adaptation of Deliverance
      is quickly investigated. Its cause is abruptly attributed to
      the characters' machismo.
          Ref.: John Boorman, p. 67; Ronny Cox, p. 68; Dustin
      Hoffman, p. 67; Carl Jung, p. 68; Lord of the Flies [film],
      p. 67; Straw Dogs [film], p. 67; Jon Voight, p. 67.

619   Carroll, Paul. "James Dickey as Critic." Chicago Review
      20 (Nov. 1968), pp. 82-87.
          ["Allen Ginsberg"], p. 84; Babel to Byzantium, pp. 82,
      85, 87; "Barnstorming for Poetry," p. 84; Buckdancer's
      Choice, p. 85; ["Charles Olson"], p. 83; ["Christopher
      Smart: 'A Song to David'"], p. 84; ["Edwin Arlington
      Robinson"], p. 84; ["Elder Olson"], p. 83; ["The Firebomb-
      ing"], p. 85; ["Francis Thompson: 'The Hound of Heaven'"],
      p. 84; ["Gene Derwood"], p. 84; "The Heaven of Animals,"
      p. 85; ["J. V. Cunningham"], p. 83; ["James Merrill"],
      p. 84; ["John Frederick Nims"], p. 83; ["John Logan"],
      p. 83; ["Kenneth Patchen"], p. 82; "Notes on the Decline
      of Outrage," p. 84; Poems 1957-1967, p. 82; "The Poet
      Turns on Himself," p. 84; ["Reed Whittemore"], p. 83;
      ["Richard Wilbur"], p. 84; ["Robert Duncan"], p. 84;
      ["Robert Frost"], p. 84; ["Robert Penn Warren"], p. 83;
      "The Sheep Child," p. 85; "Slave Quarters," p. 85;
      ["William Carlos Williams: 'The Yachts'"], p. 84.
          A defense of Dickey in the wake of Bly's essay "The
      Collapse of James Dickey." The honesty and authority--
      and the lack of condescension, myopia, and parochialism--
      evident in Dickey's Babel to Byzantium is characteristic of
      his personality.
          Ref.: Guillaume Apollinaire, p. 86; Ambrose Bierce,
      p. 86; Robert Bly's "The Collapse of James Dickey,"
      pp. 85-86 (see no. 587); Albert Camus, p. 86; Dante,
      p. 86; T. S. Eliot, p. 86; Eugene McCarthy, p. 87; The
      New Yorker, p. 86; Ezra Pound, p. 86; Jean-Paul Sartre,
      p. 86.

620   _____. "Twenty-Five Poets in Their Skins." Choice,
      no. 5 (1967), pp. 82-94 [85-86].
          "Faces Seen Once," p. 86; "The Heaven of Animals,"
      p. 85; "Them, Crying," p. 86.
          Tenderness, joy, violence, and cruelty characterize
      Dickey's poems. Often rambling, Dickey occasionally hes-
      itates or censors himself.

621   Casey, Phil. "Massive Magicman." Washington (D.C.) Post
      (20 Nov. 1971), sec. E, pp. 1, 3.
      Deliverance, p. 1.
      Dickey's financial situation, theories of poetry, and
      thoughts on public poetry readings are investigated.   Bio-

graphical data is included.
> Ref.: Leroy F. Aarons' "Ex-Adman Dickey: Don't Just Wait for Oblivion," p. 3 (see no. 555); Art Buchwald, p. 3; Al Capp, p. 3; Sammy Davis, Jr., p. 3; Maxine Dickey, pp. 1, 3.
> Photograph of Dickey by Margaret Thomas, p. 1.

622 Catholic Film Newsletter 37 (15 Aug. 1972), p. 78.
> Deliverance [novel]; Deliverance [film].
> Three levels of survival, the major theme of the film version of Deliverance, are identified. The theme's relation to the film's narrative, and the narrative's relation to film's action, are investigated. Discussion of the actors' ability and a detailed plot summary are included.
> Ref.: Ned Beatty; John Boorman; Ronny Cox; Burt Reynolds; Jon Voight; Vilmos Zsigmond.

623 Cavell, Marcia. "Visions of Battlements." Partisan Review 38, no. 1 (1971), pp. 117-121 [117-118].
> "The Celebration," p. 118; Deliverance, pp. 117-118; "Encounter in the Cage Country," p. 118; "Power and Light," p. 118; "The Sheep Child," p. 118.
> A brief mention of the theme of survival in Deliverance introduces this exploration of a major recurrent image: the narrator's watching other human beings from behind them.
> Ref.: Shirley Hazzard's The Bay of Noon, p. 117; Ernest Hemingway, p. 117; D. H. Lawrence, p. 117.

624 Champlin, Charles. "Men Against River--of Life?--in Deliverance." Los Angeles Times. Los Angeles Times Calendar (13 Aug. 1972), pp. 1, 16-17.
> Deliverance [novel], pp. 1, 17; Deliverance [film], p. 1.
> The film version of Deliverance is two separate entities: an action-packed thriller and a heavy, philosophical statement. Although the former is flawless, the latter, which is attributed to Dickey's influence, is not only unsuccessful but taints its better half. The film's statements on nature are listed.
> Ref.: Ned Beatty, pp. 1, 17; John Boorman, pp. 1, 16-17; A Clockwork Orange [film], p. 17; Herbert Coward, p. 17; Ronny Cox, pp. 1, 16-17; Billy McKinney, p. 17; Midnight Cowboy [film], p. 17; Sam Peckinpah, p. 16; Portnoy's Complaint [film], p. 17; Tom Priestly, p. 17; Burt Reynolds, pp. 1, 16-17; Jon Voight, pp. 1, 17; Vilmos Zsigmond, p. 1.
> Illustrated with stills, pp. 1, 17.
> Rept.: Filmfacts (see no. 660).

*625 Chase, D. "Deliverance." Inter/View, no. 27 (Nov. 1972), p. 41.
> A review of the film version of Deliverance.
> *[This citation is from International Index to Film Periodicals, 1972, p. 147.]

626 Choice 2 (May 1965), p. 157.
        "Horses and Prisoners."
        Favorable review of Helmets containing 168 words.
        Ref.: Steven Crane; Wallace Stevens; Dylan Thomas.

627 Choice 3 (Oct. 1966), p. 636.
        Drowning with Others; Helmets; "The Night Pool."
        Favorable review of Buckdancer's Choice containing 87
        words.

628 Choice 4 (Oct. 1967), p. 824.
        "May Day Sermon to the Women of Gilmer County,
        Georgia, by a Woman Preacher Leaving the Baptist Church."
        Favorable review of Poems 1957-1967 containing 94
        words.

629 Choice 5 (Oct. 1968), p. 950.
        Favorable review of Babel to Byzantium containing 146
        words.

630 Choice 9 (Apr. 1972), p. 212.
        Babel to Byzantium; The Suspect in Poetry.
        Favorable review of Sorties containing 190 words.

631 Choice 9 (July-Aug. 1972), pp. 652-653.
        "Pitching and Rolling," p. 653.
        Favorable review of Stolen Apples containing 251 words.

632 "Christmas Books: Looking Backward." Time 104 (16 Dec.
        1974), pp. 90-94 [90].
        Mixed review of Jericho containing 141 words.
        Ref.: "Dixie" [song]; Hubert Shuptrine; Andrew Wyeth.
        Illustrated with a reproduction of Hubert Shuptrine's
        "Black and Tan," p. 90.

633 Clarity, James F. New York Times (26 Nov. 1971), p. 41.
        Stolen Apples.
        A note on Dickey's participation in "Yevtushenko and
        Friends: Poetry in Concert."
        Ref.: Nikki Giovanni; Stanley Kunitz; Eugene McCarthy;
        Yevgeny Yevtushenko.

634 _____. New York Times (15 Aug. 1973), p. 45.
        Deliverance.
        Dickey's reaction to canoers drowning in the Chattooga
        River, a sport and river popularized by his novel, is
        related.

635 Clark, Robert. "James Dickey: American Poet." Australian
        Book Review (Mar. 1968), p. 83.
        "Falling"; "Hunting Civil War Relics at Nimblewill
        Creek"; "The Ice Skin"; "May Day Sermon to the Women
        of Gilmer County, Georgia, by a Woman Preacher Leaving

the Baptist Church"; Poems 1957-1967; "Slave Quarters"; [unidentified passage].

Collected first impressions of Poems 1957-1967 mention Dickey's rhythm, unique use of lines, obsession with every-day experiences, and choice of words. "The Ice Skin" is reprinted here in full.

Ref. : Robert Frost; Donald Hall's Contemporary American Poetry; The Sewanee Review; Louis Untermeyer's Modern American Poetry.

Rept. : Poems (see no. 1000). (It was subsequently used as the "Foreword" to this collection.)

636 Cleghorn, James D.   Abstract of "Preservation of the Wilderness: A Contemporary View of Nature Poetry. " In Dissertation Abstracts International; A: The Humanities and Social Sciences 35 (Nov. 1974), pp. 2982-2983.

In the author's dissertation (see no. 1118), a chapter of which is devoted to Dickey, it is ascertained that Dickey's nature poetry cannot be described as "ecological" since it does not remain within the limits of its definition and because his person dominates it so strongly.

Ref. : Theodore Roethke, pp. 2982-2983; Gary Snyder, p. 2982.

637 Clemons, Walter.   "James Dickey, Novelist. " New York Times Book Review (22 Mar. 1970), p. 22.

Assertations; Deliverance; The Eye-Beaters, Blood, Victory, Madness, Buckhead and Mercy; "James Dickey Tells About Deliverance"; Self-Interviews; [Sorties].

Dickey mentions the background and the problems of writing Deliverance, his view on violence, and his plan for a second novel.

Ref. : Norman Mailer; Fernando Pessoa; Sharon Tate.
Illustrated with a photograph of Dickey by Sam Falk.

638 Cocks, Jay.   "Rites of Passage. " Time 100 (7 Aug. 1972), pp. 75-76.

A review of the film version of Deliverance in which the plot is discussed at length and the script is viewed favorably.

Ref. : John Boorman, p. 76; Robert Flaherty, p. 76; Sam Peckinpah's Straw Dogs [film], p. 76.
Illustrated with stills, p. 75.

639 Connell, Evan S. , Jr.   "Deliverance. " New York Times Book Review (22 Mar. 1970), pp. 1, 23.

Deliverance, p. 1.

The plot, dramatic tension, first-person narrative, images, dialog, word choice, and motivation of characters of Dickey's novel Deliverance are surveyed.

Ref. : Marcel Proust, p. 23.
Illustrated with a sketch by Isadore Seltzer, p. 1.
Exc. : Contemporary Literary Criticism (see no. 1063).

640 Conroy, Sarah Booth. "No Tumbling Walls, Just Bridges to a
     Forgotten Past. " Washington (D. C.) Post (29 Dec. 1974),
     sec. F, pp. 1, 3.
         Deliverance [novel], pp. 1, 3; Deliverance [film], p. 1;
     Jericho, pp. 1, 3.
         Dickey's collaboration with Shuptrine on Jericho, the
     book's financial success, and the story of its creation from
     its conception to its promotion are discussed.   Much data
     on Shuptrine's contributions to the volume is included.
         Ref.:   Leslie Adams, p. 3; James Agee and Walker
     Evan's Now Let Us Praise Famous Men, p. 3; Bible, p. 3;
     Johnny Carson, p. 3; John Logue, p. 3; Rex Rush, p. 3;
     Hubert Shuptrine, pp. 1, 3; Shuptrine's "Coon Dog" [paint-
     ing], pp. 1, 3; Shuptrine's "First Bloom" [painting], p. 1;
     Shuptrine's "Idle Hours" [painting], p. 3; Shuptrine's "Last
     Bouquet" [painting], p. 1; Shuptrine's "The Porch Rocker"
     [painting], p. 1; Shuptrine's "Seiner Man" [painting], p. 1;
     Shuptrine's "Twilight" [painting], p. 1; Jim Shuptrine, p. 3;
     Southern Living, p. 3; Eudora Welty, p. 3; Charles and
     Evelyn White, p. 3.
         Photograph of Dickey with Shuptrine by an unidentified
     photographer, p. 1.   Illustrated with reproductions of
     Shuptrine's art, pp. 1, 3.

641 Coppage, Noel [N. C.].   Stereo Review 31 (Aug. 1973), p. 91.
     Deliverance [film].
         Favorable review of the L. P. record "Dueling Banjos"
     (see no. 1240) containing 372 words.
         Ref.:   John Boorman; Marshall Brickman; "Dueling
     Banjos" [song]; "End of a Dream" [song]; Steve Mandel;
     Earl Scruggs; Eric Weissberg; Weissberg and Brickman's
     "New Dimensions in Banjo and Bluegrass" [L. P. record].

642 Core, George.   Georgia Review 23 (Sum. 1969), pp. 250-251.
         A summary of the ideas Dickey expressed in Spinning the
     Crystal Ball in which Dickey is criticized for its being too
     short.
         Ref.:   Frederick Eckman's Cobras and Cockleshells,
     p. 251; John Crowe Ransom, p. 251; Delmore Schwartz,
     p. 251; Stephen Spender, p. 251; Richard Wilbur, p. 251.

643 Corrington, John William.   "James Dickey's Poems 1957-1967:
     A Personal Appraisal. " Georgia Review 22 (Spr. 1968),
     pp. 12-23.
         "Adultery, " pp. 14-15; Buckdancer's Choice, p. 13;
     "Falling, " pp. 22-23; "Falling" [sec. of Poems 1957-1967],
     p. 13; "A Folk Singer of the Thirties, " pp. 19-21, 23;
     "Hunting Civil War Relics at Nimblewill Creek, " pp. 16,
     18-19; Into the Stone and Other Poems, p. 13; Poems 1957-
     1967, pp. 12-13.
         Dickey is considered unique because he presents a total
     vision and because he is able to work with that which would
     be clichés in the works of others.   Secular and political

aspects of his poetry are commented upon.
Ref. : Eugene V. Debs, p. 22; Ecclesiasticus, p. 19;
William Faulkner, p. 12; Douglas Southall Freeman's R. E.
Lee, p. 18; Robert Frost, p. 22; Haymarket Rioters, p. 19;
Joseph McCarthy, p. 19; Karl Marx, p. 21; Thomas More,
p. 21; Marcel Proust's Swann's Way, p. 12; Nicola Sacco,
p. 20; Dylan Thomas' "Lament," p. 13; Norman Thomas,
p. 22; Leon Trotsky, p. 22; Bartolomeo Vanzetti, p. 20;
William Butler Yeats' "Saling to Byzantium," p. 13; Yeats'
"The Second Coming," p. 13.
Exc. : Contemporary Literary Criticism (see no. 1962).

644 Corry, John. "Intellectuals in Bloom at Spring Gathering."
New York Times (18 May 1972), pp. 49, 63 [63].
Dickey is listed with others newly elected to the Institute
of Arts and Letters.

645 "Corsican Wins Prix Femina." Times (30 Nov. 1971), p. 5.
Deliverance, p. 5.
Dickey is mentioned as a recipient of the Prix Médicis.

646 Cotter, James F. "American Priests, an English Novelist and
Two Critics." America 125 (13 Nov. 1971), pp. 406-412
[408].
"The Heat in Rome."
Unfavorable review of Stolen Apples with a favorable,
brief mention of Dickey's translations.

647 Coulbourn, Keith. "The Filming of Deliverance." Atlanta
Journal and the Atlanta Constitution. Atlanta Journal and
Constitution Magazine (25 July 1971), pp. 12-14, 17-18.
Deliverance [novel], pp. 13-14.
Difficulties encountered during the shooting of the film
version of Deliverance are recounted. Conflicts between
Dickey and the filming crew are related, and Bill McKin-
ney's response to his role as a rapist in the film is re-
ported. A thematic analysis concludes.
Ref. : Achilles, p. 13; John Boorman, pp. 13-14, 17;
Christopher Dickey, p. 17; Bill McKinney, p. 17; Burt
Reynolds, p. 17; Orson Welles, p. 13; Vilmos Zsigmond,
p. 14.
Illustrated with stills, pp. 12, 13. Photographs of
activities on location by Keith Coulbourn (?), pp. 13, 17-18.

648 Coulthard, Ron. "From Manuscript to Movie Script: James
Dickey's Deliverance." Notes on Contemporary Literature
3 (Nov. 1973), pp. 11-12.
Deliverance [novel], pp. 11-12; [Deliverance] [film],
pp. 11-12.
Slick suspense is substituted in the film version of
Deliverance for the character development of the novel's
narrator.

649 _____. "Reflections Upon a Golden Eye: A Note on James
Dickey's Deliverance." Notes on Contemporary Literature
3 (Sept. 1973), pp. 13-15.
Deliverance, pp. 13-15.
Philosophic pretentiousness in Deliverance is quickly
investigated by focusing on Dickey's recurrent image of a
sliver of gold in a character's eye.

650 Country Beautiful 4 (Aug. 1965), p. 73.
["Approaching Prayer"]; "The Driver."
Favorable review of Helmets containing 123 words.
Photograph of Dickey by an unidentified person.

*651 Creem 4 (Oct. 1972), p. 50.
A review of the film version of Deliverance.
*[This citation is from Multi Media Reviews Index, 1972,
p. 59.]

652 Crist, Judith. "Fat but Sightly." New York 5 (31 July 1972),
pp. 50-51.
Deliverance [film], pp. 50-51.
The film version of Deliverance is seen as an adventure
tale, a character study, and a conflict between the primi-
tive and the modern. Its actors' and technicians' abilities,
theme of survival, and script are mentioned.
Ref.: Ned Beatty, pp. 50-51; John Boorman, p. 50;
Boorman's Hell in the Pacific [film], p. 50; Boorman's Leo
the Last [film], p. 50; Ronny Cox, pp. 50-51; Fat City
[film], p. 50; The Happiness Cage [film], p. 51; Images
[film], p. 50; Steve Mandel, p. 51; Midnight Cowboy [film],
p. 50; Burt Reynolds, pp. 50-51; Jon Voight, p. 50; Eric
Weissberg, p. 51; Vilmos Zsigmond, p. 50.

653 Cromie, Robert. "Meet James Dickey, A King-Sized Poet."
Chicago Tribune (15 Mar. 1966), sec. 2, p. 2.
Buckdancer's Choice; Drowning with Others; Helmets;
Into the Stone and Other Poems; The Suspect in Poetry;
Two Poems of the Air.
Biographical data is included with Dickey's statements on
literature on the eve of his receiving the N. B. A.   An essay-
interview.
Ref.: T. S. Eliot; Kenneth Fearing; Ezra Pound; Theo-
dore Roethke; William Stafford; Alfred, Lord Tennyson;
Walt Whitman; Richard Wilbur.

654 Cross, Leslie. "Wisconsin and America's Poet of the Year,
James Dickey, Talks of His Life and Craft." Milwaukee
Journal (20 Mar. 1966), part 5, p. 4.
"Between Two Prisoners"; Buckdancer's Choice; "The
Firebombing"; The Suspect in Poetry.
Dickey comments on life, other poets, his father, and
the relationship between writing poetry and guitar playing.
Biographical data is interspersed.

Ref.: Gerard Manley Hopkins; John Keats; John Milton; William Shakespeare; Edmund Spenser; Philip Sydney; William Wordsworth.
Photograph of Dickey by an unidentified person.

655 Cushman, Jerome. Library Journal 93 (1 April 1968), p. 1485.
["Edwin Arlington Robinson"]; ["Preface"]; ["Randall Jarrell"].
Favorable review of Babel to Byzantium containing 140 words.
Rept.: "The Library Journal" Book Review: 1968 (see no. 1006).

656 D., N. K. San Francisco Sunday Chronicle. This World (6 Nov. 1960), p. 35.
Mixed review of Into the Stone and Other Poems containing 15 words.

657 Daniell, Rosemary. "Former Atlantan Hymns the Divinity of Existence." Atlanta Journal and the Atlanta Constitution (23 April 1967), sec. B, p. 10.
["Dover: Believing in Kings"]; "Falling"; "False Youth: Two Seasons, II"; ["May Day Sermon to the Women of Gilmer County, Georgia, by a Woman Preacher Leaving the Baptist Church"]; "The Owl King [: III, The Blind Child's Story]"; "The Vegetable King."
Dickey exhibits the exotic and the divine in the common-place by his vibrant images and his themes of love, guilt, and pain in Poems 1957-1967.
Ref.: James Agee; Flannery O'Conner; Dylan Thomas' [unidentified poem]; John Updike; Thomas Wolfe.

658 Davis, Douglas M. "Four Volumes Prove that Lyric Poetry Survives." National Observer (10 July 1967), p. 19.
Buckdancer's Choice; "Coming Back to America."
Dickey's viewpoint and language in Poems 1957-1967 has promoted the development of longer poems and longer individual lines.
Ref.: Brother Antoninus; Frank O'Hara; Peter Viereck; Walt Whitman.
Photograph of Dickey by an unidentified person.

659 Davison, Peter. "The Difficulties of Being Major: The Poetry of Robert Lowell and James Dickey." Atlantic 220 (Oct. 1967), pp. 116-121 [116, 119-121].
"Adultery," p. 121; ["Armor"], p. 119; "Buckdancer's Choice," p. 119; Buckdancer's Choice, p. 120; "Cherrylog Road," p. 120; "Drinking from a Helmet," p. 120; Drowning with Others, pp. 119-120; "Encounter in the Cage Country," p. 121; "Falling," p. 121; ["False Youth: Two Seasons"], p. 121; "Fence Wire," p. 120; "The Fiend," pp. 120-121; "The Firebombing," pp. 120-121; "The Heaven of Animals," p. 119; Helmets, p. 120; ["In the Lupanar at Pompeii"],

p. 120; "Inside the River," p. 120; Into the Stone and Other Poems, pp. 119-120; "The Lifeguard," p. 120; "May Day Sermon to the Women of Gilmer County, Georgia, by a Woman Preacher Leaving the Baptist Church," p. 121; Poems 1957-1967, p. 121; "Power and Light," p. 121; ["Reincarnation (II)"], p. 121; "The Scarred Girl," p. 120; "The Shark's Parlor," p. 120; "The Sheep Child," p. 121; "Slave Quarters," p. 120; "Sun," p. 121.

A brief critical chronicle of Dickey's poetry. His use of the narrative and syntaxic techniques and of the recurrent themes of reincarnation, war, and sexual aberration are duly noted. Dickey is contrasted with Robert Lowell.

Ref.: W. H. Auden, p. 121; Robert Lowell, p. 119; Edwin Muir, p. 119; Muir's "The Animals," p. 119; Theodore Roethke, p. 120.

Photograph of Dickey by an unidentified person, p. 117.

Rept.: James Dickey: The Expansive Imagination (see no. 1007). (Its title was subsequently changed to "The Great Grassy World from Both Sides: The Poetry of Robert Lowell and James Dickey.")

660 "Deliverance." Filmfacts 15, no. 10 (1972), pp. 213-217.
      Deliverance [novel], p. 216; Deliverance [film], pp. 213-16.
      A detailed synopsis of the plot of the film version of Deliverance introduces a summary of various critics' opinions and a consensus of 16 reviews. Reprints of reviews by Charles Champlin, pp. 215-216 (see no. 624), Dennis Hunt, pp. 216-217 (see no. 743), and Paul D. Zimmerman, p. 216 (see no. 976) conclude. Complete credits are included.
      Ref.: Gary Arnold's "Deliverance: A Gripping Piece of Work," pp. 214-215 (see no. 567); Ned Beatty, pp. 215-216; Blow-Up [film], p. 217; John Boorman, pp. 214-216; Boorman's Hell in the Pacific [film], p. 216; Boorman's Point Blank [film], p. 216; Vincent Canby's "James Dickey's Deliverance Arrives," p. 214 (see no. 615); Jay Cock's "Rites of Passage," pp. 214-215 (see no. 638); Herbert Coward, p. 216; Ronny Cox, pp. 215-216; Judith Crist's "Fat but Sightly," p. 215 (see no. 652); Roger Ebert's "What Is Deliverance Really Trying to Say to Us?" pp. 214-215 (see no. 677); Joseph Gelmis' [review of Deliverance], p. 214 (see no. 1249); Penelope Gilliatt's "Tax Deductible Jesus," p. 214 (see no. 709); Wanda Hale's [review of Deliverance], p. 215 (see no. 722); Stanley Kauffman's "Fair to Meddling," p. 215 (see no. 762); Arthur Knight's "... And Deliver Us from Evil," p. 215 (see no. 774); Billy McKinney, p. 216; Midnight Cowboy [film], p. 216; "Murf's" [review of Deliverance], pp. 214-215 (see no. 834); Sam Peckinpah, p. 215; Burt Reynolds, pp. 215-216; Andrew Sarris' [review of Deliverance], p. 215 (see no. 891); Jon Voight, pp. 215-216; William Wolf's [review of Deliverance], p. 214 (see no. 964); Vilmos Zsigmond, pp. 215, 217.
      Illustrated with stills, pp. 213-214.

661   "Deliverance." Films and Filming 18 (Feb. 1972), p. 23.
      Deliverance [film].
      The theme of the film version of Deliverance is given
      with this collection of three stills.

662   "Deliverance." Films and Filming 19 (Oct. 1972), pp. 57-59.
      Partial credits are included with this collection of stills.
      Illustrated with 10 stills, pp. 57-59.

663   "Deliverance by James Dickey." Literary Guild Magazine (Apr.
      1970), pp. 3-5.
      Deliverance, pp. 3-5.
      This promo piece mentions the themes of violence and
      survival.   Excerpts from the novel abound.
      Illustrated with sketches by Ken Nisson, pp. 4-5.

664   DeMott, Benjamin.   "The 'More Life' School and James
      Dickey." Saturday Review 53 (28 Mar. 1970), pp. 25-26, 38.
      Buckdancer's Choice, p. 26; "Bums, on Waking," p. 26;
      "Cherrylog Road," p. 38; Deliverance, pp. 25-26, 38;
      Drowning with Others, p. 26; The Eye-Beaters, Blood, Vic-
      tory, Madness, Buckhead and Mercy, pp. 26, 38; "Falling"
      [sec. of Poems 1957-1967], p. 26; "The Fiend," p. 26;
      "The Heaven of Animals," p. 26; Helmets, p. 26; ["Two
      Poems of Going Home: II,] Looking for the Buckhead Boys,"
      p. 38; "On the Coosawattee," p. 26; "The Shark's Parlor,"
      p. 26; "Winter Trout," p. 26.
      "More Life" is the grasping for the absolute, and the
      denial of the conventional, of human experience.   Dickey's
      novel and poetry are considered individually and contrasted.
      Ref. : Saul Bellow's Mr. Sammler's Planet, p. 25;
      Albert Camus, p. 25; Faust, p. 25; Robert Frost, p. 38;
      André Gide, p. 25; Robin Hood, p. 38; Randall Jarrell,
      p. 38; Norman Mailer, p. 25; Thomas Mann, p. 25; Rainer
      Maria Rilke, p. 25; William Butler Yeats, p. 25.
      Photograph of Dickey by Christopher Dickey, p. 26.

665   Dempsy, Michael.   "Deliverance/Boorman: Dickey in the
      Woods." Cinema 8 (Spr. 1973), pp. 10-17.
      Deliverance [novel], pp. 10, 14-16; Deliverance [script],
      pp. 11-12, 15-17; Deliverance [film], pp. 10-15, 17.
      Dickey's novel, his filmscript, and Boorman's film are
      compared in detail.   Themes and images from Boorman's
      other works are revealed and a synopsis of the film's vis-
      ual moment is included.   Boorman is credited for coauthor-
      ing the script.   Ref. : Ned Beatty, p. 11; John Boorman,
      pp. 10-14, 16; Boorman's Having a Wild Weekend [film],
      p. 13; Boorman's Hell in the Pacific [film], pp. 13, 15;
      Boorman's Leo the Last [film], pp. 13, 17; Boorman's
      Point Blank [film], p. 13; Cosmopolitan [journal], p. 14;
      Ronny Cox, p. 14; Destroy, She Said [film], p. 14; Angie
      Dickenson, p. 13; Fata Morgana [film], pp. 14, 17; Penel-
      ope Gilliatt, p. 15; Werner Herzog, pp. 14, 17; Jeremiah
      Johnson [film], p. 10; Jesus, p. 14; The King of Marvin

Gardens [film], p. 10; Last Year at Marienbad [film],
p. 14; D. H. Lawrence, p. 12; Lawrence of Arabia [film],
p. 14; McCabe and Mrs. Miller [film], p. 10; Lee Marvin,
p. 13; Prometheus, p. 16; Burt Reynolds, p. 14; The Straw-
berry Statement [film], p. 10; 2001: A Space Odyssey
[film], pp. 15-16; Vertigo [film], pp. 10, 17; Jon Voight,
p. 11; Walk About [film], p. 14; Winter Wind [film], p. 14;
Robin Wood, p. 13; Vilmos Zsigmond, pp. 10-11, 14, 16-17.
Illustrated with stills, pp. 10-11, 14-16.

666 "The Devil's Work." New York Times (17 Nov. 1973), p. 34.
      An editorial relating an incident of censorship in which
      Dickey's novel was one of the targets.
      Ref.: William Faulkner; Ernest Hemingway; John
      Steinbeck; Kurt Vonnegut's Slaughterhouse Five.

666a Dickey, R. P. "The New Genteel Tradition in American
      Poetry." Sewanee Review 82 (Oct.-Dec. 1974), pp. 730-39.
      Dickey is listed with other members of what the critic
      calls the "Non-Genteels."

667 Dickey, William. "Talking About What's Real." Hudson Re-
      view 18 (Win. 1965-1966), pp. 613-617.
      "The Grove Press New American Poets (1960)," p. 616;
      "New Poets of England and America I (1957)," p. 616; The
      Suspect in Poetry, pp. 613-614; ["Theodore Roethke"],
      p. 615; ["The Winters Approach"], p. 614.
      A comparison of the theme of Dickey's The Suspect in
      Poetry with C. Day Lewis' The Lyric Impulse and John
      Holloway's The Lion Hunt. Each deplores academicism in
      poetry which ruins the contact with the reader and disre-
      gards communicating poetic truth.
      Ref.: Dionysis, p. 616; John Gay's "Trivia," p. 617;
      John Holloway's The Lion Hunt, pp. 613-617; C. Day Lewis'
      The Lyric Impulse, pp. 613-616; Lucretius' "De Rerum
      Natura," p. 617; Wallace Stevens' "Sunday Morning," p. 617.

668 _____. "The Thing Itself." Hudson Review 19 (Spr.
      1966), pp. 146-155 [154-155].
      "The Firebombing," p. 155; "The Shark's Parlor," p. 155.
      Buckdancer's Choice is described as a volume of engag-
      ing motions. Dickey's use of the dream state, memory,
      and the various relationships of the world are mentioned.
      Ref.: Louis Simpson, p. 155.
      Exc.: Contemporary Literary Criticism (see no. 1063);
      A Library of Literary Criticism (see no. 1005).

669 Diehl, Digby. "Cream of the Coffee-Table Crop." Los Ange-
      les Times. Calendar (8 Dec. 1974), pp. 90, 92 [90].
      Favorable review of Jericho containing 74 words.
      Ref.: Hubert Shuptrine.

670 Dodsworth, Martin. "Towards the Baseball Poem." Listener
      79 (27 June 1968), p. 842.
      ["At Darien Bridge"].

Poems 1957-1967 is cluttered with symbols, lacks in
concern with the human condition, and has unrealistic ac-
tions. Major themes are listed.
Ref.: Robert Bly's "The Collapse of James Dickey"
(see no. 587); Howard Nemerov's The Winter Lightning;
William Butler Yeats.
Exc.: Contemporary Literary Criticism (see no. 1063).

671 Donoghue, Denis. "The Good Old Complex Fate." Hudson Re-
view 17 (Sum. 1964), pp. 267-277 [274-275].
"Approaching Prayer," p. 275; "Bums, on Waking,"
p. 275; "Goodbye to Serpents," p. 274; "Springer Mountain,"
p. 275.
Dickey's use of human experiences, his word choice, and
the aspects of Americana in Helmets are mentioned.
Ref.: J. V. Cunningham, p. 275; Henry James, p. 274;
William Meredith, p. 275; William Carlos Williams,
p. 275; Celeste Turner Wright, p. 275.
Exc.: A Library of Literary Criticism (see no. 1005).

672 Dorr, John H. Take One 3 (Sept.-Oct. 1971), p. 38.
Favorable review of the film version of Deliverance con-
taining 33 words.
Ref.: John Boorman.

673 Dorsey, John. "Overfilling the Image of a Poet." (Baltimore)
Sun (17 Mar. 1968), sec. D, pp. 1, 3.
Babel to Byzantium, p. 1; Buckdancer's Choice, pp. 1,
3; "The Firebombing," p. 3; ["Hunting Civil War Relics at
Nimblewill Creek"], p. 3; ["Inside the River"], p. 1; Into
the Stone and Other Poems, p. 1; ["The Movement of Fish"],
p. 1; The Suspect in Poetry, p. 1; [unidentified passage],
p. 1.
Dickey discusses his concepts of poetry and the poetic
process. Biographical data is included.
Ref.: Robert Frost, p. 1; Randall Jarrell, p. 1; Rob-
ert Lowell, p. 1; Karl Shapiro, p. 1; Robert Penn Warren,
p. 1; Walt Whitman, p. 3.

674 "Down from the Mountain." Times Literary Supplement (27
Jan. 1966), p. 65.
Buckdancer's Choice; "The Fiend"; ["The Firebombing"];
"Slave Quarters."
The tension of fantasy's conflict with everyday experi-
ences and the use of images in Buckdancer's Choice are
briefly mentioned. Its violence is discussed.
Ref.: J. Alfred Prufrock.

675 Duncan, Robert. "'Oriented by Instinct by Stars.'" Poetry
105 (Nov. 1964), pp. 131-133.
"The Being," pp. 131-133; "Drinking from a Helmet,"
pp. 131-132; "The Firebombing," pp. 132-133; "Hunting
Civil War Relics at Nimblewill Creek," p. 132; "Reincarna-

tion [(II)], " pp. 132-133; Two Poems of the Air, p. 132.
Metamorphoses are seen as invasions in Dickey's Two
Poems of the Air. Dickey's fantasies of, and fascination
with, the supernatural and conformity are emphasized. The
title is from "Reincarnation (II)."
Ref.: W. H. Auden, p. 133; Auden's Age of Anxiety,
p. 133; Ray Bradbury, p. 133; Donald Hall's [biography of
Dickey in Contemporary American Poetry], p. 132 (see
no. 461); Wallace Stevens, p. 131; Stevens' "Chocura to Its
Neighbor," p. 131.
Exc.: A Library of Literary Criticism (see no. 1005).

676 Eagleton, Terry. "New Poetry." Stand 12, no. 3 (1971),
pp. 68-70 [68, 70].
["Diabetes: II,] Under Buzzards," p. 70; The Eye-
Beaters, Blood, Victory, Madness, Buckhead and Mercy,
pp. 68, 70; "Pine," p. 70.
The energy and drama of earlier volumes appear in The
Eye-Beaters, Blood, Victory, Madness, Buckhead and
Mercy, but much of it is contrived, sentimental, and
cloudy.

677 Ebert, Roger. "What Is Deliverance Really Trying to Say to
Us?" Chicago Sun-Times. Showcase (15 Oct. 1972), p. 3.
[Deliverance] [novel]; Deliverance [film].
Much discussion concerning novels which have been adapt-
ed to film, or which have been written after their film
versions have been completed, introduces remarks on the
film version of Deliverance. It is criticized for its lack
of theme and for the irrelevance of its rape scene.
Ref.: Saul Bellow; William P. Blatty's The Exorcist;
John Boorman; Chicago Sun-Times; Herbert Coward;
William Faulkner's "The Bear"; Lois Gould's Such Good
Friends; Harold and Maude [film]; Joseph Heller's Catch 22;
Love Story [film]; Bill McKinney; The New York Times;
Mario Puzo's The Godfather; Burt Reynolds; Erich Segal's
Love Story; Straw Dogs [film]; Jon Voight.
Illustrated with a still.

678 Edwards, C. Hines, Jr. "Dickey's Deliverance: The Owl and
the Eye." Critique 15, no. 2 (1973), pp. 95-101.
Deliverance, pp. 95-100, 101n.; "Falling," p. 99; "Fog
Envelops the Animals," p. 101n.; "For the Nightly Ascent
of the Hunter Orion Over a Forest Clearing," p. 99; "On
the Coosawattee," p. 101n.; "The Owl King," p. 95; ["The
Owl King: III, The Blind Child's Story"], pp. 96, 99;
["The Owl King: II, The Owl King"], p. 96; Poems 1957-
1967, pp. 99, 101n.
Theme of Deliverance is revealed through this compre-
hensive investigation of its "owl" and "eye" imagery. Their
functions and relationship are discussed.
Ref.: William Wordsworth's "Lines Composed a Few
Miles Above Tintern Abbey," pp. 97, 101n.

679   . "A Foggy Scene in Deliverance." Notes on Con-
     temporary Literature 2 (Nov. 1972), pp. 7-9.
          Deliverance, p. 8; "Fog Envelops the Animals," pp. 7-8;
     "May Day Sermon to the Women of Gilmer County, Georgia,
     by a Woman Preacher Leaving the Baptist Church," pp. 7,
     9.
          The image of fog in Dickey's novel and in two of his
     poems is linked to his mystical concern with hunting, ani-
     mals, and sex.

680   Edwards, H. [H. E.]. High Fidelity 23 (Sept. 1973), p. 129.
          Deliverance [film].
          Mixed review of the L. P. record "Dueling Banjos" (see
     no. 1240) containing 62 words.
          Ref.: "Dueling Banjos" [song]; Steve Mandel; Eric
     Weissberg; Weissberg and Marshall Brickman's "New Di-
     mensions in Banjo and Bluegrass" [L. P. record]; Weissberg
     and Mandel's "Dueling Banjos" [L. P. record] (see no. 1240).

681   Esty, Jane and Lett, Paul. "A Mutiny Alert." Mutiny 4
     (Fall-Win. 1961-1962), pp. 3-9 [3].
          An editorial criticizing Beat poetry and calling for sup-
     port of Dickey's remarks in "Confession Is Not Enough"
     (see no. 280).
          Ref.: Allen Ginsberg; The New York Times Book Re-
     view.

682   Evans, Oliver. "University Influence on Poetry." Prairie
     Schooner 35 (Sum. 1961), pp. 179-180.
          ["Mindoro, 1944"], p. 180; ["The Signs"], p. 180;
     ["Trees and Cattle"], p. 180; "The Underground Stream,"
     p. 180.
          Dickey's Into the Stone and Other Poems is criticized
     for its obscurity, deliberate complexities, imprecise
     descriptions, and autobiographical traits.
          Ref.: Paris Leary, p. 179.

683   "Everyone's Notion of a Poet." Time 95 (20 Apr. 1970),
     p. 92.
          Deliverance; [Sorties].
          A biographical sketch and personality piece.
          Ref.: James Agee; Hart Crane; Emily Dickinson;
     Dickinson's "Because I Could Not Stop for Death"; Proteus;
     Puck.
          Photograph of Dickey by Wayne Wilson.

684   Eyster, Warren. "Two Regional Novels." Sewanee Review
     79 (July-Sept. 1971), pp. 469-474 [469-472].
          Deliverance, pp. 470-472.
          Despite the masterful descriptions and the tension-
     producing techniques of Deliverance, it is beset by super-
     ficiality caused by unbelievable characters, overly simpli-
     fied philosophy, and unanswered questions.

Ref.: Ambrose Bierce, p. 470; Natty Bumppo, p. 470;
Edgar Rice Burroughs, p. 470; Joseph Conrad's "Heart of
Darkness," p. 470; Conrad's "Youth," p. 470; Steven
Crane's "The Open Boat," p. 470; James Oliver Curwood,
p. 472; Homer's Odyssey, p. 470; Jack London, p. 472;
London's "To Build a Fire," p. 470; Don Quixote, p. 471;
Mark Twain, p. 470.
Exc.: Contemporary Library Criticism (see no. 1062).

685 Farber, Steven. "Deliverance: How It Delivers." New York
Times (20 Aug. 1972), sec. 2, pp. 9, 16.
Deliverance [novel], p. 9; Deliverance [film], p. 16.
The adventure qualities, plot, and major symbols of the
film version of Deliverance are discussed. Peckinpah's
Straw Dogs is compared to Deliverance, the novel and the
film. Character studies, concentrating on the changes in
Lewis and Ed, are emphasized.
Ref.: John Boorman, pp. 9, 16; Boorman's Having a
Wild Weekend [film], p. 9; Boorman's Hell in the Pacific
[film], p. 9; Boorman's Leo the Last [film], p. 9; Boor-
man's Point Blank [film], p. 9; Joseph Conrad's "Heart of
Darkness," p. 9; Ernest Hemingway, p. 9; Sam Peckinpah's
Straw Dogs [film], p. 9; Burt Reynolds, p. 9; Andrew
Sarris, p. 9; Jon Voight, p. 9; Vilmos Zsigmond, p. 9.
Rept.: "The New York Times" Film Reviews, 1971-1972
(see no. 1015).

686 Farkas, Andrew. Library Journal 96 (Aug. 1971), p. 2476.
Deliverance; "Falling"; "Hunting Civil War Relics at
Nimblewill Creek."
Favorable review of the L. P. record "James Dickey
Reads His Poetry" containing 115 words.

687 Fields, Kenneth. "Strategies of Criticism." Southern Review,
n. s. 2 (Oct. 1966), pp. 967-975 [968-969].
The Suspect in Poetry, p. 968.
Dickey is criticized for being too brief in The Suspect in
Poetry.
Ref.: Robert Bly's [remarks appearing on the dust
jacket of The Suspect in Poetry], p. 968.

*688 Film Information 3 (Sept. 1972), p. 1.
A review of the film version of Deliverance.
*[This citation is from Multi Media Reviews Index, 1972,
p. 59.]

689 "Film Praise 1972." Filmfacts 15, supplement (1972),
pp. 695-702.
Deliverance [film], pp. 697, 700, 702.
Lists of films nominated for, or winners of, various
awards for which Deliverance competed are given.
Ref.: John Boorman, pp. 697, 700; Tom Priestly,
p. 697; Burt Reynolds, p. 701; Jon Voight, p. 701.
Illustrated with a still, p. 701.

690 Fixmer, Clyde H.   Abstract of "The Element of Myth in
     James Dickey's Poetry. " In <u>Dissertation Abstracts Inter-</u>
     <u>national; A: The Humanities and Social Sciences</u> 35 (Oct.
     1974), p. 2265.
          Poems 1957-1967.
          In the author's dissertation (see no. 1121), Dickey's use
     of mythology is explored, and three phases of the relation
     of mythological characters to his persona are discovered.
          Ref. :   Adam; Jesus; Noah; Orion; Orpheus; Osiris.

691 Flagep, Bunky.   "River Holds Death for Many Who Run It. "
     <u>Los Angeles Times</u> (28 Oct. 1973), part 5, pp. 10-12.
          [Deliverance] [novel], p. 11; <u>Deliverance</u> [film],
     pp. 10-11.
          The dangers of and drownings on the Chattooga River,
     popularized by Dickey's <u>Deliverance</u> and its film version,
     are reported.   Mention is given to Dickey's acceptance of
     the responsibility for the drownings, to the river's destruc-
     tion of equipment during the shooting of <u>Deliverance</u>, and
     to Burt Reynolds' rumored near-drowning.
          Ref. :   Robert Bauknight, p. 10; Jim Greiner, pp. 10-12;
     Burt Reynolds, p. 11.

692 Flanigan, Marion.   "300 Poems by James Dickey. "   <u>Providence</u>
     (R. I.) <u>Sunday Journal</u> (21 May 1967), sec. W, p. 20.
          ["Buckdancer's Choice"]; <u>Buckdancer's Choice</u>; "Drinking
     from a Helmet"; "The Driver"; "Horses and Prisoners";
     ["The Ice Skin"]; ["May Day Sermon to the Women of Gil-
     mer County, Georgia, by a Woman Preacher Leaving the
     Baptist Church"]; "Sleeping Out at Easter"; ["The String"];
     [unidentified passage].
          Emphasis is on death motifs in <u>Poems 1957-1967</u> al-
     though Dickey's love of life is duly noted.   Metrical struc-
     ture of the shorter poems is compared to the human heart
     beat.
          Ref. :   Lucretius; George Troy.

693 Flint, R. W.   "Poetry Chronicle. "   <u>Partisan Review</u> 29 (Spr.
     1962), pp. 290-294 [292-293].
          "Dover: Believing in Kings, " p. 293; "The Hospital
     Window, " p. 293; "In the Lupanar at Pompeii, " p. 293;
     "The Owl King, " p. 293.
          Themes of <u>Drowning with Others</u> are emphasized, and
     especially death and nature motifs.   A brief investigation
     of Dickey's metrics is included.
          Ref. :   Aeneas, p. 292; James Michael Curley, p. 292;
     Randall Jarrell, p. 293; Count Giacomo Leopardi, p. 293;
     John Crowe Ransom, p. 292; Wallace Stevens, p. 292;
     Dylan Thomas, p. 293.

694 _____.   "Three American Poets. "   <u>New York Review of</u>
     <u>Books</u> 2 (25 June 1964), pp. 13-14.
          "Cherrylog Road, " p. 13; "Kudzu, " p. 13.

Dickey is discussed as a substantial poet, albeit one who has not yet reached the pinnacle of his abilities, more able with a volume of poetry than with an individual poem. Major themes of Helmets are given.

Ref.: Galway Kinnell, p. 13; Norman Mailer, p. 13; Wallace Stevens' "Sunday Morning," p. 13; Lionel Trilling, p. 13; William Wordsworth, p. 13.

Rept.: "New York Review of Books": Feb. 1963-Jan. 1965, (see no. 1017).

695 Flowers, Paul. "From These, Book Awards." Memphis Commercial Appeal (7 Feb. 1965), sec. 5, p. 6.

Helmets is listed with other National Book Award nominations for 1964.

696 Ford, Greg. Rolling Stone (28 Sept. 1972), p. 58.

Deliverance [novel]; Deliverance [film].

Allegory and martyrdom in the film version of Deliverance are discussed and related to its director's earlier films in which they appear.

Ref.: John Boorman; Boorman's Having a Wild Weekend [film]; Boorman's Leo the Last [film]; Boorman's Point Blank [film]; The Dave Clark Five; Barbara Ferris; Lee Marvin; Burt Reynolds; Jon Voight.

697 "Four Authors Are Given National Book Awards." Publishers Weekly 189 (21 Mar. 1966), pp. 47-48.

Buckdancer's Choice, p. 47.

A list of the judges of the poetry competition and the citation they gave Buckdancer's Choice are given.

Ref.: Ben Belitt, p. 48; Phyllis McGinley, p. 48; Elder Olson, p. 48.

Photograph of Dickey by an unidentified person, p. 47.

698 Francis, H. E. "Dickey Shows New Growth in Meaningful Chant." Atlanta Journal and Constitution (25 Feb. 1962), sec. D, p. 5. [Note: The pages were incorrectly numbered. This is actually page 6.]

"Dover: Believing in Kings"; Drowning with Others; "Facing Africa"; "In the Lupanar at Pompeii"; Into the Stone and Other Poems; "The Owl King"; "To His Children in Darkness."

Completeness and clarity of vision characterize Dickey's Drowning with Others. Recurrent imagery, metrics, and word choice are discussed.

699 Fraser, G. S. "The Magicians." Partisan Review 38 (Win. 1971-1972), pp. 469-478 [477-478].

"The Eye-Beaters," p. 477.

The Eye-Beaters, Blood, Victory, Madness, Buckhead and Mercy is diluted because of its poetry's topography, autobiographical qualities, and complexities.

Ref.: Ted Hughes, p. 478; Oedipus, p. 478; Gary Snyder, p. 478.

700   "Free Fall." Times Literary Supplement (11 Sept. 1970),
         p. 989.
         Deliverance.
         Mention of the theme, dialog, and narrative element of
         Dickey's novel Deliverance follows a plot summary.
         Ref.: Ernest Hemingway.

701   Friedman, Norman. "The Wesleyan Poets, II: The Formal
         Poets, 2." Chicago Review 19, no. 1 (1966), pp. 55-67,
         72.
         "Angina," p. 63; "Breath," p. 61; "Buckdancer's Choice,"
         p. 63; Buckdancer's Choice, p. 63; "The Celebration,"
         p. 63; "Cherrylog Road," p. 61; "Drinking from a Helmet,"
         p. 62; "The Driver," p. 62; Drowning with Others, pp. 56-
         57; "The Escape," p. 63; "Facing Africa," p. 59; "Fathers
         and Sons," p. 63; "The Fiend," p. 65; "The Firebombing,"
         p. 63; "Fog Envelops the Animals," p. 56; "A Folksinger
         of the Thirties," p. 61; "Gamecock," p. 63; "Goodbye to
         Serpents," pp. 61-62; "The Heaven of Animals," p. 57;
         Helmets, pp. 59-60; "Horses and Prisoners," p. 62; "Hunt-
         ing Civil War Relics [at Nimblewill Creek]," p. 59; "The
         Ice Skin," p. 61; "In the Lupanar at Pompeii," pp. 57-58;
         "In the Marble Quarry," p. 61; "The Island," p. 62;
         "Kudzu," p. 61; "Listening to Foxhounds," p. 56; "Mangham,"
         p. 63; "The Poisoned Man," p. 61; "Pursuit from Under,"
         pp. 63-64; "The Scarred Girl," p. 61; "The Scratch,"
         p. 59; "A Screened Porch in the Country," p. 59; "The
         Shark's Parlor," p. 65; "Slave Quarters," pp. 65-66; "Sled
         Burial, [Dream Ceremony]," p. 63; "Springer Mountain,"
         p. 65; "Them, Crying," p. 63; "A View of Fujiyama After
         the War," p. 62; "The War Wound," pp. 64-65; "Winter
         Trout," p. 60.
         Dickey's language and vision are rated highly, but the
         length, obtuseness, and lack of deep feelings are criticized.
         Themes of each section in Buckdancer's Choice, Drowning
         with Others, and Helmets are given.
         Ref.: Joseph Conrad's Lord Jim, p. 59; Walt Disney,
         p. 57; Robert Frost, p. 60; Gerard Manley Hopkins, p. 57;
         The New Yorker, p. 56; Louis Simpson, pp. 55, 66-67,
         72; Alfred, Lord Tennyson, p. 57; Tennyson's "In Memor-
         iam," p. 57.

702   Fuller, Edmund. "Black-Eyed Peas and Coon Hounds." Wall
         Street Journal (19 Nov. 1974), p. 26.
         "Among the People"; Buckdancer's Choice; Deliverance;
         ["Epilogue"]; The Eye-Beaters, Blood, Victory, Madness,
         Buckhead and Mercy; ["Introduction"] [to Jericho]; Jericho;
         "The Land and the Water"; "The Traditions Web."
         A physical description of Jericho introduces a discussion
         in which Shuptrine's artistic ability is lauded and Dickey's
         anecdotes are mentioned.
         Ref.: James Beard; William Faulkner; Joshua's [epigraph
         used in Jericho]; Hubert Shuptrine; Shuptrine's "Blue North-

er" [painting]; Shuptrine's "Coon Dog" [painting]; Shuptrine's
"Cotton Time in Linden" [painting]; Shuptrine's "Four-Mile
Bayou" [painting]; Shuptrine's "Minda" [painting]; Shuptrine's
"Mountain Gentleman" [painting]; Shuptrine's "The New
Puppy" [painting]; Shuptrine's "Patient Turn" [painting];
Shuptrine's "Seiner Man" [painting]; Shuptrine's "September
Reds" [painting]; Shuptrine's "Time Alone" [painting];
Shuptrine's "Twilight" [painting]; Thomas Wolfe.

703 _____. "Poets of Affirmation." Wall Street Journal (24
May 1967), p. 16.
　　"Approaching Prayer"; Buckdancer's Choice; "Falling";
"In the Marble Quarry"; "May Day Sermon to the Women
of Gilmer County, Georgia, by a Woman Preacher Leaving
the Baptist Church"; Poems 1957-1967.
　　Poems 1957-1967 is lauded for its personal elements,
Dickey's use of the line as a basic unit, and the power
displayed in many of its poems. Biographical and career
data is included.
　　Ref. : Walt Whitman.

704 _____. "Poets on Poetry." Wall Street Journal (15 Aug.
1968), p. 10.
　　["Allen Ginsberg"]; Babel to Byzantium; "Barnstorming
for Poetry"; ["In the Presence of Anthologies"]; "The Poet
Turns on Himself"; ["Preface"]; ["Theodore Roethke"].
　　Babel to Byzantium is described as precise, lively, and
magnanimous.

705 Galler, David. "Versions of Accident." Kenyon Review 26
(Sum. 1964), pp. 581-584.
　　"The Dusk of Horses," p. 584; Helmets, pp. 583-584;
["Horses and Prisoners"], p. 584; ["The Ice Skin"],
p. 583; ["On the Coosawattee: III, The Inundation"],
p. 584; "The Scarred Girl," p. 584.
　　Discussion of Helmets is concentrated on the poems'
details, major themes, and unrealistic experiences.
　　Ref. : D. H. Lawrence, p. 584; Edwin Muir, p. 584.

*706 Gallery 1 (Nov. 1972), p. 15.
　　A review of the film version of Deliverance.
　　*[This citation is from Multi Media Reviews Index,
1972, p. 59.]

707 Garrigue, Jean. "James Dickey Airborne and Earthbound."
New Leader 50 (22 May 1967), pp. 21-23.
　　["Between Two Prisoners"], p. 21; "Dover: Believing
in Kings," pp. 21-22; Drowning with Others, p. 21; ["The
Dusk of Horses"], p. 21; ["The Firebombing"], pp. 22-23;
"In the Mountain Tent," p. 22; Into the Stone and Other
Poems, p. 21; "May Day Sermon to the Women of Gilmer
County, Georgia, by a Woman Preacher Leaving the Baptist
Church," p. 23; "The Owl King," p. 22; ["The Owl King:

III, The Blind Child's Story"], p. 22; ["The Owl King: I, The Call"], p. 22; ["The Owl King: II, The Owl King"], p. 22; Poems 1957-1967, p. 21; "Reincarnation [(II)]," p. 23; ["Sled Burial], Dream Ceremony," p. 21; "The Summons," p. 22; Two Poems of the Air, p. 21.

By investigating the major image of Poems 1957-1967, that of one's being in the air, flight by mechanical devices or by other means, the mode of Dickey's unique perception is discovered. Themes of singing, power, and evil and the religiousness of much of his work is discussed. "The Summons" is reprinted in full on p. 22.

Ref.: King Arthur, p. 22; Bible, p. 22; Emily Dickinson, p. 21; Merlin, p. 21; Dylan Thomas, p. 21; Walt Whitman, p. 23.

*707a Gelmis, Joseph. (Garden City, N. Y.) Newsday (1972).
A review of the film version of Deliverance.
*[This citation is from Filmfacts 15, no. 10 (1972), p. 214.]

708 Ghose, Zulfikar. Ambit, no. 23 (1965), pp. 45-46 [46].
"The Being"; "Chenille"; "The Duck of Horses"; "Fence Wire"; "A Folk Singer of the Thirties"; "Kudzu."
The poems in Helmets are described as professional, overly portentous, unoriginal, and pompous.
Ref.: Theodore Roethke.

709 Gilliatt, Penelope. "Tax Deductible Jesus." New Yorker 48 (5 Aug. 1972), pp. 50-54 [52-53].
Deliverance [film], pp. 52-53.
Plot of the film version of Deliverance is summarized, and portions of its dialog and plot are criticized although its narrative element is discussed positively.
Ref.: John Boorman, p. 52; Ronny Cox, p. 53; Burt Reynolds, p. 52; Jon Voight, p. 52; Vilmos Zsigmond, p. 53.

710 Gilroy, Harry. "Book Awards Go to 4 U.S. Writers." New York Times (16 Mar. 1966), p. 42.
Buckdancer's Choice.
A list of the judges of the poetry competition of the National Book Awards and the citation they gave Buckdancer's Choice are given.
Photograph of Dickey by Barton Silverman.

711 _____. "Edsel Ford, Arkansas Writer, Wins Top Society Prize." New York Times (21 Jan. 1966), p. 44.
Buckdancer's Choice.
Dickey is mentioned as a recipient of the Melville Cane Award.

712 Goldman, Michael. "Inventing the American Heart." Nation 204 (24 April 1967), pp. 529-530.

Buckdancer's Choice, p. 529; "Cherrylog Road," p. 529;
"Falling," p. 530; "The Head-Aim," p. 530; "The Ice Skin,"
p. 530; "Power and Light," pp. 529-530; ["The Scarred
Girl"], p. 530; "A Screened Porch in the Country," p. 529;
"The Sheep Child," p. 530; "Sustainment," p. 530; [uniden-
tified passages], p. 530.
   Dickey's language, imagination, and imagery in Poems
1957-1967 are discussed. Central to this volume is the
reader's ease of identifying with the personae and the unique
use of nature.
   Ref.: W. H. Auden, p. 530; Robert Frost, p. 530;
Thomas Gray, p. 530; George Herbert, p. 530; John Keats,
p. 530; Herman Melville, p. 530; Walt Whitman, p. 530;
William Carlos Williams, p. 530; William Butler Yeats,
p. 530.

713 Gow, Gordon. "Playboy in a Monastery." Films and Filming
     18 (Feb. 1972), pp. 18-22 [19, 22].
        Deliverance [novel], p. 19; Deliverance [film], pp. 19,
     22.
        An interview with John Boorman surveying his entire
     career. Discussion of the film version of Deliverance,
     which Boorman directed, centers on its theme and plot.
        Ref.: Ronny Cox, p. 19; Bill McKinney, p. 19; Burt
     Reynolds, p. 19; Jon Voight, p. 19.
        Illustrated with a still, p. 18.

714 Gray, Paul Edward. "New Fiction in Review." Yale Review
     60 (Oct. 1970), pp. 101-108 [104-106].
        Deliverance, pp. 104-105; [unidentified passage], p. 105.
        Dickey's use of the first person narrative in Deliverance
     and its effect on the novel's moral concerns, a central
     issue, are explained.
        Ref.: Eleanor Clark's Baldur's Gate, p. 106.

715 Greiner, Donald J. "The Harmony of Bestiality in James
     Dickey's Deliverance." South Carolina Review 5 (Dec.
     1972), pp. 43-49.
        Deliverance, pp. 43-49; "Madness," p. 48.
        A brief survey of several critics' views on Deliverance
     introduces a discussion of the transformation of the novel's
     narrator from a civilized human being into a savage. Its
     shock is attributed not to its violence but to the reader's
     realization that the inner savage is a universal characteris-
     tic of humanity.
        Ref.: Djuna Barnes' Nightwood, p. 48; John Buchan's
     The Thirty-Nine Steps, p. 43; Henri Georges Clouzot's The
     Wages of Fear [film], pp. 43-44; Joseph Conrad's "Heart
     of Darkness," p. 43; Benjamin DeMott's "The 'More Life'
     School and James Dickey," pp. 43-44, 47 (see no. 664);
     "Everyone's Notion of a Poet," p. 43 (see no. 683); Wil-
     liam Faulkner's "The Bear," p. 43; L. E. Sissman's
     "Poet Into Novelist," p. 43 (see no. 907).

716 Grossman, Allen. "Dream World of James Dickey." Boston
     Sunday Globe (2 Apr. 1967), sec. B, p. 33.
          ["At Darien Bridge"]; ["The Leap"].
          Under fire are Dickey's use of long lines, violence, poor
     metrical construction and grammar, and bizarre subject
     matter in Poems 1957-1967. Its collective theme is given.
          Ref.: [unidentified critic's remarks].

717 Grumbach, Doris. "Fine Print." New Republic 171 (23 Nov.
     1974), pp. 43-47 [43].
          Unfavorable review of Jericho containing 18 words.

718 _____. "Novels, Captive Voices, Etc." New Republic 171
     (16 Nov. 1974), pp. 31-32 [32].
          Jericho.
          A brief history of the publishing of Jericho and of its
     successes.
          Ref.: Book of the Month Club, p. 32; Betty Ann Jones,
     p. 32; Our Best Recipes, p. 32; Progressive Farmer,
     p. 32; Hubert Shuptrine, p. 32; Southern Living, p. 32;
     Andrew Wyeth, p. 32; Jonathan Yardley's "A Colossal
     Ornament?", p. 32 (see no. 972).

719 Guillory, Daniel L. "Water Magic in the Poetry of James
     Dickey." English Language Notes 8 (Dec. 1970),
     pp. 131-137.
          "Awaiting the Swimmer," p. 133; "Drowning with Others,"
     pp. 135-136; "Facing Africa," p. 134; "Inside the River,"
     pp. 136, 136n.; "The Lifeguard," pp. 132-133; ["Mary
     Sheffield"], pp. 132, 134; "The Movement of Fish," p. 134;
     "Near Darien," p. 133; "The Night Pool," p. 133; "The
     Owl King," p. 133; ["The Owl King: III, The Blind Child's
     Story"], p. 134; Poems 1957-1967, p. 131; "Pursuit from
     Under," p. 135; "The Underground Stream," p. 136; "The
     Vegetable King," p. 134; "Walking on Water," p. 132.
          Religion, evil, music, initiations, sex, and death are
     linked to water imagery in Poems 1957-1967. Concise
     historical survey of water symbolism is included.
          Ref.: J. E. Cirlot's A Dictionary of Symbols, pp. 131n.,
     136n.; Robert Creeley, p. 137; James George Frazer's The
     Golden Bough, p. 131n.; Carl Jung's Man and His Symbols,
     pp. 131n., 136n.; John Keats' "To Autumn," p. 136n.;
     Carolyn Kizer and James Boatwright's "A Conversation
     with James Dickey," p. 137 (see no. 1107); Charles Olson,
     p. 137; Wallace Stevens' "Not Ideas About the Thing but
     the Thing Itself," p. 136n.; Walt Whitman, p. 135; Whit-
     man's "Crossing Brooklyn Ferry," p. 135n.

720 Gunn, Thom. "Things, Voices, Minds." Yale Review 52
     (Oct. 1962), pp. 129-138 [131-133].
          "Between Two Prisoners," p. 132; "Dover: Believing
     in Kings," p. 133; Drowning with Others, p. 131; "The
     Heaven of Animals," pp. 131-132; ["In the Tree House at

Night"], p. 132; ["The Lifeguard"], p. 132.
Fantasy, and its effects, metrical construction, and
imagery in Drowning with Others are discussed.
Ref.: Jean Cocteau, pp. 131-132; Robert Creeley,
p. 133; Paul Klee, pp. 131-132; Denise Levertov, p. 133;
William Carlos Williams, p. 131.

721 Gustafson, Richard. "The Peace of a Good Line." Poet and
Critic 6, no. 3 (1971), pp. 29-33 [32].
Metaphor as Pure Adventure.
A discussion of Dickey's definitions of a poet and of
poetry.
Ref.: Wallace Stevens; Stevens' "Of Modern Poetry."

*722 Hale, Wanda. New York Daily News (1972).
A review of the film version of Deliverance.
*[This citation is from Filmfacts 15, no. 10 (1972),
p. 215.]

723 Harper, Howard M., Jr. "Trends in Recent American Fic-
tion." Contemporary Literature 12 (Spr. 1971), pp. 204-
229 [227].
Deliverance.
Dickey's novel is cited without comment in the checklist
at its conclusion.

724 Harris, Kathryn Gibbs. Books Abroad 40 (Spr. 1966), p. 205.
Favorable review of The Suspect in Poetry containing
157 words.

725 Harrison, Keith. "Disappointments." Spectator 213 (18 Sept.
1964), p. 375.
"The Beholders"; "Bums, on Waking"; "Fence Wire";
"The Ice Skin"; "The Poisoned Man"; "The Scarred Girl";
"Winter Trout."
Texture, cadence, and subject matter in Helmets are
noted.
Ref.: Wallace Stevens.

726 Heilbrun, Carolyn. "The Masculine Wilderness of the Ameri-
can Novel." Saturday Review 55 (29 Jan. 1972), pp. 41-44
[41, 44].
Deliverance, pp. 41, 44.
Deliverance is investigated as a recent example of a
long line of popular novels which exclude or distort the
female ideal.
Ref.: James Fenimore Cooper, p. 41; Charles Dickens,
p. 41; Leslie Fiedler's Death and Love in the American
Novel, p. 41; Herman Melville, p. 41; J. B. Priestly,
p. 44.

727 Heyen, William. Saturday Review 55 (11 Mar. 1972), pp. 70-
71.

Deliverance [novel], p. 70; Deliverance [film], p. 70;
["The Greatest American Poet: Theodore Roethke"], p. 70;
"The Son, the Cave, and the Burning Bush," p. 70; Sorties,
pp. 70-71.
Dickey is seen in Sorties as a descendant of a line of
American authors who are described as unfettered, asser-
tive, and attuned to themselves.
Ref.: John Berryman, p. 70; Anne Bradstreet, p. 70;
Jonathan Edwards, p. 70; Ralph Waldo Emerson, p. 71;
Nathaniel Hawthorne, p. 70; Henry James, p. 70; Robinson
Jeffers, p. 71; Life, p. 70; Robert Lowell, p. 70; Herman
Melville, pp. 70-71; Rainer Maria Rilke, p. 70; Theodore
Roethke, pp. 70-71; Roethke's Straw for the Fire, p. 70;
Hyatt Waggoner, p. 71; Walt Whitman, pp. 70-71; William
Carlos Williams, pp. 70-71; William Butler Yeats, p. 70.
Exc.: Contemporary Literary Criticism (see no. 1063).

728 Hildreth, Gina Dessart.   Arizona Quarterly 27 (Win. 1971),
pp. 372-374.
Deliverance, p. 372; The Eye-Beaters, Blood, Victory,
Madness, Buckhead and Mercy, p. 372; "The Owl King,"
p. 373; Self-Interviews, pp. 372-374.
Two distinct parts of Self-Interviews are identified:
Dickey's autobiographical comments and his discussion of
his own verse and its evolution.   The latter is criticized,
and the source of the volume's title is given.
Ref.: Norman Mailer, p. 373; The Paris Review,
p. 372; George Plimpton, p. 372; Barbara Reiss, p. 373;
James Reiss, p. 373.

729 Hill, William B.   America 122 (2 May 1970), p. 478.
Favorable review of Deliverance containing 51 words.

730 Hochman, Sandra. "Some of America's Most Natural Re-
sources." (New York) Herald Tribune.   Book Week (20
Feb. 1966), pp. 4, 11.
Buckdancer's Choice, p. 4; "The Firebombing," pp. 4,
11.
Dickey's function as a prophet is discussed, and an ex-
plication of one poem of Buckdancer's Choice is given.
Ref.: T. S. Eliot, p. 11.

731 Holmes, John. "Words to Create a World." New York Times
Book Review (13 Nov. 1960), p. 63.
["The Other"]; "Walking on Water."
Major themes and the tension created in many of the
poems of Into the Stone and Other Poems are briefly men-
tioned.

732 Holmes, Richard. "Poets: Taking Risks in Order to Be
Heard." Times (6 Apr. 1968), p. 20.
"Falling"; Poems 1957-1967.
Favorable review of Poems 1957-1967 containing 94

words.
Ref.: The New Yorker.

733 Hooper, Brad. Booklist 70 (15 Nov. 1974), p. 314.
     Favorable review of Jericho containing 92 words.

734 Houston, Gary. "Where Do the Deep Rivers of Meaning Run
     in Deliverance?" Chicago Sun-Times. Showcase (1 Oct.
     1972), pp. 1, 7.
         [Deliverance] [novel], pp. 1, 7; Deliverance [film],
     pp. 1, 7; [unidentified passage], p. 7.
         Characters in the film version of Deliverance, especially
     Ed Gentry, are transformed by their encounters with human
     evil.
         Ref.: Ned Beatty, p. 1; John Boorman, pp. 1, 7;
     Boorman's Hell in the Pacific [film], p. 7; Boorman's Leo
     the Last [film], p. 7; Boorman's Point Blank [film], p. 7;
     Tom Burke's "Conversations with, Um, Jon Voight on Not
     Being Jon Voight and Other Theories of Acting," p. 7 (see
     no. 1095); Joseph Conrad, p. 7; Ronny Cox, p. 1; Esquire,
     p. 7; Jack London's The Sea Wolf, p. 7; Lee Marvin,
     p. 7; Burt Reynolds, pp. 1, 7; Jon Voight, pp. 1, 7.
         Illustrated with stills and with a photograph of John
     Boorman by an unidentified person, p. 1.

735 Howard, Richard. "Five Poets." Poetry 101 (Mar. 1963),
     pp. 412-418 [415-417].
         ["Autumn"], p. 415; "Dover: Believing in Kings,"
     p. 416; "The Heaven of Animals," p. 417; ["Hunting Civil
     War Relics at Nimblewill Creek"], p. 416; ["In the Tree
     House at Night"], p. 416; ["Inside the River"], p. 417;
     ["The Owl King: II, The Owl King"], p. 416; "The
     Scratch," p. 417; "Snow on a Southern State," p. 417;
     ["The Twin Falls"], p. 415.
         Mention is made of the metrics, action, and mystical
     qualities of Drowning with Others. The natural world, it
     is stated, is reflected in the inner workings of human
     beings in Dickey's verse.
         Ref.: André Gide, p. 416; Heraclitus, p. 417; Theodore
     Roethke, p. 416; Dylan Thomas, p. 416.
         Rept.: Poetry (see no. 736).

736 _____. "Five Poets." Poetry 121 (Oct. 1972), pp. 54-59
     [57-58].
         ["Autumn"], p. 57; "Dover: Believing in Kings,"
     pp. 57-58; "The Heaven of Animals," p. 58; ["Hunting
     Civil War Relics at Nimblewill Creek"], p. 57; ["In the
     Tree House at Night"], p. 57; ["Inside the River"], p. 58;
     ["The Owl King: II, The Owl King"], p. 57; "The Scratch,"
     p. 58; "Snowfall on a Southern State," p. 58; ["The Twin
     Falls"], p. 57.
         Mention is made of the metrics, action, and mystical
     qualities of Drowning with Others. The natural world, it

is stated, is reflected in the inner workings of human be-
ings in Dickey's verse.
    Ref.: André Gide, p. 57; Heraclitus, p. 58; Theodore
Roethke, p. 57; Dylan Thomas, p. 57.
    Orig.: Poetry (see no. 735).

737 _____ . "On James Dickey." Partisan Review 33 (Sum.
    1966), pp. 414-428, 479-486.
      "Approaching Prayer," p. 425; "Armor," p. 426; "At
    Darien Bridge," p. 427; "Awaiting the Swimmer," pp. 415-
    416; Buckdancer's Choice, p. 481; ["The Change"], p. 486;
    "Cherrylog Road," pp. 479-480; "The Common Grave,"
    p. 482; "A Dog Sleeping on My Feet," p. 424; "Dover:
    Believing in Kings," p. 421; ["Drinking from a Helmet"],
    p. 426; Drowning with Others, pp. 416, 420, 425; "The
    Dusk of Horses," p. 427; "The Escape," pp. 481-482;
    "The Fiend," p. 483; "The Firebombing," pp. 483-485;
    "Fog Envelops the Animals," p. 422; ["For the Nightly
    Ascent of the Hunter Orion Over a Forest Clearing"],
    p. 482; "Fox Blood," p. 481; "The Heaven of Animals,"
    pp. 423, 427; Helmets, pp. 425, 479-480; "Hunting Civil
    War Relics at Nimblewill Creek," p. 424; ["In the Marble
    Quarry"], p. 480; "Inside the River," p. 420; "Into the
    Stone," pp. 415, 417; Into the Stone and Other Poems,
    pp. 415, 419, 423, 427, 482; "Mangham," p. 485; ["Min-
    doro, 1944"], pp. 418, 426; "Near Darien," pp. 415, 427;
    "On the Coosawattee," p. 428; ["On the Coosawattee: II],
    Below Ellijay," p. 428; ["On the Coosawattee: I], By Canoe
    through the Fir Forest," p. 428; ["On the Coosawattee:
    III], The Inundation," p. 479; "Orpheus Before Hades,"
    pp. 416, 419; "The Owl King," p. 423; ["The Owl King:
    III], The Blind Child's Story," pp. 423-424; ["The Owl
    King: I], The Call," p. 423; ["The Owl King: II], The
    Owl King," p. 423; "The Performance," pp. 418-419;
    ["Poem"], p. 415; "Pursuit from Under," p. 486; ["Randall
    Jarrell"], p. 414; ["The Salt Marsh"], pp. 424-425; ["A
    Screened Porch in the Country"], p. 422; ["The Shark's
    Parlor"], p. 486; ["The Signs"], pp. 418, 426; "Slave
    Quarters," pp. 484-485; ["Springer Mountain"], pp. 427,
    480; The Suspect in Poetry, p. 414; "To Landrum Guy,
    Beginning to Write at Sixty," p. 424; "Trees and Cattle,"
    pp. 415, 417; ["The Twin Falls"], p. 420; "The Under-
    ground Stream," p. 415; "The Vegetable King," pp. 415,
    417, 419; "Walking on Water," pp. 415-416; ["The] War
    Wound," p. 481; ["Winter Trout"], p. 428.
      Dickey's major themes, symbols, images, and forms
    are investigated in this chronological survey. Much com-
    parison and contrasting of poems are included.
      Ref.: William Blake, p. 420; René Char, p. 417;
    Joseph Conrad, p. 418; Frances Cornford, p. 423; Günter
    Eich's [epigraph used in "The Firebombing"], p. 483; T.
    S. Eliot, p. 480; Ralph Waldo Emerson, p. 414; Eurydice,
    p. 416; Morgan le Fay, p. 421; André Gide, p. 479;

Frederic Harrison, p. 423; Heraclitus, p. 420; William
James, p. 424; Märchen, p. 423; John Henry Newman,
p. 481; Orpheus, pp. 415-416, 419; Plutarch, p. 421;
Prospero, p. 483; Theodore Roethke, pp. 417, 420; Percy
Bysshe Shelley, p. 420; Socrates, p. 420; Wallace Stevens,
p. 425; Jules Supervielle, p. 417; Valerianeus, p. 416;
William Wordsworth, pp. 428, 479; William Butler Yeats,
p. 416.
   Rept.: Alone with America (see no. 1024). (Its title
was subsequently changed to "James Dickey: 'We Never
Can Really Tell Whether Nature Condemns Us or Loves
Us.'" Comments covering Poems 1957-1967 not in the
original are included in its reprinted version.)
   Exc.: A Library of Literary Criticism (see no. 1005).

738 _____. "'Resurrection for a Little While.'" Nation 210
   (23 Mar. 1970), pp. 341-342.
   "Apollo," p. 342; ["Apollo: I, For the First Manned
Moon Orbit"], p. 342; ["Apollo: II, The Moon Ground"],
p. 341; Babel to Byzantium, p. 341; "The Cancer Match,"
p. 342; Deliverance, p. 341; "Diabetes," p. 342; ["Diabetes:
I, Sugar"], pp. 341-342; ["Diabetes: II, Under Buzzards"],
p. 341; "The Eye-Beaters," pp. 341-342; "The Heaven of
Animals," p. 342; "The Lord in the Air," p. 342; "Mad-
ness," p. 342; Poems 1957-1967, p. 341; ["Turning Away"],
pp. 341-342; ["Two Poems of Going Home: I, Living
There"], p. 341; [unidentified passage], p. 341; "Venom,"
p. 342; ["Victory"], p. 341.
   Movement in theme from earlier volumes to The Eye-
Beaters, Blood, Victory, Madness, Buckhead and Mercy is
emphasized. The title is from "Diabetes: I, Sugar."
   Ref.: William Blake, pp. 341-342; Blake's [epigraph
used in "The Lord in the Air"], p. 342; Eden, p. 342; I.
A. Richards, p. 342.

739 Howes, Victor. "Dickey's World and Welcome to It."
   Christian Science Monitor (13 Jan. 1972), 2d sec., p. 11.
   "The Greatest American Poet: Theodore Roethke";
Sorties; ["Spinning the Crystal Ball"].
   Definitions of "sortie" introduce this summary of the
contents of Sorties.

740 _____. "Genuine and Bogus." Christian Science Monitor
   (3 Dec. 1964), sec. B, p. 8.
   ["Anne Sexton"]; ["The Grove Press New American
Poets (1960)"]; ["Howard Nemerov"]; ["Randall Jarrell"];
["Richard Eberhart"]; ["The Second Birth"]; ["The Suspect
in Poetry"]; The Suspect in Poetry; ["Theodore Roethke"];
["W. S. Merwin"].
   Dickey's theories of criticism, and especially its per-
sonal qualities in The Suspect in Poetry, are discussed.
   Ref.: Samuel Johnson; The New Yorker; Poetry.

741 _____. [V. H.]. "Poem to a Power Plant." Christian
Science Monitor (20 Jan. 1972), p. 6.
"In the Wax Museum at Hamburg."
A mixed review of Yvegeny Yevtushenko's Stolen Apples
in which this translation by Dickey is excerpted.

742 Huff, Robert. "The Lamb, the Clocks, the Blue Light."
Poetry 109 (Oct. 1966), pp. 44-48 [46-48].
"Buckdancer's Choice," p. 47; Buckdancer's Choice,
pp. 46, 48; "The Common Grave," p. 47; "The Fiend,"
p. 48; "The Firebombing," pp. 46-48; "Mangham," p. 47;
"The Performance," p. 47; "Slave Quarters," pp. 47-48.
An attack against Hochman's comments. Guilt is
identified as the tone of Buckdancer's Choice.
Ref.: Richard Eberhart's "Dam Neck, Virginia," p. 46;
Sandra Hochman's "Some of America's Most Natural Re-
sources," p. 46 (see no. 730).

743 Hunt, Dennis. "A Thriller All the Way." San Francisco
Chronicle (4 Oct. 1972), p. 64.
[Deliverance] [novel]; Deliverance [film].
Although its dialog is trite at times, its epilogue is
distracting, and Ed's transformation is unbelievable, the
film version of Deliverance is saved by its fine acting,
lighting, photography, and action-packed, thrilling sequences.
Its theme of survival is explored, and a plot summary is
given.
Ref.: Ned Beatty; Blow Up [film]; John Boorman; Boor-
man's Point Blank [film]; Ronny Cox; Burt Reynolds; Jon
Voight; Vilmos Zsigmond.
Illustrated with a still.
Rept.: Filmfacts (see no. 660).

744 Ignatow, David. "The Permanent Hell." Nation 202 (20 June
1966), pp. 752-753.
"Buckdancer's Choice," p. 753; "The Celebration,"
p. 753; "The Escape," p. 753; "The Fiend," p. 753; "The
Firebombing," pp. 752-753; "Fox Blood," p. 753; "Game-
cock," p. 753; "Pursuit from Under," p. 753; "Slave
Quarters," p. 753.
Nature, family, the Self, guilt, and war are chief con-
cerns in Buckdancer's Choice. Dickey's identification
technique fails in "The Fiend" and "Slave Quarters."
Ref.: Henry Moore, p. 752; Walt Whitman, p. 753.

745 "In Search of an Audience." Times Literary Supplement (21
May 1971), p. 580.
The Eye-Beaters, Blood, Victory, Madness, Buckhead
and Mercy; ["The Lord in the Air"]; ["Two Poems of Going
Home: I, Living There"].
Dickey's exclamations, repetition of words and their
distribution on the page, and posturizing in The Eye-Beaters,
Blood, Victory, Madness, Buckhead and Mercy point to his

insecurity and artificiality.
   Ref.: Gerard Manley Hopkins; John Weiners' Nerves;
Walt Whitman; Richard Wilbur's Walking to Sleep.
   Rept.: T. L. S.: Essays and Reviews from "The Times
Literary Supplement," 1971 (see no. 1057). (Its title was
subsequently changed to "Poetry of 1971.")

*746   Ingenue 14 (Oct. 1972), p. 6.
   A review of the film version of Deliverance.
   *[This citation is from Multi Media Reviews Index, 1972,
p. 59.]

*747   Inter/View, no. 26 (Oct. 1972), p. 47.
   A review of the film version of Deliverance.
   *[This citation is from Multi Media Reviews Index, 1972,
p. 59.]

748   "James Dickey Named U. S. Poetry Consultant." (Washington,
   D. C.) Evening Star (20 Jan. 1966), sec. A, p. 2.
   Buckdancer's Choice; Drowning with Others; Helmets;
Into the Stone and Other Poems; The Suspect in Poetry;
Two Poems of the Air.
   A notice of Dickey's appointment to the Library of Con-
gress post of Consultant of Poetry in English, it mentions
his books and outlines his literary career. Biographical
data is included.

749   Jameson, Fredric. "The Great American Hunter, or,
   Ideological Content in the Novel." College English 34 (Nov.
   1972), pp. 180-197 [181-188, 195].
   Deliverance, pp. 181-182, 184-186, 188, 195; "The
Firebombing," p. 184.
   A Marxian analysis of Deliverance, its theme is ex-
plained as a class struggle with the bourgeois as victor.
This, it is stated, is an unconscious wish-fulfillment.
Violence, the wilderness motif, suburban stagnancy, myth
of the hero, and initiation rites are investigated.
   Ref.: James Agee and Walker Evans' Let Us Now
Praise Famous Men, p. 185; Robert Ardrey, p. 181; James
Fenimore Cooper, p. 183; Cooper's Leatherstocking Tales,
p. 183; Eugene V. Debs, p. 185; William Faulkner, p. 182;
Faulkner's Go Down Moses, p. 183; Sigmund Freud, p. 183;
Ernest Hemingway, p. 182; Hercules, p. 183; Huey P.
Long, p. 185; Norman Mailer, p. 195; Mailer's Why Are
We in Vietnam?, pp. 186, 188; Franklin D. Roosevelt,
p. 185; Jean-Paul Sartre, p. 186; Sartre's Saint Genet,
p. 186; Roger Williams, p. 185.

750   Jones, Marion. "Dickey's Works Range All Emotions."
   Hartford (Conn.) Times (12 May 1967), sec. D, p. 24.
   Buckdancer's Choice; "Faces Seen Once"; Poems 1957-
1967.
   Favorable review of Poems 1957-1967 containing 243
words.

751 Journal of Modern Literature 1, no. 5 (1971 supplement),
      p. 76.
          "The Poem as Something that Matters"; "The Poet in
      Mid-Career"; Self-Interviews.
          The usefulness of tape recorders in producing books
      such as Self-Interviews is discussed. Dickey's autobio-
      graphical remarks and comments on his own poetry are
      briefly discussed.
          Ref. : Charles Olson's Charles Olson Reading at
      Berkeley; Barbara and James Reiss' "Introduction" (see
      no. 1060).

752 Journal of Modern Literature 1, no. 5 (1971 supplement),
      p. 767.
          Deliverance; James Dickey Reads [His] Poetry.
          An L. P. record of Dickey reading his poetry and the
      location of his manuscripts at Washington University are
      mentioned.

753 "Journey into Self. " Time 95 (20 Apr. 1970), pp. 92-93.
          Deliverance, pp. 92-93.
          The narrative element, language, and empathy for
      various characters in Deliverance are investigated. Its
      failures and successes are noted.
          Ref. : Joseph Conrad's "Heart of Darkness, " p. 93;
      William Faulkner's "The Bear, " p. 93.
          Exc. : Contemporary Literary Criticism (see no. 1063).

754 "Just Like Deliverance. " Washington (D. C.) Post (14 Aug.
      1973), sec. B, p. 3.
          Deliverance [novel]; [Deliverance] [film].
          Dickey responds to the drownings in the Chattooga River
      popularized by Deliverance and its film version.
          Exc. : "Author Feels Responsible for Deaths" (see
      no. 573).

755 K. , H. A. Boston Sunday Globe (25 Mar. 1962), sec. A,
      p. 57.
          Favorable review of Drowning with Others containing
      70 words.

756 Kael, Pauline. "After Innocence. " New Yorker 49 (1 Oct.
      1973), pp. 113-118 [116].
          Deliverance [film].
          Poor acting in the film version of Deliverance accounts
      for the unbelievability of its characters. Only Dickey's
      portrayal of the sheriff is acceptable. It is seen as an
      effective film, nevertheless.
          Ref. : John Boorman.

757 _____. "A Brash Young Man. " New Yorker 50 (11 Mar.
      1974), pp. 119-124 [119].
          Deliverance [film].

Descriptions of Jon Voight's and Burt Reynolds' acting abilities in the film version of Deliverance are briefly compared.
Ref. :   Clark Gable; Burt Reynolds; Jon Voight.

758 _____ . "Labyrinths. "   New Yorker 49 (24 Dec. 1973), pp. 68, 71-73 [73].
Deliverance [film].
The talents of John Boorman, director of the film version of Deliverance, are briefly mentioned.
Ref. :   John Boorman.

759 _____ . "Soul Food. "   New Yorker 48 (30 Sept. 1972), pp. 109-111, 115-118 [115].
Deliverance [film].
While the film version of Deliverance is rated as powerful due especially to its director's ability, its character development is flimsy.

760 Kalston, David.   New York Times Book Review (23 Jan. 1972), pp. 6, 24.
Death's Baby Machine, p. 6; ["The Greatest American Poet: Theodore Roethke"], p. 6; Sorties, p. 6; "Spinning the Crystal Ball, " p. 24; [unidentified passage], p. 24.
Although the essays in Sorties are viewed favorably, its journal section is criticized for being a device created to extend Dickey's public image.
Ref. :   Hart Carne, p. 24; D. H. Lawrence, p. 24; Theodore Roethke, p. 24.
Photograph of Dickey by Thomas Victor, p. 6.

761 Katz, Bill.   Library Journal 92 (1 Apr. 1967), p. 1497.
["Bread"]; "Falling" [sec. of Poems 1957-1967]; ["The Sheep Child"].
Favorable review of Poems 1957-1967 containing 176 words.
Ref. :   The New York Times; Times Literary Supplement; [unidentified remarks].
Rept. :   Library Journal Book Review: 1967, p. 406 (see no. 1028).

762 Kauffman, Stanley.   "Fair to Meddling. "   New Republic 167 (5 and 12 Aug. 1972), pp. 24, 35-36.
[Deliverance] [novel], p. 24; Deliverance [film], p. 35.
Both Dickey's novel and its film adaptation are criticized because each is overly stated and develops a stunted theme. This discussion centers on the film.
Ref. :   John Boorman, p. 35; Boorman's Having a Wild Weekend [film], p. 35; Boorman's Leo the Last [film], p. 35; Boorman's Point Blank [film], p. 35; Jorge Luis Borges, p. 24; Victor Mature, p. 35; Burt Reynolds, p. 24; Jon Voight, p. 35.

763   Kaye, Howard.   "Why Review Poetry?"   New Republic 158
        (29 June 1968), pp. 28-29.
        "Barnstorming for Poetry," p. 29; "Cherrylog Road,"
        p. 29; ["David Ignatow"], p. 28; ["E. E. Cummings"],
        p. 28; ["Edwin Arlington Robinson"], pp. 28-29; ["Ellen
        Kay"], p. 29; ["Howard Nemerov"], p. 28; ["J. V. Cun-
        ningham"], p. 29; "Kudzu," p. 29; "Notes on the Decline
        of Outrage," p. 29; "The Poet Turns on Himself," p. 29;
        ["Randall Jarrell"], p. 28; ["Robert Duncan"], p. 28;
        ["Theodore Roethke"], p. 28; ["Thom Gunn"], p. 29; ["W.
        S. Graham"], p. 28; ["Yvor Winters"], p. 29.
        Although it is noted that Dickey attempts to be fair in
        Babel to Byzantium, his criticism is described as being
        too subjective, unreliable, and pernicious.
        Ref.: Donald Allen's The New American Poetry, p. 28;
        Robert Duncan, p. 28; Allen Ginsberg, p. 28; Anthony
        Hecht, p. 28; James Merrill, p. 28; Leopold Mozart, p. 29;
        Charles Olson, p. 28; Edwin Arlington Robinson's "Veteran
        Sirens," p. 29; Dylan Thomas, pp. 28-29; Richard Wilbur,
        p. 28.

764   Keller, Marcia.   School Library Journal (May 1970), p. 90.
        In Library Journal 95 (15 May 1970), p. 1969.
        Favorable review of Deliverance containing 143 words.

765   "Kennan Announces 9 Literary Awards."   New York Times
        (20 April 1966), p. 43.
        Buckdancer's Choice.
        Dickey is listed with other recipients of grants from the
        National Institute of Arts and Letters and the American
        Academy of Arts and Letters.

766   Kennedy, X. J.   "Joys, Griefs, and 'All Things Innocent,
        Hapless, Forsaken.'"   New York Times Book Review (23
        Aug. 1964), p. 5.
        "Approaching Prayer"; "Cherrylog Road"; Helmets; Two
        Poems of the Air.
        Intelligence and force characterize Helmets and Two
        Poems of the Air.
        Ref.: Monica Moseley Pincus; Theodore Roethke.

767   _____.   "Sometimes It's the Sound that Counts."   New York
        Times Book Review (15 July 1962), p. 4.
        "The Hospital Window."
        Dickey's controlled joy and language in Drowning with
        Others are lauded.   Its themes and recurrent words are
        listed.

768   Kessler, Jascha.   "Fantasies of Self-Gratification."   Los
        Angeles Times.   Calendar (16 Jan. 1972), p. 44.
        ["The Greatest American Poet: Theodore Roethke"];
        ["Journals"]; Sorties.
        Dickey is scolded for the vanity displayed in Sorties.

It is uninteresting and fabricated.
Ref.: D. H. Lawrence's The Plumed Serpent; T. E.
Lawrence's Seven Pillars of Wisdom; Theodore Roethke;
Philip Roth's Portnoy's Complaint.

769 Kirkus Reviews 38 (1 Jan. 1970), p. 34.
     ["Madness"].
     Unfavorable review of The Eye-Beaters, Blood, Victory,
     Madness, Buckhead and Mercy containing 268 words.

770 Kirkus Reviews 38 (1 Feb. 1970), p. 124.
     Favorable review of Deliverance containing 291 words.
     Ref.: Marquis de Sade; The Saturday Evening Post.

771 Kirkus Service 35 (15 Feb. 1967), p. 236.
     "Falling"; "The Firebombing."
     Noting the continuation of themes throughout Poems 1957-
     1967, the techniques of later poems are emphasized.
     Ref.: Robert Frost; Paul O'Neil's "The Unlikeliest Poet"
     (see no. 850).

772 Kirkus Service 36 (1 Mar. 1968), p. 300.
     ["Allen Ginsberg"]; ["Conrad Aiken"]; ["John Ashbery"];
     ["Marianne Moore"]; ["Robert Graves"]; ["The Suspect in
     Poetry"]; ["Theodore Roethke"].
     Mixed review of Babel to Byzantium containing 237 words.

773 Knapp, Dan. "Roughing It for Realism in Deliverance." Los
     Angeles Times. Calendar (20 Feb. 1972), pp. 1, 54-55.
     Deliverance, p. 1.
     The filming of Deliverance was hindered by two
     types of problems: those of nature and those of
     human interaction. Problems created by the heat,
     insects, snakes, the Chattooga River's currents, in which
     three actors were nearly lost, and the river's cliffs, from
     which one actor fell, are reported. Conflicts created by
     Dickey's presence on location during the filming and by
     changes made in the script regardless of his wishes are
     also discussed.
     Ref.: Ned Beatty, p. 54; John Boorman, pp. 1, 54-55;
     Boorman's Point Blank [film], p. 1; Ronny Cox, p. 54; Al
     Jennings, p. 54; Burt Reynolds, p. 1; Jon Voight, pp. 1,
     54-55; Sven Walnum, p. 1; Vilmos Zsigmond, p. 1.
     Illustrated with a photograph of Jon Voight by an uni-
     dentified photographer, p. 55.

774 Knight, Arthur. "... And Deliver Us from Evil." Saturday
     Review 55 (5 Aug. 1972), p. 61.
     Deliverance [novel]; Deliverance [film].
     The film version of Deliverance is discussed in regard
     to the technique employed by its director, its adventure
     quality, and its effect on the audience.
     Ref.: Ned Beatty; John Boorman; Boorman's Hell in the

Pacific [film]; Boorman's Point Blank [film]; Ronny Cox;
Burt Reynolds; Jon Voight; Vilmos Zsigmond.
Rept.: Film 72-73 (see no. 1030).

775 Korges, James. "James Dickey and Other Good Poets."
Minnesota Review 3 (Sum. 1963), pp. 473-491 [476-477,
479, 482-483, 487-491].
"A Dog Sleeping on My Feet," p. 489; Drowning with
Others, p. 488; [Helmets], p. 488; "The Hospital Window,"
p. 491; "Hunting Civil War Relics at Nimblewill Creek,"
pp. 477, 491; ["In the Lupanar at Pompeii"], p. 490; ["In
the Mountain Tent"], p. 490; "The Island," p. 489;
"Listening to Foxhounds," p. 489; "The Movement of Fish,"
p. 490; ["The Owl King: I, The Call"], p. 489; "The Owl
King [: II, The Owl King"], p. 490; "The Scratch,"
p. 491; ["The Twin Falls"], p. 491; "Utterance I," p. 488.
    Drowning with Others is criticized for its haphazard
forms, poor rhyme, and overworked, vague, and strained
images and themes. It is also described as generally
imaginative, controlled, personal, observant, and com-
passionate. Recurrent themes are listed.
    Ref.: Edgar Bowers, p. 487; Hart Crane, p. 491;
Irving Feldman, p. 491; Robert Frost, p. 491; Charles
Gullans, p. 479; Robert Lowell, pp. 483, 487; John Crowe
Ransom, p. 491; Carl Sandburg, p. 482; Wallace Stevens,
p. 491; James Tate, p. 483, 491; Dylan Thomas, p. 489;
Lionel Trilling, p. 491; Yvor Winters, pp. 489, 491; James
Dean Young, p. 489.

776 Kostelanetz, Richard. "Flyswatter and Gadfly." Shenandoah
16 (Spr. 1965), pp. 92-95.
    ["Anne Sexton"], p. 93; ["Charles Olson"], p. 94;
["E. E. Cummings"], p. 94; ["Kenneth Patchen"], p. 95;
["Randall Jarrell"], p. 93; ["The Suspect in Poetry"],
p. 93; The Suspect in Poetry, pp. 92-93; ["Thom Gunn"],
p. 93; ["Toward a Solitary Joy"], p. 95.
    The Suspect in Poetry is described as being honest and
humorous, as displaying a kindness toward bad poets, and
as possessing a single thesis evident throughout.
    Ref.: John Ashbery, p. 94; John Berryman, p. 94;
Robert Bly's [remarks appearing on the dust jacket of The
Suspect in Poetry], p. 92; Leslie A. Fiedler, p. 94;
Kenneth Koch, p. 94; C. S. Lewis, p. 93; Robert Lowell,
p. 94; Sylvia Plath, p. 94; Theodore Roethke, p. 94;
Harold Rosenberg, p. 93; William Stafford, p. 94.
    Rept.: James Dickey: The Expansive Imagination (see
no. 1032).

777 Krebs, Abin. "Notes on People." New York Times (1 Dec.
1971), p. 53.
    Deliverance.
    A note on Dickey's receiving the Prix Medicis with an
excerpt from his acceptance speech.

778   Land, Irene, ed.   "First Novelists."
         (See no. 303.)

779   Landers Film Reviews 15 (Dec. 1970), p. 83.
         "For the Last Wolverine."
         Favorable review of a film about Dickey, "Lord, Let Me
         Die but Not Die Out," containing 154 words.
         Ref.: Robert Lowell; John Milton's "Paradise Lost."

780   Lask, Thomas.   "The Voice of the Poet."   New York Times
         Book Review (2 Dec. 1962), pp. 7, 47 [47].
         Favorable review of Drowning with Others containing
         32 words.

781   _____.   "Writer Turned Reader."   New York Times (10
         May 1968), p. 45.
         ["Allen Ginsberg"]; ["In the Presence of Anthologies"];
         ["Kenneth Patchen"]; "Notes on the Decline of Outrage";
         ["Robert Penn Warren"]; ["Rolphe Humphries"]; ["Theodore
         Roethke"]; [unidentified passage].
         In Babel to Byzantium, Dickey not only locates the
         "suspect" in others' poetry but reveals those theories which
         govern his own work.
         Ref.: T. S. Eliot; Alexander Pope; Wallace Stevens;
         William Carlos Williams.
         Photograph of Dickey by an unidentified person.

782   "Leaps and Plunges."   Times Literary Supplement (8 May
         1967), p. 420.
         "Falling"; "The Leap"; "The Shark's Parlor."
         Identified as syntactically sloppy, Poems 1957-1967 is
         also described as insistent but flimsy, self-indulging and
         anecdotal.   His prosody and narrative technique are ex-
         amined.
         Ref.: Archibald MacLeish; Anne Sexton.

783   LeBlanc, Jerry.   "James Dickey Is a Poet and Quickly Lets
         You Know It."   Chicago Tribune.   Chicago Tribune Maga-
         zine (29 Oct. 1972), pp. 13, 15.
         Deliverance [novel], pp. 13, 15; [Deliverance] [film],
         pp. 13, 15.
         Dickey ruminates about teaching, gives his reactions to
         the reviews Deliverance and its film version have received,
         and recalls his concerns for the safety of the filming crew
         and his sons during the shooting of Deliverance.
         Ref.: Al Capp, p. 13; Sammy Davis, Jr., p. 13;
         Christopher Dickey, p. 15; Kevin Dickey, p. 15; Maxine
         Dickey, p. 13; Ernest Hemingway, p. 15; Frank Sinatra,
         p. 13; Jon Voight, p. 15.

784   Lehmann-Haupt, Christopher.   "Men in Groups."   New York
         Times (27 Mar. 1970), p. 31.
         Deliverance.

Unbelievable situations in Deliverance are balanced by
Dickey's story-telling ability.
Photograph of Dickey by Christopher Dickey.

785 Leibowitz, Herbert. "The Moiling of Secret Forces: The Eye-
Beaters, Blood, Victory, Madness, Buckhead and Mercy."
New York Times Book Review (8 Nov. 1970), pp. 20, 22.
        Buckdancer's Choice, p. 20; Deliverance, pp. 20, 22;
["Diabetes: II, Under Buzzards"], p. 22; "The Eye-
Beaters," p. 22; The Eye-Beaters, Blood, Victory, Mad-
ness, Buckhead and Mercy, p. 22; Helmets, p. 20; "Kudzu,"
p. 20; "[The] Lord in the Air," p. 22; "Mercy," p. 22;
Poems 1957-1967, p. 20; ["The Shark's Parlor"], p. 20;
["Two Poems of Going Home: I,] Living There," p. 22;
["Two Poems of Going Home: II,] Looking for the Buck-
head Boys," p. 22; [unidentified passages], pp. 20, 22.
        Dickey's The Eye-Beaters, Blood, Victory, Madness,
Buckhead and Mercy is tainted by hysteria, childishness,
and excessive sentimentality. It rarely indicates a step
forward in the development of Dickey's work. A concise
survey of his nature poetry introduces.
        Ref.: T. S. Eliot's "The Waste Land," p. 20; George
Frazer, p. 20; Sigmund Freud, p. 20; Carl Jung, p. 20;
Herman Melville, p. 20; Orpheus, p. 20.

786 Lensing, George. Carolina Quarterly 22 (Spr. 1970),
pp. 90-91.
        Buckdancer's Choice, p. 91; "The Eye-Beaters," p. 91;
The Eye-Beaters, Blood, Victory, Madness, Buckhead and
Mercy, pp. 90, 91; "Hunting Civil War Relics at Nimble-
will Creek," p. 91; "In the Pocket," p. 90; "The Life-
guard," p. 91; "Madness," p. 91; "The Owl King," p. 91;
"Pine," p. 90; Poems 1957-1967, p. 90; "Turning Away,"
p. 90.
        Dickey is accused of verbosity, gimmickry, and over-
statement in The Eye-Beaters, Blood, Victory, Madness,
Buckhead and Mercy.
        Ref.: Peter Davidson's "The Difficulties of Being Major:
The Poetry of Robert Lowell and James Dickey," p. 90
(see no. 659); Louis Untermeyer's "A Way of Seeing and
Saying," p. 90 (see no. 942).

787 Levin, Elena. Saturday Review 54 (13 Nov. 1971), pp. 52,
57 [57].
        Mixed review of Stolen Apples. Dickey's use of
colloquialisms in his translations is discussed.

788 L'Heureux, John. "'Having a Beer with One's Soul.'" Boston
Sunday Herald. Show Guide (4 June 1967), p. 19.
        "For the Last Wolverine"; Poems [1957-1967].
        Poems 1957-1967 is seen as a volume of celebration.
Its spiritual aspects receive most attention, but comments
on its display of fantasy, sex, and violence and the themes

of "For the Last Wolverine" are included.   Its title is
from Leroy F. Aarons' "Ex-Adman Dickey: Don't Just
Wait for Oblivion" (see no. 555).
      Ref. : Harvey Cox; Paul O'Neil's "The Unlikeliest Poet"
(see no. 850).

789   Libby, Anthony.   "Fire and Light, Four Poets to the End and
      Beyond. " Iowa Review 4 (Spr. 1973), pp. 111-126 [111-
      112, 120-123, 126].
            "Approaching Prayer, " p. 122; Buckdancer's Choice,
      p. 122; Deliverance, pp. 120, 123; Drowning with Others,
      pp. 121-122; "The Eye-Beaters, " p. 126; The Eye-Beaters,
      Blood, Victory, Madness, Buckhead and Mercy, p. 123;
      "Falling" [sec. of Poems 1957-1967], p. 122; "The Fire-
      bombing, " pp. 121-122; "For the Last Wolverine, " p. 122;
      "Gamecock, " p. 122; "The Head-Aim, " pp. 122-123; "The
      Heaven of Animals, " p. 122; Helmets, p. 122; "Inside the
      River, " p. 121; ["Journals"], p. 120; "Reincarnation (I), "
      p. 122; Sorties, pp. 121, 123; "Springer Mountain, " p. 122.
            Survival is identified as a central motif in Dickey's
      work.   Several of his works are compared to Robert Bly's
      to clarify Dickey's concern with survival and to explain
      their feud.
            Ref. : Robert Bly, pp. 112, 120-121, 123; Bly's
      "Awakening, " p. 121; Bly's "The Collapse of James Dickey, "
      pp. 121-122 (see no. 587); Bly's Fields, p. 121; Bly's
      "Return to Solitude, " p. 121; Bly's Silence in the Snowy
      Fields, p. 121; Bly's "The Teeth-Mother Naked at Last, "
      pp. 121-122; Bly's "The Work of James Dickey, " p. 121
      (see no. 589); Charles Darwin, p. 121; Leslie Fiedler,
      p. 123; Richard Howard's "On James Dickey, " p. 121 (see
      no. 737); Ted Hughes, pp. 112, 120-123; Laurence Lieber-
      man's "James Dickey: The Deepening of Being, " p. 121
      (see no. 1034); W. S. Merwin, pp. 111, 123.

790   Library of Congress Information Bulletin 24 (25 Oct. 1965),
      pp. 569-570.
            Buckdancer's Choice, p. 570; Drowning with Others,
      p. 569; Helmets, p. 570; Into the Stone and Other Poems,
      p. 569; The Suspect in Poetry, p. 570; Two Poems of the
      Air, p. 570.
            A notice of one of Dickey's public poetry readings
      presented at the Library of Congress.   Biographical and
      career data are given and his awards are listed.
            Ref. : Poetry, p. 569.

791   Library of Congress Information Bulletin 25 (20 Jan. 1966),
      pp. 41-42.
            Buckdancer's Choice, p. 42; Drowning with Others,
      p. 42; Helmets, p. 42; Into the Stone and Other Poems,
      p. 42; The Suspect in Poetry, p. 42; Two Poems of the
      Air, p. 42.
            Biographical and career data are included in this notice

of Dickey's appointment as consultant in poetry at the
Library of Congress. A list of consultants before Dickey
and the purpose of the post are given. Mention is made of
his awards and his various positions of poet-in-residence.
Ref.: Christopher Dickey, p. 42; Kevin Dickey, p. 42;
Maxine Syerson Dickey, p. 42; Library of Congress Infor-
mation Bulletin, p. 41 (see no. 790); Poetry, p. 42; The
Sewanee Review, p. 42.

792 Lieberman, Laurence. "The Expansional Poet: A Return to
Personality." Yale Review 57 (Dec. 1967), pp. 258-271
[258-260, 264-267].
"Falling," pp. 260, 264-265, 267; "The Firebombing,"
p. 265; "Fog Envelops the Animals," p. 266; "The Heaven
of Animals," pp. 265-266; Helmets, p. 258; [Poems 1957-
1967], p. 258; "Reincarnation [(II)]," p. 265; "The Sheep
Child," pp. 264-266; "Springer Mountain," p. 266.
The later poetry of Poems 1957-1967 is characterized by
extreme emotions and experience. The origins of "Falling"
and "The Sheep Child" are traced from his earlier poems
noting the influence of his personal experiences. Discus-
sion of the phrase as a basic unit of Dickey's poetry and a
poet's personality's relationship to the expansive style is
included.
Ref.: John Berryman, pp. 259-260, 266; T. S. Eliot's
"Tradition and the Individual Talent," pp. 258, 266; D. H.
Lawrence, p. 264; Theodore Roethke, pp. 259, 266;
William Stafford, pp. 259-260, 266; [unidentified passage of
an interview], p. 267.
Exc.: Contemporary Literary Criticism (see no. 1062).

793 _____. "Notes on James Dickey's Style." Far Point, no. 2
(Spr.-Sum. 1969), pp. 57-63.
Buckdancer's Choice, pp. 59-60; "Cherrylog Road,"
p. 62; "Drinking from a Helmet," pp. 58, 60; "Dust,"
pp. 59-60; "Encounter in the Cage Country," pp. 62-63;
"Falling," p. 61; "Falling" [sec. of Poems 1957-1967],
pp. 59-60; "The Flash," p. 60; Helmets, p. 59; "The
Hospital Window," p. 62; "The Island," p. 60; "The Per-
formance," p. 58; "Power and Light," p. 62; "The
Scratch," p. 60; "Snakebite," p. 60; "Sun," p. 60; The
Suspect in Poetry, p. 57.
Dickey's figurative language, line structure, poetic
forms, and symbolism are discussed. Included in this in-
vestigation is the identification of techniques common to
film and journalism in Dickey's works. Mention is given
to the development of his symbolism through several books
and to his use of the phrase as a basic unit.
Ref.: William Faulkner, p. 59; Henry James' The
Sacred Fount, p. 63; James Joyce, p. 59; Walt Whitman,
p. 59; William Butler Yeats, p. 59; Yeats' A Vision, p. 59.
Rept.: James Dickey: The Expansive Imagination (see
no. 1035).

794 _____. "Poet-Critics and Scholar-Critics." Poetry 115
(Feb. 1970), pp. 346-352 [346-347, 349].
Babel to Byzantium, p. 346; "Preface," p. 347.
Babel to Byzantium is described as frank and perceptive,
and Dickey's stand against artificiality and his influence on
the poets he criticizes are analyzed.
Ref.: Mark van Doren, p. 349; Richard Howard, p. 347;
Randall Jarrell, p. 347.

795 _____. "Poetry Chronicle: Last Poems, Fragments, and
Wholes." Antioch Review 24 (Win. 1964-1965), pp. 537-
543 [540-543].
Drowning with Others, p. 541; Helmets, p. 541; "The
Poisoned Man," p. 541; "Springer Mountain," p. 542.
Helmets, a lyrical volume, displays Dickey's mastery
of language and rhythm.
Ref.: A. R. Ammons, pp. 540, 542-543; William Carlos
Williams, p. 543.

796 _____. "The Wordly Mystic." Hudson Review 20 (Aut.
1967), pp. 513-520.
Buckdancer's Choice, p. 513; "Encounter in the Cage
Country," pp. 513, 516-517; "Falling," pp. 515, 518-520;
"Falling" [sec. of Poems 1957-1967], p. 513; "False Youth
[: Two Seasons, II]," p. 517; "The Fiend," pp. 513-514,
518-519; "The Firebombing," pp. 513, 515, 520; "The
Flash," p. 516; "Power and Light," pp. 514-515, 517,
520; "The Sheep Child," pp. 518-519; "Slave Quarters,"
pp. 513-515, 520; "Snakebite," p. 516; "Sun," p. 517;
[unidentified passages], pp. 514-515.
Two themes exist in "Falling," the last portion of Poems
1957-1967: sexual realism and comic dramatization. Each
is linked to the persona's dual personality, a quality absent
from the earlier poems. Remarks on Dickey's recurrent
use of reincarnation coupled with "air" conclude.
Ref.: "A Drunken Man's Praise of Sobriety," p. 515;
Robert Frost, p. 518; Frost's "The Road Not Taken,"
p. 518; William Butler Yeats, pp. 515, 518; Yeats' "High
Talk," p. 515.
Rept.: James Dickey: The Expansive Imagination (see
no. 1036).
Exc.: Contemporary Literary Criticism (see no. 1063);
A Library of Literary Criticism (see no. 1005).

797 Lightman, Herb A. "On Location with Deliverance." Ameri-
can Cinematographer 52 (Aug. 1971), pp. 796-799.
Deliverance [film], pp. 797-798.
Although a summary of the plot and the theme are given,
the techniques used in filming Deliverance are emphasized.
Ref.: John Boorman, pp. 796, 798-799; Boorman's
Hell in the Pacific [film], p. 798; Boorman's Point Blank
[film], p. 798; Peter Fonda, p. 798; The Hired Hand [film],
p. 798; Laszlo Kovacs, p. 798; McCabe and Mrs. Miller

[film], p. 798; Red Sky at Morning [film], p. 798; Burt
Reynolds, pp. 797-799; Jon Voight, pp. 796-799; Vilmos
Zsigmond, pp. 796, 798-799.
Photographs by an unidentified person, pp. 796-799.

798 Lindborg, Henry J. "James Dickey's Deliverance: The
Ritual of Art." Southern Literary Journal 6 (Spr. 1974),
pp. 83-90.
Deliverance, pp. 83-90; ["The Suspect in Poetry"],
p. 83; The Suspect in Poetry, p. 83n.
The chaotic setting of Deliverance is the arena from
which harmony arises. This parallels the act of creation
as investigated in the experiences and the character of the
narrator.
Ref.: Billy Budd, p. 84; Natty Bumppo, p. 90; James
Fenimore Cooper, p. 83; Mircea Eliade's Myths, Dreams
and Mysteries, p. 84n.; Ralph Waldo Emerson, pp. 88-90;
Emerson's "Demonology," pp. 86, 86n.; Emerson's "The
Poet," p. 88n.; Huck Finn, pp. 84, 90; Arthur Koestler's
The Act of Creation, pp. 85-86, 86n.; D. H. Lawrence's
Studies in Classic American Literature, pp. 83, 83n.;
Isaac McCaslin, p. 90; Norman Mailer's Why Are We in
Vietnam?, pp. 89-90; Edgar Allan Poe, p. 86; Tarzan,
p. 87; Allen Tate's "The Angelic Imagination: Poe as God,"
p. 88n.; Paul Tillich's "Religion and Secular Culture,"
p. 90; Johnny Weissmuller, p. 87; William Wordsworth's
"Lines Composed a Few Miles Above Tintern Abbey,"
p. 88.

799 Logan, John. "Poetry Shelf." Critic 21 (Dec. 1962-Jan.
1963), pp. 84-85 [84].
Drowning with Others; "The Owl King"; ["The Owl King:
III, The Blind Child's Story"].
Paternal piety is at the core of Drowning with Others.
Dickey's technique of metamorphosis and his poetic forms
are mentioned.
Ref.: John Ashbery; Robert Bly; Hieronymus Bosch's
"Garden of Earthly Delights" [paintings]; Sigmund Freud.

800 Love, Glen A. "Ecology in Arcadia." Colorado Quarterly 21
(Aut. 1972), pp. 175-185 [179-182].
Deliverance, pp. 179-182.
Plot summary of Deliverance is followed by discussions
of its nature symbolism and themes derived from trans-
cendentalism. Its differences to other earlier novels treat-
ing nature similarly are investigated.
Ref.: Ralph Waldo Emerson, p. 181; Huck Finn,
pp. 181-182; Ishmael, p. 182; Leo Marx, p. 182; I. A.
Richard's Science and Poetry, p. 182; Henry David Thoreau,
p. 181.

801 Lucas, Tom. Spirit 37 (Fall 1970), pp. 39-42 [40-42].
"Apollo," p. 40; "Blood," p. 40; "The Cancer Match,"

p. 40; "Diabetes," p. 40; "The Eye-Beaters," p. 41; "In the Pocket," p. 40; "Knock," p. 40; "The Lord in the Air," p. 40; "Madness," p. 40; "Mercy," p. 40; "Messages," pp. 41-42; "Two Poems of Going Home," p. 41; "Victory," p. 41.

A list of themes in individual poems of The Eye-Beaters, Blood, Victory, Madness, Buckhead and Mercy. Mention is given to Dickey's use of the caesura.

Ref.: John Keats, p. 40; Richard Wilbur, pp. 41-42; Wilbur's "Along the Marginal Way," p. 41.

*802 MD Medical News Magazine 16 (Sept. 1972), p. 276.
A review of the film version of Deliverance.
*[This citation is from Multi Media Reviews Index, 1972, p. 59.]

803 m., m. a. Antiquarian Bookman 39 (10 Apr. 1967), p. 1501.
Favorable review of Poems 1957-1967 containing 75 words. Data on its miniature edition is included.

*804 McGillivray, D. "Deliverance." Focus on Film, no. 11 (Aut. 1972), p. 12.
A review of the film version of Deliverance.
*[This citation is from International Index to Film Periodicals, 1972, p. 147.]

805 McHughes, Janet Ellen Larsen. Abstract of "A Phenomenological Analysis of Literary Time in the Poetry of James Dickey." Dissertation Abstracts International; A: The Humanities and Social Sciences 33 (Dec. 1972), p. 2942.
Buckdancer's Choice; Drowning with Others; The Eye-Beaters, Blood, Victory, Madness, Buckhead and Mercy; "Falling" [sec. of Poems 1957-1967]; Helmets; Into the Stone and Other Poems.
In the author's dissertation (see no. 1123), two major temporal philosophies, Proustian and Bergsonian, and several more minor concepts of time are discussed in regard to Dickey's thematic growth.
Ref.: Henri Bergson; Hercules; Marcel Proust.

806 _____. "The Contemporary Poet as Jongleur."
Speech Communication Association, Interpretation Division Newsletter (Fall 1971), pp. 4-6.
[Babel to Byzantium], pp. 4, 5n.; "Barnstorming for Poetry," pp. 4-5, 5n.; Buckdancer's Choice, p. 4; Deliverance, p. 4; [The Eye-Beaters, Blood, Victory, Madness, Buckhead and Mercy], p. 4; [Poems 1957-1967], p. 4; "Root-Light, [or the Lawyer's Daughter]," p. 5.
Relying heavily on "Barnstorming for Poetry" and on personal observation of Dickey, the development of his skills in interpreting his own poetry is outlined.
Ref.: "The Dick Cavett Show," p. 5; Don Geiger's The Sound, Sense, and Performance of Literature, pp. 4, 5n.;

Howard Nemerov, p. 5; Edith Sitwell, p. 5; Dylan Thomas, p. 5; Gerald Weales' "The Poet as Player," pp. 5, 6n.; Richard Wilbur, p. 5.

807   McKenzie, James Joseph.   Abstract of "A New American Nature Poetry: Theodore Roethke, James Dickey, and James Wright."   Dissertation Abstracts International; A: The Humanities and Social Sciences 32 (Nov. 1971), p. 2698.
   In the author's dissertation (see no. 1124), Dickey's use of the narrative, the externalization of his verse, his major themes, and the uniqueness of his voice are explored. Roethke's influences on him and Dickey's intuitive ability are also discussed.
   Ref.: Theodore Roethke; James Wright.

808   Mahon, Derek. "Suburban Arrows." Listener (10 Sept. 1970), p. 352.
   Deliverance; ["Two Days in September"].
   A plot summary of Deliverance with brief mention of its form, rhythms, and violence.
   Ref.: Ernest Hemingway.

809   Maloff, Saul. "Poet Takes His Turn as Critic." Chicago Tribune. Book World (30 June 1968), p. 10.
   ["In the Presence of Anthologies"]; ["John Berryman"]; ["Marianne Moore"]; ["Notes on the Decline of Outrage"]; The Suspect in Poetry; ["Theodore Roethke"].
   Babel to Byzantium is described as precise, generous, and honest. A summary of Dickey's major critical theories is included, and its theme is identified.
   Photograph of Dickey by Christopher Dickey (?).

810   Marin, Daniel B. "James Dickey's Deliverance: Darkness Visible." South Carolina Review 3 (Nov. 1970), pp. 49-59.
   "After," p. 52; "Before," p. 52; Deliverance, pp. 50, 51-53, 55-58, 59n.; ["Diabetes: II, Under Buzzards"], pp. 49-50; The Eye-Beaters, Blood, Victory, Madness, Buckhead and Mercy, pp. 50, 59n.; ["Messages: I, Butterflies"], p. 59; "September 14th," pp. 54-56; ["Two Days in September"], p. 59n.
   Characterization, plot, and the wilderness' effect on the narrator of Deliverance are investigated.
   Ref.: Walter Clemons' "James Dickey, Novelist," p. 52 (see no. 637); Samuel Taylor Coleridge's "The Rime of the Ancient Mariner," p. 58; Joseph Conrad's "Heart of Darkness," p. 54; Nathaniel Hawthorne's "Young Goodman Brown," p. 54; Herman Melville's "Bartleby the Scrivener," pp. 52-53.
   Rept.: James Dickey: The Expansive Imagination (see no. 1043).

811   Markos, Donald W. "Art and Immediacy: James Dickey's

Deliverance. " Southern Review, n. s. 7 (July 1971),
pp. 947-953.
      Deliverance, pp. 947, 949-952.
      A rebuttal of DeMott's "The 'More Life' School and
James Dickey" is followed by comments on the characters
in Deliverance being segments of Dickey himself, its
mysticism, the narrator's romanticism, and the sadness of
its conclusion.   Its theme is explained.
      Ref. : Benjamin DeMott's "The 'More Life' School and
James Dickey, " pp. 947-948 (see no. 664); [dust jacket of
Deliverance], p. 952; Robert Frost, p. 950; Frost's "Stop-
ping by Woods on a Snowy Evening, " p. 950; D. H. Law-
rence, p. 950; Norman Mailer, p. 947; Edgar Allan Poe,
p. 952; Theodore Roethke, p. 950; Walt Whitman, p. 950;
Whitman's "Out of the Cradle, " p. 950; William Words-
worth's The Prelude, p. 950; Wordsworth's [unidentified
passage], p. 950.
      Exc. : Contemporary Literary Criticism (see no. 1062).

812   Marsh, Pamela. "Handsome Hardbacks. " Christian Science
      Monitor (27 Nov. 1974), 2d sec. , p. 7.
            Shuptrine's art in Jericho is mentioned although Dickey's
      prose is ignored.
            Ref. : Rembrandt; Hubert Shuptrine.

813   _____. "James Dickey: Violent on Violence. " Christian
      Science Monitor (2 Apr. 1970), p. 7.
            Deliverance; [unidentified passage].
            Although characterization in and plot of Deliverance are
      briefly mentioned, its violence in its obvious and subtle
      manifestations is emphasized.

814   Martz, Louis L. "Recent Poetry: The Elegiac Mode. " Yale
      Review 54 (Dec. 1964), pp. 285-298 [289-291]. [Note:
      This issue was incorrectly dated.   The correct date is
      1965.]
            "Drinking from a Helmet, " pp. 290-291; "A Folk Singer
      of the Thirties, " p. 290; ["In the Marble Quarry"], p. 290;
      ["The Poisoned Man"], p. 289.
            Dickey's imagination and the allegorical qualities of
      poems in Helmets are mentioned.   Summaries of individual
      poems' themes are included.
            Ref. : Burl Ives, p. 290; Denise Levertov's "Overheard, "
      p. 289.

*815 Mass Media 9 (18 Sept. 1972), p. 4.
            A review of the film version of Deliverance.
            *[This citation is from Multi Media Reviews Index, 1972,
      p. 59.]

816   Meiners, R. K. "The Necessary and Permanent Revolution. "
      Southern Review, n. s. 1 (Aut. 1965), pp. 926-944 [940-
      943].

"At Darien Bridge," p. 942; ["Chenille"], p. 942;
"Drinking from a Helmet," p. 943; "The Driver," p. 943;
"Goodbye to Serpents," p. 943; Helmets, p. 940; "Horses
and Prisoners," pp. 940-941; "The Ice Skin," p. 943;
"In the Child's Night," p. 941; "Kudzu," p. 943; "On the
Coosawattee," p. 943; "The Poisoned Man," p. 943; "The
Scarred Girl," p. 943; "Springer Mountain," pp. 941-942;
["Winter Trout"], p. 942.
  The demands Dickey's images, themes, verbs and ad-
verbs, mysticism, and landscape make on the reader of
Helmets are discussed.
  Ref.: John Keats, p. 940; William Langland, p. 940;
W. S. Merwin, p. 940; Theodore Roethke, p. 941; William
Wordsworth, p. 943.

817 _____ . "The Way Out: The Poetry of Delmore Schwartz
      and Others." Southern Review, n. s. 7 (Jan. 1971),
      pp. 314-337 [318-321].
      Buckdancer's Choice, p. 318; "Deer Among Cattle,"
    pp. 318-320; "Encounter in the Cage Country," p. 319;
    "The Head Aim," p. 319; Poems 1957-1967, p. 318.
      In Poems 1957-1967, Dickey does not observe the natural
    and the animal worlds but asserts himself onto them, and
    his verse is identified as being disrespectful of them. It
    is described as literally and figuratively forced because of
    his rhetoric. "Deer Among Cattle" is reprinted in full,
    pp. 318-319.
      Ref.: John Berryman, p. 318; William Blake, p. 318;
    Robert Bly's "The Collapse of James Dickey," p. 318 (see
    no. 587); Robert Lowell, p. 318; R. K. Meiners' "The
    Necessary and Permanent Revolution," p. 318 (see no. 816);
    W. S. Merwin, p. 321; Theodore Roethke, p. 318; Delmore
    Schwartz, p. 318.

818 Meredith, William. "A Good Time for All." New York Times
      Book Review (23 Apr. 1967), pp. 4, 46.
      "Adultery," p. 46; "The Change," p. 46; "Dover: Be-
    lieving in Kings," p. 4; "The Dream Flood," p. 46;
    [Drowning with Others], p. 4; "Falling," pp. 4, 46; "False
    Youth [: Two Seasons, II]," p. 46; Into the Stone and Other
    Poems, p. 4; "May Day Sermon to the Women of Gilmer
    County, Georgia, by a Woman Preacher Leaving the Baptist
    Church," pp. 4, 46; "Power and Light," p. 46; "The Shark's
    Parlor," pp. 4, 46; "Sustainment," p. 46; [unidentified
    prose passage], p. 46.
      Poems 1957-1967 is occasionally uneven, too lengthy,
    formless, and uncontrolled. Yet it is truthful to the human
    experience and often has humorous overtones. Recurrent
    images are discussed.
      Ref.: Walter Benton, p. 46; Bob Dylan, p. 4; T. S.
    Eliot, p. 4; Eliot's "The Waste Land," p. 4; Randall
    Jarrell, pp. 4, 46; Vachel Lindsay, p. 4; Robert Lowell,
    p. 4; Edgar Lee Masters, p. 4; Ezra Pound, p. 4; Carl

Sandburg, p. 4; Wallace Stevens, p. 4; [unidentified re-
marks], p. 4; Robert Penn Warren, p. 46; John Hall
Wheelock's "Introductory Essay: Some Thoughts on Poetry,"
p. 4 (see no. 1089); Walt Whitman, p. 4; Richard Wilbur,
p. 4; William Butler Yeats, p. 46.
Photograph of Dickey by an unidentified person, p. 4.

819   _____. "James Dickey's Poems." Partisan Re-
view 32 (Sum. 1965), pp. 456-457.
"Cherrylog Road," p. 456; "A Folk Singer of the Thirties,"
p. 456; Helmets, p. 456; "The Ice Skin," pp. 456-457;
"Kudzu," p. 457; "The Scarred Girl," p. 457; "Springer
Mountain," p. 457.
In Helmets, the poems' content, reality of experience,
and unique vision place Dickey above his contemporaries.
Their metrical structures and effects on the reader is
noted. The failures of three poems, due to unfocused ex-
periences, are discussed.

820 Millar, Gavin. "Divine Thrillers." Listener (5 Oct. 1972),
pp. 452-453.
Deliverance [film], pp. 452-453.
Nature and the grail myth in the film Deliverance are
briefly discussed, and a plot synopsis is included.
Ref.: John Boorman, pp. 452-453; Boorman's Hell in
the Pacific [film], p. 452; Boorman's Point Blank [film],
p. 452; Jean-Luc Godard's Weekend [film], p. 453; Elia
Kazan's Wild River [film], p. 453; Burt Reynolds, p. 453;
Jean-Jacques Rousseau, p. 453; Jon Voight, p. 453.

821 Mills, Ralph J., Jr. "Brilliant Essays on Contemporary
Poetry." Chicago Sun Times. Book Week (5 May 1968),
p. 4.
["Allen Ginsberg"]; ["Anne Sexton"]; ["Charles Olson"];
["Donald F. Drummond"]; ["E. E. Cummings"]; ["Edwin
Arlington Robinson"]; ["Ellen Kay"]; ["John Ashbery"];
["Louis MacNeice"]; ["Marianne Moore"]; "The Poet Turns
on Himself"; "Preface"; ["Randall Jarrell"]; ["Reed Whitte-
more"]; ["Theodore Roethke"]; ["William Carlos Williams"].
Dickey is cited for his wisdom, preciseness, perception,
positive attitudes, and personal qualities displayed in Babel
to Byzantium.
Ref.: Matthew Arnold; W. H. Auden; Samuel Taylor
Coleridge; John Dryden; T. S. Eliot; Randall Jarrell;
Jarrell's Poetry and the Age; Samuel Johnson; Yvor
Winters.

822 _____. "The Poetry of James Dickey." Triquarterly,
no. 11 (Win. 1968), pp. 231-242.
"The Birthday Dream," pp. 232, 241; Buckdancer's
Choice, p. 234; "Coming Back to America," p. 241; "Deer
Among Cattle," p. 241; "Drinking from a Helmet," pp. 234,
236-237; Drowning with Others, p. 241; "Falling," p. 241;

"Falling" [sec. of Poems 1957-1967], pp. 232, 241; "The Fiend," p. 240; "The Firebombing," pp. 234, 238-240; "The Head-Aim," p. 241; Helmets, p. 241; "Hunting Civil War Relics at Nimblewill Creek," pp. 234-235, 237-238; "In the Tree House at Night," p. 234; "Inside the River," p. 236; Into the Stone and Other Poems, p. 232; "The Leap," p. 241; "May Day Sermon to the Women of Gilmer County, Georgia, by a Woman Preacher Leaving the Baptist Church," p. 241; "The Owl King," pp. 234, 236; "The Poet Turns on Himself," p. 242n.; "Reincarnation (I)," p. 234; "Reincarnation (II)," p. 241; "The Salt Marsh," p. 236; "A Screened Porch in the Country," pp. 232-233; "Slave Quarters," pp. 240-241; "Sled Burial, Dream Ceremony," p. 234; "Sleeping Out at Easter," p. 232; "Snakebite," p. 241; "Sun," p. 241; "Sustainment," p. 241.
    A loosely chronological study of Dickey's verse to Poems 1957-1967 which emphasizes Dickey's moral failure. Discussion of his imagination, themes, images, surrealistic techniques, and metaphysical qualities is included.
    Ref.: Robert Bly, pp. 232, 242; Bly's "Buckdancer's Choice," p. 239 (see no. 586); Bly's "The Work of James Dickey," pp. 234, 234n. (see no. 589); André Breton, p. 231; Samuel Taylor Coleridge, p. 241; Günter Eich's [epigraph used in "The Firebombing"], pp. 238, 240; Norman Friedman's "The Wesleyan Poets, II: The Formal Poets, 2," p. 234n. (see no. 701); Michael Goldman's "Inventing the American Heart," p. 234n. (see no. 712); Donald Hall, pp. 232, 242; Job's [epigraph used in "The Firebombing"], p. 238; D. H. Lawrence, p. 242; C. Day Lewis' The Poetic Image, pp. 235-236, 238; W. S. Merwin, pp. 232, 242; Rainer Maria Rilke's "Archaic Torso of Apollo," p. 232; Theodore Roethke, p. 232; Jon Silkin, p. 242; Louis Simpson, p. 232; Simpson's "Dead Horses and Live Issues," p. 231; Wallace Stevens, p. 232; H. L. Weatherby's "The Way of Exchange in James Dickey's Poetry," pp. 234, 234n. (see no. 954); Walt Whitman, p. 242; James Wright, pp. 232, 242.

823 Mitchell, Henry. "Dickey: Friend of Bears and Byron." Washington (D.C.) Post (19 Mar. 1974), sec. B, pp. 1-2.
    Buckdancer's Choice, p. 2; Deliverance [novel], pp. 1-2; Deliverance [film], p. 2; ["For] the Last Wolverine," p. 2; Jericho, p. 1.
    Much of Dickey's ruminations concern his admiration for Lord Byron, although he also mentions his reading habits, interest in sports, and his approach to public poetry readings. Dickey's reading at the Folger Shakespeare Library and his father's death are also noted as are his plans for a television film based on The Call of the Wild.
    Ref.: George Gordon, Lord Byron, p. 2; Jean Cocteau, p. 1; Heather Conoboy, p. 2; Tom Dickey, p. 2; Clark Gable, p. 1; Caroline Lamb, p. 2; Lassie, p. 1; Jack London's The Call of the Wild, p. 1; Katie Louccheim,

p. 2; Thomas Moore, p. 2; Plato, p. 2; Burt Reynolds, p. 2.

Photograph of Dickey by Douglas Chevalier, p. 1.

824 Monagham, Charles. Commonweal 84 (15 Apr. 1966), pp. 120-122.

Buckdancer's Choice, pp. 120-121; Drowning with Others, p. 121; "The Firebombing," p. 121; Helmets, p. 121; [Into the Stone and Other Poems], p. 120.

Imagery, involvement of the reader, and lack of over-simplification in Buckdancer's Choice are discussed. A concise, thematic analysis of "The Firebombing" is given.

Ref.: Robert Lowell, pp. 120-121; Lowell's Life Studies, p. 120; Lowell's Lord Weary's Castle, p. 120; The New York Times Book Review, p. 120; Louis Simpson, p. 122.

*825 Monthly Film Bulletin 39 (Sept. 1972), p. 186.

A review of the film version of Deliverance.

*[This citation is from Multi Media Reviews Index, 1972, p. 59.]

826 Moore, Robert Nelson, Jr. Abstract of "Aggression in the Poetry of James Dickey." Dissertation Abstracts International; A: The Humanities and Social Sciences 34 (Feb. 1974), p. 5195.

"The Enclosure"; "Encounter in the Cage Country"; "The Firebombing"; "Fog Envelops the Animals"; "For the Nightly Ascent of the Hunter Orion Over a Forest Clearing"; "The Head-Aim"; "The Heaven of Animals"; "The Jewel"; "Listening to Foxhounds"; "The Performance"; "Reunioning Dialogue"; "Springer Mountain"; "The Summons"; "The War Wound."

In the author's dissertation (see no. 1125), aggression, as it appears in Dickey's war and hunting poetry, is investigated. In some instances, the aggressive experience brings about spiritual evaluation and self-awareness.

Ref.: "Aggression" in Encyclopedia of Psychology.

827 Morris, Harry. "A Formal View of the Poetry of Dickey, Garrigue, and Simpson." Sewanee Review 77 (Spr. 1969), pp. 318-325 [318-323].

"Adultery," p. 321; "Angina," p. 322; "Bread," p. 322; "Chenille," p. 322; "Cherrylog Road," p. 322; "The Escape," p. 321; "Gamecock," p. 322; "Hedge Life," p. 321; "The Lifeguard," p. 322; "Mangham," p. 322; "The Performance," p. 322; "Pursuit from Under," p. 322; "Reincarnation (I)," p. 319; "The Sheep Child," p. 322; "Sun," p. 321; "The Wedding," p. 321.

Dickey's Poems 1957-1967 is described as shallow because of inaccuracies in his observations of nature and because of laxities with form and conciseness. His uses of stanzas, long lines, pronouns, and only a few rhetorical devices are also challenged.

Exc.: Contemporary Literary Criticism (see no. 1062).

828   Morse, J. Mitchell. "Fiction Chronicle." Hudson Review 23
      (Sum. 1970), pp. 327-338 [337-338].
            Deliverance, p. 337.
            Unlike his poetry, Dickey's Deliverance lacks in an
      ability with language and in an encouragement of sympathy
      for its characters.
            Ref.: The New York Times, p. 337.

829   Morse, Samuel French. "A Baker's Dozen?" Virginia Quart-
      erly Review 38 (Spr. 1962), pp. 324-330 [324-326].
            "Between Two Prisoners," p. 326; "A Dog Sleeping on
      My Feet," p. 326; "Dover: Believing in Kings," p. 325;
      Drowning with Others, pp. 324-326; "The Hospital Window,"
      p. 326; "In the Tree House at Night," p. 326; Into the Stone
      and Other Poems, p. 326; "The Lifeguard," p. 325; "The
      Owl King," p. 325; "The Scratch," p. 326; "To Landrum
      Guy, Beginning to Write at Sixty," p. 326; "A View of
      Fujiyama After the War," p. 326.
            The concept of the "other" is of prime concern in
      Drowning with Others, and discussion of this concept is
      emphasized. Dickey's longer poems lack in confidence.
            Ref.: Reuel Denney's In Praise of Adam, p. 324.

830   _____. "Poetry, 1962: A Partial View." Wisconsin
      Studies in Contemporary Literature 4 (Aut. 1963),
      pp. 367-380 [371-372].
            "Dover: Believing in Kings," p. 372; Drowning with
      Others, p. 372; ["The Movement of Fish"], p. 371; "The
      Owl King," p. 372.
            Drowning with Others is lauded for its concept of the
      "other" and for escaping the confessional style.

831   _____. "Poetry, 1964." Wisconsin Studies in Contemporary
      Literature 6 (Aut. 1965), pp. 354-367 [365].
            Helmets.
            Brief but favorable mention of Dickey and a prediction of
      future success.

832   _____. "Poetry, 1965." Wisconsin Studies in Contemporary
      Literature 7 (Aut. 1966), pp. 336-355 [349].
            Buckdancer's Choice.
            Buckdancer's Choice is considered a transitional volume.

833   Motion Picture Herald 242 (Aug. 1972), p. 625.
            Deliverance [novel]; Deliverance [film].
            Two levels of the film Deliverance are identified: its
      effective adventure quality and its strained theme. Char-
      acterization and stereotypes are discussed.
            Ref.: Ned Beatty; John Boorman; Ronny Cox; Burt
      Reynolds; Jon Voight; Vilmos Zsigmond.

834   Murf. Variety (19 July 1971), p. 14.
            Deliverance [novel]; Deliverance [film].

Although much of the discussion of the film Deliverance
centers on the actors' abilities, or inabilities, its conflict
between the instinct for survival and the inner moral code
and the story's implications are examined.   Credits are
included.
     Ref.: Ned Beatty; John Boorman; Bill Butler; Herbert
Coward; Ronny Cox; Happiness Cage [film]; Billy McKinney;
Steve Mandel; Tom Priestly; Burt Reynolds; Jon Voight;
Eric Weissberg; Vilmos Zsigmond.

835 Murray, Michele.   National Catholic Reporter 3 (23 Aug.
       1967), p. 9.
          Babel to Byzantium; The Suspect in Poetry.
          Babel to Byzantium is described as lacking in jargon and
       containing insight.
          Ref.: T. S. Eliot; Ezra Pound.

836 "A Mutiny Alert."   Mutiny 4 (Fall-Win. 1961-1962), pp. 3-9.
          "Confession Is Not Enough," pp. 4, 6-7; [letter to Jane
       Esty], p. 5.
          A call for those against the Beat movement in poetry to
       support Dickey's "Confession Is Not Enough."   An editorial
       introduces this rally, and it is followed by letters pro and
       con and a petition supporting Dickey's view.   Entries have
       been given to each of the individuals connected with this
       feud: Francis Brown, p. 7 (see no. 1164), Leonard Casper,
       p. 9 (see no. 1213), David Cornel DeJong, p. 9 (see
       no. 1216), Jane Esty, pp. 3, 9 (see nos. 681 and 1166),
       Harold Fleming, p. 9 (see no. 1217), Jean Garrigue, p. 9
       (see no. 1218), John J. Gill, p. 8 (see no. 1172), Leslie
       Woolf Hedley, p. 9 (see no. 1220), Eugene Kayden, p. 9
       (see no. 1224), Paul Lett, pp. 3, 7 (see nos. 681 and
       1180), Andrew Lytle, p. 9 (see no. 1226), Lynne Marquiz,
       p. 9 (see no. 1227), Gil Orlovitz, p. 9 (see no. 1229),
       Charles Philbrick, p. 9 (see no. 1230), Selden Rodman,
       p. 8 (see no. 1190), Hy Sobiloff, p. 9 (see no. 1233),
       Monroe K. Spears, p. 9 (see no. 1234), Elmer G. Sulzer,
       p. 9 (see no. 1235), Lewis Turco, p. 9 (see no. 1237),
       and Oscar Williams, p. 9 (see no. 1242).

837 "N. B. A. 1966."   Newsweek 67 (28 Mar. 1966), pp. 105-106
       [106].
          Buckdancer's Choice.
          A notice of Dickey's winning the National Book Award
       for Buckdancer's Choice with a list of the judges for the
       poetry competition.
          Ref.: W. H. Auden; Elizabeth Bishop; Randall Jarrell.
          Photograph of Dickey with other N. B. A. recipients by
       Bernard Gotfryd, p. 106.

838 Nash, Jay Robert.   Literary Times 4 (May-June 1967), p. 9.
          Buckdancer's Choice; "Falling" [sec. of Poems 1957-
       1967]; Poems 1957-1967; "The Sheep Child."

The section of Poems 1957-1967 entitled "Falling" con-
centrates on the past, the self, action, and experiences.
Ref. : Robert Lowell; Edna St. Vincent Millay;
Yevgeny Yevtushenko.

839   National Catholic Reporter 4 (9 Oct. 1968), p. 11.
Buckdancer's Choice; "Deer Among Cattle"; Drowning
with Others; "Falling"; "The Firebombing"; Helmets; Into
the Stone and Other Poems; "May Day Sermon to the Wo-
men of Gilmer County, Georgia, by a Woman Preacher
Leaving the Baptist Church. "
Poems 1957-1967 displays Dickey's good qualities--his
universality and his obsession with nature--as well as his
bad attributes--his change to longer lines and his verbose-
ness.
Ref. : A. R. Ammons; William Wordsworth.

840   Nemerov, Howard. "Poems of Darkness and a Specialized
Light. " Sewanee Review 71 (Jan. -Mar. 1963), pp. 99-104.
"Armor, " p. 104; ["Dover: Believing in Kings"], p. 99;
"Facing Africa, " p. 103; ["For the Nightly Ascent of the
Hunter Orion Over a Forest Clearing"], p. 102; ["The
Island"], p. 100; "The Lifeguard, " p. 104; ["The Owl King:
III, The Blind Child's Story"], pp. 102, 104; ["The Owl
King: II, The Owl King"], pp. 100-101; ["The Salt Marsh"],
p. 102; "The Summons, " pp. 100, 104.
Rhythm, the mysteriousness of objects and events, the
relationship distinct elements of the world have with one
another, the effect of using participles, and the use of
impared vision in Dickey's poetry are discussed.
Ref. : John Keats, p. 100; William Wordsworth, p. 100.
Rept. : Reflexions on Poetry and Poetics (see no. 1050).
(The title was subsequently changed to "James Dickey. ")

841   (New Orleans) Times-Picayune (26 Mar. 1973), sec. 1, p. 29.
Buckdancer's Choice; Deliverance.
An announcement of Dickey's appearance at Tulane Uni-
versity's "Directions '73" program. Its seven other par-
ticipants are also listed.
Ref. : Richard Bach; Bach's Jonathan Livingston Seagull;
Joe Biden; Hodding Carter III; William O. Douglas; Sam
Massell; Ronald Reagan; Carl Stokes.
Photograph of Dickey by Christopher Dickey.

842   Niflis, N. Michael. "A Special Kind of Fantasy: James
Dickey on the Razor's Edge. " Southwest Review 57 (Aut.
1972), pp. 311-317.
Deliverance, p. 313; "Drinking from a Helmet, " pp. 311-
312, 314-316; "The Eye-Beaters, " p. 317; "The Fiend, "
p. 314; ["The Grove Press New American Poets (1960)"],
p. 317; "Hunting Civil War Relics at Nimblewill Creek, "
pp. 311-312; "The Owl King, " p. 316; "The Performance, "
p. 315; "The Sheep Child, " p. 316; "Slave Quarters, "

p. 315; "Springer Mountain," pp. 313-316; The Suspect in
Poetry, p. 317; ["Teaching, Writing, Reincarnations, and
Rivers"], p. 316; ["Thom Gunn"], p. 317; "The Underground
Stream," p. 316; [unidentified passages], pp. 313-314.

Topics discussed include Dickey's originality, his motifs
of initiation and rebirth, his identification with various ani-
mals, and his preoccupation with death. He is criticized
for his overuse of adverbs and for his preoccupation with
his own anatomy.

Ref.: Matthew Arnold, p. 314; King David, p. 315;
Emily Dickinson, p. 317; Dickinson's [unidentified passage],
p. 315; Robert Frost, p. 317; Lemuel Gulliver, p. 315;
Robinson Jeffers, p. 317; Jeffers' "Roan Stallion," p. 314;
John Keats' "The Eve of St. Agnes," pp. 312-313; Keats'
"The Fall of Hyperion," p. 313; Keats' [unidentified pas-
sage], p. 313; D. H. Lawrence, p. 314; Alexander Pope's
[unidentified passage], p. 315; Edwin Arlington Robinson,
p. 317; Theodore Roethke, pp. 311, 317; Mark Schorer's
[unidentified remarks], p. 317; William Shakespeare's Mid-
summer Night's Dream, p. 315; Wallace Stevens, p. 317;
Walt Whitman, p. 317; Whitman's [unidentified passages],
pp. 311, 313, 315.

843 "1966 N. B. A. Awards Ceremonies at Philharmonic Hall."
     Publishers Weekly 189 (28 Mar. 1966), pp. 28-39 [25,
     30, 34-35].
        Buckdancer's Choice, pp. 28, 34.
        Dickey's remarks on teaching, the poet's social responsi-
     bilities, and the art of poetry are wedged among descrip-
     tions of the ceremony's activities and similar topics dis-
     cussed by other N. B. A. winners. Excerpts from his
     acceptance speech are included.
        Photograph of Dickey by an unidentified person, p. 31.

844 Nolan, James W. (New Orleans) Times-Picayune (11 June
     1967), sec. 2, p. 4.
        Favorable review of Poems 1957-1967 containing 64
     words.
        Ref.: John Berryman.

845 Norman, Geoffry. "The Stuff of Poetry." Playboy 18 (May
     1971), pp. 148-149, 230, 232, 234, 236, 238, 240, 242.
        Buckdancer's Choice, p. 148; Deliverance [novel],
     pp. 230, 232, 234, 236, 238, 240, 242; Deliverance [film],
     p. 242; Deliverance [soundtrack], p. 232; ["Drums Where I
     Live"], p. 234; The Eye-Beaters, Blood, Victory, Madness,
     Buckhead and Mercy, p. 230; "Falling," p. 232; ["The
     Firebombing"], p. 148; ["On the Coosawattee: I, The
     Inundation"], p. 242; Self-Interviews, p. 230; "The Shark
     at the Window," p. 230; [Sorties], pp. 234, 236.
        A "personality piece" in which a canoeing trip taken by
     Dickey, the author, and two other men is recounted. Much
     biographical data is included.

Ref. : James Agee, pp. 148, 234; The Beatles, p. 148;
John Boorman, p. 236; Marlon Brando, p. 234; Al
Braselton, pp. 236, 238, 240, 242; William F. Buckley,
Jr. , p. 234; Al Capp, p. 230; Hart Crane, p. 234; Ben-
jamin DeMott's "The 'More Life' School and James Dickey, "
p. 234 (see no. 664); Christopher Dickey, p. 230; Kevin
Dickey, p. 236; Maxine Dickey, pp. 230, 236, 238; Tom
Dickey, p. 236; Bob Dylan, p. 148; Paul Dietzel, p. 148;
William Faulkner, pp. 148, 238; Eddie Fisher, p. 230;
Ernest Hemingway, pp. 234, 242; William James, p. 236;
Joan King, p. 242; Lewis King, pp. 236, 238, 240, 242;
Robert Lowell, p. 148; Eugene McCarthy, pp. 234, 236;
Frank McGuire, p. 232; Sam Massell, p. 238; Willie
Morris, p. 234; Morris' North Toward Home, p. 234;
The New York Times, p. 232; Friedrich Nietzsche, p. 234;
Richard M. Nixon, p. 148; Paula Putney, pp. 236, 238;
Bertrand Russell's History of Western Philosophy, p. 236;
Mike Russo, p. 232; Erich Segal's Love Story, p. 230;
The Sewanee Review, pp. 230, 242; Stephen Spender,
p. 230; Dylan Thomas, p. 242; George Wallace, p. 234;
Warner Brothers, p. 230; "Wildwood Flower" [song],
p. 242; Roger Williams, p. 242; Thomas Wolfe, pp. 148,
234; William Wordsworth, p. 148.

846 "Novel Is Burned by School Board. " New York Times (11
Nov. 1973), p. 87.
Deliverance.
Dickey's novel was one of several chosen to be investi-
gated for alleged obscene language.
Ref. : William Faulkner; Ernest Hemingway; Bruce
Severy; John Steinbeck; Kurt Vonnegut's Slaughterhouse Five.

847 Nyren, Dorothy. Library Journal 97 (1 Feb. 1972), p. 501.
Death's Baby Machine; ["Edwin Arlington Robinson"];
["The Greatest American Poet: Theodore Roethke"]; ["The
Son, the Cave, and the Burning Bush"].
Favorable review of Sorties containing 109 words.
Rept. : The "Library Journal" Book Review (see
no. 1053).

848 _____ . "Transcriptions of Interviews with Dickey. "
Library Journal 95 (15 Sept. 1970), p. 2926.
Self-Interviews.
Favorable review of Self-Interviews containing 125 words.
Ref. : Barbara and James Reiss.
Rept. : The "Library Journal" Book Review (see
no. 1052). (The title of this review was subsequently
omitted.)

849 O'Connor, John. "'Look, Ma, Another Bag of Hot Air. '"
New York Times (5 Sept. 1971), sec. 2, p. 11.
Manipulative language is investigated culminating in a
discussion of Dickey's ability to steer clear of William F.

Buckley, Jr.'s attempts of manipulation on the latter's
"Firing Line" t. v. program (see no. 1094).
    Ref.: Fred Astaire; William F. Buckley, Jr.; Dick
Cavett; "The Dick Cavett Show"; "Firing Line"; Charlton
Heston; Jack Lemmon; Richard M. Nixon; Marcel Proust;
Anthony Quinn; Susan Sontag; Orson Welles.

850 O'Neil, Paul. "The Unlikeliest Poet." Life 61 (22 July 1966),
    pp. 68-70, 72-74, 77-79.
    ["Adultery"], p. 73; ["Allen Ginsberg"], p. 78; ["Buck-
dancer's Choice"], p. 73; Buckdancer's Choice, pp. 68, 73;
Drowning with Others, p. 77; "Falling," p. 73; ["The]
Firebombing," pp. 73-74; Into the Stone and Other Poems,
p. 77; ["Robert Mezey"], p. 78; ["The] Shark at the Win-
dow," p. 77; The Suspect in Poetry, p. 78; ["The Winters
Approach"], p. 78.
    A biographical piece with Dickey's anecdotes from poetry
readings. Two photographs of Dickey as a high school and
a college athlete are included.
    Ref.: The Atlantic, p. 77; T. S. Eliot p. 78; Robert
Frost, p. 68; Allen Ginsberg, p. 70; Harper's Magazine,
p. 77; The Hudson Review, p. 77; Robert Ingersoll, p. 74;
Sandy Koufax, p. 77; Vachel Lindsay, p. 68; The New
Yorker, p. 77; Partisan Review, p. 77; Ezra Pound, p. 78;
Theodore Roethke, p. 78; [unidentified critics' remarks],
pp. 70, 79.
    Illustrated with photographs of Dickey by Declan Haun
and Steve Carmichael, pp. 68-69 and 79, and 72-73, re-
spectively.

851 Owen, Guy. Books Abroad 36 (Sum. 1962), p. 324.
    "Dover: Believing in Kings"; Drowning with Others; "The
Hospital Window"; "In the Lupanar at Pompeii"; "Inside the
River"; Into the Stone and Other Poems; "The Island";
"Listening to Foxhounds"; "The Salt Marsh"; "To His
Children in Darkness"; "A View of Fujiyama After the
War."
    The imagination, imagery, language, and personal style
of Drowning with Others are lauded.
    Ref.: James Wright.

852   . [G. O.]. Books Abroad 39 (Win. 1965), p. 94.
    "Cherrylog Road"; "Kudzu."
    Favorable review of Helmets containing 92 words.

853 "P. P. A. Authors' Press Conference." Publishers Weekly 197
    (23 Mar. 1970), pp. 27-29 [28-29].
    Deliverance, pp. 28-29; The Eye-Beaters, Blood, Vic-
tory, Madness, Buckhead and Mercy, p. 28; ["Messages:
II,] Giving a Son to the Sea," p. 29.
    Some of Dickey's remarks made at the 1970 Publishers'
Publicity Association's press conference--his views on
freedom and on Deliverance and his environmental concern--

are repeated.
Ref.: Kevin Dickey, p. 29; Publishers Weekly's [review
of Deliverance], p. 29 (see no. 869).

854 Packard, William. Spirit 35 (Nov. 1968), pp. 150-152.
["Allen Ginsberg"], p. 151; ["Anne Sexton"], p. 151;
Babel to Byzantium, p. 151; "Barnstorming for Poetry,"
p. 152; ["Conrad Aiken"], p. 152; ["David Ignatow"],
p. 152; ["E. E. Cummings"], p. 152; ["Edwin Arlington
Robinson"], p. 152; ["Howard Nemerov"], p. 152; ["J. V.
Cunningham"], p. 152; ["John Ashbery"], p. 152; ["Kenneth
Patchen"], p. 151; ["Marianne Moore"], p. 151; "The Poet
Turns on Himself," p. 151; ["Randall Jarrell"], p. 152;
["Reed Whittemore"], p. 152; ["Richard Eberhart"],
p. 152; ["Richard Wilbur"], p. 152; ["Robert Duncan"],
p. 152; ["Robert Frost"], p. 152; ["Robert Graves"],
p. 152; ["Robinson Jeffers"], p. 152; The Suspect in Poetry,
pp. 150-151; ["Theodore Roethke"], p. 151; ["William Car-
los Williams"], p. 152; ["William Stafford"], p. 152; ["Yvor
Winters"], p. 152.
Babel to Byzantium occasionally displays lack of insight,
but it is, nevertheless, mandatory reading because of its
courage and honesty.
Ref.: Robert Bly, pp. 150-151; Allen Ginsberg, p. 151;
The Sixties, p. 151.

855 Patrick, Richard. "Heroic Deliverance." Novel 4 (Win.
1971), pp. 190-192.
Deliverance, pp. 190-192.
Deliverance is criticized for unbelievable situations and
an easy use of violence although its narrative technique and
the novel as a whole are praised. The meanings of "deliv-
erance" and each chapter's themes are discussed, and plot
summary and character studies are included.
Ref.: Georges Bataille's [epigraph used in Deliverance],
p. 190; Beowulf, p. 190; John Buchan, p. 190; Natty
Bumppo, p. 192; James Fenimore Cooper's Leatherstocking
Tales, p. 190; E. M. Forster, pp. 190, 192; The Gilgamesh
Epic, p. 190; Homer's The Odyssey, p. 190; D. H.
Lawrence, p. 192; Friedrich Nietzsche, pp. 191-192;
Obadiah's [epigraph used in Deliverance], p. 192; Mark
Twain, p. 192.

856 Pennington, Bruce and Shaw, Robert B. "James Dickey."
Harvard Crimson (9 Nov. 1967), p. 2.
"Adultery"; "Falling"; "The Fiend"; "The Firebombing";
"For the Last Wolverine"; "Fox Blood"; ["Inside the River"];
"The Performance"; "The Sheep Child."
Dickey comments on his public reading at Harvard Uni-
versity in this personality piece published in its school
newspaper.
Ref.: Randolph Bourne's [unidentified remarks]; Walt
Whitman.

857   Petty, Roy. "How Art Gets Made." Chicago Tribune. Book
      World (25 April 1971), pp. 8-9.
          "Falling," p. 9; "The Fiend," p. 9; Self-Interviews,
      pp. 8-9; "Sleeping Out at Easter," p. 9.
          Dickey's verboseness and self-centered remarks in
      Self-Interviews are criticized although most of the discus-
      sion revolves around Dickey's personality and how his
      poetic self and his actual self are seemingly at opposite
      extremes.
          Ref.: Barbara and James Reiss, p. 8.
          Photograph of Dickey by an unidentified person, p. 9.

*857a Phelan, Charlotte. "Jericho Unusual Joint Effort." Houston
      (Texas) Post (4 Oct. 1974).
          *[This citation is from Authors in the News ..., vol. 1,
      p. 132.]

858   Phillips, McCandlish. "Yevtushenko to Head Bill of Bards at
      Garden Jan. 28." New York Times (17 Jan. 1972), p. 26.
          A notice of Dickey's participation in "Yevtushenko and
      Friends: Poetry in Concert."
          Ref.: Stanley Kunitz; Eugene McCarthy; Joseph Siracuse;
      Yevgeny Yevtushenko.

859   Playboy 19 (Oct. 1972), p. 34.
          Deliverance [novel]; Deliverance [film].
          Lacking the psychological investigations and the subtlety
      of the novel Deliverance, its film version succeeds primar-
      ily only as an adventure tale.
          Ref.: Ned Beatty; John Boorman; Herbert "Cowboy"
      Coward; Ronny Cox; Ernest Hemingway; McCabe and Mrs.
      Miller [film]; Billy McKinney; Burt Reynolds; Jon Voight;
      Vilmos Zsigmond.

860   Playboy 21 (Oct. 1974), p. 3.
          Deliverance; Jericho.
          Remarks concerning the success of Dickey's career and
      his "Small Visions from a Timeless Place," which was
      published in this issue.

861   "The Poet as Journalist." Time 92 (13 Dec. 1968), p. 75.
          Buckdancer's Choice; "The Eye-Beaters"; "The Fire-
      bombing"; ["A Poet Witnesses a Bold Mission"].
          Dickey's use of journalistic techniques in "The Eye-
      Beaters" and his assignment for Life, entitled "A Poet
      Witnesses a Bold Mission," are discussed. Biographical
      data is included.
          Ref.: Samuel Taylor Coleridge's "The Rime of the
      Ancient Mariner"; Life; Stephen Spender.

862   Poetry 108 (July 1966), p. 277.
          Dickey is mentioned as a recipient of the Loines Award
      for Poetry.

863   Prairie Schooner 39 (Sum. 1965), p. 175.
            The Suspect in Poetry.
            Unfavorable review of The Suspect in Poetry containing
            83 words.

864   Pritchard, William H.   "Shags and Poets."   Hudson Review
            23 (Aut. 1970), pp. 562-577 [571-572].
            "The Cancer Match," p. 571; The Eye-Beaters, Blood,
            Victory, Madness, Buckhead and Mercy, p. 571n.; "The
            Lord in the Air," p. 571; "Two Poems of Going Home,"
            p. 571; ["Two Poems of Going Home: I,] Living There,"
            p. 571; ["Two Poems of Going Home: II,] Looking for the
            Buckhead Boys," p. 572.
            The forms of the poems of The Eye-Beaters, Blood,
            Victory, Madness, Buckhead and Mercy are considered too
            lengthy and monotonous.
            Ref.:   Mark Schorer.

865   _____.   "Why Read Criticism?"   Hudson Review 21 (Aut.
            1968), pp. 585-592 [585-587, 590].
            ["Charles Olson"], p. 586; ["E. E. Cummings"],
            p. 587; ["Edwin Arlington Robinson"], p. 585; ["Herbert
            Read"], p. 586; ["Howard Nemerov"], p. 586; ["In the
            Presence of Anthologies"], p. 586; ["James Merrill"],
            pp. 586-587; ["Kenneth Patchen"], p. 585; ["Margaret
            Tongue"], p. 586; ["May Sarton"], pp. 585-586; ["Randall
            Jarrell"], p. 587; ["Richard Eberhart"], p. 586; ["Richard
            Wilbur"], p. 587; ["Robert Penn Warren"], p. 586; The
            Suspect in Poetry, p. 585; ["Theodore Roethke"], p. 586;
            ["Thom Gunn"], p. 586; ["William Jay Smith"], p. 586;
            ["Yvor Winters"], p. 586.
            Dickey is criticized for collecting review notes out of
            context, recurrent indiscriminant praise, and lacking in
            humor in Babel to Byzantium.   "Randall Jarrell" is viewed
            favorably because of its ambivalence.
            Ref.:   Brother Antoninus, p. 590; Robert Bly, p. 586;
            Gerard Manley Hopkins, p. 586; Randall Jarrell, p. 587;
            John Keats, p. 586; Theodore Roethke, p. 587; Mark
            Schorer, pp. 585, 590; James Wright, p. 586.

866   Pryce-Jones, Alan.   "An Exception to the Rule on Poets."
            (New York) World Journal Tribune (27 April 1967), p. 29.
            "Angina."
            Favorable review of Poems 1957-1967 containing 154
            words.

867   Publishers Weekly 191 (20 Feb. 1967), p. 142.
            Buckdancer's Choice; Drowning with Others; "Falling"
            [sec. of Poems 1957-1967]; Helmets; Into the Stone and
            Other Poems.
            Favorable review of Poems 1957-1967 containing 209
            words.
            Ref.:   The New Yorker.

868 Publishers Weekly 193 (1 Apr. 1968), p. 35.
       Favorable review of Babel to Byzantium containing 144
     words.

869 Publishers Weekly 197 (9 Feb. 1970), p. 75.
       Deliverance.
       Favorable review of Deliverance containing 187 words.

870 Publishers Weekly 206 (5 Aug. 1974), p. 57.
       Mixed review of Jericho containing 168 words.
       Ref.: Hubert Shuptrine; Southern Living; Andrew Wyeth.

871 Putney, Paula G. "Wilderness World of Deliverance."
       Contempora 1 (May-Aug. 1971), pp. 30-31.
       Deliverance [novel], pp. 30-31; Deliverance [film], p. 30.
       Impressions of the locale where Deliverance was filmed
     emphasize how the crew contended with the wilderness.
       Ref.: John Boorman, pp. 30-31; Burt Reynolds, p. 30;
     Jon Voight, p. 30.
       Illustrated with stills, p. 30, and with photographs of
     Boorman and Voight on location, p. 31.

872 Raymont, Henry. "102 Vie for 10 National Book Awards."
       New York Times (27 March 1972), p. 42.
       Sorties.
       Dickey is listed as a N.B.A. nominee.
       Photograph of Dickey by Sam Falk.

873 _____. "3 Book Clubs Pick Paul Horgan Novel." New
       York Times (31 July 1970), p. 12.
       Deliverance.
       Dickey's financial success with Deliverance receives
     mention.
       Photograph of Dickey by an unidentified person.

874 _____. "Writers Appeal for Soviet Jews." New York
       Times (3 Aug. 1969), p. 6.
       Dickey is listed with other authors who signed a petition
     asking Soviet writers to help restore Jewish cultural insti-
     tutions in the U.S.S.R.

875 Rice, Susan. "What's New at the Bijou?" Media and Methods
       9 (Nov. 1972), pp. 8, 10, 12 [8].
       Mixed review of the film version of Deliverance con-
     taining 118 words.
       Ref.: Ned Beatty; John Boorman; Ronny Cox; Jon Voight.

876 Ricks, Christopher. "Man Hunt." New York Review of Books
       14 (23 Apr. 1970), pp. 37-41 [40].
       Deliverance.
       Criticism is aimed at the characters, dialog, and
     philosophical remarks in Deliverance. Its plot and descrip-
     tions, however, are commented upon favorably.

Ref. : [remarks on the dust jacket of Deliverance],
p. 40; D. H. Lawrence, p. 40; J. I. M. Stewart, p. 40.

877 _____ . "Spotting Syllabics." New Statesman 67 (1 May
1964), pp. 684-685 [685].
["Approaching Prayer"]; ["Cherrylog Road"]; Helmets;
"Kudzu. "
Dickey's metaphysical verse in Helmets is pretentious
although its nostalgic poems are of good caliber. His use
of rhythm is favorably mentioned.

878 Ripp, Judith. Parents' Magazine and Better Family Living 47
(Sept. 1972), p. 20.
Favorable review of the film version of Deliverance
containing 124 words.
Ref. : John Boorman; Burt Reynolds; Jon Voight.

879 Robbins, Fred Walker. Abstract of "The Poetry of James
Dickey, 1951-1967. " Dissertation Abstracts International;
A: The Humanities and Social Sciences 32 (May 1972),
p. 6450.
In the author's dissertation (see no. 1126), the major
themes of Dickey's works, his narrative technique, and his
poetry's metaphysical and emotional traits are investigated.
Ref. : Walt Whitman.

880 Roberts, Carey. "How James Dickey Views Poetry." Atlanta
Journal and the Atlanta Constitution (17 Apr. 1966),
pp. 16, 18.
Buckdancer's Choice, p. 18; Drowning with Others,
p. 18; "The Firebombing, " p. 18; Helmets, p. 18; Into the
Stone and Other Poems, p. 18; "On the Coosawattee, "
p. 16; Two Poems of the Air, p. 18; [unidentified remark],
p. 16.
Southern, personal, and mystical traits of Dickey's
poetry are mentioned. His public poetry readings, the
origin of his writing career, and the subject matter of his
verse are briefly commented upon. Much biographical data
is included.
Ref. : Conrad Aiken, p. 16.
Photograph of Dickey by an unidentified person, p. 16.

881 Robertson, Nan. "New National Poetry Consultant Can Also
Talk a Nonstop Prose. " New York Times (10 Sept. 1966),
sec. 1, p. 11.
Into the Stone and Other Poems.
Coverage of Dickey's first news conference as Library
of Congress poetry consultant gives Dickey's remarks on
poetry and other writers.
Ref. : Norman Mailer; Philip Rahv; Theodore Roethke;
Dylan Thomas.
Photograph of Dickey by an unidentified person.

882   Robinson, Hubell. "Deliverance." Films in Review 23 (Oct.
      1972), pp. 506-507.
            Deliverance [film], pp. 506-507.
            Plot of the film version of Deliverance and the ability
      of its actors are emphasized.
            Ref.: Ned Beatty, p. 506; John Boorman, p. 507;
      Ronny Cox, pp. 506-507; Burt Reynolds, pp. 506-507; Jon
      Voight, p. 506; Vilmos Zsigmond, p. 507.

883   Robinson, James K. "From Criticism to Historicism."
      Southern Review, n. s. 9 (July 1973), pp. 692-709 [698-700].
            Babel to Byzantium, pp. 698-699; ["Christopher Smart:]
      'A Song to David'", p. 699; ["Donald F. Drummond"],
      p. 699; ["Edwin Arlington Robinson"], pp. 699-700;
      ["Francis Thompson:] 'The Hound of Heaven'", p. 699;
      ["Gerard Manley Hopkins:] 'The Wreck of the Deutschland'",
      p. 699; ["In the Presence of Anthologies"], p. 699; ["J. V.
      Cunningham"], p. 699; ["Matthew Arnold:] 'Dover Beach'",
      p. 699; ["Robert Frost"], p. 699; ["Theodore Roethke"],
      p. 699; ["Vernon Watkins"], p. 699; ["W. S. Graham"],
      p. 699; ["W. S. Merwin"], p. 699; ["William Carlos Wil-
      liams"], p. 699; ["William Carlos Williams:] 'The Yachts'",
      p. 699; ["William Jay Smith"], p. 699; ["William Stafford"],
      p. 699; ["Winfield Townley Scott"], p. 699; ["Yvor Winters"],
      p. 699.
            Babel to Byzantium is likened to a literary survey, and
      its anti-academic theme is noted.
            Ref.: Wallace L. Anderson's Edwin Arlington Robinson:
      An Introduction, p. 699.

884   _____. "Terror Lumped and Split: Contemporary British
      and American Poets." Southern Review, n. s. 6 (Jan.
      1970), pp. 216-228 [220-221].
            "The Common Grave," p. 221; "The Escape," p. 221;
      "The Firebombing," pp. 220-221.
            Dickey's guilt, extreme awareness, and lack of style and
      tone in Buckdancer's Choice are discussed.
            Ref.: Donald Davie, pp. 220-221; Richard Eberhart,
      pp. 220-221; Eberhart's "Dam Neck, Virginia," p. 220;
      Eberhart's "The Fury of Aerial Bombardment," p. 220;
      Günter Eich's [epigraph used in "The Firebombing"],
      p. 220; William Golding's The Lord of the Flies, p. 220;
      Philip Larkin, pp. 220-221.

885   Rohr, Maria Rita. Criticism 7 (Fall 1965), pp. 392-393.
            ["Allen Ginsberg"], p. 392; ["E. E. Cummings"],
      p. 392; ["The Grove Press New American Poets (1960)"],
      p. 392; ["Hayden Carruth"], p. 393; ["Howard Nemerov"],
      pp. 392-393; ["John Logan"], p. 392; ["Kenneth Patchen"],
      pp. 392-393; ["New Poets of England and America I (1957)"],
      p. 392; ["Randall Jarrell"], p. 392-393; "The Second Birth,"
      p. 392; "The Suspect in Poetry," p. 392; The Suspect in
      Poetry, pp. 392-393; ["Theodore Roethke"], pp. 392-393;

["Thom Gunn"], p. 392; ["William Stafford"], p. 393; ["The Winters Approach"], p. 393.

Problems of The Suspect in Poetry are identified as its lack of unity and its avoidance of criteria. Dickey's humor and command of the language are noted, and the overall theme is mentioned.

886 Rosenthal, Lucy. "A Novel of Man, the Forest, Death and Heroism." Chicago Tribune. Book Week (15 Mar. 1970), sec. 9, pp. 1, 3.

Deliverance [novel], pp. 1, 3; [Deliverance] [film], p. 3.
The two major characters of Deliverance are contrasted, and its narrative technique is mentioned. Its cinematic quality is noted.
Ref.: Ernest Hemingway, p. 3.

887 Ross, Alan. London Magazine, n. s. 10 (September 1970), pp. 104-105.

Deliverance, p. 105.
Narrative element, dialog and characterization of Dickey's novel Deliverance are discussed, and a plot summary is included.
Ref.: Louis Aragon, p. 104; James Barrie, p. 105; Barrie's The Admirable Crichton, p. 105; Lawrence Durrell, p. 104; Embiricos, p. 104; William Golding's The Lord of the Flies, p. 105; Günter Grass, p. 104; Thomas Hardy, p. 104; Ernest Jünger's On the Marble Cliffs, p. 105; D. H. Lawrence, p. 104; William Meredith, p. 104; Pier Paolo Pasolini, p. 104; Steven Spender, p. 104; Spender's The Backward Son, p. 104; Jules Supervielle, p. 104; Bruno Traven's Treasure of the Sierra Madre, p. 105; Rex Warner, p. 104.

888 "Rustic and Urbane." Times Literary Supplement (20 Aug. 1964), p. 748.

["Cherrylog Road"]; ["The Dusk of Horses"]; ["On the Coosawattee: I, By Canoe through the Fir Forest"]; ["On the Coosawattee: III, The Inundation"]; [unidentified passages].

Dickey falters while ambitiously trying to fulfill the promises of his personas' situations in Helmets. His poetry's musical qualities while strong do not counterbalance their lack of humor and precision or their trite metaphysical leanings.
Ref.: The New Yorker; John Updike.

889 Samuels, Charles Thomas. "How Not to Film a Novel." American Scholar 42 (Win. 1972-1973), pp. 148-150, 152, 154 [150, 152, 154].

Deliverance [novel], pp. 150, 152; Deliverance [film], pp. 150, 154.
Failures of the film adaptation of Deliverance are listed as: unbelievable plot, avoidance of the novel's central

meaning which is linked to the rape scene, faulty dialog, ambiguities, and the alteration of the original ending.

Ref.: Ned Beatty, p. 152; John Boorman, pp. 152, 154; Robert Bresson, p. 154; Anton Chekhov's "The Lady with the Dog", p. 154; Joseph Conrad's An Outcast of the Island, p. 154; Stephen Farber's "Deliverance: How It Delivers," p. 154 (see no. 685); Fat City [film], pp. 150, 154; Peter George's Red Alert [film], p. 154; Joseph Heifetz, p. 154; John Huston, p. 154; Stanley Kubrick's Dr. Strangelove [film], p. 154; Carol Reed, p. 154; Burt Reynolds, p. 152; Charles Samuels' "What Hath Dickey Delivered?," p. 152 (see no. 890); François Truffaut, p. 154; Jon Voight, p. 152.

890   _____. "What Hath Dickey Delivered?" New Republic 162 (18 Apr. 1970), pp. 23-26.

Deliverance, pp. 23-26; "Encounter in the Cage Country," p. 24; "On the Coosawattee," p. 24; "Springer Mountain," p. 24.

Deliverance is investigated with discussion of its homosexuality, its content, its dream-like aspects, and the significance of two of its characters' names. The relationship of the introductory epigraphs to its plot and theme and the novel's origins appearing in "On the Coosawattee" are identified.

Ref.: Georges Bataille's [epigraph used in Deliverance], p. 24; Joseph Conrad's "Heart of Darkness," p. 24; Norman Mailer's Why Are We in Vietnam?, p. 24; Obadiah's [epigraph used in Deliverance], p. 24; Mark Twain's "The Notorious Jumping Frog of Calaveras County," p. 24; [unidentified passage from an interview], p. 24.

*891   Sarris, Andrew. Village Voice (1972).

A review of the film version of Deliverance.

*[This citation is from Filmfacts (see no. 660).]

892   Scarbrough, George. "One Flew East, One Flew West, One Flew Over the Cuckoo's Nest." Sewanee Review 73 (Jan. - Mar. 1965), pp. 138-150 [139-141].

["The Firebombing"], p. 140; ["Reincarnation (II)"], p. 141; Two Poems of the Air, p. 141.

Parallels are drawn between the poems of Two Poems of the Air, their flying motif is identified, and the use of carolingian script is discussed.

Ref.: Hart Crane's "The Bridge," p. 141; Ernest Hemingway, p. 140; Icarus, p. 140; Prometheus, p. 140; Walt Whitman, p. 139.

893   Schevill, James. "Experiences in Image, Sound, and Rhythm." Saturday Review 45 (15 May 1962), pp. 24-27 [24].

Drowning with Others; "Dover: Believing in Kings"; ["In the Tree House at Night"]; "The Owl King."

Drowning with Others is unique due to the way Dickey

handles animals and nature and because of the poems' tones. Its recurrent images are criticized, and his mysticism is occasionally superficial.

894 Schickel, Richard. "White Water, Black Doings. " Life 73 (18 Aug. 1972), p. 8.
    Deliverance [novel]; [Deliverance] [film].
    The positive qualities of Dickey's novel Deliverance are lost in its film version.   Plot summary and thematic inter- pretation are given.
    Ref. : John Boorman; Boorman's Hell in the Pacific [film]; Boorman's Point Blank [film]; Ernest Hemingway; Burt Reynolds; Jon Voight.
    Illustrated with a still.
    Rept. : Film 72/73 (see no. 1068).

895 Schlueter, Paul. "Elemental Conflict. "   Christian Century 87 (17 June 1970), pp. 765-766.
    Buckdancer's Choice, p. 765; Deliverance, pp. 765-766.
    Plot summary of Deliverance introduces a discussion of the novel's suspense and the psychology of survival.
    Ref. : William Faulkner, p. 765; Ernest Hemingway, p. 765; Herman Melville's Moby Dick, p. 765; Flannery O'Connor, p. 765.

896 Segura, Chris. "Novelist Dickey Shares Spotlight with Journalist. " (New Orleans) Times-Picayune (31 Mar. 1973), sec. 1, p. 21.
    Deliverance [novel]; Deliverance [film].
    At a press conference held before his appearance at Tulane University's "Directions '73" program, Dickey dis- cussed the South as a stronghold of individuality.   The origin of his nickname, "The Pheasant, " is reported.
    Ref. : Hodding Carter III; "Dueling Banjos" [song] (see no. 1240); Bob Hope; Burt Reynolds.
    Photograph of Dickey with Hodding Carter III by William F. Haber.

897 Seventeen 31 (Oct. 1972), p. 54.
    [Deliverance] [novel].
    Mixed review of the film version of Deliverance con- taining 56 words.
    Ref. : Burt Reynolds; Jon Voight.

898 Shaw, Robert B. "Poets in Midstream. " Poetry 118 (July 1971), pp. 228-233 [230].
    Buckdancer's Choice; "The Cancer Match"; "Diabetes"; "The Eye-Beaters"; The Eye-Beaters, Blood, Victory, Madness, Buckhead and Mercy; "The Lord in the Air"; "Madness"; "Messages"; "Pine"; ["Two Poems of Going Home: II,] Looking for the Buckhead Boys"; "Victory. "
    Dickey's Southern heritage is evident in much of The Eye-Beaters, Blood, Victory, Madness, Buckhead and

Mercy because of their tone, length, and internal spacing.
Ref. : Gerard Manley Hopkins; Archibald MacLeish;
John Simon's [remarks on the dust jacket of The Eye-
Beaters, Blood, Victory, Madness, Buckhead and Mercy].
Exc. : Contemporary Literary Criticism (see no. 1063).

899 Shepherd, Allen. "Counter-Monster Comes Home: The Last
Chapter of Dickey's Deliverance." Notes on Contemporary
Literature 3 (Mar. 1973), pp. 8-12.
"After," pp. 8-9; Deliverance, pp. 8-11.
The last chapter of Deliverance is investigated for the
key to the narrator's transformation.
Ref. : André Bleikasten's "Anatomie d'un Bestseller: a
propos de Deliverance," p. 12n. (see no. 1144); Walter
Clemons' "James Dickey, Novelist," pp. 8, 12n. (see
no. 637); Benjamin DeMott's "The 'More Life' School and
James Dickey," p. 12n. (see no. 664); Ernest Hemingway's
"The Short Happy Life of Francis Macomber," p. 9;
Hemingway's [unidentified work], p. 10; William Heyen's
"A Conversation with James Dickey," pp. 8, 12n. (see
no. 1105); L. E. Sissman's "Poet into Novelist," p. 8
(see no. 907).

*900 Show 2 (Nov. 1972), p. 53.
A review of the film version of Deliverance.
*[This citation is from Multi Media Reviews Index, 1972,
p. 59.]

901 Silverstein, Norman. "James Dickey's Muscular Eschatology."
Salmagundi, no. 22-23 (Spr. -Sum. 1973), pp. 258-268.
["Autumn"], p. 264; Buckdancer's Choice, p. 258; Death's
Baby Machine, p. 259; Deliverance, pp. 258, 266; ["Diabetes:
II, Under Buzzards"], p. 262; Drowning with Others,
pp. 258, 263; ["Drowning with Others"], p. 264; The Eye-
Beaters, Blood, Victory, Madness, Buckhead and Mercy,
pp. 258, 267; "Falling" [sec. of Poems 1957-1967], p. 265;
"The Heaven of Animals," p. 263; Helmets, pp. 258, 263;
["Helmets"], p. 263; "In the Pocket," pp. 267-268; "Inside
the River," p. 263; ["Into the Stone"], p. 259; Into the Stone
and Other Poems, p. 258; ["The Lifeguard"], p. 263;
"Mercy," p. 262; ["Messages: II,] Giving a Son to the
Sea," p. 262; ["Metaphor as Pure Adventure"], p. 259;
Poems 1957-1967, pp. 258, 265; "Power and Light,"
p. 266; ["The Rib"], p. 263; Self-Interviews, p. 258;
Sorties, pp. 258, 258n. , 259, 261, 267; ["Spinning the
Crystal Ball"], p. 261; ["The Summons"], p. 262; "Sun,"
pp. 264-266; ["Teaching, Writing, Reincarnations, and
Rivers"], pp. 260, 262-264; ["To His Children in Dark-
ness"], p. 264; Two Poems of the Air, p. 258; [unidenti-
fied remarks], pp. 261, 263, 266-267.
A survey of Dickey's works emphasizing suburban life's
and Southern Agrarians' influences on his art and especially
on its metaphysical qualities. Biographical data is inter-

spersed throughout, and a prediction of Dickey's movement into prose concludes.

Ref.: Thomas Aquinas, p. 264; Bible, p. 264; Robert Bly, p. 267; Albert Camus, p. 267; Walt Disney's The African Lion [film], p. 264; John Donne, p. 263; T. S. Eliot, pp. 260, 264, 267-268; Fergus mac Erc's [unidentified poem], p. 264; William Faulkner's The Sound and the Fury, p. 259; Eddie Fisher's "Coke Time" [television program], p. 261; Francesca, p. 266; the Fugitives, pp. 259-260; Thomas Hardy, p. 258; Ernest Hemingway, p. 267; Gerard Manley Hopkins, p. 264; I'll Take My Stand, p. 260; Randall Jarrell, p. 261; Richard Jefferies, p. 267; Robert Lowell, pp. 267-268; Lowell's "Skunk Hour," p. 267; Sylvia Plath, pp. 267-268; Plath's "Daddy," p. 267; Ezra Pound, pp. 267-268; John Crowe Ransom, pp. 260-261, 264; Theodore Roethke, pp. 267-268; Roethke's "The Lost Son," p. 267; the Romantics, p. 260; Monroe K. Spears, p. 259; Mrs. Monroe K. Spears, p. 259; William Stafford, p. 261; Allen Tate, pp. 261-262, 264; Tate's "Ode to the Confederate Dead," p. 262; the Victorians, p. 260; Robert Penn Warren, p. 260; James Wright, p. 267; William Butler Yeats, p. 264.

Rept.: Contemporary Poetry in America (see no. 1070).

902   . "Two Modes of Despair." Spirit 29 (Sept. 1962), pp. 122-124.

["Autumn"], p. 123; Drowning with Others, p. 122; "The Heaven of Animals," p. 123; "Inside the River," p. 122; ["The Lifeguard"], p. 122; ["The Rib"], p. 122; ["The Summons"], p. 122; ["To His Children in Darkness"], p. 123.

Discussion of Drowning with Others centers on the mysticism which it contains. The relationship of its mysticism to the images of water, hunting, and sons is emphasized.

Ref.: John Dunne, p. 122; T. S. Eliot, p. 123; Horace Gregory, p. 123.

903 Simon, John. Commonweal 87 (1 Dec. 1967), p. 315.
Favorable review of Poems 1957-1967 containing 118 words.

904   . "More Brass than Enduring." Hudson Review 15 (Aug. 1962), pp. 455-468 [466-467].

["Autumn"], p. 466; "A Birth," p. 466; "A Dog Sleeping on My Feet," p. 466; "The Dream Flood," p. 466; Drowning with Others, p. 466; "The Heaven of Animals," p. 466; Into the Stone and Other Poems, p. 466; ["The Magus"], p. 466; "The Movement of Fish," p. 466; ["The Owl King: II, The Blind Child's Story"], p. 466; "The Scratch," p. 466; "A Screened Porch in the Country," p. 466; ["A View of Fujiyama After the War"], p. 466.

The long forms, themes, metrics, and vision of Drown-

ing with Others are discussed.   Major themes are listed.
Exc. :   A Library of Literary Criticism (see no. 1005).

905   Simpson, Louis.   "New Books of Poems. "   Harper's Magazine
235 (Aug. 1967), pp. 89-91 [90].
"Cherrylog Road"; "Kudzu"; "Listening to Foxhounds";
"The Owl King"; Poems 1957-1967; "The Sheep Child";
"Slave Quarters. "
Dickey's ability in Poems 1957-1967 to enhance the
reader's experience and his narrative and metamorphosis
techniques are discussed.   His jumps from one image to
another is questioned, and false emotions are criticized.
Ref. :   Robert Creeley; Theodore Roethke; Thomas Wolfe.

906   Siskel, Gene.   "Deliverance. "   Chicago Tribune (5 Oct. 1972),
sec. 2, p. 4.
[Deliverance] [novel]; Deliverance [film].
Praise for the photography and the action in the film
version of Deliverance is interspersed throughout this plot
synopsis.   Attempts at philosophical dialog, done well in
the novel, are clumsy in this medium.   Credits are in-
cluded.
Ref. :   Ned Beatty; John Boorman; Ronny Cox; McCabe
and Mrs. Miller [film]; Burt Reynolds; Jon Voight; Vilmos
Zsigmond.
Illustrated with a still and with a photograph of John
Boorman by an unidentified person.

907   Sissman, L. E.   "Poet into Novelist. "   New Yorker 46 (2 May
1970), pp. 123-126.
Deliverance, p. 123; "May Day Sermon to the Women of
Gilmer County, Georgia, by a Woman Preacher Leaving the
Baptist Church, " p. 123.
Plot summary takes up much of this discussion of
Deliverance although comments on Dickey's style are in-
cluded.   Portions of it are criticized as being too fabricated,
slow, and rambling.
Ref. :   James Agee's A Death in the Family, p. 123;
John Buchan's The Thirty-Nine Steps, p. 123; Henri-Georges
Clouzot's The Wages of Fear [film], p. 123; Geoffrey House-
hold's Rogue Male, pp. 123-124; C. Day Lewis' Nicholas
Blake series, p. 123; George Orwell's The English People,
p. 125.

908   Skelton, Robin.   "The Verge of Greatness. "   Malahat Review,
no. 4 (Oct. 1967), pp. 119-124.
"Adultery, " pp. 122-123; [Buckdancer's Choice], p. 119;
[Drowning with Others], p. 119; "Falling, " p. 121; "The
Firebombing, " pp. 121-122; [Helmets], p. 119; [Into the
Stone and Other Poems], p. 119; "May Day Sermon to the
Women of Gilmer County, Georgia, by a Woman Preacher
Leaving the Baptist Church, " p. 123; "Slave Quarters, "
p. 121; "Walking on Water, " p. 120.

Prefaced by comments on Dickey's public image and its
effects on his critics, this discussion of Poems 1957-1967
centers on the morality expressed in his poems.
   Ref.: Robert Bly's "The Collapse of James Dickey,"
p. 121 (see no. 587); T. S. Eliot, p. 119; Paul O'Neil's
"The Unlikeliest Poet," p. 119 (see no. 850); Theodore
Roethke, p. 119; Edith Sitwell, p. 119; Walt Whitman,
p. 123; William Butler Yeats, p. 119.

909 Skinner, Olivia. "A Muscular Exponent of Poetry." St. Louis
Post-Dispatch (15 Nov. 1967), sec. F, p. 2.
   ["Allen Ginsberg"]; "The Bee"; Buckdancer's Choice;
"Cherrylog Road"; Drowning with Others; "Encounter in the
Cage Country"; Helmets; Into the Stone and Other Poems;
"Sheep Child"; The Suspect in Poetry.
   Dickey ruminates about his origins and about his life as
a freshman English instructor, a commercial writer, and a
musician. His introductions for several poems read in
public prior to this interview are included. Biographical
tidbits abound.
   Ref.: "Buckdancer's Choice" [song]; R. G. Collingwood;
Eddie Fisher; Allen Ginsberg; "The Muskrat Ramble" [song];
"Pistol Packing Momma" [song]; Plato; "St. Louis Tickle"
[song]; William Shakespeare; Paul Valéry.
   Photograph of Dickey by an unidentified person.

910 "Slaughterhouse Five Burned and Banned." School Library
Journal. In Library Journal 99 (15 Jan. 1974), p. 167.
   Deliverance.
   Mention is given to the Drake, N. D. school board's
examination of Deliverance for its alleged classroom un-
suitability.
   Ref.: William Faulkner; Ernest Hemingway; John
Steinbeck; Kurt Vonnegut, Jr.'s Slaughterhouse Five.

911 Smith, Liz. Cosmopolitan 173 (Oct. 1972), p. 12.
   Deliverance [novel]; Deliverance [film].
   The actors' ability and the tension in the film Deliver-
ance are lauded.
   Ref.: Ned Beatty; John Boorman; Ronny Cox; Clark
Gable; Midnight Cowboy [film]; Burt Reynolds; Jon Voight.

911a Smith, Raymond. "Nemerov and Nature: 'The Stillness in
Moving Things.'" Southern Review 10 (Jan. 1974),
pp. 153-169 [160].
   Poems 1957-1967; "Winter Trout."
   Dickey's and Nemerov's poems in which the image of a
trout is central are briefly compared.
   Ref.: Howard Nemerov's "The Sanctuary."

912 _____. "The Poetic Faith of James Dickey." Modern
Poetry Studies 2 (1972), pp. 259-272.
   "Approaching Prayer," p. 264; Deliverance, pp. 264-265;

["Drowning with Others"], pp. 260, 263, 265; "The Eye-Beaters," pp. 266, 269-272; The Eye-Beaters, Blood, Victory, Madness, Buckhead and Mercy, pp. 269, 272; "The Heaven of Animals," pp. 260-261; "In the Tree House at Night," p. 267; Into the Stone and Other Poems, p. 272; "The Owl King," pp. 265, 268, 272; "The Owl King [: III, The Blind Child's Story]," pp. 266-268; "The Owl King [: I, The Call]," p. 265; "The Owl King [: II, The Owl King]," pp. 265-266; "Reincarnation (II)," p. 272; "Springer Mountain," pp. 263, 268, 271; ["Teaching, Writing, Reincarnations, and Rivers"], pp. 259, 261; "Trees and Cattle," pp. 261-263; "The Vegetable King," p. 268.

Central to Dickey's ouevre is his ability to believe and the many facets of nature. Their relationship is the skeleton of his mythology.

Ref.: Joseph Campbell, p. 268; Campbell's "Man and Myth," pp. 268-269; Geoffrey Norman's "The Stuff of Poetry," p. 264 (see no. 845); Theodore Roethke, p. 266; Walt Whitman, p. 259.

913 "Soft Finger." Times Literary Supplement (29 Oct. 1964), p. 980.

["Charles Olson"]; ["The Grove Press New American Poets (1960)"]; ["Howard Nemerov"]; ["Kenneth Patchen"]; ["New Poets of England and America I (1957)"]; ["The Suspect in Poetry"]; ["Theodore Roethke"]; ["Thom Gunn"]; ["The Winters Approach"].

Inconsistency, indecision, and boastfulness characterize The Suspect in Poetry.

914 Somers, Florence. Redbook 139 (Oct. 1972), p. 19. Deliverance [film].

Favorable review of the film version of Deliverance containing 75 words.

Ref.: Ned Beatty; Burt Reynolds; Jon Voight.

915 Spector, Robert D. "A Way to Say What a Man Can See." Saturday Review 48 (13 Feb. 1965), pp. 46-48.

["The Grove Press New American Poets (1960)"], p. 46; ["Ned O'Gorman"], p. 46; ["Robert Mezey"], p. 46; ["The Suspect in Poetry"], p. 46; The Suspect in Poetry, p. 46; ["Thom Gunn"], p. 46; ["The Winters Approach: II, Ellen Kay"], p. 46.

Dickey's theories as expressed in The Suspect in Poetry are employed as a springboard for the critic's comments on several poets which he, as well as Dickey, criticizes.

916 Spender, Stephen. "On English and American Poetry." Saturday Review 49 (23 Apr. 1966), pp. 19-20, 52 [52].

Slight mention is given to Dickey's remark that American poets should write in accordance to the sound of their work and not to the way it looks on the page.

917 Squires, Radcliffe. "James Dickey and Others." <u>Michigan
     Quarterly Review</u> 6 (Oct. 1967), pp. 296-298 [297-298].
         <u>Buckdancer's Choice</u>, p. 297.
         Rhythm, images, and narrative techniques in <u>Buckdancer's
     Choice</u> are discussed.
         Ref.: Robert Lowell, p. 298.

918 Stafford, Samuel. "Soft Drinks, Potato Chips, and a 'Hunger
     for Language.'" <u>Washington</u> (D. C.) <u>Daily News</u> (9 Nov.
     1965), p. 5.
         "Bums, on Waking"; ["The Game"]; [unidentified passage].
         A personality piece with biographical data and remarks
     concerning Dickey's second public poetry reading at the
     Library of Congress.
         Illustrated with a photograph of Dickey by an unidentified
     person.

919 Stafford, William. "Supporting a Reputation." <u>Chicago Trib-
     une.</u> <u>Books Today</u> (14 May 1967), p. 9.
         "Cherrylog Road"; "The Firebombing"; "A Folk Singer of
     the Thirties"; "Into the Stone"; "The Owl King"; "The
     Scarred Girl."
         Dickey's imagination as displayed in <u>Poems 1957-1967</u>
     distinguishes him from other poets.
         Photograph of Dickey by an unidentified person.

920 Stanford, Ann. "Poet of Palpitating Hearth." <u>Los Angeles
     Times.</u> <u>Calendar Magazine</u> (23 Apr. 1967), p. 28.
         "In the Mountain Tent"; "The Salt Marsh."
         Favorable review of <u>Poems 1957-1967</u> containing 201
     words.

921 Stepanchev, Stephen. "Enemy of the Unreal." <u>New Leader</u> 51
     (20 May 1968), pp. 33-35.
         ["Allen Ginsberg"], p. 34; ["Anne Sexton"], p. 34; <u>Babel
     to Byzantium</u>, p. 33; ["Barnstorming for Poetry"], p. 34;
     ["Charles Olson"], pp. 34-35; ["Christopher Smart: 'A
     Song to David'"], p. 34; ["E. E. Cummings"], p. 34;
     ["Edwin Arlington Robinson"], p. 34; ["Francis Thompson:
     'The Hound of Heaven'"], p. 34; ["Gene Derwood"], p. 34;
     ["Gerard Manley Hopkins: 'The Wreck of the Deutschland'"],
     p. 34; ["Herbert Reed"], p. 34; ["In the Presence of
     Anthologies"], p. 34; ["James Merrill"], p. 34; ["John
     Ashbery"], pp. 34-35; ["John Berryman"], p. 34; ["Kather-
     ine Hoskins"], p. 34; ["Kenneth Burke"], p. 34; ["Louis
     Simpson"], p. 34; ["Matthew Arnold: 'Dover Beach'"],
     p. 34; ["Notes on the Decline of Outrage"], p. 34; ["The
     Poet Turns on Himself"], p. 34; ["Randall Jarrell"], p. 34;
     ["Reed Whittemore"], p. 34; ["Richard Wilbur"], p. 34;
     ["Robert Duncan"], pp. 34-35; ["Robert Frost"], p. 34;
     ["Samuel French Morse"], p. 34; <u>The Suspect in Poetry</u>,
     p. 33; ["Ted Hughes"], p. 34; ["Theodore Roethke"], p. 34;
     ["Thom Gunn"], p. 34; [" W. S. Merwin"], p. 34; ["William

Carlos Williams: 'The Yachts'"], p. 34; ["William Stafford"], p. 34.

Noting the cohesion and extensive range of Babel to Byzantium, summaries of many of its essays and reviews are given.   Discussion of Dickey's critical method is included.

Ref. :   Thomas Clark, p. 35; Kenneth Koch, p. 35; Frank O'Hara, p. 35; Poetry, p. 33; Ezra Pound, p. 35; James Schuyler, p. 35; The Sewanee Review, p. 33; The Virginia Quarterly Review, p. 33; William Carlos Williams, p. 35.

922 Stephenson, William. "Deliverance from What?" Georgia Review 28 (Spr. 1974), pp. 114-120.

Deliverance, pp. 114-116, 118-120.

Drew's role in the theme of survival in Deliverance and his influence on Ed are investigated.

Ref. :   Ahab, pp. 116, 119; Natty Bumppo, p. 120; Robert Frost, p. 120; Ernest Hemingway, p. 115; Ishmael, p. 119; D. H. Lawrence, p. 117; Lawrence's Studies in Classical American Literature, p. 114; Orpheus, pp. 116-117, 120; Percy Bysshe Shelley, p. 120; George Starbuck, p. 119.

923 Stevens, William K. "Dakota Town Dumfounded at Criticism of Book Burning by Order of the School Board. " New York Times (16 Nov. 1973), p. 27.

Deliverance.

Dickey's novel is reported being investigated for its unsuitability for high school classroom use.   Vonnegut's novel was destroyed.

Ref. :   William Faulkner; Ernest Hemingway; John Steinbeck; Kurt Vonnegut; Vonnegut's Slaughterhouse Five.

924 Stone, Robert. "Adrift in Our Ancestral Jungle. " Life 68 (27 Mar. 1970), p. 10.

Deliverance.

The theme of Deliverance is investigated, and its plot is summarized.   Mention is given to the irony of its title. Photograph of Dickey by David R. Underwood.

925 Strange, William C. "To Dream, to Remember: James Dickey's Buckdancer's Choice. " Northwest Review 7 (Fall-Win. 1965-1966), pp. 33-42.

["Armor"], p. 42; "Buckdancer's Choice," pp. 39-42; Buckdancer's Choice, pp. 33-34, 39, 42; "The Celebration," pp. 35-39, 41; "Cherrylog Road, " p. 35; "The Common Grave, " p. 34; "A Dog Sleeping on My Feet, " p. 34; ["The Dream Flood"], p. 42; Drowning with Others, p. 34; "Faces Seen Once, " pp. 34, 39; "Fathers and Sons, " p. 34; "The Fiend, " pp. 35, 42; "The Firebombing, " pp. 34, 42; "Fox Blood, " p. 34; "Gamecock, " p. 34; Helmets, p. 35; "Listening to Foxhounds, " p. 34; ["Mangham"], p. 39;

"Pursuit from Under," p. 34; "Reincarnation [(I)]," p. 34;
"Sled Burial, Dream Ceremony," p. 34; "Them, Crying,"
p. 34; "The War Wound," p. 34.

The poems of Buckdancer's Choice are divided into those
dealing with dreams and those concerned with memory, and
the relationship of the two groups is explained. Psychoana-
lytic principles are used as support for this critic's views.

Ref. : Acts 2:17, p. 41; John Berryman's Seventy-Seven
Dream Songs, pp. 33, 39; André Breton, p. 33; I Corinth-
ians 14, pp. 41-42; Dante, p. 41; Dante's Commedia,
p. 36; Sigmund Freud, p. 34; Freud's "A Hat as a Symbol
of a Man (or of Male Genitals)," p. 37; Freud's The Inter-
pretation of Dreams, p. 36; George Grosz, p. 36; David
Jones, p. 33; New Testament, p. 41; Ovid, p. 33; Alexand-
er Pope's The Rape of the Lock, p. 36; St. Paul, pp. 41-
42; St. Peter, p. 41; Jean-Paul Sartre, p. 38; William
Wordsworth, p. 38.

926 Strawn, Lynda. "Conversation with John Boorman." Action
7 (Nov. -Dec. 1972), pp. 2-5.

Deliverance [novel], p. 3; Deliverance [film], pp. 3-5.

Director Boorman discusses his use of the grail myth,
his views on violence, and his style in his film Deliverance.
Much of the interview covers films in general.

Ref. : John Boorman's Leo the Last [film], p. 3; Boor-
man's Point Blank [film], pp. 3-4; Lillian Gish, p. 4; D.
W. Griffith, p. 4; Arthur Knight, p. 3; George Lucas'
THX 1138 [film], p. 5; McCabe and Mrs. Miller [film],
p. 3; Lee Marvin, p. 3; Burt Reynolds, p. 3; Ken Russell,
p. 3; John Schlesinger, p. 3; 2001: A Space Odyssey
[film], p. 5; Jon Voight, p. 3; Orson Welles, p. 5; Vilmos
Zsigmond, p. 3.

Illustrated with photographs of Boorman on location with
Deliverance by an unidentified photographer, pp. 3-5.

927 Strick, Philip. "Deliverance." Sight and Sound 41 (Aut.
1972), pp. 228-229.

Deliverance [film], pp. 228-229.

Discussion of the film version of Deliverance centers on
such topics as the inescapability of the characters from
their situation, the changes each character undergoes, and
the film's allegorical significances. Plot summary is in-
cluded.

Ref. : Bachelor Party [film], p. 228; John Boorman,
p. 228; Boorman's Hell in the Pacific [film], p. 228; Boor-
man's Leo the Last [film], p. 228; Boorman's Point Blank
[film], p. 228; Ronny Cox, p. 228; Robinson Crusoe,
p. 228; Frogs [film], p. 228; The Grapes of Wrath [film],
p. 228; Howard Hawks' On the Buses [film], p. 228; Li'l
Abner, p. 228; Lonely Are the Brave [film], p. 228; Burt
Reynolds, p. 229; Vilmos Zsigmond, p. 228.

Illustrated with a still, p. 228.

928 Sullivan, Nancy. "The Muses of Academe." Ramparts 3 (Nov. 1964), pp. 55-58 [57].
"Bums, on Waking"; ["Drinking from a Helmet"]; "The Dusk of Horses"; Helmets; "The Scarred Girl."
A list of major themes in Helmets is given. "The Dusk of Horses" is reprinted in full, p. 57.
Ref.: The New Yorker.

929 "Suppression Is Suppression." Los Angeles Times (15 Nov. 1972), sec. 2, p. 6.
Deliverance.
Dickey's Deliverance is mentioned in this editorial attacking censorship in a North Dakota town and in the Soviet Union.
Ref.: Andrei A. Amalrik; Amalrik's Will the Soviet Union Survive Until 1984?; Ivan Dzyuba; William Faulkner; Ernest Hemingway; John Steinbeck; Kurt Vonnegut, Jr.'s Slaughterhouse Five; Robert Penn Warren's Short Story Masterpieces.

930 "Susan Appleton Tuckerman Wed." New York Times (30 Nov. 1969), p. 89.
A notice of Christopher Dickey's wedding.
Ref.: Christopher Swift Dickey; Mr. and Mrs. Eugene Dickey; Maxine Dickey; Susan Appleton Tuckerman.

931 Symons, Julian. "Moveable Feet." New Statesman 71 (16 June 1967), p. 849. [Note: The volume number given is incorrect. The correct volume is "73."]
"The Firebombing."
Dickey is criticized for overworked imagery, space-punctuation, clichés, and abstractions in Poems 1957-1967.

*931a Talbert, Bob. "Poet, Artist Blend Talents for Major Literary Coup." Toledo (Ohio) Blade (20 Oct. 1974).
*[This citation is from Authors in the News ..., vol. 1, p. 132.]

*932 Taylor, William E. "The Champ." Florida Poetry and ... 1 (Fall 1967), n.p.
*[This citation is from Guy Owen's "James Dickey," p. 189 (see no. 1132).]

933 Thompson, John. "A Catalogue of Poets." Hudson Review 13 (Win. 1960-1961), pp. 618-625 [623].
Favorable review of Into the Stone and Other Poems containing 76 words.

934 Thwaite, Anthony. "Out of Bondage." New Statesman 80 (11 Sept. 1970), pp. 310-311.
Deliverance, pp. 310-311.
Written by formula, Deliverance succeeds in audience identification. Dickey's dialog, his creation of a fantasy

world, and his support of false masculinity are criticized.
Ref. : Bernard Bergonzi, p. 311; Bible (King James
Version), p. 310; James Bond, p. 311; Warwick Deeping's
Sorrell and Son, p. 310; Ian Fleming, p. 311; Fleming's
For Your Eyes Only, p. 311; P. N. Furbank's "The 20th
Century Best Seller," p. 310; Ernest Hemingway, pp. 310-
311; Paul Johnson, p. 311; Sinclair Lewis' Babbitt, p. 311.

935 Tillinghast, Richard.   "Pilot into Poet."   New Republic 157
(9 Sept. 1967), pp. 28-29.
"The Firebombing," pp. 28-29; Helmets, p. 28; [Poems
1957-1967], p. 28; "The Poisoned Man," p. 28; "Reincarna-
tion [(I)]," p. 28; "The Salt Marsh," p. 28; "Slave Quart-
ers," p. 29.
Dickey's long lines, personae, imagination, and use of
metamorphosis are discussed.   His verse is compared to
pastoral poetry.   The reader's involvement with Dickey's
poems and Dickey's movement toward social and moral
issues are mentioned.
Ref. : W. H. Auden, p. 28; John Berryman's 77 Dream
Songs, p. 28; Berryman's Homage to Mistress Bradstreet,
p. 28; T. S. Eliot, p. 28; J. Alfred Prufrock, p. 29; John
Crowe Ransom, p. 28; Allen Tate, p. 28.

*936 Toulson, S.   Poetry Review (Sum. 1971), p. 208.
A review of The Eye-Beaters, Blood, Victory, Madness,
Buckhead and Mercy.
*[This citation is from Index to Book Reviews in the
Humanities: 1973, p. 91.]

937 Tudor, D.   Previews 2 (Oct. 1973), p. 52.
Deliverance [film].
Mixed review of the l. p. record "Dueling Banjos" con-
taining 192 words.   It indicates "Dueling Banjos" and "End
of a Dream" were original music for the film version of
Deliverance.
Ref. : "Black Rock Turnpike" [song]; "Dueling Banjos"
[song]; "End of a Dream" [song]; "Hard Ain't It Hard"
[song]; Steve Mandel; "Mountain Dew" [song]; Eric Weiss-
berg and Marshall Brickman's "New Dimensions in Banjo
and Bluegrass" [l. p. record].

938 _____ and Armitage, A.   Previews 2 (Apr. 1974), p. 18.
Deliverance [film].
Mixed review of the l. p. record "Dueling Banjos," in-
cluding comments on its title song, containing 105 words.
Ref. : Eric Weissberg.

939 Tulip, James.   "Robert Lowell and James Dickey."   Poetry
Australia, no. 24 (Oct. 1968), pp. 39-47 [39-40, 44-47].
"Buckdancer's Choice," p. 47; "Falling," p. 47;
"Fathers and Sons: I, The Second Sleep," p. 46; "A
Letter," p. 47; Poems 1957-1967, p. 44; "Power and

Light," pp. 45-46; "The Shark's Parlor," pp. 46-47.

Poems 1957-1967 is private but, paradoxically, presents public experiences. Its passivity and reality and Dickey's imagination, lyricism, variety, and modernity are discussed.

Ref.: Shelley Berman, p. 47; Lenny Bruce, p. 47; George Gordon, Lord Byron, p. 47; Truman Capote, p. 47; T. S. Eliot, p. 45; William Faulkner, p. 44; Robert Frost, p. 44; Allen Ginsberg, p. 47; Willie Loman, p. 45; Robert Lowell, pp. 39-40, 44, 46-47; Arthur Miller, p. 45; The New York Times' [epigraph used in "Falling"], p. 47; J. Alfred Prufrock, p. 45; Satan, p. 47; Louis Simpson, p. 47; Walt Whitman, p. 47; James Wright, p. 47.

940 Turco, Lewis. "The Suspect in Criticism." Mad River Review 1 (Spr. -Sum. 1965), pp. 81-85.

["Allen Ginsberg"], p. 81; ["Anne Sexton"], p. 81; ["Charles Olson"], p. 81; ["Donald Drummond"], p. 81; ["Ellen Kay"], p. 81; "The Grove Press New American Poets [(1960)]," pp. 81-82; ["Ned O'Gorman"], p. 81; ["Philip Booth"], p. 81; ["Robert Mezey"], p. 81; ["Thom Gunn"], p. 81; ["The Winters Approach"], p. 81.

An analysis of the criteria of Dickey's criticism in The Suspect in Poetry.

Ref.: W. H. Auden, p. 84; Theodore Roethke, p. 85.

941 "U. S. Book Award to Mr. Schlesinger." Times (16 Mar. 1966), p. 11.

Buckdancer's Choice.

Dickey is mentioned as a recipient of the National Book Award for Buckdancer's Choice.

942 Untermeyer, Louis. "A Way of Seeing and Saying." Saturday Review 50 (6 May 1967), pp. 31, 55.

Buckdancer's Choice, p. 31; Drowning with Others, p. 31; "Falling," pp. 31, 55; "The Fiend," p. 31; "The Firebombing," p. 31; Helmets, p. 31; Into the Stone and Other Poems, p. 31; "Near Darien," p. 31; "The Other," p. 31; [Poems 1957-1967], p. 31; "Slave Quarters," p. 31; "Sleeping Out at Easter," p. 31; "The Underground Stream," p. 31.

Flashbacks, experiences, and confrontations are the core of Poems 1957-1967. Dickey's verse is lauded for its new approaches and exuberance. A concise analysis of his development is given.

Ref.: J. M. Brinnin and B. Read's The Modern Poets, p. 31; Contemporary American Poetry, p. 31; Paul Engle and Joseph Langland's Poet's Choice, p. 31; Theodore Roethke, p. 55; William Synge's [unidentified passage], p. 55.

943 Verburg, T. Larry. "Water Imagery in James Dickey's Deliverance." Notes on Contemporary Literature 4 (Nov. 1974), pp. 11-13.

"After," pp. 12-13; "Before," pp. 11-12; Deliverance,
pp. 11-12.
Moral and intellectual development of human existence is
symbolized in Deliverance by the fountain at the beginning,
the river on which the suburbanites travel, and the artificial
lake at the end.
Ref. :   Mammon, p. 11.

944   Virginia Kirkus' Service 33 (1 Aug. 1965), p. 797.
"The Fiend"; "The Firebombing"; Helmets; "Sled Burial,
[Dream Ceremony]. "
Major themes of Buckdancer's Choice are listed, and it
is noted that they occur throughout Dickey's other volumes
of poetry.   His narrative technique is compared to that
used in short fiction.   The poems' violence, energy, and
honesty are mentioned.

945   Virginia Quarterly Review 42 (Sum. 1966), p. xciv.
Favorable review of Buckdancer's Choice containing 180
words.

946   Virginia Quarterly Review 43 (Aut. 1967), pp. clxviii-clxix.
Mixed review of Poems 1957-1967 containing 180 words.
Ref. :   T. S. Eliot, p. clxviii; Robert Frost, p. clxviii;
Wallace Stevens, p. clxviii; William Carlos Williams,
p. clxviii.

947   Virginia Quarterly Review 44 (Aut. 1968), p. cliii.
["Allen Ginsberg"]; ["E. E. Cummings"]; ["Francis
Thompson: 'The Hound of Heaven'"].
Favorable review of Babel to Byzantium containing 124 words.

948   Virginia Quarterly Review 46 (Sum. 1970), p. lxxxviii.
[Deliverance] [film].
Favorable review of Dickey's novel Deliverance contain-
ing 108 words.

949   Virginia Quarterly Review 47 (Win. 1971), p. xviii.
"The Eye-Beaters"; "Turning Away. "
Favorable review of The Eye-Beaters, Blood, Victory,
Madness, Buckhead and Mercy containing 234 words.

950   Virginia Quarterly Review 47 (Sum. 1971), p. cxx.
Favorable review of Self-Interviews containing 108 words.

951   Walsh, Moira.   "Fat City/Deliverance. "   America 127 (2 Sept.
1972), pp. 126-127 [127].
Deliverance [film].
By comparing the film version of Deliverance to other
motion pictures in which violence has a major role, its
artistic intent is recognized.
Ref. :   John Boorman's Leo the Last [film], p. 127;
Boorman's Point Blank [film], p. 127; Stanley Kubrick's A

Clockwork Orange [film], p. 127; Sam Peckinpah's Straw
Dogs [film], p. 127; Peckinpah's The Wild Bunch [film],
p. 127.

952   Washington (D. C.) Post.   Book World (8 Dec. 1974), p. 6.
         Favorable review of Jericho containing 13 words.
         Ref. : Hubert Shuptrine.

953   Watson, Robert.   "Two Books of Criticism. "   Poetry 107 (Feb.
         1966), pp. 332-333 [332].
         ["Allen Ginsberg"]; ["Anne Sexton"]; ["Charles Olson"];
         ["David Ignatow"]; ["Donald Drummond"]; ["E. E. Cummings"];
         ["Ellen Kay"]; ["Galway Kinnell"]; ["Gary Snyder"]; ["The
         Grove Press New American Poets (1960)"]; ["Harold Witt"];
         ["Howard Nemerov"]; ["John Logan"]; ["Ned O'Gorman"];
         ["New Poets of England and America I (1957)"]; ["Philip
         Booth"]; ["Randall Jarrell"]; ["Robert Merzy"]; The Suspect
         in Poetry; ["Theodore Roethke"]; ["Thom Gunn"]; ["W. S.
         Merwin"]; ["William Stafford"]; ["The Winters Approach"].
         Dickey is criticized for the terseness of The Suspect in
         Poetry which doesn't allow for a full analysis of any volume
         under his consideration.
         Exc. : A Library of Literary Criticism (see no. 1005).

954   Weatherby, H. L.   "The Way of Exchange in James Dickey's
         Poetry. "   Hudson Review 74 (July-Sept. 1966), pp. 669-680.
         ["Allen Ginsberg"], p. 680; "Approaching Prayer, "
         pp. 672-673; Buckdancer's Choice, pp. 669, 676; "Chenille, "
         p. 674; "Cherrylog Road, " pp. 674-675; "A Dog Sleeping on
         My Feet, " pp. 669-672; "Drinking from a Helmet, "
         pp. 675-676; "The Driver, " pp. 675, 677; Drowning with
         Others, pp. 669, 672; "The Fiend, " pp. 677-678; "The
         Firebombing, " p. 677; ["Harold Witt"], p. 680; "The Heaven
         of Animals, " p. 672; Helmets, pp. 669, 672, 675; "The
         Owl King [: II, The Owl King], " p. 669; "Pursuit from
         Under, " pp. 676-677; "The Shark's Parlor, " pp. 677-678;
         "Springer Mountain, " pp. 673, 676, 678; The Suspect in
         Poetry, pp. 679-680; ["Thom Gunn"], p. 680; [unidentified
         passage], p. 670.
         Dickey's technique of transferring the inner self of a
         human being into another form is studied as it is used in
         three of his volumes.   A discussion of the weaknesses of
         this technique concludes.
         Ref. : Dante, p. 679; John Keats, p. 671; William
         Shakespeare, p. 679; Edmund Spenser, p. 679; William
         Wordsworth, p. 671; William Butler Yeats, pp. 671, 679.
         Rept. : James Dickey: The Expansive Imagination (see
         no. 1084).

955   Weeks, Edward.   Atlantic 234 (Dec. 1974), pp. 123-126 [125-
         126].
         ["Introduction"] [to Jericho], p. 126; Jericho, p. 125;
         ["The Traditions Web"], p. 125.

Dickey's work in Jericho is cited for its perception,
poetic style, and narrative excellence.   However, the em-
phasis of this review is on Shuptrine's art work.
Ref. :   Hubert Shuptrine, p. 125; Shuptrine's [remarks on
the dust jacket of Jericho], p. 125; Shuptrine's "Blue
Norther" [painting], p. 126; Shuptrine's "Late Afternoon"
[painting], p. 126; Shuptrine's "Mountain Gentleman" [paint-
ing], p. 125; Shuptrine's "Nettie" [painting], p. 126;
Shuptrine's "Old Hombre" [painting], p. 126; Shuptrine's
"Sculling Home" [painting], p. 126; Shuptrine's "Shenandoah"
[painting], p. 126; Shuptrine's "Turn Gibson" [painting],
p. 125; Andrew Wyeth, pp. 125-126.

956   Westerbeck, Colin L. , Jr.   "Down a Lazy River. "   Common-
weal 96 (29 Sept. 1972), p. 526.
Deliverance [novel]; Deliverance [film].
Comparison between Dickey's novel Deliverance and its
film version supplements a discussion of their title and the
film's action.
Ref. :   John Boorman's Hell in the Pacific [film]; Boor-
man's Point Blank [film]; John Ford's Stagecoach [film];
Alfred Hitchcock's Lifeboat [film]; William Golding's Lord
of the Flies.

957   Whitehorn, Ethel.   P. T. A. Magazine 67 (Sept. 1972), p. 38.
A plot summary of the film version of Deliverance with
unfavorable critical overtones containing 134 words.
Ref. :   John Boorman; Burt Reynolds; Jon Voight.

958   Williams, Hugo.   "Selected Books. "   London Magazine, n. s. 5
(Oct. 1965), pp. 101-104.
["Allen Ginsberg"], pp. 102-104; ["Anne Sexton"], p. 104;
["Donald Drummond"], p. 102; ["E. E. Cummings"],
p. 104; ["Howard Nemerov"], p. 104; ["Ned O'Gorman"],
p. 102; ["New Poets of England and America I (1957)"],
p. 103; ["Randall Jarrell"], p. 104; ["Richard Eberhart"],
p. 104; The Suspect in Poetry, p. 101; ["Theodore Roethke"],
p. 104; ["Thom Gunn"], pp. 102-103.
Seriousness, comprehensiveness, concentration, and in-
consistencies characterize The Suspect in Poetry.
Ref. :   Robert Bly's [remarks on the dust jacket of The
Suspect in Poetry], p. 102; Laertes, p. 104.

959   Williams, Miller.   "Merrill, Smith, and Dickey. "   Shenandoah
17 (Spr. 1966), pp. 100-103 [102-103].
Buckdancer's Choice, pp. 102-103; "Reincarnation (I), "
p. 103; "Sled Burial, Dream Ceremony, " p. 103; "Them,
Crying, " p. 103.
Love, authority, and significance of events are at the
core of Buckdancer's Choice.
Ref. :   William Faulkner, p. 103.

960   Willig, Charles L.   "Ed's Transformation: A Note on Deliver-

ance." Notes on Contemporary Literature 3 (Mar. 1973), pp. 4-5.

> Deliverance [novel], pp. 4-5; Deliverance [film], p. 4.
> The passage of the novel Deliverance in which the narrator gains confidence and competence is identified.

961 Willis, Katherine Tappert. Library Journal 90 (1 Feb. 1965), pp. 648-649.

> "Barnstorming for Poetry," p. 649.
> Favorable review of The Suspect in Poetry containing 131 words.
> Ref.: Robert Bly, p. 649; The New York Times Book Review, p. 649; Dylan Thomas, p. 649.

961a Willson, Robert F., Jr. "Deliverance from Novel to Film: Where Is Our Hero?" Literature/Film Quarterly 2 (Win. 1974), pp. 52, 54-55, 57-58.

> Deliverance [novel], pp. 52, 54-55, 57; [Deliverance] [film], pp. 52, 58.
> A comparison of Deliverance and its film version, it concludes that the success of the novel, and the failure of the film, is the presentation of Ed's characterization. Two episodes in the novel which reveal Ed's inner workings are deleted from the film, and while a third is employed in the film, it is transferred with poorly chosen substitutions.
> Ref.: Nick Adams, p. 52; John Boorman, pp. 52, 54, 57-58; Huck Finn, p. 52; Jesus, p. 58; Pygmalion, p. 55; True [magazine], p. 52; Jon Voight, pp. 52, 54, 57-58.

962 Wimsatt, Margaret. Commonweal 93 (19 Feb. 1971), pp. 501-503.

> "Adultery," p. 502; Babel to Byzantium, p. 502; "Coming Back to America," p. 502; Deliverance, p. 502; ["'Falling'"], p. 502; "For the Last Wolverine," p. 502; "Hunting Civil War Relics at Nimblewill Creek," p. 502; "In the Tree House [at Night]," p. 502; "The Poet Turns on Himself," p. 502; "The Sheep Child," p. 502; "Sun," p. 502; ["Teaching, Writing, Reincarnations, and Rivers"], p. 502.
> Dickey's problems in Self-Interviews--his verboseness and immaturity--are due to a lack of editing and to the use of a tape recorder in producing this volume.
> Ref.: Theodora Bosanquet, p. 501; Dante, p. 502; Isabella Fenwick, p. 501; Erwin A. Glikes and Paul Schwaber's Of Poetry and Power, p. 502; Homer, p. 501; Henry James, p. 501; John Kennedy, p. 502; Barbara Reiss, p. 501; James Reiss, p. 501; Joseph Stalin, p. 502; William Wordsworth, p. 501.

963 Wolf, Gregory. Best Sellers 30 (1 Apr. 1970), pp. 11-12.

> Deliverance, pp. 11-12.
> The major theme and a plot summary of Deliverance are given. It is predicted that debate over the ethics of this novel will occur. Notice of its selection as a Literary

Guild choice is given.
Ref.: George Bernanos, p. 11; Charles Darwin, p. 12; William Faulkner, p. 11; [unidentified critic's remarks], p. 11.

964 Wolf, William [W. W.]. Cue 41 (5 Aug. 1972), p. 5.
Deliverance [novel]; Deliverance [film].
Favorable review of the film Deliverance containing 174 words.

965 Wolfe, Geoffrey. "Schlesinger, 3 Others Receive Book Awards." Washington (D. C.) Post (16 Mar. 1966), sec. A, p. 3.
Buckdancer's Choice.
A notice of Dickey's winning the National Book Award for Buckdancer's Choice with mention of his appointment as poetry consultant to the Library of Congress. An excerpt from his N. B. A. acceptance speech (see no. 339) is included.
Photograph of Dickey with the other winners by the Associated Press.

966 Wolff, Geoffrey. "Hunting in Hell." Newsweek 57 (30 Mar. 1970), pp. 95A, 96.
Deliverance, p. 95A.
Comments on hunting and water images of his poetry, which appear in Dickey's novel Deliverance, supplement the identification of his two major obsessions in the novel: ritual and the superman motif.
Ref.: Ernest Hemingway, p. 95A; Hemingway's "Big Two-Hearted River," p. 95A.
Photograph of Dickey by Dave Underwood, p. 95A.

967 Wolff, Geoffrey A. "Library's New Poetry Expert Is Ad Writer, Teacher, Essayist." Washington (D. C.) Post (22 Jan. 1966), sec. C, p. 19.
["Toward a Solitary Joy"].
Dickey's reaction to his appointment as poetry consultant to the Library of Congress, influences of war and sex on his poetry, his outlook on the future of his own verse, and biographical and career data are given.
Ref.: William Wordsworth.
Photograph of Dickey by an unidentified person.

968 _____. "Poet on a Motorcycle." Washington (D. C.) Post (9 May 1967), sec. A, p. 22.
Buckdancer's Choice; Drowning with Others; Helmets; Into the Stone and Other Poems; Poems 1957-1967; [Spinning the Crystal Ball].
Dickey's use of experiences, recurrent themes, and experimentation in Poems 1957-1967 and his visibility to his public are discussed. This volume is cited for its evenness and for those poems in which the natural is united with the

mechanical.   Biographical data introduces.
    Ref. :   Job's [epigraph used in Hart Crane's "The
Bridge"]; Hart Crane; Norman Rockwell.

969 Wright, James.   "Shelf of New Poets. "   Poetry 99 (Dec.
     1961), pp. 178-183 [178-180, 183].
         "Dover, Believing in Kings, " pp. 178, 178n. ; ["The
     Game"], p. 179; Into the Stone and Other Poems, p. 178;
     ["Mindoro, 1944"], p. 179; ["Near Darien"], p. 179; "The
     Performance, " p. 179; ["The Sprinter's Sleep"], p. 179;
     [unidentified passages], pp. 178-179.
         Experiences related in Into the Stone and Other Poems
     are enhanced by Dickey's compassion, musical ability, and
     imagination.
         Ref. :   W. S. Graham's "The Nightfishing, " p. 178;
     Vassar Miller, p. 183.

970 "Writers Appeal on Soviet Jews. "   New York Times (21 May
     1967), p. 12.
         Dickey is listed with other authors who signed a petition
     asking Soviet writers to help restore Jewish cultural insti-
     tutions in the U. S. S. R.

971 Yaeger, Deborah Sue.   "Panel to Study Ban of 6 Books in
     Montgomery. "   Washington (D. C.) Post (8 Nov. 1974),
     sec. C, pp. 1, 6.
         Deliverance, p. 1.
         Dickey's Deliverance is under fire for its rape scene.
         Ref. :   P. E. I. Bonewits' Real Magic, pp. 1, 6; The
     Booklist, p. 6; Claude Brown's Manchild in a Promised
     Land, p. 1; Eldridge Cleaver's Soul on Ice, pp. 1, 6;
     Frances C. Dean, p. 6; Our Working World: Families at
     Work, p. 1; Scott Foresman Reading Systems, p. 1; Nancy
     C. Walker, p. 6.

972 Yardley, Jonathan.   "A Colossal Ornament?"   New Republic
     171 (30 Nov. 1974), pp. 43-44.
         ["Introduction"] [to Jericho], p. 43; Jericho, pp. 43-44.
         Discussion of Jericho includes remarks on Dickey's
     verbosity and his unrealistic depiction of the South.
         Ref. :   The Progressive Farmer, p. 43; Southern Living,
     pp. 43-44; Andrew Wyeth, p. 43.

973 _____.   "More of Superpoet. "   New Republic 163 (5 Dec.
     1970), pp. 26-27.
         Deliverance, p. 26; ["A Dog Sleeping on My Feet"],
     p. 27; The Eye-Beaters, Blood, Victory, Madness, Buck-
     head and Mercy, p. 26; Self-Interviews, p. 26; "The Sheep
     Child, " p. 27; [Sorties], pp. 26-27; ["Teaching, Writing,
     Reincarnations, and Rivers"], pp. 26-27; [unidentified pas-
     sages], pp. 26-27.
         Criticized for revealing less in Self-Interviews than he
     does in his poems, Dickey is nevertheless lauded for the

few glimpses he gives.   Mention is given to his major
themes and his public image.
    Ref. : Horatio Alger, p. 26; Emile Coué, p. 26; E. E.
Cummings, p. 26; Robert Frost, p. 26; Rod McKuen,
p. 26; Barbara and James Reiss, p. 26; Reiss' "Introduc-
tion", p. 26 (see no. 1060); Walt Whitman, p. 26.

974   Yoder, Ed [E. Y.].   Harper's Magazine 240 (Apr. 1970),
        pp. 106-107.
        Deliverance [novel], p. 106.
        The dramatic irony in, and the setting and characters of,
Dickey's novel Deliverance are criticized slightly.   Plot
summary is included.
    Ref. : General Baden-Powell, p. 107; Joseph Conrad,
p. 106; Conrad's "Heart of Darkness," p. 106; William
Golding, p. 106; Jack London, p. 106.

975   Yurick, Sol. "Comment. "   College English 34 (Nov. 1972),
        pp. 198-199.
        An extrapolation agreeing with Fredric Jameson's com-
ments about Deliverance (see no. 749).

976   Zimmerman, Paul D.   "Down the Rapids. "   Newsweek 80 (7
        Aug. 1972), p. 61.
        Deliverance [film].
        Too much attention in the film version of Deliverance is
given to its action disregarding subtlety, characterization,
and the question of morality which arises in it.   Dickey's
dialog is criticized.
    Ref. : John Boorman's Hell in the Pacific [film].
    Illustrated with a still.
    Rept. : Filmfacts (see no. 660).

BOOKS

977 Annual Report of the Librarian of Congress for the Fiscal
Year Ending June 30, 1966, pp. xi, 74-75. Washington,
D. C. : Library of Congress, 1967.
Dickey's appointment to the post of Consultant in Poetry
in English to the Library of Congress is mentioned.

978 Annual Report of the Librarian of Congress for the Fiscal
Year Ending June 30, 1967, pp. xii, 67. Washington, D. C. :
Library of Congress, 1968.
[Reading His Poems with Comment in the Coolidge Audi-
torium on Oct. 3, 1966, Under the Auspices of the Library
of Congress; First Official Program as 1966-67 Consultant
in Poetry], p. 67; "Spinning the Crystal Ball," p. 67.
Dickey is listed as Consultant in Poetry in English. His
public poetry reading of October 3, 1966 and his public
lecture of April 24, 1967 are mentioned.

979 Annual Report of the Librarian of Congress for the Fiscal
Year Ending June 30, 1968, pp. xii, 38, 42. Washington,
D. C. : Library of Congress, 1969.
[Consultant in Poetry for 1966-68, for His Last Official
Public Appearance in the Library, Reading His Poems with
Comment in the Coolidge Auditorium on May 6, 1968, Under
the Auspices of the Library of Congress], pp. 38, 42;
"Metaphor as Pure Adventure," p. 38; [Reading His Poetry
with Comment at the University of Virginia on April 17,
1968], p. 42.
Dickey is listed as Consultant in Poetry in English. His
public poetry reading of May 6, 1968, his public lecture of
December 4, 1967, and the acquisition of two recordings of
his poetry readings, one of which was given at the Library
of Congress and the other at the University of Virginia, are
mentioned.

980 Annual Report of the Librarian of Congress for the Fiscal
Year Ending June 30, 1969, p. xii. Washington, D. C. :
Library of Congress, 1970.
Dickey is listed as Honorary Consultant in American
Letters.

981 Annual Report of the Librarian of Congress for the Fiscal
Year Ending June 30, 1970, p. xii. Washington, D. C. :

Library of Congress, 1971.
Dickey is listed as Honorary Consultant in American
Letters.

982 Annual Report of the Librarian of Congress for the Fiscal
Year Ending June 30, 1971, p. xii. Washington, D. C. :
Library of Congress, 1972.
Dickey is listed as Honorary Consultant in American
Letters.

983 Annual Report of the Librarian of Congress for the Fiscal
Year Ending June 30, 1972, p. xii. Washington, D. C. :
Library of Congress, 1973.
Dickey is listed as Honorary Consultant in American
Letters.

984 Annual Report of the Librarian of Congress for the Fiscal
Year Ending June 30, 1973, p. xii. Washington, D. C. :
Library of Congress, 1974.
Dickey is listed as Honorary Consultant in American
Letters.

985 Antrim, Harry T. "Poems 1957-1967. " In Masterplots, 1968
Annual: Magill's Literary Annual Essay-Reviews of 100
Outstanding Books Published in the United States During
1964, edited by Frank N. Magill, pp. 247-251. New York:
Salem Press, 1969.
Buckdancer's Choice, pp. 247, 250; ["Chenille"], p. 249;
"Cherrylog Road, " p. 250; "Drinking from a Helmet, "
p. 250; Drowning with Others, p. 249; "The Enclosure, "
p. 248; "Facing Africa, " p. 249; "Falling, " p. 251; "The
Firebombing, " p. 250; Helmets, pp. 249-250; "The Hospital
Window, " p. 249; "Into the Stone, " pp. 248-249; Into the
Stone and Other Poems, p. 249; "The Jewel, " p. 248; "The
Lifeguard, " p. 249; "Listening to Foxhounds, " p. 249;
"Near Darien, " p. 248; "The Performance, " p. 248; "The
Shark's Parlor, " pp. 250-251; "Sleeping Out at Easter, "
p. 248; "The Vegetable King, " p. 248.
Dickey's personal mythology, which is derived from his
own experiences, and its religious overtones receive most
of the discussion of this survey of Poems 1957-1967. Also
discussed are motion, and its accompanying images, love,
death, and his linear experiments in these poems.
Ref. : Theodore Roethke, p. 249; Dylan Thomas, p. 249;
Walt Whitman, p. 251; William Carlos Williams, pp. 250-
251; William Wordsworth, p. 248.

986 Ashley, Franklin. "Compiler's Note. " In James Dickey: A
Checklist, compiled by Franklin Ashley, pp. ix-x. Detroit:
Gale Research Co. , Book Tower, 1972.
"The Hospital Window, " p. ix; Poems 1957-1967, p. ix.
An explanation of the problems he encountered with cer-
tain entries and a list of acknowledgments.

Ref. : Jennifer Atkinson, p. x; Maxine Dickey, p. x;
W. L. Jowers, p. x; Myra Millinger, p. x; Bobbie Ann
Redd, p. x.

987 Atherton, John. "Preface. " In A Private Brinksmanship: An
     Address by James Dickey, Poet-in-Residence, San Fernando
     Valley State College at the First Pitzer College Commence-
     ment, June 6, 1965, pp. 2-3. Claremont, Calif. : Pitzer
     College, 1965. [Note: The pages of this publication are
     unnumbered.]
          Details concerning the choice of Dickey as the speaker
     at Pitzer College's first graduation commencement are
     given.
          Ref. : Marlene Bates, p. 3; Katherine Gibs, p. 3;
     Nicole Scheel, p. 3.

988 Avant, John Alfred. In The "Library Journal" Book Review:
     1970, p. 447. New York: R. R. Bowker Co. , 1970.
          ["Apollo: II, The Moon Ground"]; "The Eye-Beaters";
     "Madness"; "Mercy. "
          Favorable review of The Eye-Beaters, Blood, Victory,
     Madness, Buckhead and Mercy containing 135 words.
          Orig. : Library Journal (see no. 574).

989   . In The "Library Journal" Book Review, 1970,
     pp. 714-715. New York: R. R. Bowker Co. , 1970.
          Unfavorable review of Deliverance containing 158 words.
          Ref. : Edgar Rice Burroughs, p. 715; Ernest Heming-
     way, p. 715.
          Orig. : Library Journal (see no. 575).

990 Bobbitt, John T. "Motion Pictures. " In 1973 Britannica Book
     of the Year, edited by Michel Silva, pp. 482-487 [483,
     486]. Chicago: Encyclopaedia Britannica, 1973.
          [Deliverance] [novel], p. 483; Deliverance [film], p. 483.
          The film version of Dickey's Deliverance is briefly
     criticized for its philosophical superficiality.
          Ref. : John Boorman, p. 483; Burt Reynolds, p. 486.
          Illustrated with a still, p. 486.

991 Bradbury, John M. Renaissance in the South: A Critical
     History of the Literature, 1920-1960, p. 14. Chapel Hill,
     N. C. : The University of North Carolina Press, 1963.
          Dickey is only slightly mentioned although praised.

992 Calhoun, Richard. "James Dickey: The Expansive Imagina-
     tion. " In Modern American Poetry: Essays in Criticism,
     edited by Guy Owen, pp. 239-252. DeLand, Fla. : Everett-
     Edwards, 1972.
          "Approaching Prayer, " p. 247; Babel to Byzantium,
     p. 241; "Barnstorming for Poetry, " p. 240; "Buckdancer's
     Choice, " pp. 241-242; Buckdancer's Choice, pp. 240, 244,
     246-247; "Cherrylog Road, " p. 244; "A Dog Sleeping on My

Feet," pp. 246-247; "Drinking from a Helmet," pp. 246-247; "The Driver," p. 247; Drowning with Others, pp. 240, 245-246; "The Dusk of Horses," p. 244; "Encounter in the Cage Country," pp. 249-250; "The Eye-Beaters," pp. 251-252; "Falling," pp. 245, 250-252; "Falling" [sec. of Poems 1957-1967], p. 250; "The Fiend," p. 252; "The Firebomb-ing," pp. 246-249; "Fog Envelops the Animals," p. 249; "The Heaven of Animals," p. 248; Helmets, p. 240, 245; "The Hospital Window," p. 244; Into the Stone and Other Poems, pp. 240, 242, 245; "May Day Sermon to the Women of Gilmer County, Georgia, by a Woman Preacher Leaving the Baptist Church," p. 252; "The Performance," pp. 242-243; Poems 1957-1967, pp. 240, 250; ["The Poet Turns on Himself"], pp. 242-243, 245; "Power and Light," pp. 251-252; "Reincarnation (II)," p. 249; "The Sheep Child," pp. 249-250, 252; "Slave Quarters," p. 249; "Sleeping Out at Easter," p. 243; ["The Son, the Cave, and the Burning Bush"], p. 252; "Springer Mountain," pp. 246-247; "The String," p. 243; ["Theodore Roethke"], pp. 241-244; [unidentified passage], p. 252.

Dickey's verse is described as personal not confessional. His two major obsessions, his brother's death and his survival of military action, and the development of the sentence into the split line are discussed. Explanations of "expansive," "suspect," and "exchange" are included.

Ref.: John Berryman, p. 239; Robert Bly's "The Collapse of James Dickey," p. 249 (see no. 587); Richard Eberhart, p. 239; Peter Davison's "The Difficulties of Being Major: The Poetry of Robert Lowell and James Dickey," pp. 241, 252 (see no. 659); T. S. Eliot, p. 239; Robert Frost, p. 239; Anthony Hecht, p. 239; The Kenyon Review, p. 240; Laurence Lieberman's "Notes on James Dickey's Style," pp. 245-246 (see no. 793); Lieberman's "The Worldly Mystic," p. 250 (see no. 796); Robert Lowell, pp. 239-240, 252; Lowell's Life Studies, p. 239; The New York Review of Books, p. 240; John Crowe Ran-som, p. 240; Theodore Roethke, pp. 239-241; The Sewanee Review, pp. 240-241; Allen Tate, p. 240; Robert Penn Warren, p. 252; H. L. Weatherby's "The Way of Exchange in James Dickey's Poetry," pp. 242, 246 (see no. 954); Walt Whitman, pp. 240, 250; William Carlos Williams, p. 239.

993 Calhoun, Richard J. "'His Reason Argues with His Invention': James Dickey's Self-Interviews and The Eye-Beaters." In James Dickey: The Expansive Imagination; A Collection of Critical Essays, edited by Richard J. Calhoun, pp. 203-212. DeLand, Fla.: Everett-Edwards, 1973.

["Apollo: I, For the First Manned Moon Orbit"], p. 212; Babel to Byzantium, p. 204; Buckdancer's Choice, p. 209; "The Cancer Match," p. 210; Deliverance, p. 203; "Diabetes: I, [Sugar]," p. 208; ["Diabetes: II,] Under Buzzards," pp. 208, 211; Drowning with Others, pp. 206, 208; ["Drown-

ing with Others"], pp. 205-206; "The Eye-Beaters,"
pp. 207, 211; The Eye-Beaters, Blood, Victory, Madness,
Buckhead and Mercy, pp. 203, 206-207, 210; "Falling,"
p. 209; "Falling" [sec. of Poems 1957-1967], p. 209; "The
Firebombing," p. 209; ["The Heaven of Animals"], p. 205;
Helmets, p. 208; Into the Stone and Other Poems, p. 208;
["J. V. Cunningham"], p. 204; "The Lifeguard," p. 206;
["The Lord in the Air"], p. 207; ["Messages"], p. 207;
["Messages: II,] Giving a Son to the Sea," p. 211; ["Pine:
I"], p. 207; "The Poem as Something That Matters,"
p. 205; Poems 1957-1967, pp. 205, 209; "The Poet in Mid-
Career," p. 205; "Power and Light," p. 209; ["Randall
Jarrell"], p. 204; Self-Interviews, pp. 203-206, 210; "Two
Poems of Going Home," p. 210; ["Two Poems of Going
Home: I,] Living There," p. 210; ["Two Poems of Going
Home: II,] Looking for the Buckhead Boys," pp. 208, 211;
["William Carlos Williams"], p. 204.
    The strengths and weaknesses of Self-Interviews and the
themes of death, aging, and illness in The Eye-Beaters,
Blood, Victory, Madness, Buckhead and Mercy are investi-
gated.   A brief examination of the reincarnation motif of
five volumes of Dickey's poetry is included.   The quoted
portion of the title is from "The Eye-Beaters."
    Ref.: James Agee, p. 206; T. S. Eliot, p. 205; Hera-
clitus, p. 206; Randall Jarrell, p. 207; John Keats, p. 206;
Life, p. 212; Robert Lowell's Life Studies, p. 208; Mal-
colm Lowry, p. 206; Marshall McLuhan, p. 203; Wolfgang
Mozart, p. 206; Barbara Reiss and James Reiss' "Introduc-
tion," p. 203 (see no. 1060); Stephen Spender's "The Making
of a Poem," p. 206; Allen Tate's "Ode to the Confederate
Dead," p. 206.
    Orig.: The South Carolina Review (see no. 613).

994 _____. ed. James Dickey: The Expansive Imagination; A
    Collection of Critical Essays.   DeLand, Fla.: Everett-
    Edwards, 1973.
    Entries are provided for chapters of this volume under
each chapter's author: Richard J. Calhoun's "'His Reason
Argues with His Invention':   James Dickey's Self-Interviews
and The Eye-Beaters," pp. 203-212 (see no. 993), Calhoun's
"Whatever Happened to the Poet-Critic?," pp. 119-133 (see
no. 995), Peter Davison's "'The Great Grassy World from
Both Sides:'   The Poetry of Robert Lowell and James
Dickey," pp. 35-51 (see no. 1007), Arthur Gregor's "James
Dickey, American Romantic: An Appreciation," pp. 77-80
(see no. 1020), Robert W. Hill's "James Dickey: A Check-
list," pp. 213-228 (see no. 1130), Hill's "James Dickey:
Comic Poet," pp. 143-155 (see no. 1023), Carolyn Kizer
and James Boatwright's "A Conversation with James Dickey,"
pp. 1-33 (see no. 1108), Richard Kostelanetz's "Flyswatter
and Gadfly," pp. 135-141 (see no. 1032), George Lensing's
"James Dickey and the Movements of Imagination," pp. 157-
175 (see no. 1033), Laurence Lieberman's "Notes on James

Dickey's Style, " pp. 195-201 (see no. 1035), Lieberman's
"The Worldly Mystic, " pp. 65-76 (see no. 1036), Daniel B.
Marin's "James Dickey's Deliverance: Darkness Visible, "
pp. 105-117 (see no. 1043), William J. Martz's "A Note
on Meaningless Being in 'Cherrylog Road, '" pp. 81-83 (see
no. 1044), Paul Ramsey's "James Dickey: Meter and
Structure, " pp. 177-194 (see no. 1059), Thomas O. Sloan's
"The Open Poem Is a Now Poem: Dickey's May Day Ser-
mon, " pp. 85-104 (see no. 1072), and H. L. Weatherby's
"The Way of Exchange in James Dickey's Poetry, " pp. 53-
64 (see no. 1084).

995   Calhoun, Richard James.   "Whatever Happened to the Poet-
Critic?" In James Dickey: The Expansive Imagination; A
Collection of Critical Essays, edited by Richard J. Calhoun,
pp. 119-133.   DeLand, Fla. : Everett-Edwards, 1973.
["Allen Ginsberg"], p. 120; Babel to Byzantium, pp. 119,
122-123, 127, 129, 131; "Barnstorming for Poetry, " p. 130;
["E. E. Cummings"], pp. 123, 125, 128-129; ["Edwin
Arlington Robinson"], pp. 123, 125, 129; ["Edwin Arlington
Robinson: The Many Truths"], p. 130; ["Harold Witt"],
p. 126; ["Howard Nemerov"], p. 123-124; ["I. A. Richards"],
p. 132; ["In the Presence of Anthologies"], p. 124; ["J. V.
Cunningham"], p. 132; ["James Merrill"], p. 120; ["Mari-
anne Moore"], p. 123; "Notes on the Decline of Outrage, "
p. 130; "The Poet Turns on Himself, " pp. 126-130;
"Preface, " p. 120; ["Randall Jarrell"], p. 133; ["Richard
Wilbur"], p. 120; ["Robert Frost"], pp. 125-126; ["Robert
Graves"], p. 132; "Sleeping Out at Easter, " p. 126; The
Suspect in Poetry, p. 119; ["Theodore Roethke"], pp. 123,
125-129; ["Thom Gunn"], p. 120; [unidentified passage],
p. 119; ["William Carlos Williams"], p. 133; ["William
Carlos Williams: 'The Yachts'"], p. 127; ["William Mere-
dith"], p. 126; ["Yvor Winters"], p. 132.
Returning subjectivity and personality to poetry, the tar-
get of Dickey's criticism is academicism, the opposite of
subjectivity and personality.   Several major poet-critics
are discussed as are points of concern for the critic, such
as the voice of the poet, the reader's belief in the poem,
etc.
Ref. : W. H. Auden, p. 124; Robert Bly, p. 125;
Dionysios, p. 119; T. S. Eliot, pp. 121-122, 124-125,
130-131, 133; Eliot's "The Love Song of J. Alfred Pru-
frock, " p. 121; Eliot's On Poetry and Poets, p. 121; Rob-
ert Frost, pp. 122-123; Frost's "The Secret Sits, " p. 122;
Northrop Frye, pp. 121, 133; Allen Ginsberg, p. 124; T.
E. Hulme, p. 130; Randall Jarrell, pp. 119, 121, 123,
129, 131, 133; Jarrell's Poetry and the Age, p. 123;
Murray Krieger, pp. 121, 133; D. H. Lawrence, p. 120;
Robert Lowell, pp. 123, 125; W. S. Merwin, p. 125;
Charles Olson, p. 124; Walter Pater, p. 132; Edgar Allan
Poe, p. 119; John Crowe Ransom, pp. 119, 121-122;
Theodore Roethke, pp. 123, 125; The Sewanee Review,

pp. 119, 123; Anne Sexton, p. 125; Karl Shapiro, pp. 120,
123-124, 132; Louis Simpson, p. 125; W. D. Snodgrass,
p. 125; William Stafford, p. 125; Wallace Stevens, pp. 119-
123, 130-131; Allen Tate, pp. 119-122, 130-131; Robert
Penn Warren, p. 122; René Wellek, pp. 121-123, 123n.,
131; Walt Whitman, pp. 120, 123; William Carlos Williams,
p. 123; Yvor Winters, p. 129; Thomas Wolfe, p. 128;
James Wright, p. 125.
   Orig.: The Southern Literary Journal (see no. 614).

996 Canby, Vincent. In "The New York Times" Film Reviews,
     1971-1972, p. 291. New York: The New York Times and
     Arno Press, 1973.
        Deliverance [novel]; Deliverance [film].
        The theme of survival and the influences of the charac-
     ters' experiences are central to Deliverance and its film
     version. The film lacks in realism and has static dialog
     and rough narrative. Credits for the film are included.
        Ref.: Ned Beatty; John Boorman; Ronny Cox; Ernest
     Hemingway; McCabe and Mrs. Miller [film]; Burt Reynolds;
     Jon Voight; Irving Wallace; Vilmos Zsigmond.
        Illustrated with a still.
        Orig.: The New York Times (see no. 615). (Its title,
     omitted here, originally was "James Dickey's Deliverance
     Arrives.")

997 Carrol, Paul. "Faire, Foul and Full of Variations: The
     Generation of 1962." In The Poem in Its Skin, pp. 203-
     259 [210-213]. Chicago: Follett Publishing Co., 1968.
        Babel to Byzantium, p. 211; "Faces Seen Once," p. 213;
     "The Fiend," p. 211; "The Firebombing," p. 211; Into the
     Stone [and Other Poems], p. 210; "The Sheep Child,"
     pp. 211, 213; "Slave Quarters," p. 211; The Suspect in
     Poetry, p. 211; "Them, Crying," p. 213.
        Dickey's imagination and the mingling of joy and violence
     in individual poems of his are mentioned. Portions of
     Carroll's "Twenty-Five Poets in Their Skins" (see no. 620)
     appear here verbatim or paraphrased.
        Ref.: Peter Davison, p. 210.
        Exc.: Contemporary Literary Criticism (see no. 1063).

998 _____. "The Smell of Blood in Paradise." In The Poem
     in Its Skin, pp. 43-49 [43-48]. Chicago: Follett Publishing
     Co., 1968.
        "The Heaven of Animals," pp. 43-48.
        Violence and joy are integral to Dickey's poem about a
     discordant paradise. Interpretations of its cycles, metrics,
     and its readers' roles are given. "The Heaven of Animals"
     is reprinted in full, pp. 41-42.
        Ref.: Dante, pp. 45, 45n.; Dante's The Divine Comedy,
     p. 44; Dante's Paradiso, p. 45; Edward Hicks, pp. 43-44;
     Hicks' "The Peaceable Kingdom" [painting], p. 43; Etienne-
     Pierre-Théodore Rousseau, p. 44; William Butler Yeats'

"Byzantium, " p. 44.
Photograph of Dickey by Christopher Dickey, p. 40.

999 Carruth, Hayden. "Literature. " In The 1967 World Book
Year Book: The Annual Supplement to the World Book
Encyclopedia, pp. 396-400 [399-400]. Chicago: Field
Enterprises Educational Corp. , 1967.
Buckdancer's Choice, p. 399.
Notices of Dickey's post as poetry consultant to the
Library of Congress and of his winning the N. B. A. are
given.
Photograph of Dickey with other authors by Bernard
Gotfryd, p. 399.

1000 Clark, Robert. "Foreword. " In Poems, by James Dickey,
pp. 5-8. Melbourne, Victoria, Australia: Sun Books,
1968.
"Falling, " p. 8; Poems 1957-1967, p. 5; "Slave Quart-
ers, " p. 6; [unidentified passage], p. 7.
Collected first impressions of Poems 1957-1967 mention
Dickey's rhythm, unique use of line, obsession with every-
day experiences, and choice of words.
Ref. : Robert Frost, p. 6; The Sewanee Review, p. 5;
Louis Untermeyer's Modern American Poetry, p. 5.
Orig. : Australian Book Review (see no. 635). (It was
originally entitled "James Dickey: American Poet. ")

1001 Cott, Jonathan. "The New American Poetry. " In The New
American Arts, edited by Richard Kostelanetz, pp. 117-
161 [118]. London: Collier-Macmillan, 1965.
Dickey is listed with other young writers who are
respected but are unable to "explore" themselves, their
worlds, and their languages fully.
Ref. : Anthony Hecht; W. S. Merwin.

1002 Cowie, Peter. "Deliverance. " In International Film Guide:
1974, edited by Peter Cowie, pp. 338-339. New York:
A. S. Barnes and Co. , 1973.
Violence and the employment of adventure techniques
in the film version of Deliverance are discussed as its
distinguishing traits. A comprehensive list of credits is
included.
Ref. : John Boorman, p. 338; Akira Kurosawa, p. 339.

1003 Coxe, Louis. Edwin Arlington Robinson: The Life of Poetry,
p. 22. New York: Pegasus, 1969.
Dickey is compared to Edwin Arlington Robinson.

1004 Crowder, Richard. "Poetry: 1900 to the 1930's. " In
American Literary Scholarship: An Annual, 1970, edited
by J. Albert Robbins, pp. 280-307 [295]. Durham, N. C. :
Duke University Press, 1972.
["Edwin Arlington Robinson: The Many Truths"].

Mention is given to Dickey's contribution to a volume
of critical essays concerning Edwin Arlington Robinson.
Ref.: Francis Murphy's Edwin Arlington Robinson: A
Collection of Critical Essays, p. 295 (see no. 483).

1005 Curley, Dorothy Nyren; Kramer, Maurice; and Kramer,
      Elaine Fialka, eds. "Dickey, James." In A Library of
      Literary Criticism: Modern American Literature, 4th enl.
      ed., vol. 1, pp. 287-290. New York: Frederick Ungar
      Publishing Co., 1969.
        "The Being," p. 288; Buckdancer's Choice, pp. 288-289;
      "Drinking from a Helmet," p. 288; Drowning with Others,
      p. 287; ["E. E. Cummings"], p. 288; "Falling" [sec. of
      Poems 1957-1967], p. 290; "The Firebombing," p. 288;
      Helmets, pp. 287, 289; Into the Stone and Other Poems,
      p. 287; Poems 1957-1967, p. 290; ["Randall Jarrell"],
      p. 288; "Reincarnation (II)," p. 288; ["The Shark's Par-
      lor"], p. 289; The Suspect in Poetry, p. 288; Two Poems
      of the Air, p. 288.
        A compilation of excerpts from the following essays on
      Dickey's works: Joseph Bennett's "A Man with a Voice"
      (see no. 580), Wendell Berry's "James Dickey's New
      Book" (see no. 583), William Dickey's "The Thing Itself"
      (see no. 668), Denis Donoghue's "The Good Old Complex
      Fate" (see no. 671), Robert Duncan's "'Oriented by
      Instinct by Stars'" (see no. 675), Richard Howard's "On
      James Dickey" (see no. 737), Laurence Lieberman's "The
      Worldly Mystic" (see no. 796), M. L. Rosenthal's "Epi-
      logue: American Continuities and Cross Currents" (see
      no. 1066), John Simon's "More Brass than Enduring" (see
      no. 904), and Robert Watson's "Two Books of Criticism"
      (see no. 953).
        Ref.: William Carlos Williams, p. 287.

1006 Cushman, Jerome. In The "Library Journal" Book Review:
      1968, pp. 339-340. New York: R. R. Bowker Co.,
      1969.
        ["Edwin Arlington Robinson"], p. 339; ["Preface"],
      p. 339; ["Randall Jarrell"], p. 339.
        Favorable review of Babel to Byzantium containing 140
      words.
        Orig.: Library Journal (see no. 655).

1007 Davison, Peter. "'The Great Grassy World from Both Sides':
      The Poetry of Robert Lowell and James Dickey." In
      James Dickey: The Expansive Imagination; A Collection
      of Critical Essays, edited by Richard J. Calhoun, pp. 35-
      51 [37-38, 44-51]. DeLand, Fla.: Everett-Edwards, 1973.
        "Adultery," p. 50; ["Armor"], p. 46; "Buckdancer's
      Choice," p. 45; Buckdancer's Choice, p. 48; "Cherrylog
      Road," p. 47; "Drinking from a Helmet," p. 47; Drowning
      with Others, pp. 46-47; "Encounter in the Cage Country,"
      p. 50; "Falling," p. 50; ["False Youth: Two Seasons"],

p. 50; "Fence Wire," p. 47; "The Fiend," pp. 48-49;
"The Firebombing," pp. 48-49; "The Heaven of Animals,"
p. 45; Helmets, pp. 47-48; ["In the Lupanar at Pompeii"],
p. 47; "Inside the River," p. 46; Into the Stone and Other
Poems, pp. 46-47; "The Lifeguard," p. 47; "May Day
Sermon to the Women of Gilmer County, Georgia, by a
Woman Preacher Leaving the Baptist Church," p. 51;
Poems 1957-1967, pp. 49, 51; "Power and Light," p. 50;
["Reincarnation (II)"], p. 50; "The Scarred Girl," p. 47;
"The Shark's Parlor," p. 49; "The Sheep Child," p. 50;
"Slave Quarters," p. 48; "Sun," p. 50.

A brief chronicle of Dickey's poetry in which his use
of narrative and syntatical techniques and of the recurrent
themes of reincarnation, war, and sexual aberration are
examined.   Dickey is contrasted with Robert Lowell at the
beginning.   The first portion of its title is from "The
Sheep Child."

Ref.: W. H. Auden, p. 51; Robert Lowell, p. 45;
Edwin Muir, pp. 45-46; Muir's "The Animals," p. 45;
Theodore Roethke, p. 48.

Orig.: The Atlantic (see no. 659).   (It was originally
entitled "The Difficulties of Being Major: The Poetry of
Robert Lowell and James Dickey." This is an "adapta-
tion" of the original essay.)

1008 Dillard, R. H. W. [R. H. W. D.]. "Literature." In Britannica
Book of the Year, 1971, pp. 452-453 [453]. Chicago:
Encyclopaedia Britannica, 1971.
Deliverance.
The use of violence in Deliverance is briefly mentioned.
Ref.: Saul Bellow's Mr. Sammler's Planet, p. 453.

1009 Dodsworth, Martin. "Introduction: The Survival of Poetry."
In The Survival of Poetry: A Contemporary Survey, edited
by Martin Dodsworth, pp. 11-36 [16-19]. London: Faber
and Faber, 1970.
"The Ice Skin," pp. 16-17.
Dickey's poems are well suited to academic study be-
cause of the ease with which they are explicated due to
their obvious symbolism, techniques, and commonplace-
ness.   Explication and failures of "The Ice Skin" are
given.
Ref.: Edward Lucie-Smith, pp. 18-19; George MacBeth,
p. 18.

1010 Donadio, Stephen. "Some Younger Poets in America." In
Modern Occasions, edited by Philip Rahv, pp. 226-246
[236-238, 243]. New York: Farrar, Straus and Giroux,
1966.
Buckdancer's Choice, pp. 236, 238; ["A Dog Sleeping on
My Feet"], p. 237; Drowning with Others, p. 236; "The
Fiend," p. 238; ["The Heaven of Animals"], p. 237;
Helmets, pp. 236, 238; ["In the Tree House at Night"],

p. 237; Into the Stone and Other Poems, p. 236; ["The
Owl King: III, The Blind Child's Story"], p. 237; The
Suspect in Poetry, p. 236.
 Dickey's imagination and his preoccupation with meta-
morphosis and death are discussed. Ideas expressed by
Robert Bly in an essay on Dickey are summarized and
supported.
 Ref.: Robert Bly's "The Work of James Dickey,"
p. 238 (see no. 589); Robert Creeley, p. 236.

1011 Elley, Derek. "John Boorman." In International Film Guide
  1974, edited by Peter Cowie, pp. 15-21 [17-19]. London:
  Tantivy Press, 1973.
   Deliverance [novel], p. 17; Deliverance [film], pp. 15,
  18-19.
   In this study of all of Boorman's films to date, his use
  of color, the introspections of the characters, and the
  building tension in the film version of Deliverance are
  briefly mentioned. Complete credits for the film appear
  in the Boorman filmography which concludes.
   Ref.: Ned Beatty, p. 18; Burt Reynolds, p. 18; Jon
  Voight, p. 18.
   Illustrated with a still, p. 18.

1012 Ellman, Richard and O'Clair, Robert, eds. "James Dickey."
  In The Norton Anthology of Modern Poetry, pp. 1028-1030.
  New York: W. W. Norton and Co., 1973.
   "Chenille," p. 1030; ["Creative Possibilities"], p. 1029;
  "Falling," p. 1028; "The Fiend," p. 1028; "The Jewel,"
  p. 1030; Self-Interviews, p. 1029n.; ["Teaching, Writing,
  Reincarnations, and Rivers"], p. 1029.
   Dickey's ideas concerning poetry in general are given
  with some biographical data.
   Ref.: William Blake, p. 1028; Andrew Lytle, p. 1029;
  Flannery O'Connor, p. 1029; The Sewanee Review,
  p. 1029; Monroe K. Spears, p. 1029; Oscar Wilde, p. 1028.

1013 Ethridge, James M. and Kopala, Barbara, eds. "Dickey,
  James (Lafayette)." In Contemporary Authors: A Bio-
  Bibliographical Guide to Current Authors and Their Works,
  vol. 11-12, pp. 110-111. Detroit: Gale Research Co.,
  Book Tower, 1965.
   Dickey's achievements and interests are lightly covered.
  Lists devoted to biographical data, career information, and
  major works are included.
   Ref.: Howard Nemerov, p. 111; Theodore Roethke,
  p. 111; Richard Wilbur, p. 111; Chad Walsh's "James
  Dickey," p. 111 (see no. 1083).
   Rept.: 200 Contemporary Authors (see no. 1021).
  (Information was subsequently up-dated in the reprinted
  work.)

1014 Evans, Oliver. "Poetry: The 1930's to the Present." In

American Literary Scholarship: An Annual, 1966, edited
by James Woodress, pp. 205-217 [206, 209-210]. Durham,
N.C.: Duke University Press, 1968.
Drowning with Others, p. 210; Helmets, p. 210.
Autobiographical traits in Dickey's poetry and his
attitude toward poetry in general are considered defects.
Most of this discussion revolves around Norman Fried-
man's essay on Dickey.
Ref.: Stephen Donadio's "Some Younger Poets in
America," p. 209 (see no. 1010); William Faulkner,
p. 210; Norman Friedman's "The Wesleyan Poets, II:
The Formal Poets, 2," p. 210 (see no. 701); John Keats'
"Ode on a Grecian Urn," p. 210; Carolyn Kizer and James
Boatwright's "A Conversation with James Dickey," p. 210
(see no. 1107); Karl Shapiro, p. 210.

1015 Farber, Stephen. "Deliverance: How It Delivers." In "The
New York Times" Film Reviews, 1971-1972, pp. 299-300.
New York: The New York Times and Arno Press, 1973.
Deliverance [novel], p. 299; Deliverance [film],
pp. 299-300.
The adventure qualities, plot, and symbolism of the
film version of Deliverance are discussed. It is compared
to the novel version, and character studies, concentrating
on the changes of Lewis and Ed, receive most of the re-
marks made.
Ref.: John Boorman, pp. 299-300; Boorman's Having
a Wild Weekend [film], p. 299; Boorman's Hell in the
Pacific [film], p. 299; Boorman's Leo the Last [film],
p. 299; Boorman's Point Blank [film], p. 299; Joseph
Conrad's "Heart of Darkness", p. 299; Ernest Hemingway,
p. 300; Sam Peckinpah's Straw Dogs [film], p. 300; Burt
Reynolds, p. 300; Andrew Sarris, p. 299; Jon Voight,
p. 300; Vilmos Zsigmond, p. 300.
Orig.: The New York Times (see no. 685).

1016 Fleishman, W. B. [B.W.F.]. "Dickey, James." In
Encyclopedia of World Literature in the Twentieth Century
in Three Volumes, edited by Wolfgang Bernard Fleishman,
vol. 1, p. 284. New York: Frederick Ungar Publishing
Co., 1967.
Buckdancer's Choice; The Suspect in Poetry.
Tone, imagery, and setting of Dickey's works are
mentioned as is his place in the lineage of Southern
writers. Biographical data and a short bibliography are
included.
Ref.: Matthew Arnold; Robert Frost; Ezra Pound; John
Crowe Ransom; Allen Tate; Alfred, Lord Tennyson; Paul
Valéry.

1017 Flint, R. W. "Three American Poets." In "New York Re-
view of Books:" Feb. 1963-Jan. 1965, pp. 13-14. New
York: Arno Press, 1969.

"Cherrylog Road," p. 13; "Kudzu," p. 13.

Dickey is regarded as a substantial poet, albeit one who has not yet reached the pinnacle of his abilities, more able with a volume of poetry than with an individual poem. Major themes of Helmets are given.

Ref.: Galway Kinnell, p. 14; Norman Mailer, p. 13; Wallace Stevens' "Sunday Morning," p. 13; Lionel Trilling, p. 13; William Wordsworth, p. 14.

Orig.: The New York Review of Books (see no. 694).

1018 Garrett, George. "Against the Grain: Poets Writing Today." In American Poetry, edited by Irvin Ehrenpreis, pp. 221-239 [224, 226]. London: Edward Arnold, Publishers, 1965.

Helmets, p. 228.

Brief mention is given to Dickey describing him as an influential descendant of a critical dynasty.

Ref.: T. S. Eliot, p. 224; Randall Jarrell, p. 224; John Crowe Ransom, p. 224; Allen Tate, p. 224; Robert Penn Warren, p. 224.

1019 Glancy, Eileen. "Introductory Essay." In James Dickey: The Critic as Poet; An Annotated Bibliography with an Introductory Essay, pp. 1-33. Troy, N. Y.: The Whitston Publishing Co., 1971.

["Allen Ginsberg"], p. 6; "Approaching Prayer," pp. 21-25; Babel to Byzantium, p. 1; ["Buckdancer's Choice"], pp. 24, 28; Buckdancer's Choice, pp. 26-27; "The Celebration," pp. 28-29; ["Charles Olson"], p. 6; "Chenille," p. 20; "Cherrylog Road," p. 30; Deliverance, p. 1; "A Dog Sleeping on My Feet," pp. 18-19; ["E. E. Cummings"], p. 8, 25; "Falling," p. 25; ["Galway Kinnell"], p. 11; ["Gary Snyder"], p. 11; ["Hayden Carruth"], p. 7; "In the Tree House at Night," pp. 16, 26-27; ["J. V. Cunningham"], p. 13; ["Marianne Moore"], pp. 10-11; "May Day Sermon to the Women of Gilmer County, Georgia, by a Woman Preacher Leaving the Baptist Church," pp. 30-32; ["The Owl King: II, The Owl King"], p. 15; Poems 1957-1967, pp. 1, 14, 30; "The Poet Turns on Himself," pp. 3-5, 13-14, 33; ["Preface"], p. 2; "Pursuit from Under," p. 16; ["Randall Jarrell"], p. 12; ["Richard Eberhart"], pp. 9, 25; ["Richard Wilbur"], p. 13; ["Robert Duncan"], p. 12; "The Salt Marsh," p. 16; "A Screened Porch in the Country," pp. 17-18; [Spinning the Crystal Ball], pp. 2, 14; "Springer Mountain," pp. 24-25; ["The Suspect in Poetry"], p. 5; The Suspect in Poetry, p. 5; ["Theodore Roethke"], pp. 9-10; ["Thom Gunn"], pp. 7-8; [unidentified passages], pp. 5, 7-8, 15; ["The Winters Approach"], p. 6.

Dickey's criticism, and his critics' works about him, is surveyed to discover if he follows his own theories in his verse. Dickey's imagery, the development of his persona, his poetry's action, his use of superlatives,

empathy, and exchange, and his primitivism are dis-
cussed.

Ref.: Donald W. Baker's "The Poetry of James
Dickey, " p. 14 (see no. 576); T. S. Eliot, p. 1; Ralph
Waldo Emerson, p. 8; Emerson's "Brahma, " p. 23;
Esquire, p. 5; Gerard Manley Hopkins, p. 15; Hopkins'
"Hurrahing in Harvest, " pp. 15-16; Henry James, p. 13;
Randall Jarrell, p. 1; Carolyn Kizer and James Boat-
wright's "A Conversation with James Dickey, " p. 2 (see
no. 1107); Life, p. 15; Ralph J. Mills, Jr. 's "Brilliant
Essays on Contemporary Poetry, " p. 1 (see no. 821);
Marianne Moore, pp. 11, 33; The New Yorker, p. 15;
Poetry, p. 15; Ezra Pound, p. 13; Theodore Roethke,
pp. 10-11, 33; Louis Simpson's "Dead Horses, Live
Issues, " p. 17; H. L. Weatherby's "The Way of Exchange
in James Dickey's Poetry, " p. 19 (see no. 954); Walt
Whitman, p. 30.

1020   Gregor, Arthur. "James Dickey, American Romantic: An
Appreciation. " In James Dickey: The Expansive Imagina-
tion; A Collection of Critical Essays, edited by Richard J.
Calhoun, pp. 77-80. DeLand, Fla. : Everett-Edwards,
1973.

"Armor, " p. 77; "Blood, " p. 78; Buckdancer's Choice,
p. 78; The Eye-Beaters, Blood, Victory, Madness, Buck-
head and Mercy, p. 78; "The Fiend, " p. 78; "Knock, "
p. 78; "May Day Sermon to the Women of Gilmer County,
Georgia, by a Woman Preacher Leaving the Baptist
Church, " p. 78; "The Owl King, " p. 77; "The Shark's
Parlor, " p. 78; "Springer Mountain, " p. 77; "Walking on
Water, " p. 77.

Aspects of sacredness in Dickey's poetry are noted
with a distinction made between his and previous roman-
tics' verse. The quality of energy, his heritage--regional
and familial--and his personal, Hemingway-like persona
give his brand of romanticism a distinctly American flavor
to which the affirmative statement of his vision adds.

Ref.: Samuel Taylor Coleridge, p. 78; Emily Dickin-
son's [unidentified passage], p. 79; Theodore Roethke,
p. 78; Dylan Thomas, p. 78.

1021   Harte, Barbara and Riley, Carolyn, eds. "Dickey, James. "
In 200 Contemporary Authors: Bio-Bibliographies of
Selected Leading Writers of Today with Critical and Per-
sonal Sidelights, p. 89. Detroit: Gale Research Co. ,
Book Tower, 1969.

Dickey's achievements and interests are lightly covered.
Lists devoted to biographical data, career information, and
major works are included.

Ref.: Howard Nemerov; Theodore Roethke; Richard
Wilbur; Chad Walsh's "James Dickey" (see no. 1083).

Orig.: Contemporary Authors (see no. 1013). (Some
information does not appear in the original publication.)

1021a Haskell, Molly.   From Reverence to Rape: The Treatment
of Women in the Movies, pp. 13, 23, 364. New York:
Holt, Rinehart and Winston, 1974.
[Deliverance] [novel], p. 364; Deliverance [film], pp. 13,
23, 364.
The film version of Deliverance is listed as one of
many male-oriented films of recent years.
Ref. : The Dirty Dozen [film], p. 13; The French Con-
nection [film], p. 13; The Godfather [film], p. 13.

1022 Hassan, Ihab.   Contemporary American Literature, 1945-
1972: An Introduction, pp. 126-127. New York: Fred-
erick Ungar Publishing Co. , 1973.
Babel to Byzantium, p. 127; Buckdancer's Choice,
p. 126; Deliverance, p. 127; Drowning with Others,
p. 126; The Eye-Beaters, Blood, Victory, Madness, Buck-
head and Mercy, p. 127; Helmets, p. 126; Into the Stone
[and Other Poems], p. 126; ["The Poet Turns on Him-
self"], p. 126; The Suspect in Poetry, p. 127.
Mysticism, violence, guilt, and dreams characterize
Dickey's oeuvre.
Ref. : William Faulkner, p. 127.

1023 Hill, Robert W.   "James Dickey: Comic Poet." In James
Dickey: The Expansive Imagination; A Collection of Criti-
cal Essays, edited by Richard J. Calhoun, pp. 143-155.
DeLand, Fla. : Everett-Edwards, 1973.
"Cherrylog Road," pp. 148, 151; "Encounter in the
Cage Country," pp. 148, 150-151; "Falling," pp. 144,
146, 148; "The Heaven of Animals," pp. 148-149; "The
Lifeguard," p. 144; "May Day Sermon to the Women of
Gilmer County, Georgia, by a Woman Preacher Leaving
the Baptist Church," p. 143; "The Performance,"
pp. 144-145; "Power and Light," pp. 148, 151, 153;
["Two Poems of Going Home: II,] Looking for the Buck-
head Boys," p. 143.
Dickey's brand of comedy is characterized by optimism
and positivism. The joy expressed in much of his work
is also discussed.
Ref. : Beowulf, p. 143; Pecos Bill, p. 154; Paul
Bunyan, p. 154; Dante, p. 148; Falstaff, p. 154; Northrop
Frye, p. 143; Laurence Lieberman's "James Dickey: The
Deepening of Being, " p. 151 (see no. 1034); Herman
Melville, p. 149; Constance Rourke, pp. 143, 154; Wil-
liam Shakespeare's Hamlet, p. 143; Thor, p. 155; Walt
Whitman, p. 155.

1024 Howard, Richard.   "James Dickey: 'We Never Can Really
Tell Whether Nature Condemns Us or Loves Us. '" In
Alone with America: Essays on the Art of Poetry in the
United States Since 1950, pp. 75-98. New York: Athen-
eum, 1969.
"Adultery," p. 96; "Approaching Prayer," pp. 85-86;

"Armor," p. 86; "At Darien Bridge," pp. 87-88; "Await-
ing the Swimmer," pp. 76-77; Buckdancer's Choice,
pp. 90-91, 96; ["The Change"], pp. 95-96; "Cherrylog
Road," pp. 89-90; "The Common Grave," p. 92; "A Dog
Sleeping on My Feet," p. 85; "Dover: Believing in
Kings," pp. 81-82; ["Drinking from a Helmet"], pp. 86-
87; Drowning with Others, pp. 77, 80, 85-86, 96; "The
Dusk of Horses," p. 87; "The Escape," p. 91; "Falling,"
pp. 96-97; "The Fiend," p. 92; "The Firebombing,"
pp. 93-95; "Fog Envelops the Animals," p. 83; ["For the
Last Wolverine"], p. 96; ["For the Nightly Ascent of the
Hunter Orion Over a Forest Clearing"], p. 92; "Fox
Blood," p. 91; "The Heaven of Animals," pp. 83, 87;
Helmets, pp. 85, 89-90, 96; "Hunting Civil War Relics
at Nimblewill Creek," p. 85; ["In the Lupanar at
Pompeii"], p. 75; ["In the Marble Quarry"], p. 90;
"Inside the River," pp. 80-81; "Into the Stone," pp. 76,
78; Into the Stone and Other Poems, pp. 76, 80, 84, 87,
92, 96; ["A Letter"], p. 98; "Mangham," p. 95; ["May
Day] Sermon to the Women of Gilmer County, Georgia, by
a Woman Preacher Leaving the Baptist Church," pp. 96-
97; ["Mindoro, 1944"], pp. 79, 86; "Near Darien," pp. 76,
87; "On the Coosawattee," p. 88; ["On the Coosawattee:
II], Below Ellijay," p. 88; ["On the Coosawattee: I], By
Canoe Through the Fir Forest," p. 88; ["On the Coosa-
wattee: III], The Inundation," p. 89; "Orpheus Before
Hades," p. 77; "The Owl King," p. 84; ["The Owl King:
III], The Blind Child's Story," p. 84; ["The Owl King: I],
The Call," p. 84; "The Performance," pp. 79-80; ["Poem"],
p. 75; Poems 1957-1967, p. 96; "Pursuit from Under,"
p. 95; ["Randall Jarrell"], p. 75; ["Reincarnation (II)"],
pp. 96-98; ["The Salt Marsh"], p. 85; ["A Screened Porch
in the Country"], pp. 82-83; ["The Shark's Parlor"],
p. 96; ["The Signs"], pp. 78-79, 86; "Slave Quarters,"
pp. 94-95; ["Springer Mountain"], pp. 87, 90; The Suspect
in Poetry, p. 75; "To Landrum Guy, Beginning to Write
at Sixty," p. 85; "Trees and Cattle," pp. 76-77; ["The
Twin Falls"], p. 80; "The Underground Stream," p. 76;
[unidentified passage], p. 81; "The Vegetable King,"
pp. 76, 78, 80; "Walking on Water," pp. 76-77; ["The]
War Wound," p. 91; ["Winter Trout"], p. 88.
    Dickey's major themes, symbols, images, and forms
are investigated in this chronological survey.   Much com-
parison and contrasting of poems are included.
    Ref.: William Blake, p. 80; Renê Char, p. 77; Joseph
Conrad, p. 78; Francis Cornford, p. 84; Günter Eich's
[epigraph used in "The Firebombing"], p. 93; T. S. Eliot,
p. 90; Ralph Waldo Emerson, p. 75; Eurydice, p. 77;
Morgan le Fay, p. 82; André Gide, p. 89; Frederic
Harrison, p. 84; Heraclitus, p. 80; William James, p. 84;
Märchen, p. 84; John Henry Newman, p. 91; Orpheus,
pp. 76-77, 80; Plutarch, p. 82; Prospero, p. 93; Theodore
Roethke, pp. 77, 81; Percy Bysshe Shelley, p. 80; Socra-

tes, p. 81; Wallace Stevens, p. 85; Jules Supervielle,
p. 77; Valerianeus, p. 77; William Wordsworth, p. 88;
William Butler Yeats, p. 77.
    Orig. : Partisan Review (see no. 737). (It was
originally entitled "On James Dickey" and did not include
the section concerning Poems 1957-1967.)

1025 Johnson, J. J. "Deliverance. " In Masterplots, 1971 Annual:
      Magill's Literary Annual Essay-Reviews of 100 Outstanding
      Books Published in the United States During 1970, edited
      by Frank N. Magill, pp. 58-61. Englewood Cliffs, N. J. :
      Salem Press, 1971.
          "Before, " p. 60; Deliverance, pp. 58-60; "The Fire-
      bombing, " p. 60; "In the Mountain Tent, " p. 60.
          The theme of Deliverance is given two interpretations,
      and its title's relationship to the theme and to each of the
      four main characters is explained. The wilderness motif
      is discussed in regard to its relationship to the novel and
      to two of Dickey's poems, "The Firebombing" and "In the
      Mountain Tent. "
          Ref. : Charles Darwin, p. 59.

1026 Justus, James H. "Fiction: The 1930's to the Present. "
      In American Literary Scholarship: An Annual, 1970,
      edited by J. Albert Robbins, pp. 253-279 [255]. Durham,
      N. C. : Duke University Press, 1972.
          Deliverance.
          Mention is given to Dickey's participation on a panel
      discussion.
          Ref. : Robert Drake's "The Writer and His Tradition, "
      p. 255 (see no. 1100).

1027 _____ . "Fiction: The 1930's to the Present. " In Ameri-
      can Literary Scholarship: An Annual, 1972, edited by J.
      Albert Robbins, pp. 264-311 [270-271].
          Deliverance, p. 271.
          Two articles written about Dickey's works are dis-
      cussed briefly.
          Ref. : Howard M. Harper, Jr. 's "Trends in Recent
      American Fiction, " p. 270 (see no. 723); Fredric Jame-
      son's "The Great American Hunter, or Ideological Content
      in the Novel, " p. 271 (see no. 749).

1028 Katz, Bill. In The "Library Journal" Book Review, 1967,
      p. 406. New York: R. R. Bowker Co. , 1969.
          ["Bread"]; "Falling" [sec. of Poems 1957-1967]; ["The
      Sheep Child"].
          Favorable review of Poems 1957-1967 containing 176
      words.
          Ref. : The New York Times; Times Literary Supple-
      ment; [unidentified passages from criticism of Dickey].
          Orig. : Library Journal (see no. 761).

1029 Kinsman, Clare D. and Tennehouse, Mary Ann, eds.
      "Dickey, James (Lafayette)." In Contemporary Authors:
      A Bio-bibliographical Guide to Current Authors and Their
      Works, vol. 9-12, first revision, pp. 228-232. Detroit:
      Gale Research Co., The Book Tower, 1974.
         Babel to Byzantium, p. 231; Buckdancer's Choice,
      p. 230; Deliverance [novel], p. 230; Deliverance [film],
      p. 232; The Eye-Beaters, Blood, Victory, Madness, Buck-
      head and Mercy, p. 231; "The Fiend," p. 230; "The Firebomb-
      ing," p. 230; ["First Novelists"], p. 230; Helmets, p. 231;
      Poems 1957-1967, pp. 230-231; [The Poems of James Dickey
      (1957-1967)] [L. P. record], p. 232; ["The Poet Turns on Him-
      self"], p. 229; "Slave Quarters," p. 230; Two Poems of the
      Air, p. 230; [unidentified passages], pp. 230-231.
         A survey of criticism of Dickey's works, it is intro-
      duced by lists detailing his life, career, published works,
      and works in progress.
         Ref.: James Aronson's [review of Self-Interviews],
      p. 229 (see no. 569); John Alfred Avant's [review of
      Deliverance], p. 231 (see no. 575); Donald W. Baker's
      "The Poetry of James Dickey," p. 230 (see no. 576);
      Calvin Bedient's "Gold-Glowing Mote," p. 230 (see
      no. 578); John Berryman, p. 231; Robert Bly's "Buck-
      dancer's Choice," p. 230 (see no. 586); John William
      Corrington's "James Dickey's Poems 1957-1967: A Per-
      sonal Appraisal," pp. 229, 231 (see no. 643); Peter
      Davison's "The Difficulties of Being Major: The Poetry
      of Robert Lowell and James Dickey," pp. 229, 231 (see
      no. 659); Richard Eberhart, p. 231; Norman Friedman's
      "The Wesleyan Poets, II: The Formal Poets, 2,"
      pp. 230-231 (see no. 701); Jean Garrigue's "James Dickey
      Airbourne and Earthbound," p. 230 (see no. 707); Richard
      Howard's "On James Dickey," p. 230 (see no. 737); Vic-
      tor Howes' "Genuine and Bogus," p. 231 (see no. 740);
      Rolfe Humphries, p. 231; Howard Kaye's "Why Review
      Poetry?," p. 231 (see no. 763); "Leaps and Plunges,"
      p. 231 (see no. 782); Laurence Lieberman's "James
      Dickey: The Deepening of Being," p. 231 (see no. 1034);
      "Lord, Let Me Die but Not Die Out" [film], p. 232 (see
      no. 1140); Robert Lowell, p. 231; Saul Maloff's "Poet
      Takes His Turn as Critic," p. 231 (see no. 809); Ralph
      J. Mills, Jr.'s "The Poetry of James Dickey," p. 230
      (see no. 822); Harry Morris' "A Formal View of the
      Poetry of Dickey, Garrigue, and Simpson," p. 231 (see
      no. 827); Jay Robert Nash's [remarks in Literary Times],
      p. 232 (see no. 838); Howard Nemerov, p. 231; Paul
      O'Neil's "The Unlikeliest Poet," pp. 229-231 (see no. 850);
      Christopher Ricks' "Man Hunt," p. 230 (see no. 876);
      Lucy Rosenthal's "A Novel of Man, the Forest, Death and
      Heroism," p. 230 (see no. 886); May Sarton, p. 231; John
      Simon's "More Brass than Enduring," p. 231 (see no. 904);
      L. E. Sissman's "Poet Into Novelist," p. 230 (see
      no. 907); William Jay Smith, p. 231; Margaret Tongue,

p. 231; Louis Untermeyer's "A Way of Seeing and Saying,"
p. 231 (see no. 942); The Virginia Quarterly Review's
[review of Babel to Byzantium], p. 231 (see no. 947);
Robert Penn Warren, p. 231; Geoffrey Wolff's "Hunting
in Hell," p. 229 (see no. 966).

1030 Knight, Arthur.   "... And Deliver Us from Evil." In Film
72-73: An Anthology, edited by David Denby, pp. 19-21.
New York: The Bobbs-Merrill Co., 1973.
    Deliverance [novel], p. 19; Deliverance [film], pp. 19-
21.
    The film version of Deliverance is discussed in regard
to the technique employed by its director, its adventure
quality, and its effect on the audience.
    Ref.: Ned Beatty, p. 20; John Boorman, pp. 19-21;
Boorman's Hell in the Pacific [film], p. 19; Boorman's
Point Blank [film], p. 19; Ronny Cox, p. 20; Burt
Reynolds, pp. 20-21; Jon Voight, pp. 20-21; Vilmos
Zsigmond, p. 21.
    Orig.: Saturday Review (see no. 774).

1031 Kostelanetz, Richard.   The End of Intelligent Writing: Lit-
erary Politics in America, pp. 95, 147-148, 255, 324-
325, 347, 358-359.   New York: Sheed and Ward, 1974.
    Babel to Byzantium, p. 148; "The Son, the Cave, and
the Burning Bush," pp. 324, 347.
    Dickey's role in the politics of literary publishing is
briefly discussed.
    Ref.: The American Literary Anthology, p. 147 (see
no. 548); John Ashbery, p. 147; Robert Bly, p. 358;
Robert Creeley, pp. 147, 359; Creeley's A Quick Graph,
p. 148; Allen Ginsberg, p. 359; Richard Howard, p. 148;
Howard's ["On James Dickey"], p. 148 (see no. 737);
Laurence Lieberman, p. 148; Lieberman's ["James
Dickey: The Deepening of Being"], p. 148 (see no. 1034);
Robert Lowell, pp. 95, 359; Theodore Roethke, p. 255.

1032 _____.   "Flyswatter and Gadfly." In James Dickey: The
Expansive Imagination; A Collection of Critical Essays,
edited by Richard J. Calhoun, pp. 135-141. DeLand, Fla.:
Everett-Edwards, 1973.
    ["Allen Ginsberg"], p. 139; ["Anne Sexton"], pp. 136-
137; Babel to Byzantium, p. 139n.; ["E. E. Cummings"],
p. 138; ["The Grove Press New American Poets (1960)"],
p. 137; ["John Logan"], p. 140; ["Kenneth Patchen"],
pp. 139, 141; ["New Poets of England and America I
(1957)"], p. 139; ["Randall Jarrell"], pp. 136, 140; The
Suspect in Poetry, pp. 135, 137, 140; ["Thom Gunn"],
p. 137; ["Toward a Solitary Joy"], p. 141.
    The Suspect in Poetry is described as being honest and
humorous, as displaying a kindness toward bad poets, and
as possessing a single thesis evident throughout.
    Ref.: John Ashbery, p. 138; John Berryman, p. 138;

Robert Bly's [remarks on the dust jacket of The Suspect
in Poetry], p. 135; Leslie A. Fiedler, p. 138; Randall
Jarrell, p. 140; Kenneth Koch, p. 138; C. S. Lewis,
pp. 136-137; Robert Lowell, p. 138; Sylvia Plath, p. 138;
Theodore Roethke, p. 138; Harold Rosenbury, p. 137;
William Stafford, p. 138.
    Orig. : Shenandoah (see no. 776).

1033 Lensing, George. "James Dickey and the Movements of
      Imagination. " In James Dickey: The Expansive Imagina-
      tion; A Collection of Critical Essays, edited by Richard J.
      Calhoun, pp. 157-175. DeLand, Fla. : Everett-Edwards,
      1973.
          ["Armor"], pp. 165, 175; "Between Two Prisoners, "
      p. 162; "The Birthday Dream, " p. 162; "Buckdancer's
      Choice, " p. 165; Buckdancer's Choice, p. 171; ["Cherry-
      log Road"], p. 160; ["Deer Among Cattle"], p. 164; "A
      Dog Sleeping on My Feet, " pp. 161, 164; "Drinking from
      a Helmet, " pp. 162-163; "The Driver, " p. 162; "The Dusk
      of Horses, " p. 162; ["The Enclosure"], p. 160; "The Eye-
      Beaters, " p. 169; The Eye-Beaters, Blood, Victory, Mad-
      ness, Buckhead and Mercy, pp. 166, 173; "Falling, "
      pp. 159, 172, 174; "Fence Wire, " p. 163; "The Fire-
      bombing, " p. 162; "Fog Envelops the Animals, " p. 162;
      "A Folk Singer of the Thirties, " p. 162; "For the Last
      Wolverine, " p. 174; "Gerard Manley Hopkins: 'The Wreck
      of the Deutschland, '" p. 173; "Horses and Prisoners, "
      p. 162; "Hunting Civil War Relics at Nimblewill Creek, "
      pp. 159-160; ["The Ice Skin"], p. 175; "In the Lupanar at
      Pompeii, " p. 166; ["In the Mountain Tent, "] p. 164; "In
      the Tree House at Night, " p. 165; "Kudzu, " p. 166; "The
      Lifeguard, " pp. 167, 169, 171; "The Lord in the Air, "
      p. 166; "Madness, " p. 166; "Messages, " p. 166; "Near
      Darien, " pp. 161-162; "The Other, " pp. 159, 161; "The
      Owl King, " p. 164; "The Performance, " p. 162; "Pine, "
      p. 173; "The Poet Turns on Himself, " pp. 158-159, 162,
      164, 172, 175; "Pursuit from Under, " p. 159; "Reincarna-
      tion (II), " p. 174; Self-Interviews, p. 167; "The Shark's
      Parlor, " p. 166; "The Sheep Child, " p. 163; "Slave
      Quarters, " p. 172; "Sled Burial, Dream Ceremony, "
      p. 162; "Springer Mountain, " pp. 162, 164, 170-171; "The
      String, " p. 165; "To His Children in Darkness, " p. 162;
      "Trees and Cattle, " p. 170; "Turning Away, " p. 173;
      [unidentified passage], p. 160; "Victory, " p. 162; "Walk-
      ing on Water, " p. 166; "The War Wound, " p. 162;
      "Winter Trout, " p. 166.
          The narrative technique is vital to Dickey's work, and
      its success relies heavily on the first lines being written
      in a journalistic style. Devices used to shift from the
      real to the imaginary are discussed at length, and men-
      tion of the qualities of romanticism in his verse is in-
      cluded.
          Ref. : Robert Bly, p. 158; William Faulkner, p. 174;

John Keats, p. 174; Keats' "Ode to a Nightingale," p. 175, 175n.; Ralph J. Mills, Jr.'s "The Poetry of James Dickey," p. 172 (see no. 822); Louis Simpson, p. 158; William Stafford, p. 158; Wallace Stevens, p. 171; William Wordsworth, p. 174; James Wright, p. 158.

1034 Lieberman, Laurence. "James Dickey: The Deepening of Being." In The Achievement of James Dickey: A Comprehensive Selection of His Poems with a Critical Introduction, pp. 1-21. Glenview, Ill.: Scott, Foresman and Co., 1968.

"Drinking from a Helmet," pp. 3-5, 10; Drowning with Others, p. 10; "Encounter in the Cage Country," pp. 17-21; "Falling," pp. 10-11, 13; "Falling" [sec. of Poems 1957-1967], pp. 1, 8; "The Firebombing," pp. 1-3, 5-6, 8, 10, 13-14; "Fog Envelops the Animals," pp. 16-17; "The Heaven of Animals," pp. 17, 20; "The Ice Skin," pp. 1-2; "In the Tree House at Night," pp. 10-12; Into the Stone and Other Poems, p. 9; "The Jewel," pp. 2-3; "The Lifeguard," pp. 11-12, 14; "The Owl King," pp. 18-19; "The Performance," pp. 2-3; "Power and Light," pp. 8-9, 17; "Pursuit from Under," p. 7; "Reincarnation (II)," p. 18; ["The] Shark's Parlor," p. 11; "The Sheep Child," pp. 11, 18-20; "Slave Quarters," pp. 1, 13; "Snakebite," p. 20; "Springer Mountain," pp. 16-17, 20; "The String," pp. 8-10, 13.

Joy, considered to be the central quality of Dickey's works, conducts and transforms the major themes. His verse dealing with war, death, animals, guilt, sex, and their various combinations are discussed at length. Ritualism and the persona's dual nature are also investigated. "The Heaven of Animals" is reprinted in full, pp. 14-16.

Ref.: Bible, p. 19; Claudius, p. 6; Crazy Jane, p. 19; King Hamlet, p. 6; Randall Jarrell, p. 4; Franz Kafka's "Metamorphosis," p. 18; D. H. Lawrence, p. 14; Lawrence's Women in Love, p. 16; Wilfred Owen, p. 4; Robert Ripley, p. 19; Theodore Roethke, p. 1; Walt Whitman, p. 6; William Butler Yeats, pp. 1, 19; Yeats' "Leda and the Swan," p. 19; Yeats' "The Second Coming," p. 19.

1035 _____. "Notes on James Dickey's Style." In James Dickey: The Expansive Imagination; A Collection of Critical Essays, edited by Richard J. Calhoun, pp. 195-201. DeLand, Fla.: Everett-Edwards, 1973.

Buckdancer's Choice, pp. 197-198; "Cherrylog Road," p. 201; "Drinking from a Helmet," pp. 196, 198; "Dust," pp. 197-198; "Encounter in the Cage Country," pp. 200-201; "Falling," p. 199; "Falling" [sec. of Poems 1957-1967], pp. 197-198; "The Flash," p. 198; Helmets, p. 197; "The Hospital Window," p. 201; "The Island," p. 198; "The Performance," p. 195; "Power and Light,"

p. 200; "The Scratch," p. 198; "Snakebite," p. 198;
"Sun," p. 198; The Suspect in Poetry, p. 195.

Dickey's figurative language, line structure, poetic
forms, and symbolism are discussed. Included in this
investigation is the identification of techniques common to
film and journalism in Dickey's works. Mention is given
to the development of his symbolism through several books
and to his use of the phrase as a basic unit.

Ref. : William Faulkner, p. 199; Henry James' The
Sacred Fount, p. 201; James Joyce, p. 199; Walt Whit-
man, p. 197; William Butler Yeats, p. 197; Yeats' A
Vision, p. 197.

Orig. : The Far Point (see no. 793).

1036 _____ . "The Worldly Mystic. " In James Dickey: The
Expansive Imagination; A Collection of Critical Essays,
edited by Richard J. Calhoun, pp. 65-76. DeLand, Fla. :
Everett-Edwards, 1973.

Buckdancer's Choice, p. 66; "Encounter in the Cage
Country," pp. 65, 70-71; "Falling," pp. 69, 72-74, 76;
"Falling" [sec. of Poems 1957-1967], p. 65; "False
Youth [: Two Seasons, II]," pp. 71-72; "The Fiend, "
pp. 66, 72-74; "The Firebombing," pp. 66, 68, 76; "The
Flash, " p. 69; "Power and Light," pp. 67, 69, 71, 76;
"The Sheep Child," pp. 72-74; "Slave Quarters," pp. 66,
68, 76; "Snakebite," pp. 69-70; "Sun,." p. 71; [unidentified
passages], pp. 66, 68.

Two themes exist in "Falling," the last portion of
Poems 1957-1967: sexual realism and comic dramatiza-
tion. Each is linked to the persona's dual personality, a
quality absent from the earlier poems. Remarks on
Dickey's recurrent use of reincarnation coupled with "air"
conclude.

Ref. : "A Drunken Man's Praise of Sobriety," p. 68;
Robert Frost, p. 72; Frost's "The Road Not Taken," p.
72; William Butler Yeats, pp. 68, 72; Yeats' "High Talk, "
p. 68.

Exc. : Contemporary Literary Criticism (see no. 1063);
A Library of Literary Criticism (see no. 1005).

Orig. : The Hudson Review (see no. 796).

1037 Linebarger, J. M. John Berryman, pp. 142, 162. New York:
Twayne Publishers, 1974.

["John Berryman"], p. 162n. ; ["Journals"], pp. 142,
162n. ; Sorties, pp. 142, 162n.

Comments are made about Dickey's view of John Berry-
man and about Berryman's poem about Dickey.

Ref. : John Berryman's "Damn You, Jim D. , You
Woke Me Up," p. 142 (see no. 1211).

1038 Magill, Frank N. , ed. "Drowning with Others. " In Master-
plots, 1963 Annual: Essay-Reviews of 100 Outstanding
Books Published in the United States During 1962, pp. 44-

47. New York: Salem Press, 1963.

"Antipolis," p. 47; "A Birth," p. 45; ["A Dog Sleeping on My Feet"], p. 45; "Drowning with Others," p. 46; "Fog Envelops the Animals," p. 45; "The Heaven of Animals," p. 45; "The Hospital Window," p. 46; "In the Mountain Tent," p. 47; ["In the Tree House at Night"], p. 45; Into the Stone and Other Poems, p. 44; "The Lifeguard," p. 44; ["Listening to Foxhounds"], p. 44; "The Owl King," p. 46; "The Owl King [: I, The Call]," p. 46; "The Rib," p. 45; "The Scratch," p. 46.

Recurrent images and themes, especially those of a religious nature, in Drowning with Others are discussed. Dickey's metrics and the persons who have influenced his work are mentioned.

Ref.: Dante, p. 44; T. S. Eliot, p. 46; Homer, p. 47; Icarus, p. 46; Robert Lowell, p. 46; Pericles, p. 47; Ezra Pound, p. 45; Rainer Maria Rilke, pp. 45, 47; Theodore Roethke, pp. 46-47; The Sewanee Review, p. 44; Dylan Thomas, pp. 46-47; Thomas' "I Dreamed My Genesis," p. 47; William Butler Yeats, p. 45.

Exc.: "The Poetry of Dickey" (see no. 1040).

1039 _____. "The Poetry of Dickey." In Masterplots: Five Hundred Plot Stories and Essay Reviews from the World's Fine Literature, 4th Series, vol. 2, pp. 778-781. New York: Salem Press, 1968.

"Approaching Prayer," p. 779; "The Beholders," p. 779; "The Being," p. 779; "A Birth," p. 778; "Buckdancer's Choice," p. 780; Buckdancer's Choice, pp. 780-781; "Bums, on Waking," p. 779; "Cherrylog Road," p. 779; "Drowning with Others," p. 778; Drowning with Others, p. 778; "The Escape," p. 780; "Faces Seen Once," p. 780; "The Firebombing," p. 780; "Fog Envelops the Animals," p. 778; "The Heaven of Animals," p. 778; Helmets, p. 779; "The Hospital Window," p. 779; "In the Child's Night," p. 779; Into the Stone and Other Poems, p. 778; "The Lifeguard," p. 778; "The Night Pool," p. 780; "Reincarnation [(I)]," p. 781; "The Scratch," p. 779; "Springer Mountain," p. 779.

The central themes of each volume of Dickey's oeuvre and the development of Dickey's personal experiences and symbolism into a personal mythology are discussed. His success is attributed to two techniques: the projection of his personae and the vast scope of his perspectives.

Ref.: Aesop, p. 779; Ariel, p. 779; Bible, p. 779; T. S. Eliot, p. 778; Icarus, p. 778; Robert Lowell, p. 778; Dylan Thomas, pp. 778, 780; Ulysses, p. 779; William Butler Yeats, p. 778.

1040 _____. "The Poetry of Dickey." In Masterplots Comprehensive Library Edition: Two Thousand and Ten Plot Stories and Essay Reviews from the World's Fine Literature, vol. 6, pp. 3842-3845. New York: Salem Press,

1968.
"Approaching Prayer," p. 3843; "The Beholders,"
p. 3843; "The Being," p. 3843; "A Birth," p. 3842;
["Buckdancer's Choice"], p. 3844; Buckdancer's Choice,
pp. 3844-3845; "Bums, on Waking," p. 3843; "Cherrylog
Road," p. 3843; "Drowning with Others," p. 3842; Drown-
ing with Others, p. 3842; "The Escape," p. 3844; "Faces
Seen Once," p. 3844; "The Firebombing," p. 3844; "Fog
Envelops the Animals," p. 3842; "The Heaven of Animals,"
p. 3842; Helmets, p. 3843; "The Hospital Window,"
p. 3843; "In the Child's Night," p. 3843; Into the Stone
and Other Poems, p. 3842; "The Lifeguard," p. 3842;
"The Night Pool," p. 3844; "Reincarnation (I)," p. 3844;
"The Scratch," p. 3843; "Springer Mountain," p. 3843.
Although primarily a composite of excerpts from
Magill's "Drowning with Others" (see no. 1038), Newman's
"Helmets" (see no. 1051), and Workman's "Buckdancer's
Choice" (see no. 1090), a section on Into the Stone and
Other Poems was added.
Ref.: Aesop, p. 3843; Ariel, p. 3843; Bible, p. 3843;
T. S. Eliot, p. 3842; Icarus, p. 3842; Robert Lowell,
p. 3842; Dylan Thomas, p. 3844; Ulysses, p. 3843; Wil-
liam Butler Yeats, p. 3842.

1041 Malkoff, Karl. "Dickey, James." Crowell's Handbook of
Contemporary American Poetry, pp. 100-108. New York:
Thomas Y. Crowell Co., 1973.
"Blood," p. 107; Buckdancer's Choice, pp. 103-104,
106; "The Celebration," p. 106; "Cherrylog Road,"
p. 104; "The Common Grave," p. 106; Deliverance,
p. 107; "A Dog Sleeping on My Feet," p. 103; Drowning
with Others, pp. 102, 104; "The Eye-Beaters," p. 107;
The Eye-Beaters, Blood, Victory, Madness, Buckhead
and Mercy, p. 107; "Falling," pp. 103, 106; "Falling"
[sec. of Poems 1957-1967], p. 106; "The Firebombing,"
pp. 103-106; "The Heaven of Animals," pp. 103-104;
Helmets, p. 104; "The Hospital Window," p. 104; Into the
Stone and Other Poems, p. 101; "Kudzu," p. 104; "The
Lifeguard," pp. 102, 107; "Madness," p. 107; "On the
Coosawattee," p. 104; "The Owl King [: III, The Blind
Child's Story"], p. 104; "The Performance," pp. 102,
106; Poems 1957-1967, p. 106; "The Poet Turns on Him-
self," pp. 100-101, 105; "Pursuit from Under," p. 106;
"The Sheep Child," p. 106; "Slave Quarters," pp. 104,
106; "The Summons," p. 103; "The Vegetable King,"
pp. 101-102; "Winter Trout," pp. 104, 106.
Dickey's earlier works are concentrated upon and their
similarities and differences are noted. His use of the
guilt motif and the development of his poetic forms are
investigated in detail. Their autobiographical qualities
and violence and his critics' major concerns are mentioned.
Ref.: Paul Carroll's "The Smell of Blood in Paradise,"
p. 103 (see no. 998); Robert Frost, p. 104; Ernest Heming-

way's "Big Two-Hearted River," p. 104; Sylvia Plath,
p. 106; Marcel Proust, p. 101; Theodore Roethke, p. 101;
Wallace Stevens, p. 107.

1042   _____. "Introduction: A Short History of Contemporary
American Poetry." In Crowell's Handbook of Contemporary
American Poetry, pp. 1-43 [39]. New York: Thomas Y.
Crowell Co., 1973.
Dickey is listed as a member of a loosely knit "school."
Except for their somewhat formal approach to verse,
cohesive characteristics of this group are not identified.
Ref.: Robert Bly; Louis Simpson; James Wright.

1043   Marin, Daniel B. "James Dickey's Deliverance: Darkness
Visible." In James Dickey: The Expansive Imagination;
A Collection of Critical Essays, edited by Richard J.
Calhoun, pp. 105-117. DeLand, Fla.: Everett-Edwards,
1973.
"After," p. 109; "Before," p. 109; Deliverance, pp. 106,
109, 114, 116-117; ["Diabetes: II, Under Buzzards"],
p. 106; The Eye-Beaters, Blood, Victory, Madness, Buck-
head and Mercy, p. 107; ["Messages: I, Butterflies"],
p. 117; "September 14th," p. 112.
Characterization, plot, and setting of Deliverance are
discussed in regard to their strengthening or weakening
the novel as a whole. Its major themes are related to a
few of Dickey's poems.
Ref.: Walter Clemons' "James Dickey, Novelist,"
p. 109 (see no. 637); Samuel Taylor Coleridge's "The
Rime of the Ancient Mariner," p. 117; Joseph Conrad's
"Heart of Darkness," p. 111; Nathaniel Hawthorne's
"Young Goodman Brown," p. 111; Herman Melville's
"Bartleby the Scrivener," p. 110.
Orig.: The South Carolina Review (see no. 810).

1044   Martz, William J. "A Note on Meaningless Being in 'Cherry-
log Road.'" In James Dickey: The Expansive Imagina-
tion; A Collection of Critical Essays, edited by Richard J.
Calhoun, pp. 81-83. DeLand, Fla.: Everett-Edwards,
1973.
"Cherrylog Road," p. 81.
The last line of Dickey's poem "Cherrylog Road" is
central to the whole poem's meaning. Discussion of the
poem's last two words comprises most of this investiga-
tion.

1045   Mesic, Michael. "A Note on James Dickey." In American
Poetry Since 1960: Some Critical Perspectives, edited by
Robert B. Shaw, pp. 145-153. Chester Springs, Penn.:
Dufour Editions, 1974.
Buckdancer's Choice, pp. 149-150, 152; Deliverance,
pp. 150, 153; "Diabetes," p. 153; Drowning with Others,
pp. 148-151; "The Enclosure," p. 146; The Eye-Beaters,

Blood, Victory, Madness, Buckhead and Mercy, pp. 150, 152-153; "The Fiend," pp. 150, 152; "The Firebombing," p. 150; "The Heaven of Animals," p. 151; Helmets, pp. 149, 150, 152; ["Into the Stone"], p. 147; Into the Stone and Other Poems, pp. 146, 148, 150; "On the Coosawattee," pp. 150, 152; "The Owl King," p. 148; ["The Owl King: III,] The Blind Child's Story," pp. 148-149; ["The Owl King: I, The Call"], p. 148; ["The Owl King: II, The Owl King"], p. 148; "The Performance," p. 146; Poems 1957-1967, pp. 146, 149, 152; "The String," p. 147; "The Underground Stream," p. 150.

By attempting, subconsciously or not, to write poetry of the common person, Dickey's verse has developed into prose.   Dickey's metrics and his verse's linear structure are discussed at length, and his recurrent themes and tones are noted.

Ref. :   [blurb on the dust jacket of Poems 1957-1967], p. 145; T. S. Eliot, p. 145; Robert Frost, p. 145; Ezra Pound, p. 145; Wallace Stevens, pp. 145, 147; Stevens' Collected Poems, p. 146.

1046   Mills, Ralph J. , Jr.   Contemporary American Poetry, p. 212. New York: Random House, 1967.

"Drowning with Others"; "The Owl King."

Dickey's ability in creating images and the reader's mental associations accompanying those images are mentioned in a list of similarly talented poets.

Ref. :   Robert Bly; W. S. Merwin; Louis Simpson; James Wright.

1047   _____ .   Creation's Very Self: On the Personal Element in Recent American Poetry, pp. 3-4, 9, 14, 18-19.   Fort Worth, Tex. :   The Texas Christian University Press, 1969.

"The Dream Flood," p. 19; Drowning with Others, p. 18; "The Second Birth," pp. 3-4.

Dickey's metamorphosis technique and his imagination are mentioned, but the theme of "The Second Birth" is discussed in greater detail.   This is one of the annual Cecil Williams Lectures in American Literature delivered May 7, 1969.

Ref. :   Robert Bly, p. 14; David Ignatow, p. 14; John Logan, p. 14; W. S. Merwin, p. 14; Frank O'Hara, p. 14; Louis Simpson, p. 14; Simpson's "The Morning Light," p. 14; William Stafford, p. 14; [unidentified remarks on the dust jacket of Drowning with Others], p. 18; James Wright, p. 14.

1048   _____ .   "James Dickey. " In Contemporary Poets of the English Language, edited by Rosalie Murphy, pp. 295-297.   Chicago: St. James Press, 1970.

Babel to Byzantium, p. 296; "The Poet Turns on Himself, " p. 296; ["A Screened Porch in the Country"],

p. 296; [unidentified passages], pp. 295-296.
Coverage of Dickey's verse includes their rhythm,
language, images, and personal experiences. His longer
poems are criticized for their verboseness and diffusion.
A summary of "The Poet Turns on Himself" is given.
      Ref. : Robert Bly, p. 297; Laurence Lieberman's
"James Dickey: The Deepening of Being, " p. 296 (see
no. 1034); W. S. Merwin, p. 297; Rainer Maria Rilke,
p. 297; Theodore Roethke, p. 296; Louis Simpson,
p. 297; Walt Whitman, p. 296; James Wright, p. 297.

1049 Muste, John M. "American Literature. " In The Americana
      Annual, 1968: An Encyclopedia of the Events of 1967,
      pp. 51-54 [52]. n. p. : Americana, 1968.
      Poems 1957-1967.
      A gradual darkening of Dickey's vision and an accom-
      panying thoughtfulness characterizes Poems 1957-1967.

1050 Nemerov, Howard. "James Dickey. " Reflexions on Poetry
      and Poetics, pp. 71-76. New Brunswick, N. J. : Rutgers
      University Press, 1972.
      "Armor, " p. 76; ["Dover: Believing in Kings"],
      p. 71; "Facing Africa, " p. 75; ["For the Nightly Ascent
      of the Hunter Orion Over a Forest Clearing"], p. 74;
      ["The Island"], p. 72; "The Lifeguard, " p. 76; ["The
      Owl King: III, The Blind Child's Story"], pp. 74, 76;
      ["The Owl King: II, The Owl King"], pp. 72-73; ["The
      Salt Marsh"], p. 74; "The Summons, " pp. 72, 76.
      Rhythm, the mysteriousness of objects and events, the
      relationship distinct elements of the world have with one
      another, the effect of using participles, and the use of
      impaired vision in Dickey's poetry are discussed.
      Ref. : John Keats, p. 72; William Wordsworth, p. 72.
      Orig. : The Sewanee Review (see no. 840). (It was
      originally entitled "Poems of Darkness and a Specialized
      Light. ")

1051 Newman, Preston. "Helmets. " In Masterplots, 1965 Annual:
      Essay-Reviews of 101 Outstanding Books Published in the
      United States During 1964, edited by Frank N. Magill,
      pp. 121-123. New York: Salem Press, 1965.
      "Approaching Prayer, " p. 123; "The Beholders, "
      p. 122; "The Being, " p. 122; "Bums, on Waking, " p. 122;
      "Cherrylog Road, " p. 122; "Drinking from a Helmet, "
      p. 123; "The Driver, " p. 123; "A Folk Singer of the
      Thirties, " p. 122; Helmets, pp. 121-123; "Horses and
      Prisoners, " p. 123; "In the Child's Night, " p. 122;
      "Kudzu, " p. 121; "The Poisoned Man, " pp. 121-122;
      "Springer Mountain, " p. 121.
      Helmets is investigated for its personal mythology and
      its involvement with animals. Plot summaries are
      abundant.
      Ref. : Aesop, p. 121; Ariel, p. 121; W. H. Auden,

p. 121; Bible, p. 121; Robert Frost, p. 121; Karl Shapiro, p. 121; Dylan Thomas, pp. 121, 123; Ulysses, p. 121. Exc.: "The Poetry of Dickey" (see no. 1040).

1052 Nyren, Dorothy. In The "Library Journal" Book Review: 1970, p. 447. New York: R. R. Bowker Co., 1970.
Self-Interviews.
Favorable review of Self-Interviews containing 125 words.
Orig.: Library Journal (see no. 848). (It was originally published under the title "Transcriptions of Interviews with Dickey.")

1053 _____ . In The "Library Journal" Book Review: 1972, p. 299. New York: R. R. Bowker Co., 1973.
Death's Baby Machine; ["Edwin Arlington Robinson"]; ["The Greatest American Poet: Theodore Roethke"]; ["The Son, the Cave, and the Burning Bush"].
Favorable review of Sorties containing 108 words.
Orig.: Library Journal (see no. 847).

1054 Oates, Joyce Carol. "Out of Stone, Into Flesh: The Imagination of James Dickey." New Heaven, New Earth: The Visionary Experience in Literature, pp. 205-263. New York: Vanguard Press, 1974.
"Adultery," p. 242; ["Allen Ginsberg"], p. 305n.; "Angina," p. 238; "Apollo," pp. 250, 252; ["Apollo: I, For the First Manned Moon Orbit"], p. 216; "Apollo [: II, The Moon Ground]," pp. 216, 253; "Approaching Prayer," pp. 225, 304n.; "Armor," p. 304n.; "At Darien Bridge," p. 222; "Blood," p. 250; "Buckdancer's Choice," p. 238; Buckdancer's Choice, pp. 208, 225, 227, 233-234, 237, 242, 254; "The Cancer Match," pp. 220, 250, 253; "Chenille," pp. 222, 237; "Cherrylog Road," pp. 215, 223-224, 227; "The Common Grave," p. 238; Deliverance, pp. 217, 223, 232, 239-240, 248-249, 305n.; "Diabetes," pp. 220, 250; "Diabetes [: I, Sugar]," p. 251; ["Diabetes: II,] Under Buzzards," p. 251; "Drinking from a Helmet," pp. 219, 225-226, 304n.; ["Drowning with Others"], p. 216; Drowning with Others, pp. 208, 216-217; "The Dusk of Horses," pp. 219-220; "The Enclosure," p. 214; "The Escape," p. 238; "The Eye-Beaters," pp. 209, 213, 218, 239, 250, 255-257, 260, 262-263, 304n.; The Eye-Beaters, Blood, Victory, Madness, Buckhead and Mercy, pp. 208, 212, 233, 249, 254, 259-260; "Falling," pp. 233, 236, 242, 257; "Falling" [sec. of Poems 1957-1967], pp. 241, 304n.; "False Youth: Two Seasons," p. 304n.; "Fence Wire," pp. 220-221; "The Fiend," pp. 214, 240-241; "The Firebombing," pp. 227-231; "Fog Envelops the Animals," pp. 215, 217; "For the Last Wolverine," pp. 243-244; "Goodbye to Serpents," pp. 224-225; ["The Grove Press New American Poets (1960)"], p. 211; "The Heaven of Animals," pp. 216-217; Helmets, pp. 208,

219-220, 222, 225, 227; ["Howard Nemerov"], p. 304n.;
["Into the Stone"], p. 215; Into the Stone and Other Poems,
pp. 208, 213-215, 235; "Knock," p. 250; "The Lord in the
Air," p. 252; "Madness," pp. 250, 252, 258; "Mangham,"
p. 254; "May Day Sermon to the Women of Gilmer County,
Georgia, by a Woman Preacher Leaving the Baptist
Church," pp. 220, 224, 235-237, 257; "Mercy,"
p. 250; "Messages," p. 252; ["Messages: I, Butterflies"],
p. 252; ["Messages: II, Giving a Son to the Sea"], p. 253;
"The Movement of Fish," p. 216; "On the Coosawattee [:
II, Below Ellijay]," pp. 222-223; "The Owl King," p. 255;
["The Owl King: III, The Blind Child's Story"], p. 218;
"The Owl King [: I, The Call]," p. 218; "The Owl King
[: II, The Owl King]," p. 217; "The Performance,"
pp. 215, 227; Poems 1957-1967, pp. 234-235, 241; ["The
Poet Turns on Himself"], p. 304n.; "The Poisoned Man,"
p. 224; "Pursuit from Under," pp. 238-239; ["Randall
Jarrell"], pp. 219, 304n.; "Reincarnation (I)," pp. 225,
241-242; "Reincarnation (II)," pp. 241-242, 261; ["The]
Second Birth," pp. 212-213, 304n.; "The Self as Agent,"
p. 304n.; Self-Interviews, pp. 217-218, 239, 304n.;
"Slave Quarters," p. 241; "Sleeping Out at Easter,"
pp. 213-214; "Snakebite," pp. 211, 224; ["The Son, the
Cave, and the Burning Bush"], pp. 234-235; Sorties,
pp. 205, 208, 210-211, 240, 243, 304n.; "The String,"
p. 226; The Suspect in Poetry, pp. 210, 212, 219, 234,
305n.; "Them, Crying," p. 238; "Trees and Cattle,"
pp. 215, 222; "Turning Away," pp. 205, 209, 212, 250,
259-260, 261-263; ["Two Poems of] Going Home," p. 254;
["Two Poems of Going Home: I, Living There"], p. 254;
["Two Poems of Going Home: II,] Looking for the Buck-
head Boys," pp. 250, 255; "The Underground Stream,"
pp. 214, 226; [unidentified passages], p. 213, 224; "The
Vegetable King," p. 214; "Venom," pp. 251-252.
    A loosely chronological but comprehensive survey of
Dickey's oeuvre focuses on the persona's evolution. Its
relationship to life experiences, to nature, and to
animals is clarified. The development from one volume,
or from an individual poem, to another is investigated,
and major and recurrent themes, sex, symbolism, and
metaphysical traits of his works are discussed at length.
Notes to this chapter appear on pp. 303-305.
    Ref.: Bible, p. 248; William Blake, pp. 252, 263;
Blake's [epigraph used in "The Lord in the Air"], p. 252;
Gautama Buddha, p. 246; Paul Cézanne, p. 253; René
Descartes, p. 243; Fyodor Dostoyevsky, p. 232; Mircea
Eliade, p. 258; T. S. Eliot, p. 212; Eliot's "Four Quar-
tets," p. 260; Ralph Waldo Emerson, p. 217; Allen Gins-
berg, pp. 235-236; Ginsberg's "Aether," p. 236; Ginsberg's
Ankor Wat, p. 235; Thomas Gray's "Elegy," p. 253;
Hamlet, p. 209; Ernest Hemingway, p. 234; William
Heyen's "A Conversation with James Dickey," p. 305n.
(see no. 1105); Adolf Hitler, p. 246; Ted Hughes' Crow,

p. 248; William James' The Varieties of Religious Ex-
perience, p. 246; Jesus, p. 246; Job's [epigraph used in
"The Firebombing"], p. 228; Carl Jung, p. 240; Søren
Kierkegaard, p. 216; D. H. Lawrence, pp. 215-216, 247;
Lawrence's "A Doe at Evening," p. 215; Life, p. 252;
Norman Mailer, pp. 239, 243, 249, 253; Mailer's Of a
Fire on the Moon, p. 253; Mailer's Why Are We in Viet-
nam?, pp. 239, 249; Charles Manson, p. 246; Herbert
Marcuse, p. 232; Friedrich Nietzsche, p. 304n.; Sylvia
Plath, p. 243; Plato, p. 216; Prospero, p. 209; Rodion
Romanovitch Raskolnikov, p. 232; Rainer Maria Rilke,
p. 234; Arthur Rimbaud, p. 212; Theodore Roethke,
pp. 217, 233; Albert Schweitzer, pp. 213, 231;
Smerdyakov, p. 232; Raymond Smith's "The Poetic Faith
of James Dickey," pp. 257, 305n. (see no. 912); Joseph
Stalin, p. 246; Wallace Stevens, p. 220; Stevens' "Anec-
dote of the Jar," p. 220; Dylan Thomas, pp. 212, 237;
Thomas' "Ballad of the Long-Legged Bait," p. 237; Walt
Whitman, pp. 209-210, 230-231; Whitman's "Song of My-
self," p. 231; William Wordsworth, p. 212; William
Butler Yeats, pp. 233-234; Yeats' The Green Helmet,
p. 234; Yeats' Last Poems, p. 234; Father Zossima,
p. 232.

1055   Owen, Guy. "James Dickey." In A Bibliographical Guide to
the Study of Southern Literature, with an Appendix Con-
taining Sixty-Eight Additional Writers of the Colonial South,
edited by Louis D. Rubin, pp. 188-189 [188].   Baton
Rouge: Louisiana State University Press, 1969.
Buckdancer's Choice; Drowning with Others; The Sus-
pect in Poetry.
Remarks concerning the "feud" between Dickey and
academe, the need for sound criticism of his works, and
his public image preface this bibliography (see no. 1132).
Ref.: Richard J. Calhoun's "James Dickey: The Ex-
pansive Imagination" (see no. 992); Ernest Hemingway;
Mary Lillis Latimer's "James Dickey: A Bibliography"
(see no. 1131); Paul O'Neil's "The Unlikeliest Poet" (see
no. 850).

1056   Perrine, Laurence [L. P.].   One Hundred American Poems of
the Twentieth Century, edited by Laurence Perrine and
James M. Reid, pp. 279-280. New York: Harcourt,
Brace and World, 1966.
"The Lifeguard," pp. 279-280.
Religious overtones of "The Lifeguard" are investigated,
and comments on its themes of guilt and love are included
in this anthology. It is reprinted in full, pp. 277-279.
Ref.: Jesus, pp. 279-280.

1057   "Poetry of 1971" In T. L. S.: Essays and Reviews from "The
Times Literary Supplement," 1971, vol. 10, pp. 149-171
[160-161]. London: Oxford University Press, 1972.

The Eye-Beaters, Blood, Victory, Madness, Buckhead
and Mercy, p. 160; ["The Lord in the Air"], p. 161;
["Two Poems of Going Home: I, Living There"], p. 160.
    Dickey's exclamations, repetition of words and their
distribution on the page, and posturizing in The Eye-
Beaters, Blood, Victory, Madness, Buckhead and Mercy
point to his insecurity and artificiality.
    Ref.: Gerard Manley Hopkins, p. 160; John Weiners'
Nerves, p. 160; Walt Whitman, p. 160; Richard Wilbur's
Walking to Sleep, p. 161.
    Orig.: Times Literary Supplement (see no. 745).   (It
was originally entitled "In Search of an Audience.")

1058   Rader, Dodson.   Blood Dues, p. 127.   New York: Alfred A.
       Knopf, 1973.
           A description of Dickey's reactions to segments of the
       first performance of "Yevtushenko and Friends."

1059   Ramsey, Paul.   "James Dickey: Meter and Structure."   In
       James Dickey: The Expansive Imagination; A Collection of
       Critical Essays, edited by Richard J. Calhoun, pp. 177-
       194.   DeLand, Fla.:   Everett-Edwards, 1973.
           "Awaiting the Swimmer," p. 187; Babel to Byzantium,
       p. 184; "The Birthday Dream," p. 185; "Blood," p. 186;
       "Buckdancer's Choice," p. 181; "The Cancer Match,"
       p. 186; "Chenille," p. 179; "Cherrylog Road," pp. 180-
       181; "Coming Back to America," p. 185; "Dover: Believ-
       ing in Kings," p. 179; "Drinking from a Helmet," p. 190;
       "The Driver," pp. 189-191; "Falling," pp. 184-185, 192;
       "The Fiend," p. 185; "The Firebombing," p. 191; "A
       Folk Singer of the Thirties," p. 191; "The Game,"
       p. 187; "Into the Stone," p. 186; "May Day Sermon to the
       Women of Gilmer County, Georgia, by a Woman Preacher
       Leaving the Baptist Church," pp. 185, 192-193; Metaphor
       as Pure Adventure, p. 194; "Near Darien," p. 186; "On
       the Hill Below the Lighthouse," p. 187; "The Other,"
       p. 187; "The Owl King," p. 189; "The Performance,"
       p. 187; "Pine: Taste, Touch and Sight," p. 186; "Poem,"
       p. 187; "Reincarnation [(II)]," p. 185; "The Scarred Girl,"
       p. 181; "The Shark's Parlor," pp. 184-185; "The Sheep
       Child," p. 185; "Sled Burial, Dream Ceremony," p. 182;
       "Sleeping Out at Easter," pp. 178-179, 187-190; "Trees
       and Cattle," pp. 187-188; "Uncle," p. 187; [unidentified
       passage], p. 177; "The Vegetable King," p. 187; "Walking
       on Water," p. 187.
           Dickey's basic metrical forms, end-stopped trimeter and
       free verse with lengthy lines, and forms derived from them
       are identified and examined at length.   Discussion of the
       success of his shorter poems and failure of the longer ones
       is included.
           Ref.:   Aristotle, p. 187; Robert Creeley, p. 181; H.D.,
       p. 181; William Faulkner, p. 193; Robinson Jeffers,
       p. 183; John Keats' "The Eve of Saint Agnes," p. 193;

D. H. Lawrence, p. 183; James McConkey, p. 192; Harry Morris' "A Formal View of the Poetry of Dickey, Garrigue, and Simpson," p. 191 (see no. 827); Flannery O'Connor, p. 193; Theodore Roethke, pp. 178, 183; Anne Stanford, p. 183; Walt Whitman, p. 183; John Hall Wheelock's "Introductory Essay: Some Thoughts on Poetry," p. 177 (see no. 1089); William Carlos Williams, p. 181; Yvor Winters, p. 178.

1060 Reiss, Barbara and Reiss, James. "Introduction." In Self-Interviews, by James Dickey, pp. 9-17. New York: Doubleday, 1970.

Deliverance, p. 15; "Falling," p. 14; Poems 1957-1967, pp. 9, 15; "Preface," p. 15; Self-Interviews, pp. 10-11, 15-16.

Dickey's reactions to Self-Interviews, the process of its creation, and its aims and objectives are discussed. An excerpt from a portion of the tape not transcribed for this volume is included.

1061 Reynolds, Michael S. "The Eye-Beaters, Blood, Victory, Madness, Buckhead and Mercy." In Masterplots, 1971 Annual: Magill's Literary Annual Essay-Reviews of 100 Outstanding Books Published in the United States During 1970, edited by Frank N. Magill, pp. 69-73. Englewood Cliffs, N.J.: Salem Press, 1971.

["Apollo: I, For the First Manned Moon Orbit"], p. 72; "Blood," p. 71; "Diabetes," p. 72; ["Diabetes: II,] Under Buzzards," p. 71; "The Eye-Beaters," p. 73; "In the Pocket," p. 72; "The Lord in the Air," pp. 70-71; "Madness," p. 71; "Mercy," p. 72; "Messages," p. 70; "The Place," p. 71; "Two Poems of Going Home," p. 72; ["Two Poems of Going Home: II,] Looking for the Buckhead Boys," p. 72; "Victory," pp. 71-72.

The thematic movement within The Eye-Beaters, Blood, Victory, Madness, Buckhead and Mercy is investigated in regard to its title. Failure of the volume is blamed on its lack of development beyond Dickey's previous works. Dickey's major motifs, which link all his volumes, and his symbolism are discussed. His relationship to the Transcendentalists is noted.

Ref.: The Atlantic Monthly, p. 72; Romantics, p. 71; Transcendentalists, p. 71; William Wordsworth, p. 71.

1062 Riley, Carolyn, ed. "Dickey, James." In Contemporary Literary Criticism: Excerpts from Criticism of the Works of Today's Novelists, Poets, Playwrights, and Other Creative Writers, vol. 1, pp. 73-74. Detroit: Gale Research Co., Book Tower, 1973.

A compilation of excerpts from the following essays on Dickey's works: James Aronson's [review of Self-Interviews] pp. 73-74 (see no. 569); John William Corrington's "James Dickey's Poems 1957-1967: A Personal Appraisal," p. 73 (see no. 643); Warren Eyster's "Two Regional Novels," p. 74 (see no. 684); Laurence Lieberman's "The Expansional Poet: A Return to Personality," p. 73 (see no. 792); Donald W. Markos' "Art and Immediacy: James Dickey's Deliverance," p. 74 (see no. 811); and Harry Morris' "A Formal View of Dickey, Garrigue, and Simpson," p. 73 (see no. 827).

1063   _____ and Harte, Barbara, eds. "Dickey, James." In Contemporary Literary Criticism: Excerpts from Criticism of the Works of Today's Novelists, Poets, Playwrights, and Other Creative Writers, vol. 2, pp. 115-117. Detroit: Gale Research Co., Book Tower, 1974.
    A compilation of excerpts from the following essays on Dickey's works: Paul Carroll's "Faire, Foul and Full of Variations: The Generation of 1962," p. 116 (see no. 997); Evan S. Connell, Jr.'s "Deliverance," p. 116 (see no. 639); William Dickey's "The Thing Itself," p. 115 (see no. 668); Martin Dodsworth's "Towards the Baseball Poem," pp. 115-116 (see no. 670); William Heyen's [review of Sorties], p. 117 (see no. 727); "Journey into Self," p. 116 (see no. 753); Laurence Lieberman's "The Worldly Mystic," p. 115 (see no. 796); M. L. Rosenthal's "Epilogue: American Continuities and Cross Currents," p. 115 (see no. 1066); Robert B. Shaw's "Poets in Midstream," p. 117 (see no. 898); Monroe K. Spears' Dionysus and the City, pp. 116-117 (see no. 1074); and Stephen Stephanchev's "James Dickey," p. 115 (see no. 1079).

1064 Rizza, Peggy. "Another Side of This Life: Women as Poets." In American Poetry Since 1960: Some Critical Perspectives, edited by Robert B. Shaw, pp. 167-179 [172, 177-178]. Chester Springs, Penn.: Dufour Editions, 1974.
    Criticism is aimed at Dickey for his praise of Mona Van Duyn's To See, to Take printed on its dust jacket and reprinted here.
    Ref.: Mona Van Duyn's "Marriage, with Beasts," p. 172 (see no. 1238); Van Duyn's To See, to Take, p. 177.

1065 Rodman, Selden. "American Poetry 1945-1970." In One Hundred American Poems: Masterpieces of Lyric, Epic and Ballad from Pre-Colonial Times to the Present, 2d ed., edited by Selden Rodman, pp. 43-57 [50-51]. New York: New American Library, 1972.
    ["Buckdancer's Choice"], p. 51; "The Firebombing," p. 51.
    Dickey and Sylvia Plath are compared on the basis of the honesty each displays in poetry. Robert Bly's and Dickey's comments on "The Firebombing," the former's in "The Collapse of James Dickey" and the latter's in "Buckdancer's Choice," conclude.

Ref.: Robert Bly's "The Collapse of James Dickey,"
p. 51 (see no. 587); Sylvia Plath, p. 50.

1065a Rosen, Molly. Popcorn Venus: Women, Movies and the Amer-
ican Dream, p. 334. New York: Coward, McCann and
Geoghegan, 1973.
Deliverance [film].
Audiences' reactions to the homosexual rape scene in
the film version of Deliverance is briefly compared to
reactions to heterosexual rape scenes in other films.

1066 Rosenthal, M. L. "Epilogue: American Continuities and
Cross Currents." In The New Poets: American and
British Poetry Since World War II, pp. 310-333 [320,
325-327]. New York: Oxford University Press, 1967.
"The Being," pp. 326-327; "The Firebombing," p. 326.
Form, and its relationship to the experiences related
in Dickey's poems, is discussed at great length. The
language and afflatus of his work is mentioned.
Ref.: Robert Bly, p. 320; Donald Hall, p. 320; Louis
Simpson, p. 320; Simpson's "Carentan O Carentan,"
p. 326; James Wright, pp. 320, 326.
Exc.: Contemporary Literary Criticism (see no. 1063);
A Library of Literary Criticism (see no. 1005).

1067 Rubin, Louis D., Jr. "Four Southerners." In American
Poetry, edited by Irvin Ehrenpreis, pp. 11-43 [41-42].
London: Edward Arnold, Publishers, 1965.
Slight mention of Dickey listing him in the lineage of
Southern poets.
Ref.: John Berryman, p. 42; Randall Jarrell, p. 41;
Robert Lowell, p. 42; William Meredith, p. 42; Howard
Nemerov, p. 42; Karl Shapiro, p. 42; William Jay Smith,
p. 41; Reed Whittemore, p. 42; Richard Wilbur, p. 42.

1068 Schickel, Richard. "White Water, Black Doings." In Film
72/73: An Anthology, edited by David Denby, pp. 21-22.
New York: The Bobbs-Merrill Co., 1973.
Deliverance [novel], p. 21; [Deliverance] [film],
pp. 21-22.
The positive qualities of Dickey's novel Deliverance are
lost in its film version. Plot summary and thematic
interpretation are given.
Ref.: John Boorman, p. 21; Boorman's Hell in the
Pacific [film], p. 22; Boorman's Point Blank [film], p. 22;
Ernest Hemingway, p. 22; Burt Reynolds, p. 22; Jon
Voight, p. 22.
Orig.: Life (see no. 894).

1069 Schorer, Mark. "James Dickey." In The Literature of
America: Twentieth Century, edited by Mark Schorer,
pp. 730-731. New York: McGraw-Hill Book Co., 1970.
Babel to Byzantium, p. 730; Buckdancer's Choice,

p. 730; Drowning with Others, p. 730; The Eye-Beaters,
Blood, Victory, Madness, Buckhead and Mercy, p. 730;
Helmets, p. 730; Into the Stone and Other Poems, p. 730;
Poems 1957-1967, p. 730; ["The Poet Turns on Himself'],
pp. 730-731; ["The Shark's Parlor"], p. 730; The Suspect
in Poetry, p. 730.
    Highlights of Dickey's life and career introduce remarks
by Dickey concerning his themes. His metrics, narrative
technique, and use of action are briefly investigated by
Schorer.
    Ref.: Paul Carroll's "Faire, Foul, and Full of Varia-
tion: The Generation of 1962," p. 731 (see no. 997);
Carroll's "The Smell of Blood in Paradise," p. 731 (see
no. 998); Richard Howard's "James Dickey: 'We Never
Can Really Tell Whether Nature Condemns Us or Loves
Us,'" p. 731 (see no. 1024).

1070 Silverstein, Norman. "James Dickey's Muscular Eschatology."
      In Contemporary Poetry in America: Essays and Inter-
      views, edited by Robert Boyers, pp. 303-313. New York:
      Schocken Books, 1974.
          ["Autumn"], p. 309; Buckdancer's Choice, p. 303;
      Death's Baby Machine, p. 304; Deliverance, pp. 303, 311;
      ["Diabetes: II, Under Buzzards"], p. 307; Drowning with
      Others, pp. 303, 308; ["Drowning with Others"], p. 309;
      The Eye-Beaters, Blood, Victory, Madness, Buckhead and
      Mercy, pp. 303, 312; "Falling" [sec. of Poems 1957-1967],
      p. 310; "The Heaven of Animals," p. 308; Helmets,
      pp. 303, 308; ["Helmets"], p. 308; "In the Pocket,"
      pp. 312-313; "Inside the River," p. 308; ["Into the Stone"],
      p. 304; Into the Stone and Other Poems, p. 303; ["The
      Lifeguard"], p. 308; "Mercy," p. 307; ["Messages: II,]
      Giving a Son to the Sea," p. 307; ["Metaphor as Pure
      Adventure"], p. 304; Poems 1957-1967, pp. 303, 310;
      "Power and Light," p. 311; ["The Rib"], p. 308; Self-
      Interviews, p. 303; Sorties, pp. 303, 303n., 304, 306,
      312; ["Spinning the Crystal Ball"], p. 306; ["The Summons"],
      p. 308; "Sun," pp. 309-311; ["Teaching, Writing, Rein-
      carnations, and Rivers"], pp. 305, 307-309; ["To His
      Children in Darkness"], p. 309; Two Poems of the Air,
      p. 303; [unidentified remarks], pp. 306-307, 311-312.
          A survey of Dickey's works emphasizing suburban life's
      and Southern Agrarians' influences on his art and especially
      on its metaphysical qualities. Biographical data is inter-
      spersed throughout, and a prediction of Dickey's move-
      ment into prose concludes.
          Ref.: Thomas Aquinas, p. 309; Bible, p. 309; Robert
      Bly, p. 312; Albert Camus, p. 312; Donald Davidson's
      I'll Take My Stand, p. 305; Walt Disney's The African
      Lion [film], p. 309; John Donne, p. 308; T. S. Eliot,
      pp. 305, 309, 312-313; Fergus mac Erc's [unidentified
      poem], p. 309; William Faulkner's The Sound and the
      Fury, p. 304; Eddie Fisher's Coke Time [television show],

p. 306; Francesca, p. 311; the Fugitives, pp. 304-305;
Thomas Hardy, p. 303; Ernest Hemingway, p. 312;
Gerard Manley Hopkins, p. 309; Randall Jarrell, p. 306;
Richard Jeffries, p. 312; Robert Lowell, pp. 312-313;
Lowell's "Skunk Hour," p. 312; Paolo, p. 311; Sylvia
Plath, pp. 312-313; Plath's "Daddy," p. 312; Ezra Pound,
pp. 312-313; John Crowe Ransom, pp. 305-306, 309;
Theodore Roethke, pp. 312-313; Roethke's "The Lost Son,"
p. 312; the Romantics, p. 305; Monroe K. Spears, p. 304;
Mrs. Monroe K. Spears, p. 304; William Stafford, p. 306;
Allen Tate, pp. 305-307, 309; Tate's "Ode to the Confed-
erate Dead," p. 307; the Victorians, p. 305; Robert Penn
Warren, p. 305; James Wright, p. 312; William Butler
Yeats, pp. 303, 309.
    Orig.: Salmagundi (see no. 901).

1071   Sloan, Thomas O. "The Open Poem Is a Now Poem: Dickey's
       May Day Sermon." In Literature as Revolt and Revolt as
       Literature: Three Studies in the Rhetoric of Non-Oratorial
       Forms; The Proceedings of the Fourth Annual University
       of Minnesota Spring Symposium in Speech-Communication,
       pp. 17-31. Minneapolis, Minn.: University of Minnesota,
       1969.
          "Falling," p. 31n.; "May Day Sermon to the Women of
       Gilmer County, Georgia, by a Woman Preacher Leaving
       the Baptist Church," pp. 17, 20-27, 30, 31n.; "The Poet
       Turns on Himself," pp. 21, 31n.
          The relationship between Dickey's "May Day Sermon to
       the Women of Gilmer County, Georgia, by a Woman
       Preacher Leaving the Baptist Church" and its reader is
       investigated concluding with discussion of the seemingly
       extemporaneous text of the "sermon." Its themes, recur-
       rent images, and use of violence, confrontations, and
       opposites are noted.
          Ref.: Matthew Arnold, p. 18; Robert Beloof, p. 21;
       Beloof's The Performing Voice in Literature, p. 31n.;
       Bible, pp. 19, 21; William Blake, p. 18; Robert Brown-
       ing, p. 27; H. L. Chaytor, pp. 18, 31n.; Chaytor's From
       Script to Print, p. 31n.; Peter Davison's "The Difficulties
       of Being Major," pp. 30, 31n. (see no. 659); T. S. Eliot,
       pp. 18, 27; Jack Goody and Ian Watt's "The Consequences
       of Literacy," p. 19; Johann Gutenberg, p. 18; Jehovah,
       p. 24; James Joyce, p. 20; Albert Lord, pp. 22, 31n.;
       Lord's The Singer of Tales, p. 31n.; Marshall McLuhan,
       pp. 17-18, 28; McLuhan's The Gutenberg Galaxy, p. 31n.;
       McLuhan's Understanding Media, p. 31n.; Charles Olson's
       "Projective Verse," p. 31n.; Paul O'Neil's "The Unlike-
       liest Poet," pp. 17, 30n. (see no. 850); Walter Ong,
       p. 18; Ong's The Presence of the Word, pp. 19, 28-29,
       31n.; Ong's Ramus, Method and the Decay of Dialogue,
       p. 31; Milman Parry, pp. 22, 31n.; Ezra Pound, p. 20;
       Raymond C. Swain's [letter], p. 17 (see no. 1192); Chad
       Walsh's "The Sound of Poetry in the Age of McLuhan,"

p. 31n.

Rept.: James Dickey: The Expansive Imagination (see no. 1072). (The sequence of certain remarks was changed when reprinted.)

1072 _____. "The Open Poem Is a Now Poem: Dickey's May Day Sermon. " In James Dickey: The Expansive Imagination; A Collection of Critical Essays, edited by Richard J. Calhoun, pp. 85-104. DeLand, Fla.: Everett-Edwards, 1973.

"Falling, " p. 92n.; "May Day Sermon to the Women of Gilmer County, Georgia, by a Woman Preacher Leaving the Baptist Church, " pp. 86, 89, 92n., 93-98, 100, 103; "The Poet Turns on Himself, " pp. 21, 31n.

The relationship between Dickey's "May Day Sermon to the Women of Gilmer County, Georgia, by a Woman Preacher Leaving the Baptist Church" and its reader is investigated concluding with discussion of the seemingly extemporaneous text of the "sermon. " Its themes, recurrent images, and use of violence, confrontations, and opposites are noted.

Ref.: Matthew Arnold, p. 86; Robert Beloof, p. 89; Beloof's The Performing Voice in Literature, p. 89n.; Bible, pp. 90, 99; William Blake, p. 88; Robert Browning, p. 98; H. L. Chaytor, pp. 87, 87n.; Chaytor's From Script to Print, p. 87n.; Peter Davison's "The Difficulties of Being Major, " pp. 103, 103n. (see no. 659); T. S. Eliot, pp. 86, 98; Jack Goody and Ian Watt's "The Consequences of Literacy, " p. 87n.; Johann Gutenberg, p. 88; Jehovah, p. 94; James Joyce, p. 100; Albert Lord, p. 91; Lord's The Singer of Tales, p. 91n.; Marshall McLuhan, pp. 85, 87, 87n., 101; McLuhan's The Gutenberg Galaxy, p. 87n.; McLuhan's Understanding Media, p. 87n.; Charles Olson's "Projective Verse, " p. 91n.; Paul O'Neil's "The Unlikeliest Poet, " p. 85 (see no. 850); Walter Ong, p. 87; Ong's The Presence of the Word, p. 87n.; Ong's Ramus, Method and the Decay of Dialogue, pp. 87n., 101; Milman Parry, p. 91; Ezra Pound, p. 100; Raymond C. Swain's [letter], p. 86 (see no. 1192); Chad Walsh's "The Sound of Poetry in the Age of McLuhan, " p. 91n.

Orig.: Literature as Revolt and Revolt as Literature (see no. 1071). (The sequence of certain remarks is changed from the original.)

1073 Sparks, Barry [B. S.]. "Dickey, James. " In The Penguin Companion to American Literature, edited by Malcolm Bradbury, Eric Mottram, and Jean Franco, p. 73. New York: McGraw-Hill Book Co. , 1971.

Babel to Byzantium; Buckdancer's Choice; Deliverance; Drowning with Others; The Eye-Beaters, Blood, Victory, Madness, Buckhead and Mercy; "The Firebombing"; Helmets; Into the Stone and Other Poems; Poems 1957-1967; "Slave Quarters"; The Suspect in Poetry; Two Poems of

the Air.
Brief mention of the voice, narrative techniques,
mystical overtones, and setting of Dickey's oeuvre is in-
cluded in this list of his books.

1074 Spears, Monroe K.   Dionysus and the City: Modernism in
Twentieth Century Poetry, pp. 13n. , 250, 252-260, 269.
New York: Oxford University Press, 1970.
"Adultery," p. 259; ["Allen Ginsberg"], p. 253; Babel
to Byzantium, p. 252; "The Bee," p. 259; Buckdancer's
Choice, p. 252; "A Dog Sleeping on My Feet," p. 256;
"Encounter in the Cage Country," p. 256; "Falling,"
pp. 257-258; "The Fiend," p. 259; "For the Last Wolver-
ine," p. 256; "Fox Blood," p. 256; "Goodbye to Serpents,"
p. 256; Helmets, p. 254; Into the Stone and Other Poems,
p. 252; "The Leap," p. 258; "The Movement of Fish,"
p. 256; "The Owl King," p. 256; Poems 1957-1967,
p. 252; ["The Poet Turns on Himself"], pp. 253-255; ["A
Poet Witnesses a Bold Mission"], p. 269; "Power and
Light," p. 258; "The Shark's Parlor," pp. 255-256; "The
Sheep Child," pp. 256-257, 259; ["The Son, the Cave, and
the Burning Bush"], p. 260; "Sustainment," p. 259;
["Theodore Roethke"], pp. 253, 255.
Dionysian and Apollonian principles of Dickey's verse
and his major influence are identified.   Also discussed are
his role of identification with the "other," his metrical
concerns, his open and narrative techniques, and his use
of myths and ritual.
Ref. :   the Beats, p. 253; Ted Hughes, p. 250; D. H.
Lawrence, p. 253; Lawrence's [unidentified remarks],
p. 255; Leda, p. 257; Sir Herbert Read, p. 253; Rainer
Maria Rilke, p. 253; Theodore Roethke, p. 253; William
Carlos Williams, p. 253.
Exc. :   Contemporary Literary Criticism (see no. 1063).

1075 Spiller, Robert E. , et al. , eds.   Literary History of the
United States: History, 4th ed. rev. , p. 1446.   New
York: Macmillan Publishing Co. , 1974.
"Falling"; "The Firebombing"; [Poems 1957-1967].
Forms and metrics of Dickey's verse and his motifs of
violence and guilt are briefly mentioned.   Poems 1957-
1967 is incorrectly identified as Selected Poems.

1076 Stalker, James C.   "Syntactic and Semantic Pattern Matches
in James Dickey's 'False Youth: Autumn: Clothes of the
Age. '"   In Meaning: A Common Ground of Linguistics and
Literature; Proceedings of a University of Northern Iowa
Conference Held April 27-28, 1973, in Honor of Norman C.
Stageberg, edited by Don L. E. Nilsen, pp. 153-157.
n. p. :   University of Northern Iowa, 1973.
"False Youth: Autumn: Clothes of the Age," pp. 153-
155, 157.
The theme of "False Youth: Autumn: Clothes of the

Age" is briefly mentioned in this investigation of the
poem's humor discovered through its syntactic and seman-
tic analyses. It is reprinted in full, p. 157.
  Ref. : T. S. Eliot, p. 155; Dylan Thomas, p. 155;
Norbert Weiner, p. 153.

1077 Stanford, Ann. "Poetry: 1900 to the 1930's. " In American
      Literary Scholarship: An Annual, 1965, edited by James
      Woodress, pp. 204-219 [208]. Durham, N. C. : Duke
      University Press, 1967.
        ["Edwin Arlington Robinson: The Many Truths"].
        A summary of the ideas Dickey expressed in an essay
      on Edwin Arlington Robinson is given.

1078 Stauffer, Donald Barlow.   A Short History of American Poetry,
      pp. 394-395, 401-405.   New York: E. P. Dutton and Co. ,
      1974.
        Buckdancer's Choice, pp. 404-405; "Cherrylog Road, "
      p. 403; Drowning with Others, p. 403; The Eye-Beaters,
      Blood, Victory, Madness, Buckhead and Mercy, p. 404;
      "Falling, " p. 405; "The Fiend, " pp. 401, 405; "The
      Firebombing, " p. 404; Helmets, p. 404; "Hunting Civil
      War Relics at Nimblewill Creek, " p. 403; "In the Marble
      Quarry, " p. 405; "The Lifeguard, " p. 404; ["Louis Simp-
      son"], p. 394; ["The Poet Turns on Himself"], p. 403;
      "A Screened Porch in the Country, " pp. 401, 404; "The
      Sheep Child, " p. 404; "Slave Quarters, " p. 405.
        Dickey's use of fantasy, his metrics, and his delving
      into the inner life of other persons in his verse are men-
      tioned. Discussion of his major device, the "open" poem,
      is included.
        Ref. : Robert Bly, p. 404; W. S. Merwin, p. 404;
      The New York Times' [epigraph used in "Falling"],
      p. 405; Louis Simpson, p. 404; Allen Tate, p. 403; Robert
      Penn Warren, p. 403.

1079 Stepanchev, Stephen. "James Dickey. " In American Poetry
      Since 1945: A Critical Survey, pp. 190-192. New York:
      Harper and Row, Publishers, 1965.
        "Cherrylog Road, " p. 192; "The Lifeguard, " p. 192.
        The subject matter and forms used in Dickey's first
      three volumes of verse are discussed.
        Exc. : Contemporary Literary Criticism (see no. 1063).

1080 Sutton, Walter. "Criticism and Poetry. " In American Poetry,
      edited by Irvin Ehrenpreis, pp. 175-195 [192]. London:
      Edward Arnold, Publishers, 1965.
        Dickey is listed with others having received much
      recognition since 1955.
        Ref. : Galway Kinnell; Adrienne Rich; James Wright.

1081 Waggoner, Hyatt H.   American Poets: From the Puritans to
      the Present, pp. 423-424, 426-427, 607-610.   Boston:

Houghton Mifflin, 1968.
["The Grove Press New American Poets (1960)"],
pp. 609-610; ["The Second Birth"], p. 426; ["The Suspect
in Poetry"], p. 608; The Suspect in Poetry, p. 607;
[unidentified passage], p. 423.
A concise analysis of Dickey's critical theories, it
identifies Emerson as his predecessor.
Ref.: T. S. Eliot, pp. 426-427; Ralph Waldo Emerson,
pp. 609-610; Robert Frost, p. 610; Ezra Pound, p. 610;
Theodore Roethke, p. 607.

1082   Wagner, Linda Welshimer. "Poetry: The 1930's to the
Present." In American Literary Scholarship: An Annual,
1972, edited by J. Albert Robbins, pp. 332-353 [332, 334-
346, 349]. Durham, N. C.: Duke University Press, 1974.
Deliverance, p. 345; [Deliverance] [film], p. 345; ["The
Poet Turns on Himself"], p. 349.
Critical works pertaining to Dickey are listed.
Ref.: Franklin Ashley's James Dickey: A Checklist,
p. 345 (see no. 1127); Eileen Glancy's James Dickey: The
Critic as Poet, p. 345 (see no. 1129); N. Michael Niflis'
"A Special Kind of Fantasy: James Dickey on the Razor's
Edge," p. 345 (see no. 842); William Packard's "Craft
Interview with James Dickey," p. 346 (see no. 1112);
Raymond Smith's "The Poetic Faith of James Dickey,"
p. 345 (see no. 912).

1083   Walsh, Chad. "James Dickey." In Today's Poets: American
and British Poetry Since the 1930's, p. 414. New York:
Charles Scribner's Sons, 1964.
Drowning with Others; Helmets; Into the Stone and Other
Poems; The Suspect in Poetry; [unidentified passage].
A personality piece with some biographical data.
Ref.: Poetry; The Sewanee Review.

1084   Weatherby, H. L. "The Way of Exchange in James Dickey's
Poetry." In James Dickey: The Expansive Imagination;
A Collection of Critical Essays, edited by Richard J.
Calhoun, pp. 53-64. DeLand, Fla.: Everett-Edwards,
1973.
["Allen Ginsberg"], p. 64; "Approaching Prayer," p. 57;
Buckdancer's Choice, pp. 53, 60; "Chenille," p. 58;
"Cherrylog Road," p. 59; "A Dog Sleeping on My Feet,"
pp. 53-56; "Drinking from a Helmet," p. 60; "The Driver,"
pp. 59-61; Drowning with Others, pp. 53, 56; "The Fiend,"
p. 62; "The Firebombing," p. 61; ["Harold Witt"], p. 64;
"The Heaven of Animals," pp. 56-57; Helmets, pp. 53,
57, 60; "The Owl King [: II, The Owl King]," p. 53;
"Pursuit from Under," p. 60; "The Shark's Parlor,"
pp. 61, 63; "Springer Mountain," pp. 57, 60, 63; The Sus-
pect in Poetry, p. 64; ["Thom Gunn"], p. 64; [unidentified
passage], p. 55.
Dickey's technique of transferring the inner self of a

human being into another form is studied as it is used in
three of his volumes.   A discussion of the weaknesses of
this technique concludes.
    Ref.: Dante, p. 63; John Keats, p. 56; William
Shakespeare, p. 63; Edmund Spenser, p. 63; William
Wordsworth, p. 56; William Butler Yeats, pp. 56, 63.
    Orig.: The Hudson Review (see no. 954).

1085   Weatherhead, A. Kingsley.   "Poetry: The 1930's to the
        Present."   In American Literary Scholarship: An Annual,
        1968, edited by J. Albert Robbins, pp. 244-259 [245-246,
        253, 255-256].   Durham, N.C.: Duke University Press,
        1970.
            Babel to Byzantium, p. 245; "The Firebombing,"
        p. 256; "The Poet Turns on Himself," pp. 245-246; ["The
        Son, the Cave, and the Burning Bush"], p. 245; Spinning
        the Crystal Ball, p. 246; [unidentified passage], p. 245.
            Works pertaining to Dickey are listed, and a composite
        of Dickey's critical theories is given.
            Ref.: Laurence Lieberman's The Achievement of James
        Dickey, p. 255 (see no. 472); Lieberman's "James Dickey:
        The Deepening of Being," pp. 253, 255 (see no. 1034);
        Ralph J. Mills, Jr.'s "The Poetry of James Dickey,"
        p. 256 (see no. 822).

1086   _____.   "Poetry: The 1930's to the Present."   In Ameri-
        can Literary Scholarship: An Annual, 1969, edited by J.
        Albert Robbins, pp. 278-292 [278, 286-287].   Durham,
        N.C.: Duke University Press, 1971.
            ["The] Firebombing," p. 286; "Slave Quarters," p. 286.
        Six critical essays pertaining to Dickey are surveyed.
            Ref.: Robert Bly's "Buckdancer's Choice," p. 286 (see
        no. 586); Bly's "The Work of James Dickey," p. 286 (see
        no. 589); Richard Calhoun's "On Robert Bly's Protest
        Poetry," p. 287 (see no. 612); Paul Carroll's "The Smell
        of Blood in Paradise," pp. 278, 287 (see no. 998); Ralph
        J. Mills, Jr.'s Creation's Very Self, p. 278 (see no. 1047).

1087   _____.   "Poetry: The 1930's to the Present."   In Ameri-
        can Literary Scholarship: An Annual, 1970, edited by J.
        Albert Robbins, pp. 308-329 [310, 326].   Durham, N.C.:
        Duke University Press, 1972.
            Self-Interviews, p. 326.
            Two critical essays pertaining to Dickey are listed.
        Self-Interviews is described.
            Ref.: Martin Dodsworth's "Introduction: The Survival
        of Poetry," p. 310 (see no. 1009); Monroe K. Spears'
        Dionysus and the City, p. 310 (see no. 1074).

1088   _____.   "Poetry: The 1930's to the Present."   In Ameri-
        can Literary Scholarship: An Annual, 1971, edited by J.
        Albert Robbins, pp. 299-321 [319].   Durham, N.C.: Duke
        University Press, 1973.

Eileen Glancy's James Dickey: The Critic as Poet is
summarized.
Ref. :   Eileen Glancy's "Introductory Essay" (see
no. 1019); Glancy's James Dickey: The Critic as Poet
(see no. 1129).

1089 Wheelock, John Hall.   "Introductory Essay: Some Thoughts
on Poetry. " In Poets of Today, vol. 7, edited by John
Hall Wheelock, pp. 13-32 [22-26].   New York: Charles
Scribner's Sons, 1960.
["The Enclosure"], p. 25; ["The Game"], p. 25; ["Into
the Stone"], p. 25; ["The Landfall"], p. 25; ["Near
Darien"], p. 25; ["On the Hill Below the Lighthouse"],
p. 25; ["The Other"], p. 25; "Sleeping Out at Easter, "
p. 24; "The Underground Stream, " p. 24; [unidentified
passage], pp. 25-26; ["The Vegetable King"], p. 25.
Dickey's use of his experiences, lines, and forms and
their metrical schemes in Into the Stone and Other Poems
is investigated.   Major themes in this volume are listed.
Ref. :   William Blake, p. 25; Theodore Roethke,
pp. 23-24.
Orig. :   The Arizona Quarterly (Dickey is not mentioned
in the original version.)

1090 Workman, Charles.   "Buckdancer's Choice. " In Masterplots,
1966 Annual: Magill's Literary Annual; Essay-Reviews of
100 Outstanding Books Published in the United States Dur-
ing 1965, edited by Frank N. Magill, pp. 38-43.   New
York: Salem Press, 1967.
"Buckdancer's Choice, " p. 39; Buckdancer's Choice,
pp. 38, 42-43; "The Escape, " pp. 40-42; "Faces Seen
Once, " p. 42; "The Firebombing, " pp. 40-41; "The Night
Pool, " p. 42; "Reincarnation [(I)], " p. 43; "The Shark's
Parlor, " pp. 39-40.
Dickey's responses to experiences and his technique of
metamorphosis in Buckdancer's Choice are investigated.
Exc. :   "The Poetry of Dickey" (see no. 1040).

INTERVIEWS AND PANEL DISCUSSIONS

1091   Arnett, David Leslie. "James Dickey and the Writing of
       Deliverance." In "James Dickey: Poetry and Fiction,"
       pp. 192-220. Ph.D. dissertation, Tulane University, 1973.
           "A Beginning Poet, Aged Sixty-Five," p. 213; Deliver-
       ance [novel], pp. 192, 196, 199, 205-207, 209-212, 215;
       [Deliverance] [film], pp. 194, 198; "The Dream Flood,"
       p. 211; "The Driver," p. 211; Drowning with Others,
       p. 211; "The First Morning of Cancer," p. 200; "A Folk
       Singer of the Thirties," p. 200; "For the Linden Moth,"
       p. 200; ["In Medias Res"], p. 201; ["Into the Stone"],
       p. 208; ["Journals"], p. 216; "The Lifeguard," p. 200;
       "The Movement of Fish," p. 211; "On the Coosawattee,"
       pp. 205-206; ["On the Coosawattee: I,] By Canoe through
       the Fir Forest," p. 205; Self-Interviews, p. 211; "Sleeping
       Out at Easter," p. 200; ["Teaching, Writing, Reincarna-
       tions, and Rivers"], p. 218; "To Landrum Guy, [Beginning
       to Write at Sixty"], p. 213.
           Dickey traces the history of his novel Deliverance from
       its conception to its publication and discusses its title and
       its relationship with various of his poems. Those recur-
       rent themes appearing in his novel and poems are investi-
       gated, as are his fascination with sharks and snakes.
       Christ and water symbols are explored.
           Ref.: James Agee, pp. 197, 218-219; Agee's The
       African Queen, p. 219; Aristotle, p. 217; Richard A.
       Ashman, p. 201; Al Braselton, pp. 192, 196; Paul Brooks,
       pp. 207-208; Rachel Carson, p. 207; Joseph Conrad's
       "Heart of Darkness," p. 210; Stephen Crane's "The Open
       Boat," pp. 209-210; Crane's The Red Badge of Courage,
       p. 210; Donald Davidson, p. 218; Christopher Dickey,
       p. 196; Arnold van Gennep, p. 209; William Golding's
       Lord of the Flies, p. 207; Heraclitus, p. 211; Herman
       Hesse's Siddhartha, p. 211; Geoffrey Household's Rogue
       Male, p. 210; Stanley Edgar Hyman's "Myth, Ritual, and
       Nonsense," p. 209; Carl Jung, p. 203; Immanuel Kant,
       p. 199; John Keats, pp. 218-219; Lewis King, pp. 192,
       196, 205; Bob Lesher, p. 197; Malcolm Lowry, pp. 218-
       219; Andrew Lytle, p. 218; John Milton's Paradise Lost,
       p. 203; The New Yorker, p. 205; Obadiah's [epigraph used
       in Deliverance], p. 214; Osiris, p. 208; Plato, p. 217;
       Theodore Roethke, pp. 210, 219; Ross Allen's Reptile
       Institute, p. 215; Satan, pp. 203-204; William Shakespeare,

p. 217; Percy Bysshe Shelley, pp. 216-217; Dylan
Thomas, pp. 210, 219; John Updike, p. 197; Robert Penn
Warren, p. 218; Warren's All the King's Men, pp. 217-
218; Richard Wilbur, p. 213.

1092 "'The Best People I Have Ever Known, and Also the Worst,
Were Poets.'" Mademoiselle 75 (Aug. 1972), pp. 282-
283, 417-420.
    Buckdancer's Choice, p. 282; Deliverance [novel],
pp. 282, 417; Deliverance [film], pp. 282, 417; "Falling,"
p. 283; "A Folk Singer of the Thirties," p. 283; "The
Sheep Child," p. 283; Sorties, pp. 282, 417-419.
    Dickey discusses the various aspects of poetry and the
poet: the elitism of poets, the relationship of poets and
poetry to politics, the effects his critics and reviewers
have had on him, the aging process's toll on poets, and
his coping with being a public figure.
    Ref.: James Agee, p. 418; Charles Baudelaire, p. 282;
John Berryman, pp. 282, 418; George Gordon, Lord By-
ron, p. 417; Al Capp, p. 418; Hart Crane, p. 282; Sammy
Davis, Jr., p. 419; Esquire, p. 418; Allen Ginsberg,
p. 420; Mark Hatfield, p. 282; Carolyn Heilbrun's "The
Masculine Wilderness of the American Novel," p. 417
(see no. 726); Robinson Jeffers' [unidentified passage],
p. 420; Eugene McCarthy, p. 282; Osip Mandel'shtam,
p. 282; Leslie Marchand's Byron: A Biography, p. 418;
"Me and Bobby McGee" [song], p. 420; Herman Melville,
p. 418; Ben Nicholson, p. 417; Plato, p. 420; Dylan
Thomas, p. 282; John Updike, p. 418; Virginia Woolf,
p. 418; William Butler Yeats, p. 418; Yevgeny
Yevtushenko, p. 282; "Yevtushenko and Friends: Poetry
in Concert," p. 282.
    Photograph of Dickey by Duana Michals, p. 283.

1093 Buck, Carol. "The 'Poetry Thing' with James Dickey."
Poetry Australia, no. 21 (Apr. 1968), pp. 4-6.
    Buckdancer's Choice, pp. 4, 6; Drowning with Others,
p. 4; Helmets, p. 4; "The Owl King," p. 5; Poems 1957-
1967, p. 4; ["The Poet Turns on Himself"], p. 5.
    Dickey's thoughts on poets who are teachers, the
poem's effect on its reader, his Southern heritage, and
his use of spaces within a line of poetry are examined.
A short, biographical paragraph introduces the interview.

1094 Buckley, William F., Jr. S.E.C.A. Presents "Firing Line."
[n.p.]: Southern Educational Communications Association,
1971.
    Buckdancer's Choice, p. 1; Deliverance, p. 1; The
Eye-Beaters, Blood, Victory, Madness, Buckhead and
Mercy, p. 1; ["False Youth: Autumn: Clothes of the
Age"], p. 2; [A Private Brinksmanship], p. 1.
    Dickey answers the topic at hand--"What has happened
to the American spirit?"--by attributing its loss to soci-

ety's extreme use of technology and introspection, but he
foresees the flowering of the individual's spirit. The
Vietnamese War is discussed at length. Buckley hosted
this program, recorded at WYES-TV, New Orleans, on
April 22, 1971 and originally telecast on PBS on August
25, 1971, from which this transcript was made. A panel
discussion, including Dickey, Buckley, Margaret Blain,
Clark DuRant, and Ralph Wafer, concludes.
    Ref.: Horatio Alger, p. 2; W. H. Auden, p. 7;
William Calley, p. 2; Albert Camus, p. 4; Camus' Le
Mythe de Sisyphe, p. 4; Easy Rider [film], p. 10;
F. Scott Fitzgerald's The Great Gatsby, p. 3; John Hey-
wood, p. 4; Adolf Hitler, p. 5; Homer, p. 8; John F.
Kennedy, p. 9; Sinclair Lewis' Babbitt, p. 2; Andrew
Marvell's "To His Coy Mistress," p. 7; The New York
Times, p. 6; The New Yorker, p. 10; Richard M. Nixon,
p. 10; Playboy, p. 7; François Rabelais, p. 1; Kenneth
Rexroth, p. 5; George Santayana, p. 5; Susan Sontag,
p. 2; Ed White, p. 8; White's [remark used in "Apollo"],
p. 8; Thomas Wolfe, p. 2; William Wordsworth, p. 7;
Frank Lloyd Wright, p. 10; William Butler Yeats, p. 7;
Howard Zinn, p. 3.

1095   Burke, Tom. "Conversations with, Um, Jon Voight on Not
       Being Jon Voight and Other Theories of Acting." Esquire
       77 (Jan. 1972), pp. 116-119, 150, 155-158 [117-118, 155-
       158].
           Deliverance [novel], pp. 118, 155, 157; Deliverance
       [screenplay], pp. 118, 155, 157; Deliverance [film],
       pp. 155, 157, 158.
           Although primarily a compendium of short discussions
       with Jon Voight, a conversation with Dickey is included.
       Voight relates his concept of his role as Ed Gentry in the
       film version of Deliverance, his differences with Dickey
       over their opposed views of the film's theme, and the
       changes he made in its screenplay. Dickey remarks on
       changes the film's director, John Boorman, and Voight
       made.
           Ref.: John Boorman, pp. 155, 157; Maxine Dickey,
       pp. 155; Pauline Kael, p. 158; Mary McCarthy, p. 155;
       Joyce Carol Oates, p. 155; John Updike, p. 155; Jon
       Voight, p. 155.

1096   Cassidy, Jerry. "What the Poetry Editor of Esquire Is Like:
       Interview with James Dickey." Writer's Digest 54 (Oct.
       1974), pp. 16-20.
           Alnilam, p. 17; "Apollo," p. 18; Babel to Byzantium,
       p. 17; Buckdancer's Choice, p. 17; Crux Australis, p. 17;
       Death's Baby Machine, p. 17; Deliverance [novel], pp. 17,
       19; Deliverance [film], p. 17; Drowning with Others,
       p. 17; The Eye-Beaters, Blood, Victory, Madness, Buck-
       head and Mercy, p. 17; "Falling," p. 19; "Falling" [sec.
       of Poems 1957-1967], p. 17; Helmets, p. 17; "The Hos-

pital Window," p. 19; Into the Stone and Other Poems,
p. 17; "On the Coosawattee," p. 17; Self-Interviews,
p. 17; The Suspect in Poetry, p. 17; Sorties, p. 17.
    Dickey reveals the order in which he wrote various
portions of Deliverance, his plans for two novels, of
which one will be a sequel to the other, and a long poem,
two anecdotes about "Falling," and his theories of creative
writing.
    Ref.: John Boorman, p. 17; Thomas Carlyle, p. 18;
Christopher Dickey, p. 17; Maxine Dickey, p. 18; William
Faulkner, p. 20; Ernest Hemingway, p. 20; John Hersey's
The War Lover, p. 20; Eugene McCarthy, p. 20; Howard
Moss, p. 19; The New Yorker, pp. 19-20; Flannery
O'Connor, p. 19; Andrew Sherwood, p. 19; Aleksandr
Solzhenitsyn, p. 20; Jon Voight, p. 17; Richard Wilbur,
p. 20; Yevgeny Yevtushenko, p. 20.
    Illustrated with a sketch by L. Specker, p. 16.

*1097 Chambless, Laura. "The Many Faces of James Dickey."
       Tampa (Fla.) Tribune-Times (13 May 1973), sec. I, p. 3.
           *[This citation is from Margaret C. Patterson's "James
       Dickey," second page (see no. 1133).]

1098   Coulbourn, Keith. "James Dickey: The Poetic Gadfly."
       Atlanta Journal and the Atlanta Constitution. Atlanta
       Journal and Constitution Magazine (15 Mar. 1970), pp. 6-7,
       38-41, 43.
           Deliverance, pp. 7, 38; Self-Interviews, p. 38; [Sorties],
       p. 38.
           Dickey's poetry is discussed at length as are the
       reader's relationship with Dickey's poetry, its goal, and
       poets which have influenced him. Factual basis for
       Deliverance and its plot are discussed, and a translation
       of the quote from Georges Bataille is given. Also covered
       are Dickey's ideas concerning teaching creative writing, a
       "typical" daily schedule Dickey follows, and biographical
       data.
           Ref.: James Agee, pp. 6, 41; Cliff Baldowski, p. 6;
       "Don't Get Mad at Me Boys if Your Buggy Don't Ride Like
       Mine" [song], p. 6; T. S. Eliot, p. 40; William Empson,
       p. 39; Allen Ginsberg, p. 40; Henry James, p. 41; Robert
       Lowell, p. 40; Ralph McGill, p. 43; Norman Mailer,
       p. 38; G. E. Moore, p. 41; John Updike, p. 38; Thomas
       Wolfe, pp. 7, 43.
           Photographs of Dickey by Kenneth Rogers, pp. 6-7, 39,
       41, 43.

1099   "Deliverance": An Interview with James Dickey, a Poet Ex-
       ploring the Novel Form [Cassette].
           (See no. 1137.)

1100   Drake, Robert, ed. "The Writer and His Tradition." In The
       Writer and His Tradition: 1969 Southern Literary Festi-

val; Festival Proceedings, pp. 11-30.   Knoxville, Tenn. :
University of Tennessee, 1969.
   A panel discussion, with Dickey, Robert Drake, Cleanth
Brooks and Reynolds Price participating, held on April
16-17, 1969.   Topics investigated include U. S. life styles
from the Depression to the present, the disappearance of
the rural South, and the celebratory aspects of art, es-
pecially in Dickey's and Price's works.
   Ref. :   the Agrarian Group, p. 21; Edward Aswell,
p. 28; Samuel Beckett's Waiting for Godot, p. 25; Truman
Capote, p. 22; Cosmopolitan, p. 24; E. E. Cummings,
p. 26; Donald Davidson, pp. 20, 22; Davidson's The Attack
on Leviathan, p. 21; Davidson's I'll Take My Stand, p. 21;
Stephen Dedalus, p. 15; Bob Dylan, p. 16; Ralph Ellison's
The Invisible Man, p. 17; William Faulkner, pp. 14, 18;
the Fugitive Group, p. 21; Ernest Hemingway's For Whom
the Bell Tolls, p. 28; Fred Hoyle's The Nature of the
Universe, p. 27; Robinson Jeffers, p. 27; Grandpa Jones,
p. 16; Franz Kafka, p. 17; T. E. Lawrence, p. 30;
Bernard Malamud, pp. 18-19; The New Yorker, pp. 19-
20; Katherine Ann Porter's "María Concepción," p. 26;
Alexander Portnoy, p. 25; Herbert Read, p. 14; Philip
Roth's Portnoy's Complaint, p. 18; Louis Rubin, p. 18;
Doc Watson, p. 16; Eudora Welty's "Why I Live at the
P. O. ," p. 22; Thomas Wolfe, p. 28; William Butler
Yeats, pp. 14, 27.

*1101   "Druid Interview: James Dickey. "   Druid (Fall 1969), p. 8.
       *[This citation is from David C. Berry, Jr. 's "Orphic
   and Narcissistic Themes in the Poetry and Criticism of
   James Dickey. " p. 189 (see no. 1116).]

1102   Graham, John.   "James Dickey. "   In Craft So Hard to Learn:
   Conversations with Poets and Novelists About the Teaching
   of Writing, edited by George Garrett, pp. 82-87.   New
   York: Morrow Paperback Editions, 1972.
       Poems 1957-1967, p. 83.
       Dickey discusses his ideas concerning teaching creative
   writing, but his comments on the poetic process in gen-
   eral, the prime characteristics of a writer, "spaceous"
   poetry, and protest poetry are given.   This interview was
   originally recorded in June 1970 at the Hollins Conference
   in Creative Writing and Cinema for Graham's "The
   Scholar's Bookshelf, " a radio show.
       Ref. :   W. H. Auden, p. 83; Allen Ginsberg, p. 86;
   Rod McKuen, p. 86.

1103   _____ .   "James Dickey. "   In The Writer's Voice: Con-
   versations with Contemporary Writers, edited by George
   Garrett, pp. 228-247.   New York: William Morrow and
   Co. , 1973.
       Babel to Byzantium, p. 228; Buckdancer's Choice,
   pp. 228, 235; Deliverance [novel], pp. 228, 237, 242,

245-246; Deliverance [film], p. 228; Drowning with Others, p. 228; The Eye-Beaters, Blood, Victory, Madness, Buckhead and Mercy, pp. 228-229; "Falling," p. 230; Helmets, p. 228; "In the Pocket," p. 238; Into the Stone and Other Poems, p. 228; "Messages [: I, Butterflies]," pp. 232-233; "On the Coosawattee," p. 242; Poems 1957-1967, p. 228; Self-Interviews, p. 228; Sorties, p. 228; Spinning the Crystal Ball, p. 228; The Suspect in Poetry, p. 228; Two Poems of the Air, p. 228.

Dickey relates his fascination with, and need for, long poems, his use of spacing within a poem's lines, concrete poetry, his problems with writing prose, and his use of experiences. The poem "In the Pocket" is reprinted in full, p. 239.

Ref. : Guillaume Apollinaire's Calligrammes, p. 234; Henri Bergson, p. 230; Marlon Brando, p. 229; James Gould Cozzens' Guard of Honor, p. 241; E. E. Cummings, p. 234; George Herbert's "Altar," p. 234; Herbert's "Angel Wings," p. 234; Herbert's "Church Monuments," p. 234; Herbert's "Easter Wings," p. 234; John Hollander, p. 234; King Kong, p. 229; Walter Pater, p. 240; Luigi Pirandello's Six Characters in Search of an Author, p. 243; Erich Maria Remarque All Quiet on the Western Front, p. 241; John Updike, p. 245.

1104 Greiner, Donald J. "'That Plain-Speaking Guy': A Conversation with James Dickey on Robert Frost." In Frost: Centennial Essays, comp. by the Committee on the Frost Centennial of the University of Southern Mississippi, pp. 51-59. Jackson, Miss.: University Press of Mississippi, [n. d.].

[Deliverance] [film], p. 55; ["Robert Frost"], pp. 52-53.

Dickey discusses Robert Frost the public personality as well as the poet and attempts to reevaluate Frost's poetry in a contemporary light.

Ref. : W. H. Auden, p. 59; T. S. Eliot, pp. 56-57; Ralph Waldo Emerson, p. 55; Robert Frost, pp. 51-59; Frost's "Acquainted with the Night," p. 59; Frost's "After Apple-Picking," pp. 53, 59; Frost's "All Revelation," p. 56; Frost's "Birches," pp. 52, 56-57; Frost's "Death of the Hired Man," p. 54; Frost's "Design," p. 53; Frost's "Directive," pp. 56, 59; Frost's "The Fear," p. 54; Frost's "Fire and Ice," pp. 56-57; Frost's "The Gift Outright," p. 52; Frost's "Home Burial," pp. 54, 56; Frost's "Mending Wall," pp. 52, 57; Frost's "The Most of It," p. 54; Frost's "Neither Out Far Nor In Deep," p. 56; Frost's North of Boston, p. 58; Frost's "October," p. 56; Frost's "One Step Backward Taken," p. 56; Frost's "Provide, Provide," p. 55; Frost's "Stopping by Woods on a Snowy Evening," pp. 56-57; Frost's "The Earthward," p. 53; Randall Jarrell, p. 56; Pablo Picasso, pp. 58-59; Ezra Pound, pp. 56, 59; J. B. Priestly's Literature and Western Man, p. 55; Tom Priestly, p. 55; Wallace

Stevens, pp. 56-58; Algernon Swinburne, p. 51; Alfred, Lord Tennyson, p. 51; Lawrence Thompson, p. 53; Lionel Trilling, p. 55; Yvor Winters, p. 54; William Wordsworth, p. 54; William Butler Yeats, p. 57.

1105 Heyen, William. "A Conversation with James Dickey." Southern Review, n. s. 9 (Jan. 1973), pp. 135-156.
     "The Bee," p. 141; Deliverance, pp. 149-151, 153-154; Drowning with Others, p. 145; "Falling" [sec. in Poems 1957-1967], p. 138; ["Galway Kinnell"], p. 140; "The Heaven of Animals," pp. 142-145; Into the Stone and Other Poems, p. 145; "Matthew Arnold: 'Dover Beach,'" p. 148; "The Performance," pp. 135, 137-138, 140, 145; Self-Interviews, pp. 135, 138; "The Sheep Child," p. 138; "Sled Burial, Dream Ceremony," p. 149.
     Dickey gives the background of several of his poems and of Deliverance and its film version. Dickey expresses his ideas concerning the poetic process, death, the poetic use of experience, the differences between his first and second volumes, and the criticism of poetry. This interview is a transcript of a video tape. The poems "The Heaven of Animals," "The Performance," and "Sled Burial, Dream Ceremony" are reprinted in full, pp. 143-144, 135-136, and 149-150, respectively.
     Ref.: Robert Ardrey's The Social Contract, p. 148; Buddy Baer, p. 151; John Berryman, p. 154; Cleanth Brooks and Robert Penn Warren's Understanding Poetry, p. 146; Paul Carroll's "The Smell of Blood in Paradise," p. 144 (see no. 998); "Dangerous Dan" [song], p. 146; Democritus, p. 148; Joan Didion, p. 148; Walt Disney's African Lion [film], p. 142; Disney's White Wilderness [film], p. 142; Jesse Hill Ford, p. 153; William James, p. 142; Randall Jarrell, p. 139; Deborrah Kerr, p. 151; Rudyard Kipling, p. 145; D. H. Lawrence, pp. 139, 148; Arthur Lovejoy, p. 139; Robert Lowell, p. 147; Peter Marchant, pp. 135, 149; The New Yorker, p. 145; Sylvia Plath, pp. 147-148; J. B. Priestley's Midnight on the Desert, p. 146; Edwin Arlington Robinson, p. 148; Theodore Roethke, pp. 145, 147; Nicola Sacco, p. 154; Erich Segal's Love Story, p. 152; Robert Service, p. 145; Anne Sexton, p. 147; William Shakespeare, p. 145; Robert Taylor, p. 151; St. Thomas Aquinas, p. 143; Bartolomeo Vanzetti, p. 154; Richard Wilbur, p. 145; William Butler Yeats, pp. 145-146.

1106 "An Interview with James Dickey." Eclipse, no. 5 (1966), pp. 5-20.
     "Confession Is Not Enough," p. 9; Buckdancer's Choice, pp. 5, 8, 10, 17; Drowning with Others, pp. 5, 8; "Falling" [sec. of Poems 1957-1967], pp. 8, 16; "The Fiend," pp. 7, 11, 19; "A Folk Singer of the Thirties," p. 10; Helmets, pp. 5, 8, 10; Into the Stone and Other Poems, p. 5; ["Randall Jarrell"], p. 12; "Slave Quarters," p. 7;

The Suspect in Poetry, pp. 5, 12; Two Poems of the Air,
p. 5.
  Dickey discusses at length his concepts of his own
poetics and of poetry in general. Topics examined include:
folk music's influencing his verse, moralizing traits in
poems, American apathy toward poetry, poets who have
influenced him and the influence of his Southern heritage,
and the teaching of creative writing. Dickey's prediction
for the future of poetry concludes.
  Ref.: George Barker, p. 13; John Berryman, pp. 10,
12; Alain Blanchart, p. 20; Robert Bly, pp. 7, 20; Bly's
"The Work of James Dickey," p. 9 (see no. 589); André
Breton, p. 20; René Guy Cadou, p. 14; John Cage, p. 10;
Jean Cocteau, p. 8; Samuel Taylor Coleridge's "The Rime
of the Ancient Mariner," p. 17; Gregory Corso, pp. 9-10;
Steven Crane, p. 18; Robert Creeley, p. 9; Salvador Dali,
p. 20; Donald Davidson, p. 15; Robert Desnos, p. 20;
Robert Duncan, p. 9; T. S. Eliot, p. 14; Paul Eluard,
p. 20; André Frenaud, p. 14; Robert Frost, p. 12; Allen
Ginsberg, pp. 9-10; Woody Guthrie's Bound for Glory,
p. 10; Gerard Manley Hopkins, p. 14; Burl Ives, p. 11;
Ives' The Wayfaring Stranger, p. 10; Randall Jarrell,
pp. 12-13; "Jimmy Crack Corn" [song], p. 11; Bill
Knott, p. 20; John Logan, p. 9; Robert Lowell, p. 13;
Andrew Marvell's "To His Coy Mistress," p. 14; John
Milton's "Il Penseroso," p. 14; Friedrich Nietzsche,
p. 17; John Nofel, p. 20; Pablo Picasso, p. 8; Edgar
Allan Poe, pp. 7-8; Ezra Pound, p. 14; John Crowe Ran-
som, p. 13; Pierre Reverdy, p. 14; Theodore Roethke,
pp. 13-14; George Santayana, p. 17; Delmore Schwartz,
p. 13; Robert Service, p. 8; William Shakespeare's Ham-
let, p. 14; Karl Shapiro, p. 12; "The Shooting of Dan
McGrew" [song], p. 8; Louis Simpson, p. 10; William
Stafford, pp. 10, 12, 19; Jules Supervielle, p. 14; Allen
Tate, p. 13; Dylan Thomas, p. 14; Tristan Tzara, p. 20;
[unidentified script concerning Dickey's poetry], pp. 7-8
(see no. 1135); Paul Valéry, p. 18; Robert Penn Warren,
p. 15; Walt Whitman, p. 18; William Wordsworth's
"Intimations of Immortality," p. 14.

1107 Kizer, Carolyn and Boatwright, James. "A Conversation
   with James Dickey." Shenandoah 18 (Aut. 1966), pp. 3-28.
     Discussion with Dickey centers on his ideas concerning
   the mythologized poet and the relationship between himself
   and his public image. Also included are Dickey's thoughts
   on his literary heritage, his relationship to the academic
   community, the poetic process, and the process of aging.
     Ref.: James Agee, p. 27; W. H. Auden, pp. 11, 13,
   18; Charles Baudelaire, p. 16; the Beat poets, p. 6;
   Simone de Beauvoir, p. 25; de Beauvoir's The Mandarins,
   p. 25; George Gordon, Lord Byron, pp. 17-18; Byron's
   Don Juan, p. 18; T. S. Eliot, pp. 11-13; Kenneth Fearing,
   p. 15; E. M. Forster's Howards End, p. 16; John Fowles,

p. 20; André Gide, p. 25; Gotham Book Mart, p. 5;
Hell's Angels, p. 3; Ernest Hemingway, pp. 4-5, 28;
Dick Hugo, p. 20; Henry James, p. 27; Ben Jonson, p. 6;
Carolyn Kizer, p. 3; Stanley Kunitz, p. 17; D. H. Law-
rence, p. 23; Vachel Lindsay, p. 8; Mary McCarthy,
p. 27; John Masefield, p. 23; John Milton, p. 13; Paul
O'Neil's "The Unlikeliest Poet," p. 15 (see no. 850);
Alexander Pope, p. 13; Katherine Anne Porter, p. 15;
John Crowe Ransom, p. 16; Kenneth Rexroth, p. 6; Rainer
Maria Rilke, p. 6; Theodore Roethke, pp. 26-27; Patrice
de la Tour du Pin's La Somme de la Poésie, p. 26;
François Villon, p. 6; W. A. S. P. 's, p. 13; Robert Penn
Warren, p. 25; William Wordsworth, pp. 13, 16; William
Butler Yeats, pp. 13, 19, 22, 23.
    Rept. : James Dickey: The Expansive Imagination (see
no. 1108).

1108   . "A Conversation with James Dickey." In James
    Dickey: The Expansive Imagination; A Collection of Criti-
    cal Essays, edited by Richard J. Calhoun, pp. 1-33.
    DeLand, Fla. : Everett-Edwards, 1973.
        Discussion with Dickey centers on his ideas concerning
    the mythologized poet and the relationship between himself
    and his public image. Also included are Dickey's thoughts
    on his literary heritage, his relationship to the academic
    community, the poetic process, and the process of aging.
        Ref. : James Agee, p. 32; W. H. Auden, pp. 12, 14,
    20; Charles Baudelaire, p. 18; the Beat poets, p. 5;
    Simone de Beauvoir, p. 29; de Beauvoir's The Mandarins,
    p. 29; George Gordon, Lord Byron, pp. 19-20; Byron's
    Don Juan, p. 20; T. S. Eliot, pp. 12-14; Kenneth Fearing,
    p. 16; E. M. Forster's Howards End, p. 17; John Fowles,
    p. 23; André Gide, p. 29; Gotham Book Mart, p. 4; Hell's
    Angels, p. 1; Ernest Hemingway, p. 3; Dick Hugo, p. 23;
    Henry James, p. 31; Ben Jonson, p. 4; Carolyn Kizer,
    p. 1; Stanley Kunitz, p. 18; D. H. Lawrence, p. 27;
    Vachel Lindsay, p. 7; Mary McCarthy, pp. 31-32; John
    Masefield, p. 27; John Milton, p. 14; Paul O'Neil's "The
    Unlikeliest Poet," p. 17 (see no. 850); Alexander Pope,
    p. 13; Katherine Ann Porter, p. 17; John Crowe Ransom,
    p. 18; Kenneth Rexroth, p. 5; Rainer Maria Rilke, p. 4;
    Theodore Roethke, pp. 30-32; Patrice de la Tour du Pin's
    La Somme de la Poésie, p. 30; François Villon, p. 4;
    W. A. S. P. 's, p. 14; Robert Penn Warren, p. 29; William
    Wordsworth, pp. 13, 18; William Butler Yeats, pp. 14,
    22, 26.
        Orig. : Shenandoah (see no. 1107).

1109 Logue, John. "James Dickey Describes His Life and Works
    as He 'Moves Towards Hercules.'" Southern Living 6
    (Feb. 1971), pp. 44-49, 60, 65.
        Buckdancer's Choice, pp. 46, 48; "A Closer Walk,"
    p. 65; Deliverance [novel], pp. 45-48, 60, 65; Deliverance

[film], p. 46; Drowning with Others, p. 48; ["Edwin
Arlington Robinson: The Many Truths"], p. 48; The Eye-
Beaters, Blood, Victory, Madness, Buckhead and Mercy,
p. 47; The Field of Dogs, pp. 60, 65; Helmets, p. 48;
"The Indian Maiden," pp. 60, 65; Into the Stone and Other
Poems, p. 48; Self-Interviews, p. 49; Slowly Toward
Hercules, p. 65; The Suspect in Poetry, p. 48; ["Two
Poems of Going Home: II,] Looking for the Buckhead
Boys," pp. 48-49; Two Poems of the Air, p. 48; [uni-
dentified documentary films] p. 46 (see nos. 530 and 531).
     Discussion with Dickey centers on his publishing career.
Also discussed are his financial and literary successes,
his Southern heritage, and his plans for future publications.
Biographical data is included.
     Ref. : Neil Armstrong, p. 65; John Boorman, pp. 46-47;
Boorman's Hell in the Pacific [film], p. 46; Boorman's
Point Blank [film], p. 46; John Calley, p. 46; Christopher
Dickey, p. 49; Kevin Dickey, p. 49; Maxine Dickey, pp. 49, 60;
John Donne, p. 65; John Dryden, p. 60; T. S. Eliot,
p. 65; Robert Frost, p. 48; Ben Gazzara, p. 46; Alex
Gotfryd, p. 47; Bill Hall, p. 46; Ernest Hemingway, p. 60;
Charlton Heston, p. 47; Frank Howard, p. 49; Hubert
Humphrey, p. 60; William Hunter, p. 60; Randall Jarrell,
p. 48; "Jim Conway Show," p. 47; "Just a Closer Walk
with Me" [song], p. 65; Nikos Kazantzakis' Report to
Greco, p. 65; The Kenyon Review, p. 45; Burt Lancaster,
p. 47; Robert Lowell, p. 48; Rod McKuen, p. 47; Norman
Mailer, p. 46; Claude Mauriac, p. 60; François Mauriac,
p. 60; Herman Melville, p. 65; Lewis Mumford, p. 65;
Pablo Picasso, p. 60; Alexander Pope, p. 60; Ezra Pound,
p. 65; Edwin Arlington Robinson, p. 48; Robinson's "Luke
Havergal," p. 48; Robinson's "Mr. Flood's Party," p. 48;
Philip Roth, p. 46; The Sewanee Review, p. 60; Louis
Simpson, p. 48; Oliver Smith, p. 38; Monroe Spears,
p. 60; Spears' Auden: A Collection of Critical Essays,
p. 60; John Steinbeck, p. 48; William Styron, p. 46; May
Swenson, p. 48; Allen Tate, p. 65; Leo Tolstoy, p. 60;
John Updike, p. 46; Raymond Weaver, p. 65.

*1109a Moore, Robert H. "The Last Months at Harper's: Willie
     Morris in Conversation." Mississippi Review 3 (1974),
     pp. 121-130.
          *[This citation is from American Literary Scholarship:
     An Annual, 1974, p. 316.]

*1110 Newman, Edwin. Comment. Washington, D. C.: Merkle
     Press, [n.d.].
          A transcription of Newman's "Comment," a television
     program of the National Broadcasting Company, it seems
     to have been aired on April 16, 1972. Included in the
     original citation is "2 (16 April 1972), pp. 1-7. "
          *[This citation is from David C. Berry, Jr. 's "Orphic
     and Narcissistic Themes in the Poetry and Criticism of
     James Dickey," p. 192 (see no. 1116).]

1111   Norman, Geoffry. "Playboy Interview: James Dickey."
       Playboy 20 (Nov. 1973), pp. 81-82, 86, 89, 92, 94, 212-
       216.
          Buckdancer's Choice, p. 81; Deliverance [novel], pp. 82,
       89, 212-215; Deliverance [film], pp. 81, 214-215; "Drums
       Where I Live," p. 216; "The Firebombing," pp. 92, 213;
       Into the Stone and Other Poems, p. 81; "The Shark at
       the Window," p. 89.
          Dickey discusses his public image, his fascination with
       nature, hunting, and various animals. Comments regard-
       ing war, his success, his acting career, poets and politics,
       alcoholism, and suicide are related. Biographical data is
       included.
          Ref.: James Agee, pp. 82, 94; Fred Bear, p. 86;
       Hilaire Belloc, p. 215; John Berryman, pp. 92, 94; Robert
       Bly, p. 213; John Boorman, p. 215; Robert Burns, p. 89;
       Al Capp, p. 212; Hart Crane, pp. 92, 94; Kevin Dickey,
       p. 82; Maxine Dickey, p. 82; T. S. Eliot, p. 89; William
       Faulkner, p. 89; F. Scott Fitzgerald, p. 213; Robert
       Frost, pp. 89, 92, 213; Frost's "Acquainted with the
       Night," p. 89; Nordahl Grieg, p. 89; Ernest Hemingway,
       pp. 86, 213; John Hersey's The War Lover, p. 92; Randall
       Jarrell, p. 92; James Jones, p. 213; John Keats, p. 89;
       Fletcher Knebel and Charles W. Bailey's Seven Days in
       May, p. 216; Robert Lowell, p. 89; Malcolm Lowry, p. 89;
       Marshall McLuhan, p. 82; Norman Mailer, pp. 89, 213;
       Herman Melville, p. 89; Melville's Moby Dick, p. 89;
       Wright Morris, p. 214; Newsweek, p. 89; Geoffrey Nor-
       man's "The Stuff of Poetry," p. 82 (see no. 845); George
       Orwell, p. 92; Sylvia Plath, p. 94; Edgar Allan Poe,
       p. 82; Poe's "The Gold Bug," p. 82; Ezra Pound, p. 89;
       Burt Reynolds, p. 82; George Santayana, p. 92; Upton
       Sinclair's The Jungle, p. 92; C. P. Snow, p. 94; Aleksandr
       Solzhenitsyn, p. 92; William Styron, p. 213; Dylan Thomas,
       p. 94; Lawrence Thompson's Robert Frost, p. 94; John
       Unterecker's Voyager: A Life of Hart Crane, p. 92; Paul
       Valéry, p. 94; Jon Voight, p. 81; Thomas Wolfe, pp. 94,
       213; Yevgeny Yevtushenko, p. 92.
          Illustrated with photographs of Dickey by David Cahn,
       p. 81.

1112   Packard, William. "Craft Interview with James Dickey."
       New York Quarterly, no. 10 (Spr. 1972), pp. 16-35.
          Babel to Byzantium, p. 19; "Barnstorming for Poetry,"
       p. 22; Deliverance, pp. 17-18; "Falling," p. 30; ["In the
       Presence of Anthologies"], p. 20; "The Lifeguard," p. 27;
       "May Day Sermon to the Women of Gilmer County, Georgia,
       by a Woman Preacher Leaving the Baptist Church,"
       pp. 29-30, 34; "The Movement of Fish," p. 28; ["Notes
       on the Decline of Outrage"], p. 32; ["The Poet Turns on
       Himself"], pp. 24-27; "Preface," pp. 17-18; Sorties,
       p. 34; "The Stepson," p. 30.
          While aiming at the theories and processes of writing,

topics also covered by Dickey include: the adaptation of
Deliverance to film, the differences between writing prose
and poetry, his theories of criticism, teaching's and work-
shops' influences on him, socially and politically oriented
poetry, public readings of creative works, the use of per-
sonal experiences in poetry, the poet's psyche, and
Dickey's Southern heritage.

Ref.: James Agee, p. 29; Aristotle, p. 22; W. H.
Auden, p. 20; Wendell Berry, pp. 31-32; John Berryman,
pp. 24, 29; Robert Bly, pp. 22, 33; William F. Buckley,
Jr.'s "Firing Line," p. 28 (see no. 1094); Samuel Taylor
Coleridge, pp. 20, 30; Hart Crane, pp. 17, 29; Donald
Davidson, p. 31; Robert Frost, p. 31; Allen Ginsberg,
p. 33; Anthony Hecht, p. 25; Martin Heidegger, p. 26;
Ernest Hemingway, p. 24; Randall Jarrell, p. 29; Robin-
son Jeffers, p. 31; Jeffers' "Apology for Bad Dreams,"
p. 31; John the Baptist, p. 35; The Kenyon Review, p. 22;
Robert Lowell, p. 24; James Merrill, p. 25; The New York
Quarterly, p. 26; Sylvia Plath, p. 31; Edwin Arlington
Robinson, p. 27; Christopher Salmon, pp. 26-27; Carl
Sandburg, p. 31; Bobby Seale, p. 33; Carl Seifert, p. 27;
Anne Sexton, p. 31; Karl Shapiro's Edsel, p. 17; Monroe
Spears, p. 27; Spears' Dionysus and the City, p. 27 (see
no. 1074); Jesse Stuart, p. 32; Allen Tate, p. 31; Red
Warren, p. 31; Alfred North Whitehead, pp. 24, 26;
Alfred North Whitehead and Bertrand Russell's Principia
Mathematica, p. 26; Richard Wilbur, p. 25; Yvor Winters,
p. 19; Ludwig Wittgenstein, p. 26; William Butler Yeats'
"Easter 1916," p. 33.

Rept.: The Craft of Poetry: Interviews from "The New
York Quarterly" (see no. 1113).

Photographs of Dickey by Layle Silbert, pp. 16, 35.

1113 _____ . "Craft Interview with James Dickey." In The
Craft of Poetry: Interviews from "The New York Quar-
terly," edited by William Packard, pp. 133-151. Garden
City, N.Y.: Doubleday and Co., 1974.

Babel to Byzantium, p. 135; "Barnstorming for Poetry,"
p. 138; Deliverance, p. 133; "Falling," p. 145; ["In the
Presence of Anthologies"], p. 136; "The Lifeguard,"
p. 143; "May Day Sermon to the Women of Gilmer County,
Georgia, by a Woman Preacher Leaving the Baptist Church,"
pp. 145-146, 150; "The Movement of Fish," p. 143;
["Notes on the Decline of Outrage"], p. 148; ["The Poet
Turns on Himself"], pp. 140-143; "Preface," pp. 135-136;
Sorties, p. 150; "The Stepson," p. 146.

While aiming at the theories and processes of writing,
topics also covered by Dickey include: the adaptation of
Deliverance to film, the differences between writing prose
and poetry, his theories of criticism, teaching's and work-
shops' influences on him, socially and politically oriented
poetry, public readings of creative works, the use of per-
sonal experiences in poetry, the poet's psyche, and

Dickey's Southern heritage.
    Ref.: James Agee, p. 145; Aristotle, p. 138; W. H.
Auden, p. 136; Wendell Berry, p. 148; John Berryman,
pp. 140, 145; Robert Bly, pp. 137, 149; William F.
Buckley, Jr.'s "Firing Line," p. 144 (see no. 1094);
Samuel Taylor Coleridge, pp. 136, 146; Hart Crane,
pp. 133, 145; Donald Davidson, p. 147; Robert Frost,
p. 147; Allen Ginsberg, p. 149; Anthony Hecht, p. 141;
Martin Heidegger, p. 142; Ernest Hemingway, p. 140;
Randall Jarrell, p. 145; Robinson Jeffers, p. 147; Jeffers'
"Apology for Bad Dreams," p. 147; John the Baptist,
p. 151; The Kenyon Review, p. 138; Robert Lowell,
p. 140; James Merrill, p. 141; The New York Quarterly,
p. 142; Sylvia Plath, p. 147; Edwin Arlington Robinson,
p. 143; Christopher Salmon, pp. 142-143; Carl Sandburg,
p. 147; Bobby Seale, p. 149; Carl Seifert, p. 143; Anne
Sexton, p. 147; Karl Shapiro's Edsel, p. 133; Monroe
Spears, p. 143; Spears' Dionysus and the City, p. 143 (see
no. 1074); Jesse Stuart, p. 148; Allen Tate, p. 147; Red
Warren, p. 147; Alfred North Whitehead, pp. 140, 142;
Alfred North Whitehead and Bertrand Russell's Principia
Mathematica, p. 142; Richard Wilbur, p. 141; Yvor
Winters, p. 135; Ludwig Wittgenstein, p. 142; William
Butler Yeats' "Easter 1916," p. 149.
    Orig.: The New York Quarterly (see no. 1112).
    Photograph of Dickey by Layle Silbert on the first page
following p. 200.

1114 Roberts, Francis. "James Dickey: An Interview." Per/Se
      3 (Spr. 1968), pp. 8-12.
          Buckdancer's Choice, p. 8; "Cave Master," p. 10;
      "Drinking from a Helmet," p. 9; Drowning with Others,
      p. 8; "The Firebombing," p. 9; Helmets, p. 8; Into the
      Stone and Other Poems, pp. 8-9, 11; A Private Brinks-
      manship, p. 12; "Slave Quarters," p. 10; The Suspect in
      Poetry, p. 8.
          Dickey discusses his use of personal and imagined ex-
      periences, and especially his war experiences, other
      writers and philosophers whom he admires or dislikes,
      and the process of creative writing. He concludes with
      advice for young writers.
          Ref.: Achilles, p. 11; Anaximander, p. 10; Guillaume
      Apollinaire, p. 10; Ben Belitt, p. 8; Joseph Bennett's "A
      Man with a Voice," p. 8 (see no. 580); Christopher
      Dickey, p. 8; Maxine Dickey, p. 8; Emily Dickinson,
      p. 9; John Donne, p. 10; T. S. Eliot, p. 9; Paul Eluard,
      p. 9; Euclid, p. 10; Robert Frost, p. 11; Ernest Heming-
      way, pp. 9-10, 12; Heraclitus of Ephesus, p. 10; Geoffrey
      Hill, p. 9; Gerard Manley Hopkins, p. 10; Ted Hughes, p. 9;
      Juan Ramón Jiménez, p. 11; Carl Jung, p. 10; Marie-René-
      Auguste-Alexis Léger, p. 9; John Livingstone Lowes' The Road
      to Xanadu, p. 10; Phyllis McGinley, p. 8; Rene Ménard,
      p. 10; Eugenio Montale, p. 9; Wolfgang Mozart, p. 9;

Edwin Muir, p. 9; Odysseus, p. 11; Elder Olson, p. 8;
Ezra Pound, p. 9; Marcel Proust, p. 10; Pythagoras,
p. 10; Salvatore Quasimodo, p. 9; Theodore Roethke,
p. 9; George Seféris, p. 9; Jon Silkin, p. 9; Socrates,
p. 10; Jules Supervielle, p. 9; Emanuel Swendenborg,
p. 10; Alfred, Lord Tennyson, p. 9; Dylan Thomas,
p. 9; Guiseppe Ungaretti, p. 9; Walt Whitman, pp. 9, 11;
William Butler Yeats, pp. 9-10.

DISSERTATIONS, THESES, AND TERM PAPERS

1115 Arnett, David Leslie. "James Dickey: Poetry and Fiction."
Ph. D. dissertation, Tulane University, 1973.
Abs.: <u>Dissertation Abstracts International</u> (see no. 566).

1116 Berry, David Chapman, Jr. "Orphic and Narcissistic Themes
in the Poetry of James Dickey, 1951-1970." Ph. D. dis-
sertation, University of Tennessee, 1973.
Abs.: <u>Dissertation Abstracts International</u> (see no. 582).

1117 Carnes, Bruce Marshall. "James Dickey: The Development
of His Poetry." Ph. D. dissertation, Indiana University,
1971.
Abs.: <u>Dissertation Abstracts International</u> (see no. 617).

1118 Cleghorn, James D. "James Dickey." In "Preservation of
the Wilderness: A Contemporary View of Nature Poetry,"
pp. 111-182. Ph. D. dissertation, University of Massa-
chusetts, 1974.
"Approaching Prayer," pp. 129-132, 139; <u>Buckdancer's
Choice</u>, p. 159; ["Creative Possibilities"], p. 115; <u>Deliver-
ance</u>, pp. 160-164; "A Dog Sleeping on My Feet," pp. 125-
129; "The Driver," pp. 168-174, 177; <u>Drowning with
Others</u>, pp. 120, 151-152, 159; ["Drowning with Others"],
pp. 133, 153, 156, 158; "The Dusk of Horses," p. 176;
<u>The Eye-Beaters, Blood, Victory, Madness, Buckhead and
Mercy</u>, p. 173; "Falling," pp. 174-176; "'Falling,'" p. 138;
"Fog Envelops the Animals," p. 180n. ; "Fox Blood,"
p. 180n. ; "The Heaven of Animals," p. 156; "Hunting Civil
War Relics at Nimblewill Creek," pp. 120, 122-123, 127;
["In Medias Res"], pp. 144, 148; "In the Lupanar at
Pompeii," p. 111; "In the Mountain Tent," p. 153; <u>Into
the Stone and Other Poems</u>, pp. 151, 159; "Listening to
Foxhounds," p. 180n. ; "May Day Sermon to the Women of
Gilmer County, Georgia, by a Woman Preacher Leaving
the Baptist Church," pp. 172-173, 180n. ; ["Metaphor as
Pure Adventure"], pp. 127-128, 148, 165-167; ["Notes on
the Decline of Outrage"], pp. 116-117; ["The Poet Turns
on Himself'], p. 149; "The Salt Marsh," pp. 153-158; "The
Scarred Girl," p. 176; "A Screened Porch in the Country,"
pp. 116-122, 125; "The Shark's Parlor," p. 180n. ; "The
Sheep Child," pp. 134-139, 141, 150-151; "Sleeping Out at
Easter," p. 149; ["Spinning the Crystal Ball"], p. 137;

229

"Springer Mountain, " pp. 132, 176, 180n. ; "The Summons, " p. 180n. ; ["Teaching, Writing, Reincarnations, and Rivers"], pp. 123-125; "The Vegetable King, " pp. 141, 143-147.

Dickey's is an ambitious approach to nature poetry. He attempts to surrender to nature and succeeds in doing so in his earlier books. However, he fails in his later works because his egocentrism blocks his passage. Techniques he employs in his surrender are identified and many of his critics' comments are surveyed.

Ref. : Donald W. Baker's "The Poetry of James Dickey, " pp. 121, 127, 149-150, 174-175 (see no. 576); Wendell Berry's "James Dickey's New Book, " p. 182 (see no. 583); Robert Bly's "The Work of James Dickey, " pp. 112, 120-121, 145-146, 155, 172-173 (see no. 589); John William Corrington's "James Dickey's Poems 1957-1967, " pp. 122-123, 127, 142 (see no. 643); Peter Davison's "The Difficulties of Being Major, " p. 126 (see no. 659); Ralph Waldo Emerson, p. 121; William Everson, p. 130; Norman Friedman's "The Wesleyan Poets, II: The Formal Poets, 2, " pp. 132, 176-177 (see no. 701); Michael Goldman's "Inventing the American Heart, " pp. 114, 153-154, 158 (see no. 712); Richard Howard's "James Dickey: 'We Never Can Really Tell Whether Nature Condemns Us or Loves Us, '" pp. 112, 147-148, 151-152 (see no. 1024); James Korges' "James Dickey and Other Good Poets, " pp. 167, 176 (see no. 775); D. H. Lawrence's "Snake, " p. 126; C. Day Lewis, p. 126; William Meredith's "James Dickey's Poems, " p. 176 (see no. 819); Ralph J. Mills, Jr. 's "The Poetry of James Dickey, " pp. 119-120, 122, 126, 132-133, 137, 159-160, 176 (see no. 822); John Muir's [unidentified passage], pp. 160-162; Howard Nemerov's "Poems of Darkness and a Specialized Light, " p. 182 (see no. 840); Charles Olson's "Projective Verse, " p. 150; The Seafarer, p. 150; John Simon's "More Brass than Enduring, " p. 167 (see no. 904); Gary Snyder, pp. 113-116, 119-123, 136, 141-142, 150, 152, 160; Snyder's Earth House Hold, p. 115; Snyder's Myths and Texts, pp. 119, 121, 133, 141-142, 160; Snyder's [unidentified passage], p. 160; William C. Strange's "To Dream, to Remember, " pp. 121-122, 131 (see no. 925); Dylan Thomas, p. 176; The Wanderer, p. 150; H. L. Weatherby's "The Way of Exchange in James Dickey's Poetry, " pp. 125-126, 128, 177 (see no. 954); Walt Whitman, p. 121; Whitman's "Out of the Cradle Endlessly Rocking, " p. 126; William Wordsworth, p. 168.

1119   _____ . "Preservation of the Wilderness: A Contemporary View of Nature Poetry. " Ph. D. dissertation, University of Massachusetts, 1974.

Abs. : Dissertation Abstracts International (see no. 636). (Only one chapter pertains solely to Dickey [see no. 1118].)

*1120 Dacey, Philip. Master's thesis, n. p. , n. d.
       A draft of an untitled thesis on Dickey's poetry. A
       photocopy with suggested revisions is held at the John M.
       Olin Library.
       *[This citation is from a photocopy of the register of
       the Dickey papers at the John M. Olin Library, p. 33
       (see no. 547).]

 1121 Fixmer, Clyde H. "The Element of Myth in James Dickey's
       Poetry. " Ph. D. dissertation, University of Oklahoma,
       1974.
       Abs. : <u>Dissertation Abstracts International</u> (see no. 690).

*1122 Kipling, George. "James Dickey: The Spirit and the Image. "
       Term paper [?], n. p. , n. d.
       A duplicated copy of this paper is held at the John M.
       Olin Library.
       *[This citation is from a photocopy of the register of
       the Dickey papers at the John M. Olin Library, p. 33
       (see no. 547).]

 1123 McHughes, Janet Ellen Larsen. "A Phenomenological Analysis
       of Literary Time in the Poetry of James Dickey. " Ph. D.
       dissertation, Northwestern University, 1972.
       Abs. : <u>Dissertation Abstracts International</u> (see no. 805).

 1124 McKenzie, James Joseph. "A New American Nature Poetry:
       Theodore Roethke, James Dickey, and James Wright. "
       Ph. D. dissertation, University of Notre Dame, 1971.
       Abs. : <u>Dissertation Abstracts International</u> (see no. 807).

 1125 Moore, Robert Nelson, Jr. "Aggression in the Poetry of
       James Dickey. " Ph. D. dissertation, University of Cin-
       cinnati, 1973.
       Abs. : <u>Dissertation Abstracts International</u> (see no. 826).

 1126 Robbins, Fred Walker. "The Poetry of James Dickey, 1951-
       1967. " Ph. D. dissertation, University of Texas at Austin,
       1970.
       Abs. : <u>Dissertation Abstracts International</u> (see no. 879).

BIBLIOGRAPHIES

1127 Ashley, Franklin, comp. James Dickey: A Checklist.
      Introduced by James Dickey. Detroit: Gale Research
      Co. , Book Tower, 1972.
          "Introduction," p. xi; "James Dickey, National Book
      Award in Poetry, 1966: Acceptance Speech," p. xiii-xv.
          A list of books and pamphlets by Dickey with photo-
      graphs of their title pages.

1128 Glancy, Eileen K. "James Dickey: A Bibliography."
      Twentieth Century Literature 15 (Apr. 1969), pp. 45-61.
          A list of 206 works by Dickey and 131 works about
      him. Its scope was later expanded, and its title was
      changed to James Dickey: The Critic as Poet; An Anno-
      tated Bibliography with an Introductory Essay (see
      no. 1129).

1129 _____. James Dickey: The Critic as Poet; An Annotated
      Bibliography with an Introductory Essay. Troy, N. Y. :
      The Whitston Publishing Co. , 1971.
          A list of 229 works by Dickey and 167 works about
      him originally entitled "James Dickey: A Bibliography"
      (see no. 1128). It was slightly shorter in its original
      version.

1130 Hill, Robert W. "James Dickey: A Checklist." In James
      Dickey: The Expansive Imagination; A Collection of Criti-
      cal Essays, edited by Richard J. Calhoun, pp. 213-228.
      DeLand, Fla. : Everett-Edwards, 1973.
          A list of 51 works by Dickey and 112 works about him
      compiled as a "supplement" to Glancy's "James Dickey:
      A Bibliography" (see no. 1128).

1131 Latimer, Mary Lillis, comp. "James Dickey: A Bibliography."
      Mimeographed. Washington, D. C. : Bibliography and Ref-
      erence Correspondence Section, Reference Department,
      Library of Congress, 1966.
          A list of 183 works by Dickey, 63 works about him,
      and 6 anthologies in which his works appear.

1132 Owen, Guy. "James Dickey." In A Bibliographical Guide to
      the Study of Southern Literature with an Appendix Con-
      taining Sixty-Eight Additional Writers of the Colonial South,

232

edited by Louis D. Rubin, pp. 188-189. Baton Rouge:
Louisiana State University Press, 1969.
    A list containing 1 work by Dickey and 15 about him.

1133 Patterson, Margaret C. "James Dickey." In "Creative
    Writers Bibliography, 1949-1972: University of Florida."
    Mimeographed. Gainesville, Fla.: University of Florida,
    1973.
        A list of 20 works by Dickey and 38 works about him
    on 4 unnumbered pages.

SCRIPTS

*1134 A Poetry Experience on Film; "Lord, Let Me Die but Not
    Die Out": James Dickey, Poet. Chicago: Encyclopaedia
    Britannica, 1970.
        *[This citation is from Franklin Ashley's James Dickey:
    A Checklist, p. 97 (see no. 1127).]

*1135 [unidentified].
        Produced for the Voice of America, it is about Dickey's
    poetry.
        *[This citation is from "An Interview with James
    Dickey," pp. 7-8 (see no. 1106).]

NON-PRINT MATERIALS

*1135a Calhoun, Richard James. "Deliverance" (James Dickey) [Phono-
    tape]. Everett-Edwards, 1971, 1 cassette, 2 1/2 x 4 in.,
    43 min. (Cassette Curriculum.)
        *[This citation is from the card catalog of Loyola Uni-
    versity, Chicago.]

*1136 _____. James Dickey [Cassette]. Nos. 175-176. Everett-
    Edwards Press, [1971].
        *[This citation is from Robert W. Hill's "James Dickey:
    A Checklist," p. 226 (see no. 1130).]

*1136a _____. James Dickey [Phonotape]. Everett-Edwards,
    1971, 2 cassettes, 2 1/2 x 4 in., 84 min. (Modern
    American Poetry Criticism.)
        *[This citation is from the card catalog of Loyola Uni-
    versity, Chicago.]

*1137 "Deliverance": An Interview with James Dickey, a Poet Ex-

ploring the Novel Form [Cassette].   The Center for
Cassette Studies 21676, [1973], 1 7/8 ips., 30 min.
(Authors and Their Books.)
   *[This citation is from the card catalog of Loyola University, Chicago.]

*1138   James Dickey [Filmstrip].   Audiovisual Instructional Devices,
   1972, 50 fr., col., and audio tape.   (The Contemporary
   Voices Series.)
      *[This citation is from N.I.C.E.M.'s Index to 35mm
   Educational Filmstrips, vol. 2, 1975, p. 131.]

1139   James Dickey, Poet: "Lord, Let Me Die but Not Die Out."
   [Motion Picture].
      Citations vary, but it is cited as "Lord, Let Me Die
   but Not Die Out" in The National Union Catalog (see
   no. 1140).

*1140   "Lord, Let Me Die but Not Die Out" [Motion Picture].
   Stanley Croner, producer and director.   Encyclopaedia
   Britannica Educational Corp., [1970], 37 min., sd., col.,
   16mm.   (Humanities Series.)
      Its title is a line from Dickey's "For the Last Wolverine."
      *[This citation was compiled from data from The National Union Catalog ...:   Motion Pictures and Film Strips,
   vol. 4, p. 197; N.I.C.E.M.'s Index to 16mm Educational
   Films, vol. 2, 1975, p. 808; and From the "Humanities
   Series":   New Films That Explore the Nature of Man and
   Interweave the Areas of Human Experience (a catalog from
   the Encyclopaedia Britannica Educational Corporation), the
   page preceding p. 15.]

NON-ENGLISH LANGUAGE PUBLICATIONS

*1141 Allombert, G. "Délivrance." Image et Son (Paris),
no. 265 (Nov. 1972), pp. 108-109.
A review of the film Deliverance and a short interview
with John Boorman, the film's director.
*[This citation is from International Index to Film
Periodicals, 1972, p. 146.]

*1142 Beaulieu, J. "Deliverance." Séquences (Montreal) 71 (Jan.
1973), pp. 35-36.
A review of the film Deliverance.
*[This citation is from International Index to Film
Periodicals, 1973, p. 150.]

1143 Benoit, C.
Benoit wrote one of the two reviews of the film Deliver-
ance which appear together as "Face à face de deux
Amériques" (see no. 1154).

1144 Bleikasten, André. "Anatomie d'un bestseller: A propos de
Deliverance." Recherches Anglaises et Americaines,
no. 4 (1971), pp. 116-129.

*1145 Braucourt, G. "Breve rencontre avec John Boorman."
Ecran (Paris), no. 9 (Nov. 1972), pp. 30-32.
An interview with John Boorman, the director of
Deliverance, concerning its filming. Illustrated.
*[This citation is from International Index to Film
Periodicals, 1972, p. 147.]

*1145a Ciment, M. "Deux entretiens avec John Boorman." Positif
(Paris), no. 57 (Mar. 1974), pp. 12-19.
Discussion concerning the film version of Deliverance
is included.
*[This citation is from International Index to Film
Periodicals, 1974, p. 182.]

*1146 _____. "Voyage au bout de la nuit." Positif (Paris),
no. 143 (Oct. 1972), pp. 63-67.
A review of the film Deliverance. Illustrated.
*[This citation is from International Index to Film
Periodicals, 1972, p. 147.]

1147   Fauchereau, Serge.   "Entretien avec M. L. Rosenthal: 'Des
       figures intéressantes rien de plus. '"   Quinzaine Litteraire,
       no. 126 (1-15 Oct. 1971), pp. 9-11.

*1148   Fukuda, Rikutaro.   "James Dickey no Shi to Shiron. "   Eigo
       Seinen (Tokyo) 114 (1968), pp. 576-577.
           This is concerned with Dickey's poems and techniques.
           *[This citation is from M. L. A. International Bibliogra-
           phy, 1970, vol. 1, p. 124.]

*1149   Grisolia, M.   "John Boorman: 'L'Amérique s'est dissociée
       de la nature, par une sorte de névrose commune.... '"
       Cinéma (Paris), no. 170 (Nov. 1972), pp. 60-65.
           An interview with John Boorman, the director of
           Deliverance, concerning its filming.   Illustrated.
           *[This citation is from International Index to Film
           Periodicals, 1972, p. 147.]

*1149a "Kosmorama Essay: Niels Jensen/Den tavse mand og: Det
        onde, det gode og det grusomme. "   Kosmorama (Copen-
        hagen) 19 (May 1973), pp. 191-197.
           A review of the film version of Deliverance.   Illus-
           trated.
           *[This citation is from Film Literature Index, 1973,
           p. 100.]

*1149b Leirens, J.   "Delivrance ou le retour a la nature?"   Amis
        du Film et de la Television (Brussels), no. 200 (Jan.
        1973), pp. 14-15.
           A review of the film version of Deliverance.   Illus-
           trated.
           *[This citation is from Film Literature Index, 1973,
           p. 100.]

*1149c Leon (Frias), I.   "Amarga pesadella. "   Hablemos de Cine
        (Lima) 10, no. 66 (1974), pp. 46-47.
           A review of the film version of Deliverance.   Illus-
           trated.
           *[This citation is from International Index to Film
           Periodicals, 1975, p. 192.]

*1150   Leroux, A.   "Deliverance. "   Cinéma Quê (Montreal) 2 (Nov.
        1972), pp. 46-47.
           A review of the film Deliverance.
           *[This citation is from International Index to Film
           Periodicals, 1972, p. 147.]

*1151   Manns, T.   "Den Sista Färden. "   Chaplin (Stockholm) 14
        (1972), p. 258.
           A review of the film Deliverance.   Illustrated.
           *[This citation is from International Index to Film
           Periodicals, 1972. p. 147.]

*1152   Mee, R. du.   "Terug naar de natuur...." Skoop (Amster-
        dam) 8 (1972), pp. 2-4.
            A review of the film Deliverance.   Illustrated.
            *[This citation is from International Index to Film
        Periodicals, 1972, p. 147.]

*1153   Morawski, S.   "Janie-Jakubie, pomylka!" Kino (Warsaw) 8
        (Aug. 1973), pp. 58-59.
            A review of the film Deliverance.   Illustrated.
            *[This citation is from International Index to Film
        Periodicals, 1973, p. 150.]

*1154   Prédal, R. and Benoit, C.   "Face à face de deux Amériques:
        Delivrance." Jeune Cinéma (Paris), no. 67 (Dec. -Jan.
        1972-1973), pp. 29-33.
            Two reviews of the film Deliverance.   Illustrated.
            *[This citation is from International Index to Film
        Periodicals, 1972, p. 147.]

*1155   Renaud, T.   "Delivrance: La rivière sans retour." Cinéma
        (Paris), no. 170 (Nov. 1972), pp. 108-110.
            A review of the film Deliverance.   Illustrated.
            *[This citation is from International Index to Film
        Periodicals, 1972, p. 147.]

*1155a Stella, Mario.   "James Dickey: dalla poesia alla narrativa."
        Trimestre (Pescara) 7 (1973), pp. 420-436.
            An analysis of Dickey's works and his movement from
        poetry into fiction.
            *[This citation is from M. L. A. International Bibliogra-
        phy, 1975, vol. 1, p. 164 and American Literary Scholar-
        ship: An Annual, 1975, p. 490.]

*1156   Tessier, M.   "Délivrance." Ecran (Paris), no. 8 (Sept. -
        Oct. 1972), pp. 53-55.
            A review of the film Deliverance.   Illustrated.
            *[This citation is from International Index to Film
        Periodicals, 1972, p. 147.]

*1156a Vecchiali, P.   "Delivrance." Revue de Cinema/Image et Son
        (Paris), no. 276-277 (Oct. 1973), p. 101.
            A review of the film version of Deliverance.   Credits
        are included.
            *[This citation is from Film Literature Index, 1973,
        p. 100.]

*1157   Westendorp, T. A.   "Recent Southern Fiction: Percy, Price
        and Dickey." In Handelingen van het XXIXe Vlaams
        Filologencongres Antwerpen 16-18 april 1973, edited by J.
        Van Haver, pp. 188-198.   Zellick, Belgium: [n. p.], 1973.
            *[This citation is from M. L. A. International Bibliogra-
        phy, 1974, vol. 1, pp. 2 and 186.]

*1158   Young, James D. "Ecstasy and Metamorphosis in the Poems
         of James Dickey." In Wolfram: Studien II, edited by
         Werner Schröeder, pp. 139-148. Berlin: Schmidt, 1974.
            *[This citation is from M. L. A. International Bibliogra-
         phy, 1974, vol. 1, pp. 3 and 171.]

PUBLISHED CORRESPONDENCE

1159 Berg, Stephen. "That Dickey Poem." Atlantic 220 (July
     1967), pp. 24-25 [24].
          A favorable letter to the editor concerning "May Day
     Sermon to the Women of Gilmer County, Georgia, by a
     Woman Preacher Leaving the Baptist Church." It con-
     tains 60 words.

1160 Berry, Wendell. "Or Would You Rather Be James Dickey?"
     Sewanee Review 72 (July-Sept. 1964), pp. 551-552 [552].
     ["Your Next-Door Neighbor's Poems"].
          A defense of Robert Hazel's Poems 1951-1961 which
     Dickey had reviewed. Dickey is described as being
     nasty, condescending, and irresponsible. Hazel's reply
     to Dickey's review (see no. 1176) is published on the page
     preceding this letter.

1161 Boles, Bertha. "May Day Sermons Department." Atlantic
     219 (June 1967), pp. 40, 42-43 [42].
          An unfavorable letter to the editor concerning "May Day
     Sermon to the Women of Gilmer County, Georgia, by a
     Woman Preacher Leaving the Baptist Church." It con-
     tains 49 words.

1162 Bookwalter, Mary. "May Day Sermons Department." Atlantic
     219 (June 1967), pp. 40, 42-43 [42].
     "The Sheep Child."
          A favorable letter to the editor concerning "May Day
     Sermon to the Women of Gilmer County, Georgia, by a
     Woman Preacher Leaving the Baptist Church." It con-
     tains 77 words.

1163 Bradford, Mary L. "James Dickey." Life 61 (12 Aug. 1966),
     p. 20.
          A favorable letter to the editor concerning Paul O'Neil's
     "The Unlikeliest Poet" (see no. 850). It contains 34 words.

1164 Brown, Francis. "A Mutiny Alert." Mutiny 4 (Fall-Win.
     1961-1962), pp. 3-9 [7].
          A copy of a letter from the editor of The New York
     Times Book Review to Paul Lett. It is a response to
     Lett's letter to Brown (see no. 1180).
          Ref.: Jane Esty.

239

1165 Eaton, Charles Edward. "Two Open Letters Concerning the
         Critic's Role." Sewanee Review 73 (Jan. -Mar. 1965),
         pp. 176-177.
            The Suspect in Poetry, p. 176; ["Your Next-Door
         Neighbor's Poems"], pp. 176-177.
            Dickey's unfavorable review of Eaton's Countermoves
         prompted Eaton's reply. Dickey is criticized for not
         having understood the volume and for not having recognized
         it as a successful collection while other reviewers had.
         Dickey's reply follows (see no. 537).
            Ref. : Charles Edward Eaton's "An Almost Sacerdotal
         Incident," p. 176; Eaton's Countermoves, p. 176; Eaton's
         "Della Robbia in August," p. 176; Eaton's "The Poet,"
         p. 176; Eaton's The Shadow of the Swimmer, p. 176;
         Eaton's [unidentified poem], p. 177; Wallace Fowlie's
         [unidentified review of Countermoves], p. 176.

1166 Esty, Jane. "A Mutiny Alert." Mutiny 4 (Fall-Win. 1961-
         1962), pp. 3-9 [6].
            "Confession Is Not Enough."
            A copy of a letter to Francis Brown, editor of The
         New York Times Book Review, supporting Dickey's un-
         favorable review of beat poetry.
            Ref. : the Beats; Allen Ginsberg; William Shakespeare.

1167 Eva Mary, Sister. "That Dickey Poem." Atlantic 220 (July
         1967), pp. 24-25 [24].
            A letter to the editor applauding the publication of "May
         Day Sermon to the Women of Gilmer County, Georgia, by
         a Woman Preacher Leaving the Baptist Church." It con-
         tains 52 words.

1168 Everson, William [Brother Antoninus]. Sewanee Review 69
         (Apr. -June 1961), pp. 351-353.
            ["The Suspect in Poetry or Everyman as Detective"],
         pp. 351-353.
            A defense of Everson's The Crooked Lines of God which
         Dickey had reviewed. He claims Dickey's judgment is
         based on prejudice and ignorance of theology. Dickey's
         response is included (see no. 535).
            Ref. : Geoffrey Chaucer, p. 352; Dante, p. 352;
         Gerard Manley Hopkins, p. 352; Hopkins' "The Wreck of
         the Deutschland," p. 352; Isaiah, p. 352; Jeremiah,
         p. 352; John Milton, p. 352; William Shakespeare, p. 352.

1169 _____ [Brother Antoninus]. Sewanee Review 69 (July-Sept.
         1961), pp. 510-512.
            ["The Suspect in Poetry or Everyman as Detective"],
         p. 510; [Dickey's letter in The Sewanee Review (see
         no. 535)], p. 511.
            Everson replies to Dickey's response to Everson's
         initial letter (see no. 1168). In this, as in the initial
         remarks, Everson defends himself against Dickey's review

of his The Crooked Lines of God.   Dickey's response is
included (see no. 536).
    Ref.: R. P. Blackmur, pp. 510-511; Isaiah, p. 511;
Jeremiah, p. 511; John Milton, p. 511.

1170 Fariban, Sally. "May Day Sermons Department." Atlantic
       219 (June 1967), pp. 40, 42-43 [42].
       An unfavorable letter to the editor concerning "May
       Day Sermon to the Women of Gilmer County, Georgia, by
       a Woman Preacher Leaving the Baptist Church." It con-
       tains 89 words.

1171 Gaines, Nancy. "Robert Frost, Man or Myth." Atlantic 219
       (Jan. 1967), p. 30.
       An unfavorable letter to the editor concerning "Robert
       Frost, Man and Myth." It contains 68 words.

1172 Gill, John J. "Allen Ginsberg." New York Times Book Re-
       view (13 Aug. 1961), p. 18.
       ["Confession Is Not Enough"].
       A letter to the editor criticizing Dickey's comments on
       Allen Ginsberg's Kaddish.
       Ref.: Allen Ginsberg's Kaddish.
       Rept.: "A Mutiny Alert," p. 8 (see no. 1173).

1173   . "A Mutiny Alert." Mutiny 4 (Fall-Win. 1961-
       1962), pp. 3-9 [8].
       ["Confession Is Not Enough"].
       A reprint of a letter to the editor of The New York
       Times Book Review criticizing Dickey's comments on
       Allen Ginsberg's Kaddish.
       Ref.: Allen Ginsberg's Kaddish.
       Orig.: The New York Times Book Review (see
       no. 1172).

1174 Groseth, Haakon B. "Mislabeled Witch-Hunt." New York
       Times (7 Dec. 1973), p. 40.
       A letter to the editor discussing the censorship of
       several books, one of which was Dickey's Deliverance, in
       Drake, N. D.
       Ref.: the Nazis; the Supreme Court.

1175 Hazard, Patrick D. "May Day Sermons Department."
       Atlantic 219 (June 1967), pp. 40, 42-43 [43].
       A letter to the editor applauding the publication of "May
       Day Sermon to the Women of Gilmer County, Georgia, by
       a Woman Preacher Leaving the Baptist Church." It con-
       tains 75 words.
       Ref.: John Birch Society.

1176 Hazel, Robert. "Or Would You Rather Be James Dickey?"
       Sewanee Review 72 (July-Sept. 1964), pp. 551-552 [551].
       ["Your Next-Door Neighbor's Poems"].

Dickey's unfavorable review of Hazel's Poems 1951-1961 prompted Hazel's reply in which Dickey is satirically pictured as a god of vengeance.
Ref.: Conrad Aiken; Robert Bridges; Hart Crane; Gerard Manley Hopkins; T. E. Hulme; Jesus; Dylan Thomas; Yvor Winters.

1177   Herzog, Garry S.   "Dickey Delivers."   Playboy 21 (Feb. 1974), p. 14.
A letter to the editor criticizing the publication of Playboy's interview with Dickey.   It contains 112 words.
Ref.: Robert Bly; Geoffry Norman's "Playboy Interview: James Dickey" (see no. 1111).

1178   Humphries, Rolphe.   "An Exchange on Delta Return."   Poetry 89 (Mar. 1957), pp. 391-392 [391].
["Five Poets"] (see no. 306).
A defense of Charles Bell's Delta Return which Dickey had reviewed.   Dickey's reply is published with the same title, following this letter (see no. 534).
Ref.: Charles Bell's Delta Return; Lucretius.

1179   Igo, Harold.   "James Dickey."   Life 61 (12 Aug. 1966), p. 20.
A letter to the editor applauding Paul O'Neil's "The Unlikeliest Poet" (see no. 850).   It contains 74 words.

1180   Lett, Paul.   "A Mutiny Alert."   Mutiny 4 (Fall-Win. 1961-1962), pp. 3-9 [7].
"Confession Is Not Enough."
A copy of a letter to Francis Brown, editor of The New York Times Book Review, supporting Dickey's unfavorable review of beat poetry.   Editor Francis Brown's reply (see no. 1164) is included.
Ref.: the Beats.

1181   Lieberman, Laurence.   "May Day Sermons Department."   Atlantic 219 (June 1967), pp. 40, 42-43 [43].
A letter to the editor applauding the publication of "May Day Sermon to the Women of Gilmer County, Georgia, by a Woman Preacher Leaving the Baptist Church."   It contains 51 words.

1182   McGowan, Royal.   "Dickey Delivers."   Playboy 21 (Feb. 1974), p. 14.
A letter to the editor applauding Playboy's interview with Dickey.   It contains 18 words.
Ref.: Geoffry Norman's "Playboy Interview: James Dickey" (see no. 1111).

1183   Maloff, Saul.   "That Dickey Poem."   Atlantic 220 (July 1967), pp. 24-25.
A letter to the editor applauding the publication of "May

Day Sermon to the Women of Gilmer County, Georgia, by a Woman Preacher Leaving the Baptist Church. " It contains 95 words.

1184   Mathewson, W. A.   "May Day Sermons Department. " Atlantic 219 (June 1967), pp. 40, 42-43 [42-43].
          A letter to the editor applauding the publication of "May Day Sermon to the Women of Gilmer County, Georgia, by a Woman Preacher Leaving the Baptist Church. " It contains 80 words.
          Ref. :   Eric Barker's [unidentified remarks], p. 43; Jean Burden's [unidentified remarks], p. 43.

1185   Meyer, Lloyd.   "Dickey Delivers. "   Playboy 21 (Feb. 1974), p. 14.
          A letter to the editor applauding Playboy's interview with Dickey.   It contains 34 words.
          Ref. :   Geoffry Norman's "Playboy Interview: James Dickey" (see no. 1111).

1186   Morgan, Barbara.   "Triumph of Apollo 7. "   Life 65 (22 Nov. 1968), p. 32A.
          A letter to the editor applauding the publication of Dickey's "A Poet Witnesses a Bold Mission. " It contains 45 words.

1187   Nye, Alison M.   "May Day Sermons Department. "   Atlantic 219 (June 1967), pp. 40, 42-43 [42].
          A letter to the editor criticizing the publication of "May Day Sermon to the Women of Gilmer County, Georgia, by a Woman Preacher Leaving the Baptist Church. " It contains 42 words.

1188   Orlovitz, Gil.   "Beat Poetry. "   New York Times Book Review (24 Sept. 1961), p. 48.
          ["Confession Is Not Enough"].
          A letter to the editor supporting Dickey's criticism of beat poetry.
          Ref. :   Guillaume Apollinaire; the Beats; Tristan Corbière; Emily Dickinson; John Donne; John J. Gill; Allen Ginsberg; Ginsberg's Kaddish; Henry James; The New York Times Book Review; Selden Rodman; William Shakespeare; Sophocles; Walt Whitman.

1189   Rodman, Selden.   "Allen Ginsberg. "   New York Times Book Review (13 Aug. 1961), p. 18.
          ["Confession Is Not Enough"].
          A letter to the editor criticizing Dickey's comments on Allen Ginsberg's Kaddish.
          Ref. :   Allen Ginsberg; Henry James; Walt Whitman.
          Rept. :   "A Mutiny Alert" (see no. 1190).

1190   _____ .   "A Mutiny Alert. "   Mutiny 4 (Fall-Win. 1961-

1962), pp. 3-9 [8].

["Confession Is Not Enough"].

A reprint of a letter to the editor of The New York Times Book Review criticizing Dickey's comments on Allen Ginsberg's Kaddish.

Ref. : Allen Ginsberg; Henry James; Walt Whitman.

Orig. : The New York Times Book Review (see no. 1189).

1191 Rothstein, Bette M. "James Dickey. " Life 61 (12 Aug. 1966), p. 20.

A letter to the editor applauding Paul O'Neil's "The Unlikeliest Poet" (see no. 850). It contains 28 words.

1192 Swain, Raymond C. "That Dickey Poem. " Atlantic 220 (July 1967), pp. 24-25 [25].

A letter to the editor criticizing the publication of "May Day Sermon to the Women of Gilmer County, Georgia, by a Woman Preacher Leaving the Baptist Church. " It contains 171 words. The editor's reply follows this letter (see no. 1193).

Ref. : the Baptists, p. 25.

1193 "That Dickey Poem. " Atlantic 220 (July 1967), pp. 24-25 [25].

The editor replies to an irate reader's letter (see no. 1192) in which the publication of "May Day Sermon to the Women of Gilmer County, Georgia, by a Woman Preacher Leaving the Baptist Church" is criticized.

1194 Thomas, R. B. "May Day Sermons Department. " Atlantic 219 (June 1967), pp. 40, 42-43 [40, 42].

A letter to the editor criticizing the publication of "May Day Sermon to the Women of Gilmer County, Georgia, by a Woman Preacher Leaving the Baptist Church. " It contains 54 words.

1195 Walton, Mrs. Charles M. "James Dickey. " Life 61 (12 Aug. 1966), p. 20.

A letter to the editor applauding Paul O'Neil's "The Unlikeliest Poet" (see no. 850). It contains 52 words.

1196 Williams, Oscar. "Beat Poetry. " New York Times Book Review (24 Sept. 1961), p. 48.

["Confession Is Not Enough"].

A letter to the editor supporting Dickey's criticism of the Beats.

Ref. : the Beats; Allen Ginsberg; Life; Selden Rodman; Time; Walt Whitman.

1197 Wilson, Ellen K. "Robert Frost, Man or Myth. " Atlantic 219 (Jan. 1967), p. 30.

A letter to the editor criticizing the publication of

"Robert Frost, Man and Myth." It contains 82 words.
    Ref.: Emily Dickinson; William Shakespeare.

1198 Wolfson, George H. "Robert Frost, Man or Myth." Atlantic
        219 (Jan. 1967), p. 30.
        A letter to the editor criticizing the publication of
      "Robert Frost, Man and Myth." It contains 135 words.
        Ref.: Robert Frost's "The Death of the Hired Man";
      Frost's "West-Running Brook."

1199 Yazzetti, E. C. "Robert Frost, Man or Myth." Atlantic
        219 (Jan. 1967), p. 30.
        A letter to the editor tenuously concerned with the pub-
      lication of "Robert Frost, Man and Myth." It deals with
      poets in general, and specifically with Frost's rather than
      with Dickey's work.
        Ref.: Stephen Crane; Peter Davison's "Some Recent
      Poetry"; Emily Dickinson; Edgar Allan Poe.

BIOGRAPHIES

1200 "Dickey, James." In American Authors and Books: 1640 to
the Present Day, edited by W. J. Burke and Will D.
Howe, 3d rev. ed. , edited by Irving Weiss and Anne
Weiss, p. 168. New York: Crown Publishers, 1972.

1201 "Dickey, James." In The Blue Book: Leaders of the Eng-
lish Speaking World, 1973-74, p. 370. New York: St.
Martin's Press, 1973.

1202 "Dickey, James." In Current Biography Yearbook: 1968,
edited by Charles Moritz, pp. 109-112. New York: H.
W. Wilson Co. , 1969.
      Babel to Byzantium, p. 111; Buckdancer's Choice,
pp. 109, 111; Drowning with Others, p. 111; Helmets,
p. 111; Into the Stone and Other Poems, p. 110; "[The]
Shark at the Window," p. 110; "The Sheep Child," p. 111;
The Suspect in Poetry, p. 111; Two Poems of the Air,
p. 111.
      Biographical data is embellished with comments Dickey
made during his public readings and with excerpts from
his critics' works.
      Ref. : Leroy F. Aarons' "Ex-Adman Eickey: Don't
Just Wait for Oblivion," pp. 110-111 (see no. 555); "Four
Authors Are Given National Book Awards," p. 111 (see
no. 697); Michael Goldman's "Inventing the American
Heart," p. 111 (see no. 712); Richard Howard's "On
James Dickey," p. 111 (see no. 737); L. Quincy Mum-
ford, p. 111; Paul O'Neil's "The Unlikeliest Poet,"
pp. 110-112 (see no. 850); Poetry, p. 112; Nan Robert-
son's "New National Poetry Consultant Can Also Talk a
Nonstop Prose," pp. 111-112 (see no. 881); The Sewanee
Review, p. 110; Stephen Spender, p. 111; Geoffrey A.
Wolff's "Library's New Poetry Expert Is Ad Writer,
Teacher, Essayist," pp. 110-111 (see no. 967); William
Wordsworth, p. 111.
      Orig. : Current Biography (see no. 1208).
      Photograph of Dickey by an unidentified person, p. 110.

1203 "Dickey, James." In International Who's Who, 38th ed. :
1974-1975, pp. 428-429. London: Europa Publications,
1974.

1204 "Dickey, James." In International Who's Who in Poetry, 4th
        ed.: 1974-1975, edited by Ernest Kay, p. 119. London:
        International Who's Who in Poetry, 1974.

1205 "Dickey, James." In Who's Who in America, 38th ed.: 1974-
        1975, vol. 1, p. 795. Chicago: Marquis Who's Who,
        1974.

1206 "Dickey, James." In Who's Who in the World, 2d ed.:
        1974-1975, p. 271. Chicago: Marquis Who's Who, 1973.

1207 "Dickey, James." In The Writer's Directory 1974-1976,
        p. 206. New York: St. Martin's Press, 1973.

*1208 "James Dickey." Current Biography 29 (Apr. 1968),
        pp. 10-12.
            *[This citation is from Biography Index, vol. 8,
        p. 173.]
            Rept.: Current Biography Yearbook, pp. 109-112 (see
        no. 1202).

1209 "James Dickey." In A Directory of American Poets, 1975
        ed., p. 71. New York: Poets and Writers, 1974.

MISCELLANEA

1210   Atlantic 225 (Feb. 1970).
              A photograph of Dickey by Christopher Dickey appears
       on the cover in a collage by Adrian Taylor and M.
       Halberstadt.

1211   Berryman, John. "Damn You, Jim D., You Woke Me Up."
       Delusions, Etc., of John Berryman, p. 55. New York:
       Farrar, Straus and Giroux, 1972.
              A poem.

1212   Booklist 70 (15 Nov. 1974).
              An illustration from Jericho, "Lonesome Song" by
       Hubert Shuptrine, appears on the cover with an explanatory
       note on p. 305.

1213   Casper, Leonard. "A Mutiny Alert." Mutiny 4 (Fall-Win.
       1961-1962), pp. 3-9 [9].
              Casper signed a petition published here in support of
       Dickey's "Confession Is Not Enough."
              Ref.: the Beats; Mutiny.

1214   Cinema 8 (Spr. 1973).
              A still from the film Deliverance appears on the cover.

1215   Combs, Richard E. Authors: Critical and Biographical Ref-
       erences; A Guide to 4,700 Critical and Biographical Pas-
       sages in Books. Metuchen, N.J.: Scarecrow Press,
       1971.
              Babel to Byzantium is indexed here.

1216   DeJong, David Cornel. "A Mutiny Alert." Mutiny 4 (Fall-
       Win. 1961-1962), pp. 3-9 [9].
              DeJong signed a petition published here in support of
       Dickey's "Confession Is Not Enough."
              Ref.: the Beats; Mutiny.

1217   Flemming, Harold. "A Mutiny Alert." Mutiny 4 (Fall-Win.
       1961-1962), pp. 3-9 [9].
              Flemming signed a petition published here in support
       of Dickey's "Confession Is Not Enough."
              Ref.: the Beats; Mutiny.

1218   Garrigue, Jean. "A Mutiny Alert."   Mutiny 4 (Fall-Win.
1961-1962), pp. 3-9 [9].
Garrigue signed a petition published here in support of
Dickey's "Confession Is Not Enough."
Ref.: the Beats; Mutiny.

1219   "Harry Umbrage: Poet on the Make."   Harvard Lampoon
158, no. 4 (1968), pp. 68-70.
A parody of Paul O'Neil's "The Unlikeliest Poet" (see
no. 850), it includes a lampoon of Dickey's "Falling"
entitled "Washing," p. 70.

1220   Hedley, Leslie Woolf. "A Mutiny Alert."   Mutiny 4 (Fall-
Win. 1961-1962), pp. 3-9 [9].
Hedley signed a petition published here in support of
Dickey's "Confession Is Not Enough."
Ref.: the Beats; Mutiny.

1221   Henderson, Jeanne J. and Piggins, Brenda G., eds. Literary
and Library Prizes, 8th ed., pp. 25, 97, 140, 284, 287.
New York: R. R. Bowker Co., 1973.
Many of Dickey's awards are listed.

1222   Howard, Richard. On "James Dickey Reads His Poetry," by
James Dickey. Caedmon Records, 1971, disc TC 1333,
12 in., 33 1/3 rpm., stereo., 2 sides.
"Apollo"; Babel to Byzantium; [Deliverance]; ["Diabetes:
I, Sugar"]; ["Diabetes: II, Under Buzzards"]; ["The Eye-
Beaters"]; ["The Lord in the Air"]; ["Pine"]; Poems 1957-
1967; ["Turning Away"]; ["Two Poems of Going Home: I,
Living There"]; [unidentified passages].
Comments on the slipcase define Dickey's as poetry of
ecstasy, renewal, and transcendence.
Ref.: William Blake.

1223   James Dickey Reads His Poems. London: Cultural Affairs
Office of the American Embassy, 1968.
"The Flash," p. [4]; "The Head-Aim," p. [2].
A program of a public poetry reading Dickey gave on
April 26, 1968, at the American Embassy in London. Its
pages are unnumbered. Some biographical data is given.
The poems "The Head-Aim" and "The Flash" are reprinted
in full on the second and fourth pages respectively.

1224   Kayden, Eugene M. "A Mutiny Alert."   Mutiny 4 (Fall-Win.
1961-1962), pp. 3-9 [9].
Kayden signed a petition published here in support of
Dickey's "Confession Is Not Enough."
Ref.: the Beats; Mutiny.

1225   Literary Guild Magazine (Apr. 1970).
A painting, or perhaps two paintings, by Ken Nisson
depicting scenes from Deliverance appears on both covers.

1226 Lytle, Andrew. "A Mutiny Alert." Mutiny 4 (Fall-Win.
      1961-1962), pp. 3-9 [9].
            Lytle signed a petition published here in support of
      Dickey's "Confession Is Not Enough."
            Ref.: the Beats; Mutiny.

1227 Marquiz, Lynne. "A Mutiny Alert." Mutiny 4 (Fall-Win.
      1961-1962), pp. 3-9 [9].
            Marquiz signed a petition published here in support of
      Dickey's "Confession Is Not Enough."
            Ref.: the Beats; Mutiny.

1228 Meinke, Peter. "To an Athlete Turned Poet." In Sports
      Poems, edited by R. R. Knudson and P. K. Ebert, p. 43.
      New York: Dell Publishing Co., 1971.
            A poem dedicated to Dickey.

1229 Orlovitz, Gil. "A Mutiny Alert." Mutiny 4 (Fall-Win. 1961-
      1962), pp. 3-9 [9].
            Orlovitz signed a petition published here in support of
      Dickey's "Confession Is Not Enough."
            Ref.: the Beats; Mutiny.

1230 Philbrick, Charles. "A Mutiny Alert." Mutiny 4 (Fall-Win.
      1961-1962), pp. 3-9 [9].
            Philbrick signed a petition published here in support of
      Dickey's "Confession Is Not Enough."
            Ref.: the Beats; Mutiny.

1231 Poetry Australia, no. 21 (Apr. 1968).
            Dickey's photograph appears on the cover.

1232 Smith, William James, ed. Granger's Index to Poetry:
      Sixth Edition Completely Revised and Enlarged, Indexing
      Anthologies Published through December 31, 1970.   New
      York: Columbia University Press, 1973.
            Fifty-one of Dickey's poems are indexed.

1233 Sobiloff, Hy. "A Mutiny Alert." Mutiny 4 (Fall-Win. 1961-
      1962), pp. 3-9 [9].
            Sobiloff signed a petition published here in support of
      Dickey's "Confession Is Not Enough."
            Ref.: the Beats, Mutiny.

1234 Spears, Monroe K. "A Mutiny Alert." Mutiny 4 (Fall-Win.
      1961-1962), pp. 3-9 [9].
            Spears signed a petition published here in support of
      Dickey's "Confession Is Not Enough."
            Ref.: the Beats; Mutiny.

1235 Sulzer, Elmer G. "A Mutiny Alert." Mutiny 4 (Fall-Win.
      1961-1962), pp. 3-9 [9].
            Sulzer signed a petition published here in support of

Dickey's "Confession Is Not Enough."
Ref. : the Beats; Mutiny.

1236 Taylor, Henry. "Mr. James Dickey in Orbit." In The
      Horse Show at Midnight, pp. 25-27. Baton Rouge:
      Louisiana State University Press, 1966.
      A poem which parodies Dickey and his style.

1237 Turco, Lewis. "A Mutiny Alert." Mutiny 4 (Fall-Win.
      1961-1962), pp. 3-9 [9].
      Turco signed a petition published here in support of
      Dickey's "Confession Is Not Enough."
      Ref. : the Beats; Mutiny.

1238 Van Duyn, Mona. "Marriage, with Beasts." In To See, to
      Take, pp. 91-94. New York: Atheneum, 1971.
      A poem in which Dickey is mentioned. The lines men-
      tioning Dickey are excerpted in Peggy Rizza's "Another
      Side of This Life" (see no. 1064).

1239 "Washing."
      A poem that parodies Dickey's "Falling," it is included
      in "Harry Umbrage: Poet on the Make" (see no. 1219).

*1240 Weissberg, Eric and Mandel, Steve. "Dueling Banjos" [Sound
      Recording]. Warner Brothers, 1973, disc BS 2683, 12
      in. , 33 1/3 rpm.
      Weissberg and Marshall Brickman's "New Dimensions in
      Banjo and Bluegrass" was reissued under this title although
      two of its songs were deleted and "Dueling Banjos" and
      "End of a Dream," original music from the film Deliver-
      ance played by Weissberg and Mandel, were substituted
      for them. "Dueling Banjos" is also available as a single
      (WB7659).
      *[This citation is from Library Journal (Oct. 1973),
      p. 52.]

1241 White, William, comp. Edwin Arlington Robinson: A Supple-
      mentary Bibliography. [n. p.]: Kent State University
      Press, 1971.
      "Edwin Arlington Robinson: The Many Truths," pp. 8-9,
      50, 55; "The Poet of Secret Lives and Misspent Opportun-
      ities," p. 106.
      Dickey's works on Robinson are listed.

1242 Williams, Oscar. "A Mutiny Alert." Mutiny 4 (Fall-Win.
      1961-1962), pp. 3-9 [9].
      Williams signed a petition, published here, in support
      of Dickey's "Confession Is Not Enough."
      Ref. : the Beats; Mutiny.

INDEX TO WORKS BY JAMES DICKEY

(All numbers refer to bibliographic citations, not to pages. Numbers for citations giving original publication data are underscored.)

Babel to Byzantium: Poets and Poetry Now 1, 18, 557, 564, 582,
     600, 603, 609, 613-614, 619, 629-630, 655, 673, 704, 738,
     763, 772, 781, 794, 806, 809, 821, 835, 854, 865, 868, 883,
     921, 947, 962, 992-993, 995, 997, 1006, 1019, 1022, 1029,
     1031-1032, 1048, 1059, 1069, 1073-1074, 1085, 1096, 1103,
     1112-1113, 1202, 1215, 1222
"Barnstorming for Poetry" 269, 1, 379, 614, 619, 704, 763, 806,
     854, 921, 961, 992, 995, 1112-1113
"The Bee" 41, 13, 301, 501, 576, 909, 1074, 1105
"Before" 270, 3, 426, 810, 943, 1025, 1043
"A Beginning Poet, Aged Sixty-Five" 42, 1091
"The Beholders" 43, 7, 13, 194, 444, 725, 1039-1040, 1051. See
     also "Poems of North and South Georgia"
"The Being" 44, 7, 13, 500, 576, 675, 708, 1039-1040, 1051,
     1066
"Below Ellijay" 45, 7, 13, 177, 491, 566, 737, 1024, 1054. See
     also "On the Coosawattee"
"Below the Lighthouse" 46. See also "On the Hill Below the Light-
     house"
"Between Two Prisoners" 47, 4, 13, 444, 455, 470, 481, 507,
     542, 654, 707, 720, 829, 1033
"A Birth" 48, 4, 13, 476, 494, 541, 904, 1038-1040
"The Birthday Dream" 49, 13, 576, 822, 1033, 1059
"The Blind Child's Story" 50, 4, 13, 183, 589, 657, 678, 707,
     719, 737, 799, 840, 904, 912, 1010, 1024, 1041, 1045, 1050,
     1054. See also "The Owl King"
"Blood" 51, 6, 801, 1020, 1041, 1054, 1059, 1061
"Blowjob on a Rattlesnake" 272
"Bread" 52, 13, 455, 761, 827, 1028
"Breath" 53, 7, 701
"Brother Antoninus" 273, 1, 18, 496, 597
"Buckdancer's Choice" 54, 2, 13, 449, 455-457, 460, 465, 467,
     485, 659, 692, 701, 742, 744, 850, 925, 939, 992, 1007, 1019,
     1033, 1039-1040, 1054, 1059, 1090
Buckdancer's Choice 2, 555-556, 576, 580-582, 586, 591, 598,
     601, 603, 609, 613, 617, 619, 627, 643, 653-654, 658-659,
     664, 668, 673-674, 692, 697, 701-703, 710-712, 730, 737, 742,
     744, 748, 750, 765, 785-786, 789-791, 793, 796, 805-806, 817,
     822-824, 832, 837-839, 841, 843, 845, 850, 861, 867, 880,
     884, 895, 898, 901, 908-909, 917, 925, 941-942, 944-945, 954,
     959, 965, 968, 985, 992-993, 999, 1007, 1010, 1016, 1019-
     1020, 1022, 1024, 1029, 1033, 1035-1036, 1039-1041, 1045,
     1054-1055, 1069-1070, 1073-1074, 1078, 1084, 1090, 1092-1094,
     1096, 1103, 1106, 1109, 1111, 1114, 1118, 1202
"Buckdancer's Choice" 274, 15, 1065
"Bums, on Waking" 55, 7, 13, 472, 485, 510, 544, 583, 664, 671,
     725, 918, 928, 1039-1040, 1051
"Butterflies" 56, 6, 168, 810, 1043, 1054, 1103. See also
     "Messages"
"By Canoe Through the Fir Forest" 57, 7, 13, 177, 485, 509,
     607, 737, 888, 1024, 1091. See also "On the Coosawattee"

"The Owl King" [poem] 182, 4, 13, 183, 588-589, 678, 707, 737, 775, 840, 912, 954, 1019, 1024, 1045, 1050, 1054, 1084. See also "The Owl King" [collective title for two poems]

"The Owl King" [collective title for two poems] 183, 50, 182, 184. See also "The Owl King" [collective title for three poems]

"The Owl King" [collective title for three poems] 184, 4, 13, 50, 58, 182-183, 589, 609, 693, 698, 707, 719, 728, 735-737, 786, 799, 822, 829-830, 842, 893, 905, 919, 1020, 1024, 1033, 1038, 1045-1046, 1054, 1059, 1074, 1093

"Paestum" 185

"The Performance" 186, 8, 11, 13, 334, 453, 456-457, 461-462, 472, 515, 539, 541-542, 545, 576, 607, 737, 742, 793, 826-827, 842, 856, 969, 985, 992, 1023-1024, 1033, 1035, 1041, 1045, 1054, 1059, 1105

"Philip Booth" 375, 1, 18, 940, 953

"Pine" [collective title for two poems] 187, 188, 613. See also "Pine" [collective title for five poems]

"Pine" [collective title for five poems] 188, 6, 187, 189, 676, 786, 898, 993, 1033, 1222

"Pine: Taste, Touch, and Sight" 189, 188, 1059. See also "Pine" [collective title for five poems]

"Pitching and Rolling" 190, 20, 631

"The Place" 191, 6, 1061

"Poem" 192, 8, 495, 581, 589, 737, 1024, 1059

"A Poem About Bird-Catching by One Who Has Never Caught a Bird" 193

"The Poem as Something that Matters" 15, 613, 751, 993

Poems 11

Poems 1957-1967 [miniature edition] 12, 803

Poems 1957-1967 13, 556, 576, 599, 603, 609, 613, 619, 628, 635, 643, 657-659, 670, 678, 690, 703, 707, 712, 716, 719, 732, 738, 750, 761, 771, 782, 785-786, 788, 792, 796, 803, 806, 817, 822, 827, 838-839, 844, 866-867, 901, 903, 905, 908, 919-920, 931, 935, 939, 942, 946, 968, 985, 992-993, 1000, 1007, 1019, 1024, 1028-1029, 1036, 1041, 1045, 1049, 1054, 1060, 1069-1070, 1073-1075, 1093, 1102-1103, 1222, 1258

"The Poems of James Dickey (1957-1967)" 541, 1029

"Poems of North and South Georgia" 194, 34, 43, 86, 137, 196

"Poems of the Sixties--4" 216

"The Poet in Mid-Career" 15, 613, 751, 993

"The Poet of Secret Lives and Misspent Opportunities" 376, 294, 1241. See also "Edwin Arlington Robinson" [review of Coxe's biography]

"The Poet Tries to Make a Kind of Order" 377, 301. See also "'Falling'"

"The Poet Turns on Himself" [essay] 378, 1, 379, 453, 457, 484, 492, 614, 619, 704, 763, 821-822, 854, 921, 962, 992, 995, 1019, 1022, 1029, 1033, 1041, 1048, 1054, 1069, 1071-1072, 1074, 1078, 1082, 1085, 1093, 1112-1113, 1118

GENERAL INDEX

(All numbers refer to bibliographic citations, not
to pages. Books, poems, etc., are listed by
author, while films, songs, and works of unknown
authorship are listed by title. The film Deliver-
ance, however, appears in the preceding index.)

Abner, Li'l 927
Abse, Dannie. Works: with
    Howard Sargent, Mavericks
    331
Achilles 647, 1114
Adam 565, 690
Adams, Leslie 640
Adams, Nick 565, 961a
Aeneas 693
Aesop 1039-1040, 1051
The African Lion [film] 901,
    1070, 1105
Agee, James 613, 657, 683,
    749, 845, 993, 1091-1092,
    1098, 1107-1108, 1111-1113.
    Works: The African Queen
    [film script] 1091; A Death
    in the Family 907; with
    Walker Evans, Now Let Us
    Praise Famous Men 640,
    749
"Aggression" [encyclopedia
    article] 826
Ahab 922
Aiken, Conrad 880, 1176.
    Works: The Morning Song
    of Lord Zero 416; Sheep-
    fold Hill 315
Alger, Horatio 973, 1094
Allen, Donald. Works: The
    New American Poetry:
    1945-1960 285, 763
Amalrik, Andrei A. 929.
    Works: Will the Soviet
    Union Survive Until 1984?
    929

Ambrose, Jack 584a
American Academy of Arts
    and Letters 765
Amis, Kingsley 578. Works:
    A Case of Samples 331
Ammons, A. R. 795, 839
Anaximander 1114
Anderson, Wallace L. Works:
    Edwin Arlington Robinson:
    An Introduction 883
Antoninus, Brother see
    Everson, William
Apollinaire, Guillaume see
    Kostrowitski, Wilhelm
    Appollinaris de
Apollo 582, 1074
Aquinas, Thomas see Thomas
    Aquinas, St.
Aragon, Louis 887
Ardrey, Robert 749. Works:
    The Social Contract 1105
Ariel 1039-1040, 1051
Aristotle 1059, 1091, 1112-
    1113
Armstrong, Neil 1109
Arnold, Matthew 821, 842,
    1016, 1071-1072
Arthur, King 707
Ashbery, John 776, 799,
    1031-1032. Works: Some
    Trees 310
Ashman, Richard A. 1091
Ashwell, Edward 1100
Astaire, Fred 849
Atkinson, Jennifer 986
Atlanta Film Festival 568

270

283 General Index

Millinger, Myra 986
Milton, John 654, 1107-1108, 1168-1169. Works: Paradise Lost 779, 1091; "Il Penseroso" 1106
Montale, Eugenio 1114
Moore, G. E. 1098
Moore, J. C. 584a
Moore, Henry 744
Moore, Marianne 1019. Works: A Marianne Moore Reader 411; Tell Me, Tell Me 432
Moore, Thomas 823
More, Thomas 643
Morris, Willie 845, 1109a. Works: North Toward Home 845
Morris, Wright 1111
Morse, Samuel French. Works: The Scattered Causes 306
Moss, Howard 1096
"Mountain Dew" [song] 937
Mozart, Leopold 763
Mozart, Wolfgang 613, 993, 1114
Muir, Edwin 659, 705, 1007, 1114, 1118. Works: "The Animals" 659, 1007; Collected Poems 331
Mumford, L. Quincy 538, 1202
Mumford, Lewis 1109
Murphy, Francis. Works: Edwin Arlington Robinson: A Collection of Critical Essays 1004
"The Muskrat Ramble" [song] 909
Mutiny [journal] 1213, 1216-1218, 1220, 1224, 1226-1227, 1229-1230, 1233-1235, 1237, 1242

Narcissus 582
National Book Award 653, 697, 710, 843, 872, 941, 965, 909
National Institute of Arts and Letters 570, 765
Nemerov, Howard 589, 806, 1013, 1021, 1029, 1067. Works: New and Selected Poems 285; The Salt Garden 407; "The Sanctuary" 911a; The Winter Lightning 670
New York Quarterly [journal] 1112-1113
New York Review of Books [journal] 992
New York Times [newspaper] 677, 761, 828, 845, 939, 1028, 1078, 1094
New York Times Book Review [journal] 681, 824, 961, 1164, 1173, 1180, 1188, 1190
New Yorker [journal] 586, 619, 701, 732, 740, 850, 867, 888, 928, 1019, 1091, 1094, 1096, 1100, 1105
Newman, John Henry 737, 1024
Newsweek [journal] 1111
Nicholson, Ben 1092
Nietzsche, Friedrich 845, 855, 1054, 1106
Nims, John Frederick 589. Works: Knowledge of the Evening 411
Nixon, Richard M. 845, 849, 1094
Noah 690
Nofel, John 1106
Novalis 578

Oates, Joyce Carol 1095
O'Connor, Flannery 657, 895, 1012, 1059, 1096
Odysseus 1114
Oedipus 699
O'Gorman, Ned. Works: The Night of the Hammer 328
O'Hara, Frank 658, 921, 1047
Olson, Charles 614, 719, 763, 995. Works: Charles Olson Reading at Berkeley [L. P. record (?)] 751; The Distances 280; The Maximus Poems 280, 285,